T0267374

Web Engineering

Web Engineering

Edited by
Carson Thomas

Larsen & Keller
www.larsen-keller.com

Web Engineering
Edited by Carson Thomas
ISBN: 978-1-63549-292-7 (Hardback)

© 2017 Larsen & Keller

 Larsen & Keller

Published by Larsen and Keller Education,
5 Penn Plaza,
19th Floor,
New York, NY 10001, USA

Cataloging-in-Publication Data

Web engineering / edited by Carson Thomas.
        p. cm.
Includes bibliographical references and index.
ISBN 978-1-63549-292-7
        1. World Wide Web. 2. Software engineering. 3. Web services. 4. Web site development.
I. Thomas, Carson.
TK5105.888 .W43 2017
004.678--dc23

This book contains information obtained from authentic and highly regarded sources. All chapters are published with permission under the Creative Commons Attribution Share Alike License or equivalent. A wide variety of references are listed. Permissions and sources are indicated; for detailed attributions, please refer to the permissions page. Reasonable efforts have been made to publish reliable data and information, but the authors, editors and publisher cannot assume any responsibility for the vailidity of all materials or the consequences of their use.

Trademark Notice: All trademarks used herein are the property of their respective owners. The use of any trademark in this text does not vest in the author or publisher any trademark ownership rights in such trademarks, nor does the use of such trademarks imply any affiliation with or endorsement of this book by such owners.

The publisher's policy is to use permanent paper from mills that operate a sustainable forestry policy. Furthermore, the publisher ensures that the text paper and cover boards used have met acceptable environmental accreditation standards.

Printed and bound in the United States of America.

For more information regarding Larsen and Keller Education and its products, please visit the publisher's website www.larsen-keller.com

Table of Contents

Preface

World wide web has become a crucial part of our lives be it socially, culturally or economically. Web engineering refers to the technology and the practice of systematically and quantifiably developing good quality web search engines, web based applications and systems, etc. It incorporates elements from various fields like software engineering, human-computer interaction, information engineering, project management and graphic design, etc. This book unfolds the innovative aspects of web engineering which will be crucial for the holistic understanding of the subject matter. Some of the diverse topics covered in it address the varied branches that fall under this category. Selected concepts that redefine this subject have been presented in this text. Coherent flow of topics, student-friendly language and extensive use of examples make this textbook an invaluable source of knowledge.

Given below is the chapter wise description of the book:

Chapter 1- The web has become a major platform in several domains. Web engineering focuses on the methodologies and techniques that are the basics of web application. This chapter is an overview of the subject matter incorporating all the major aspects of web engineering.

Chapter 2- Web design comprises of different skills that are used in the production of websites and also in the maintenance of these websites. Some of the aspects elucidated in the section are CSS frameworks, cascading style sheets, user experience design, responsive web design and rollover. This section will provide an integrated understanding of web design.

Chapter 3- Web framework is a software that is used for supporting the development of web applications. These include web services, web resources and web APIs. Some of the web frameworks are PRADO, play framework, Padrino, Silex and Snap. The major components of web framework are discussed in this chapter.

Chapter 4- The World Wide Web is the space where documents are identified by using uniform resource locators and can be read by using the Internet. Web science, uniform resource locator, web standards and history of the World Wide Web are some of the topics covered in the chapter. The section will provide an integrated understanding of the World Wide Web.

Chapter 5- HTML is an essential element in web engineering; it is the standard language that used in creating web pages. HTML5, markup language, HTML element, HTML attribute and semantic HTML are the topics explained in the section. The aspects elucidated in this chapter are of vital importance, and provide a better understanding of HTML.

Chapter 6- Software engineering is a branch of engineering that focuses on the design, development and maintenance of software. The aspects related to software engineering that have been elucidated in the section are software requirements, software construction, software design, software quality, software testing and the history of software engineering. The chapter serves as a source to understand the major categories related to software engineering.

Chapter 7- The essential aspects of web engineering are web container, web content development, web navigation, web usability, web application, multimedia etc. The topics discussed in the chapter are of great importance to broaden the existing knowledge on web engineering.

At the end, I would like to thank all those who dedicated their time and efforts for the successful completion of this book. I also wish to convey my gratitude towards my friends and family who supported me at every step.

Editor

Introduction to Web Engineering

The web has become a major platform in several domains. Web engineering focuses on the methodologies and techniques that are the basics of web application. This chapter is an overview of the subject matter incorporating all the major aspects of web engineering.

Web Engineering

The World Wide Web has become a major delivery platform for a variety of complex and sophisticated enterprise applications in several domains. In addition to their inherent multifaceted functionality, these Web applications exhibit complex behaviour and place some unique demands on their usability, performance, security and ability to grow and evolve. However, a vast majority of these applications continue to be developed in an ad-hoc way, contributing to problems of usability, maintainability, quality and reliability. While Web development can benefit from established practices from other related disciplines, it has certain distinguishing characteristics that demand special considerations. In recent years, there have been developments towards addressing these considerations.

As an emerging discipline, Web engineering actively promotes systematic, disciplined and quantifiable approaches towards successful development of high-quality, ubiquitously usable Web-based systems and applications. In particular, Web engineering focuses on the methodologies, techniques and tools that are the foundation of Web application development and which support their design, development, evolution, and evaluation. Web application development has certain characteristics that make it different from traditional software, information system, or computer application development.

Web engineering is multidisciplinary and encompasses contributions from diverse areas: systems analysis and design, software engineering, hypermedia/hypertext engineering, requirements engineering, human-computer interaction, user interface, information engineering, information indexing and retrieval, testing, modelling and simulation, project management, and graphic design and presentation. Web engineering is neither a clone, nor a subset of software engineering, although both involve programming and software development. While Web Engineering uses software engineering principles, it encompasses new approaches, methodologies, tools, techniques, and guidelines to meet the unique requirements of Web-based applications.

As a Discipline

Proponents of Web engineering supported the establishment of Web engineering as a discipline at an early stage of Web. First Workshop on Web Engineering was held in conjunction with World

Wide Web Conference held in Brisbane, Australia, in 1998. San Murugesan, Yogesh Deshpande, Steve Hansen and Athula Ginige, from University of Western Sydney, Australia formally promoted Web engineering as a new discipline in the first ICSE workshop on Web Engineering in 1999. Since then they published a series of papers in a number of journals, conferences and magazines to promote their view and got wide support. Major arguments for Web engineering as a new discipline are:

- Web-based Information Systems (WIS) development process is different and unique.

- Web engineering is multi-disciplinary; no single discipline (such as software engineering) can provide complete theory basis, body of knowledge and practices to guide WIS development.

- Issues of evolution and lifecycle management when compared to more 'traditional' applications.

- Web-based information systems and applications are pervasive and non-trivial. The prospect of Web as a platform will continue to grow and it is worth being treated specifically.

However, it has been controversial, especially for people in other traditional disciplines such as software engineering, to recognize Web engineering as a new field. The issue is how different and independent Web engineering is, compared with other disciplines.

Main topics of Web engineering include, but are not limited to, the following areas:

Modeling Disciplines

- Design Manufacturing of Steel Plant equipments
- Process Modelling of Web applications
- Requirements Engineering for Web applications
- B2B applications

Design Disciplines, Tools and Methods

- UML and the Web
- Conceptual Modeling of Web Applications (aka. Web modeling)
- Prototyping Methods and Tools
- Web design methods
- CASE Tools for Web Applications
- Web Interface Design
- Data Models for Web Information Systems

Implementation Disciplines

- Integrated Web Application Development Environments
- Code Generation for Web Applications
- Software Factories for/on the Web
- Web 2.0, AJAX, E4X, ASP.NET, PHP and Other New Developments
- Web Services Development and Deployment

Testing Disciplines

- Testing and Evaluation of Web systems and Applications
- Testing Automation, Methods and Tools

Applications Categories Disciplines

- Semantic Web applications
- Ubiquitous and Mobile Web Applications
- Mobile Web Application Development
- Device Independent Web Delivery
- Localization and Internationalization Of Web Applications

Attributes

Web Quality

- Web Metrics, Cost Estimation, and Measurement
- Personalisation and Adaptation of Web applications
- Web Quality
- Usability of Web Applications
- Web accessibility
- Performance of Web-based applications

Content-related

- Web Content Management
- Content Management System (CMS)
- Multimedia Authoring Tools and Software
- Authoring of adaptive hypermedia

Education

- Master of Science: Web Engineering as a branch of study within the MSc program Web Sciences at the Johannes Kepler University Linz, Austria

- Diploma in Web Engineering: Web Engineering as a study program at the International Webmasters College (iWMC), Germany

Web Modeling

Web modeling (aka model-driven Web development) is a branch of Web engineering which addresses the specific issues related to design and development of large-scale Web applications. In particular, it focuses on the design notations and visual languages that can be used for the realization of robust, well-structured, usable and maintainable Web applications. Designing a data-intensive Web site amounts to specifying its characteristics in terms of various orthogonal abstractions. The main orthogonal models that are involved in complex Web application design are: data structure, content composition, navigation paths, and presentation model.

In the beginning of web development, it was normal to access Web applications by creating something with no attention to the developmental stage. In the past years, web design firms had many issues with managing their Web sites as the developmental process grew and complicated other applications. Web development tools have helped with simplifying data-intensive Web applications by using page generators. Microsoft's Active Server Pages and JavaSoft's Java Server Pages have helped by bringing out content and using user-programmed templates.

Several languages and notations have been devised for Web application modeling. Among them, we can cite:

- HDM - W2000

- RMM

- OOHDM

- the Interaction Flow Modeling Language (IFML), adopted by the Object Management Group (OMG) in March 2013

- ARANEUS

- STRUDEL

- TIRAMISU

- WebML

- Hera

- UML Web Application Extension

- UML-based Web Engineering (UWE)

- ACE

- WebArchitect

- OO-H

One of the main discussion venues for this discipline is the Model-Driven Web Engineering Workshop (MDWE) held yearly in conjunction with the International Conference on Web Engineering (ICWE) conference.

Web Developer

A web developer is a programmer who specializes in, or is specifically engaged in, the development of World Wide Web applications, or distributed network applications that are run over HTTP from a web server to a web browser.

Nature of Employment

Web developers are found working in various types of organizations, including large corporations and governments, small and medium - sized companies, or alone as freelancers. Some web developers work for one organization as a permanent full-time employee, while others may work as independent consultants, or as contractors for an employment agency. Web developers typically handle both server-side and front-end logic. This usually involves implementing all the visual elements that users see and use in the web application, as well as all the web services and APIs that are necessary to power the front-end. Depending on the type of development work, location, and level of seniority, web developer salaries in many large metropolitan areas routinely surpass $100,000.

Type of Work Performed

Modern web applications often contain three or more tiers, and depending on the size of the team a developer works on, he or she may specialize in one or more of these tiers - or may take a more interdisciplinary role. For example, in a two-person team, one developer may focus on the technologies sent to the client such as HTML, JavaScript, CSS, and on the server-side frameworks (such as Perl, Python, Ruby, PHP, Java, ASP, ASP.NET) used to deliver content and scripts to the client. Meanwhile, the other developer might focus on the interaction between server-side frameworks, the web server, and a database system. Further, depending on the size of their organization, the aforementioned developers might work closely with a content creator/copy writer, marketing advisor, user experience designer, web designer, web producer, project manager, software architect, or database administrator - or they may be responsible for such tasks as web design and project management themselves.

Educational and Licensure Requirements

There are no formal educational or licensure requirements to become a web developer. However, many colleges and trade schools offer coursework in web development. There are also many tutorials and articles, which teach web development, freely available on the web - for example: Basic JavaScript.

Even though there are no formal educational requirements, dealing with web developing projects requires those who wish to be referred to as web developers to have advanced knowledge/skills in:

- HTML/XHTML, CSS, JavaScript

- server/client side architecture

- Programming/Coding/Scripting in one of the many server-side frameworks (at least one of: Perl, Python, Ruby, PHP, Go, CFML - ColdFusion, Java, ASP, ASP.NET)

- Ability to utilize a database

- Creating single-page application with use of front-end tools such as ReactJS or AngularJS

Web Design: A Comprehensive Study

Web design comprises of different skills that are used in the production of websites and also in the maintenance of these websites. Some of the aspects elucidated in the section are CSS frameworks, cascading style sheets, user experience design, responsive web design and rollover. This section will provide an integrated understanding of web design.

Web Design

Web design encompasses many different skills and disciplines in the production and maintenance of websites. The different areas of web design include web graphic design; interface design; authoring, including standardised code and proprietary software; user experience design; and search engine optimization. Often many individuals will work in teams covering different aspects of the design process, although some designers will cover them all. The term web design is normally used to describe the design process relating to the front-end (client side) design of a website including writing mark up. Web design partially overlaps web engineering in the broader scope of web development. Web designers are expected to have an awareness of usability and if their role involves creating mark up then they are also expected to be up to date with web accessibility guidelines.

History

Web design books in a store

1988—2001

Although web design has a fairly recent history, it can be linked to other areas such as graphic design. However web design can also be seen from a technological standpoint. It has become a large part of people's everyday lives. It is hard to imagine the Internet without animated graphics, different styles of typography, background and music.

The Start Of the Web and Web Design

In 1989, whilst working at CERN Tim Berners-Lee proposed to create a global hypertext project, which later became known as the World Wide Web. During 1991 to 1993 the World Wide Web was born. Text-only pages could be viewed using a simple line-mode browser. In 1993 Marc Andreessen and Eric Bina, created the Mosaic browser. At the time there were multiple browsers, however the majority of them were Unix-based and naturally text heavy. There had been no integrated approach to graphic design elements such as images or sounds. The Mosaic browser broke this mould. The W3C was created in October 1994 to "lead the World Wide Web to its full potential by developing common protocols that promote its evolution and ensure its interoperability." This discouraged any one company from monopolizing a propriety browser and programming language, which could have altered the effect of the World Wide Web as a whole. The W3C continues to set standards, which can today be seen with JavaScript. In 1994 Andreessen formed Communications Corp. that later became known as Netscape Communications, the Netscape 0.9 browser. Netscape created its own HTML tags without regard to the traditional standards process. For example, Netscape 1.1 included tags for changing background colours and formatting text with tables on web pages. Throughout 1996 to 1999 the browser wars began, as Microsoft and Netscape fought for ultimate browser dominance. During this time there were many new technologies in the field, notably Cascading Style Sheets, JavaScript, and Dynamic HTML. On the whole, the browser competition did lead to many positive creations and helped web design evolve at a rapid pace.

Evolution of Web Design

In 1996, Microsoft released its first competitive browser, which was complete with its own features and tags. It was also the first browser to support style sheets, which at the time was seen as an obscure authoring technique. The HTML markup for tables was originally intended for displaying tabular data. However designers quickly realized the potential of using HTML tables for creating the complex, multi-column layouts that were otherwise not possible. At this time, as design and good aesthetics seemed to take precedence over good mark-up structure, and little attention was paid to semantics and web accessibility. HTML sites were limited in their design options, even more so with earlier versions of HTML. To create complex designs, many web designers had to use complicated table structures or even use blank spacer .GIF images to stop empty table cells from collapsing. CSS was introduced in December 1996 by the W3C to support presentation and layout. This allowed HTML code to be semantic rather than both semantic and presentational, and improved web accessibility.

In 1996, Flash (originally known as FutureSplash) was developed. At the time, the Flash content development tool was relatively simple compared to now, using basic layout and drawing tools, a limited precursor to ActionScript, and a timeline, but it enabled web designers to go beyond the point of HTML, animated GIFs and JavaScript. However, because Flash required a plug-in, many web developers avoided using it for fear of limiting their market share due to lack of compatibility. Instead, designers reverted to gif animations (if they didn't forego using motion graphics altogether) and JavaScript for widgets. But the benefits of Flash made it popular enough among specific target markets to eventually work its way to the vast majority of browsers, and powerful enough to be used to develop entire sites.

End of the First Browser Wars

During 1998 Netscape released Netscape Communicator code under an open source licence, enabling thousands of developers to participate in improving the software. However, they decided to start from the beginning, which guided the development of the open source browser and soon expanded to a complete application platform. The Web Standards Project was formed and promoted browser compliance with HTML and CSS standards by creating Acid1, Acid2, and Acid3 tests. 2000 was a big year for Microsoft. Internet Explorer was released for Mac; this was significant as it was the first browser that fully supported HTML 4.01 and CSS 1, raising the bar in terms of standards compliance. It was also the first browser to fully support the PNG image format. During this time Netscape was sold to AOL and this was seen as Netscape's official loss to Microsoft in the browser wars.

2001—2012

Since the start of the 21st century the web has become more and more integrated into peoples lives. As this has happened the technology of the web has also moved on. There have also been significant changes in the way people use and access the web, and this has changed how sites are designed.

Since the end of the browsers wars new browsers have been released. Many of these are open source meaning that they tend to have faster development and are more supportive of new standards. The new options are considered by many to be better than Microsoft's Internet Explorer.

The W3C has released new standards for HTML (HTML5) and CSS (CSS3), as well as new JavaScript API's, each as a new but individual standard.While the term HTML5 is only used to refer to the new version of HTML and *some* of the JavaScript API's, it has become common to use it to refer to the entire suite of new standards (HTML5, CSS3 and JavaScript).

In 2016, the term "web brutalism" was applied to web design that emphasized simple presentation and fast page loading.

Tools and Technologies

Web designers use a variety of different tools depending on what part of the production process they are involved in. These tools are updated over time by newer standards and software but the principles behind them remain the same. Web designers use both vector and raster graphics editors to create web-formatted imagery or design prototypes. Technologies used to create websites include W3C standards like HTML and CSS, which can be hand-coded or generated by WYSIWYG editing software. Other tools web designers might use include mark up validators and other testing tools for usability and accessibility to ensure their web sites meet web accessibility guidelines.

Skills and Techniques

Marketing and Communication Design

Marketing and communication design on a website may identify what works for its target market. This can be an age group or particular strand of culture; thus the designer may understand the trends of its audience. Designers may also understand the type of website they are designing, meaning, for example, that (B2B) business-to-business website design considerations might differ greatly from a consumer targeted website such as a retail or entertainment website. Careful consideration might be made to ensure that the aesthetics or overall design of a site do not clash with the clarity and accuracy of the content or the ease of web navigation, especially on a B2B website. Designers may also consider the reputation of the owner or business the site is representing to make sure they are portrayed favourably.

User Experience Design and Interactive Design

User understanding of the content of a website often depends on user understanding of how the website works. This is part of the user experience design. User experience is related to layout, clear instructions and labeling on a website. How well a user understands how they can interact on a site may also depend on the interactive design of the site. If a user perceives the usefulness of the website, they are more likely to continue using it. Users who are skilled and well versed with website use may find a more distinctive, yet less intuitive or less user-friendly website interface useful nonetheless. However, users with less experience are less likely to see the advantages or usefulness of a less intuitive website interface. This drives the trend for a more universal user experience and ease of access to accommodate as many users as possible regardless of user skill. Much of the user experience design and interactive design are considered in the user interface design.

Advanced interactive functions may require plug-ins if not advanced coding language skills. Choosing whether or not to use interactivity that requires plug-ins is a critical decision in user experience design. If the plug-in doesn't come pre-installed with most browsers, there's a risk that the user will have neither the know how or the patience to install a plug-in just to access the content. If the function requires advanced coding language skills, it may be too costly in either time or money to code compared to the amount of enhancement the function will add to the user experience. There's also a risk that advanced interactivity may be incompatible with older browsers or hardware configurations. Publishing a function that doesn't work reliably is potentially worse for the user experience than making no attempt. It depends on the target audience if it's likely to be needed or worth any risks.

Page Layout

Part of the user interface design is affected by the quality of the page layout. For example, a designer may consider whether the site's page layout should remain consistent on different pages when designing the layout. Page pixel width may also be considered vital for aligning objects in the layout design. The most popular fixed-width websites generally have the same set width to match the current most popular browser window, at the current most popular screen resolution, on the current most popular monitor size. Most pages are also center-aligned for concerns of aesthetics on larger screens.

Fluid layouts increased in popularity around 2000 as an alternative to HTML-table-based layouts and grid-based design in both page layout design principle and in coding technique, but were very slow to be adopted.This was due to considerations of screen reading devices and varying windows sizes which designers have no control over. Accordingly, a design may be broken down into units (sidebars, content blocks, embedded advertising areas, navigation areas) that are sent to the browser and which will be fitted into the display window by the browser, as best it can. As the browser does recognize the details of the reader's screen (window size, font size relative to window etc.) the browser can make user-specific layout adjustments to fluid layouts, but not fixed-width layouts. Although such a display may often change the relative position of major content units, sidebars may be displaced below body text rather than to the side of it. This is a more flexible display than a hard-coded grid-based layout that doesn't fit the device window. In particular, the relative position of content blocks may change while leaving the content within the block unaffected. This also minimizes the user's need to horizontally scroll the page.

Responsive Web Design is a newer approach, based on CSS3, and a deeper level of per-device specification within the page's stylesheet through an enhanced use of the CSS @media rule.

Typography

Web designers may choose to limit the variety of website typefaces to only a few which are of a similar style, instead of using a wide range of typefaces or type styles. Most browsers recognize a specific number of safe fonts, which designers mainly use in order to avoid complications.

Font downloading was later included in the CSS3 fonts module and has since been implemented in Safari 3.1, Opera 10 and Mozilla Firefox 3.5. This has subsequently increased interest in web typography, as well as the usage of font downloading.

Most site layouts incorporate negative space to break the text up into paragraphs and also avoid center-aligned text.

Motion Graphics

The page layout and user interface may also be affected by the use of motion graphics. The choice of whether or not to use motion graphics may depend on the target market for the website. Motion graphics may be expected or at least better received with an entertainment-oriented website. However, a website target audience with a more serious or formal interest (such as business, community, or government) might find animations unnecessary and distracting if only for entertainment or decoration purposes. This doesn't mean that more serious content couldn't be enhanced with animated or video presentations that is relevant to the content. In either case, motion graphic design may make the difference between more effective visuals or distracting visuals.

Motion graphics that are not initiated by the site visitor can produce accessibility issues. The World Wide Web consortium accessibility standards require that site visitors be able to disable the animations.

Quality of Code

Website designers may consider it to be good practice to conform to standards. This is usually done via a description specifying what the element is doing. Failure to conform to standards may not make a website unusable or error prone, but standards can relate to the correct layout of pages for readability as well making sure coded elements are closed appropriately. This includes errors in code, more organized layout for code, and making sure IDs and classes are identified properly. Poorly-coded pages are sometimes colloquially called tag soup. Validating via W3C can only be done when a correct DOCTYPE declaration is made, which is used to highlight errors in code. The system identifies the errors and areas that do not conform to web design standards. This information can then be corrected by the user.

Generated Content

There are two ways websites are generated: statically or dynamically.

Static Websites

A static website stores a unique file for every page of a static website. Each time that page is requested, the same content is returned. This content is created once, during the design of the website. It is usually manually authored, although some sites use an automated creation process, similar to a dynamic website, whose results are stored long-term as completed pages. These automatically-created static sites became more popular around 2015, with generators such as Jekyll and Adobe Muse.

The benefits of a static website are that they were simpler to host, as their server only needed to serve static content, not execute server-side scripts. This required less server administration and had less chance of exposing security holes. They could also serve pages more quickly, on low-cost server hardware. These advantage became less important as cheap web hosting expanded to also offer dynamic features, and virtual servers offered high performance for short intervals at low cost.

Almost all websites have some static content, as supporting assets such as images and stylesheets are usually static, even on a website with highly dynamic pages.

Dynamic Websites

Dynamic websites are generated on the fly and use server-side technology to generate webpages. They typically extract their content from one or more back-end databases: some are database queries across a relational database to query a catalogue or to summarise numeric information, others may use a document database such as MongoDB or NoSQL to store larger units of content, such as blog posts or wiki articles.

In the design process, dynamic pages are often mocked-up or wireframed using static pages. The skillset needed to develop dynamic web pages is much broader than for a static pages, involving server-side and database coding as well as client-side interface design. Even medium-sized dynamic projects are thus almost always a team effort.

When dynamic web pages first developed, they were typically coded directly in languages such as Perl, PHP or ASP. Some of these, notably PHP and ASP, used a 'template' approach where a server-side page resembled the structure of the completed client-side page and data was inserted into places defined by 'tags'. This was a quicker means of development than coding in a purely procedural coding language such as Perl.

Both of these approaches have now been supplanted for many websites by higher-level application-focussed tools such as content management systems. These build on top of general purpose coding platforms and assume that a website exists to offer content according to one of several well recognised models, such as a time-sequenced blog, a thematic magazine or news site, a wiki or a user forum. These tools make the implementation of such a site very easy, and a purely organisational and design-based task, without requiring any coding.

Homepage Design

Usability experts, including Jakob Nielsen and Kyle Soucy, have often emphasised homepage design for website success and asserted that the homepage is the most important page on a website. However practitioners into the 2000s were starting to find that a growing number of website traffic was bypassing the homepage, going directly to internal content pages through search engines, e-newsletters and RSS feeds. Leading many practitioners to argue that homepages are less important than most people think. Jared Spool argued in 2007 that a site's homepage was actually the least important page on a website.

In 2012 and 2013, carousels (also called 'sliders' and 'rotating banners') have become an extremely popular design element on homepages, often used to showcase featured or recent content in a confined space. Many practitioners argue that carousels are an ineffective design element and hurt a website's search engine optimisation and usability.

Occupations

There are two primary jobs involved in creating a website: the web designer and web developer, who often work closely together on a website. The web designers are responsible for the visual aspect, which includes the layout, coloring and typography of a web page. Web designers will also have a working knowledge of markup languages such as HTML and CSS, although the extent of their knowledge will differ from one web designer to another. Particularly in smaller organizations one person will need the necessary skills for designing and programming the full web page, while larger organizations may have a web designer responsible for the visual aspect alone.

Further jobs which may become involved in the creation of a website include:

- Graphic designers to create visuals for the site such as logos, layouts and buttons
- Internet marketing specialists to help maintain web presence through strategic solutions on targeting viewers to the site, by using marketing and promotional techniques on the internet
- SEO writers to research and recommend the correct words to be incorporated into a particular website and make the website more accessible and found on numerous search engines
- Internet copywriter to create the written content of the page to appeal to the targeted viewers of the site
- User experience (UX) designer incorporates aspects of user focused design considerations which include information architecture, user centered design, user testing, interaction design, and occasionally visual design.

CSS Frameworks

CSS frameworks are pre-prepared software frameworks that are meant to allow for easier, more standards-compliant web design using the Cascading Style Sheets language. Most of these frameworks contain at least a grid. More functional frameworks also come with more features and additional JavaScript based functions, but are mostly design oriented and unobtrusive. This differentiates these from functional and full JavaScript frameworks.

Two notable and widely used examples are Bootstrap and Foundation.

CSS frameworks offer different modules and tools:

- reset style sheet
- grid especially for responsive web design
- web typography
- set of icons in sprites or icon fonts
- styling for tooltips, buttons, elements of forms
- parts of graphical user interfaces like accordion, tabs, slideshow or modal windows (Lightbox)
- equalizer to create equal height content
- often used css helper classes (*left*, *hide*)

Bigger frameworks use a CSS interpreter like LESS or SASS.

Grid Systems

Name	Latest release/ Date	License	Fixed, fluid or responsive	Units (px, em, %)	Features	# of columns
960 grid system	October 21, 2011	GPL, MIT License	fixed	px	source ordering	12, 16, 24
Avalanche	1.1.2 (May 23, 2016)	MIT	responsive	%	Responsive, BEM-syntax CSS grid system written in Sass with coupled media queries	Any
awsm.css	March 20, 2016	MIT License	responsive	px, em, %	A lightweight, mobile-first, responsive, library for semantic HTML markup.	
Baseguide	1.7.0 (October 16, 2016)	MIT License	fluid	px, em, rem, %	Lightweight and robust CSS framework for prototyping and production code.	Any
Blueprint	1.0.1 (May 14, 2011)	MIT License			typography, forms, print. plugins for buttons, tabs and sprites.	
Bluesky grid system	April 17, 2013	Openpassorn license v1.0	responsive	px, %	responsive grid system	12
Bootstrap	3.3.6 (November 24, 2015)	MIT License (Apache License v2.0 prior to 3.1.0)	fixed, fluid, responsive	px, %	Layout, typography, forms, buttons, navigation, media queries + more, + .less files + js libraries	12

Cardinal Framework	3.1.0 (March 8, 2015)	MIT	fluid and responsive		fluid typography, responsive grid system. Style agnostic	
Cascade Framework	1.5 (August 28, 2013)	MIT	fixed, elastic, fluid, responsive	px, %	Grid, layout, typography, forms, buttons, media queries + more	Any
Cascade Framework Light	1.1 (July 23, 2013)	MIT	fixed, elastic, fluid, responsive	px, %	Grid, layout, typography, forms, buttons, media queries + more	Any
Chopstick	Continuous	MIT	hybrid	px, %	Sass (SCSS), semantic (if you want to), responsive, nesting, source ordering, configurable with variables	Any
Cre-atix-CSS	1.0.2 (April 6, 2014)	CC BY-SA 4.0	responsive	em, %	Easy to use, Layout, typography, forms, responsive grid system	12
Flexify	0.1 (April 24, 2016)	MIT	fixed, fluid, responsive	px, %	Bootstrap-like 12-cols grid and Flexbox 12-cols grid. Typography, forms, tables, css dropdown menu, columns, helper classes.	12
floatz	1.4.0 (September, 2015)	Apache License v2.0	fixed, fluid and responsive	%, em	floatz is a flexible and easy to use CSS framework. It provides a set of reusable CSS classes, Javascript modules and HTML code snippets that support web designers and developers to create state-of-the-art responsive web sites, web applications and HTML based mobile apps - on all browsers, platforms and devices.	Any
Fluidable	1.1.0 (September 8, 2013)	CC0 1.0	fluid	%	Lightweight responsive grid system, mobile first, fixed gutters, any number of columns	Any
Foundation	6.2.0 (February 26, 2016)	MIT License	fluid	px, %	Responsive Layout, source ordering, typography, forms, buttons, navigation, media queries, js libraries	Any
Jaidee Framework	(3.8) April, 2014	Openpassorn license v1.0	fluid	px, %	A lightweight CSS Framework with Responsive CSS Layout, grid system, typography, forms, buttons, navigation, media queries, js librarie, slideshow, js tab, Responsive modal popup	4,6,12
Jalsonic Opinion	(V1 Beta) May 14, 2016		fixed, fluid, responsive	px, %	Layout, grid system, web browser detect, Network, showing content by regions, scroll animations with Moves Reveal	12

Jeet Grid System	5	GPL3 License	fluid	%, px, em	A light, semantic, responsive, Stylus/SCSS framework built from the best parts. IE8+, fractional columns, consistently sized/infinitely nestable gutters.	Any, on the fly
Modest Grid	February 16, 2015	Creative Commons Attribution 4.0 International License	Responsive and fluid	px, %	Responsive grid system	1 to 24
Pure	0.6.0 (February 23, 2015)	BSD License	elastic, fluid, responsive	em, %	A lightweight, mobile-first, optionally responsive, grid system with modular support for forms, buttons, tables, and menus.	1, 2, 3, 4, 5, 6, 8, 12, 24
motus	V1.1 (8/01/2016)	MIT license	responsive	px, rem, %	Sass, multiple grid sizes, JQuery	12
Responsee	3.1.0 (April 15, 2016)	MIT License	responsive	px, em, %	A lightweight, grids, columns, responsive forms, navigation, typography, responsive tabs, buttons, free templates, premium templates	12
RÖCSSTI	June 2, 2016	MIT License	fixed, elastic, fluid, responsive	px, em, %	Layout, typography, forms, media queries, + .less file + .scss file	Any
Semantic	2.14 (September 13, 2015)	Apache License v2.0		px, %	responsive	
Ink	V2 (June 2013)	MIT license	elastic	px, em, %	Responsive, percentage based grid (for three screens, expandable to more), Typography, Forms, Tables, FontAwesome, Navigation, Alerts. Includes own JS library with several ready to use UI components.	Any, percentage based
skeleton	V1.2 (6/20/2012)	MIT license	responsive		Responsive Grid Down To Mobile, Fast to Start, Style Agnostic. Base grid is a variation of the 960 grid system.	12
VCL Flex Layout	0.1.0 (3/20/2016)	MIT license	fluid	em, %, flex units	Flexible Box (Flexbox) based grid.	12, percentage
YAML	4.1.2 (July 28, 2013)	CC-BY 2.0	fixed, elastic, fluid	px, em, %	Layout, grids, columns, forms, buttons, progressive linearization for responsive layouts, float handling, navigation, typography, accessibility, add-ons (accessible tabs, rtl-support, microformats)	any

Yet Another CSS Grid System	1.0	public domain	fluid, responsive		a very small easy to use responsive css grid system. Javascript is not required.	6
YUI CSS grids	3.5.1	BSD-3	fixed and fluid			
Zass	1.0 (January 24, 2012)	LGPL License	fluid	%	semantic (doesn't pollute HTML with classes), clean (no CSS hacks neither negative margins), any number of columns, infinite nesting of columns	Any
KNACSS	4.0 (March 2015)	WTPL	fixed, elastic, fluid, responsive	px, em, rem, %	CSS reset, reusable classes, best practices and conventions, CSS snippets, positioning models, advanced positioning (FlexBox), high browser support, grids and gutters, responsive webdesign, table classes, forms classes, LESS version, Sass version	Any
simplecss	2.1.4 (April 2, 2015)	MIT	elastic,responsive	%	Grids, Input, Buttons, Menu, Tables, Lists, Dialog, Messages, Paginator, Utility, Autocomplete, Badge, Extensions, Breadcrumb,ecc	12
Wee	3.3.4 (June 8, 2016)	Apache License v2.0	fluid, responsive	rem, em, px, %	HTML5 element styling, Less CSS mixin library, JavaScript toolset, and automated build process	Any
sGrid	v1.1.2 (November 11, 2015)	MIT	fluid, responsive	rem, em, px, %	Flexbox grid system built with Stylus CSS preprocessor. It is also based on CSS native calc() function.	Any
Diisba framework	1.3.1 (August 25, 2016)	CC 4.0	responsive	em, rem, px, %	HTML5 element styling, JavaScript toolset , Flex and float grid , Ted JS	12,11

Grid Generators

Name	Supported grid systems
Modest Grid	Set your columns, gutter width, maximum screen width and viewport sizes.

Blueprint (CSS Framework)

Blueprint is a CSS framework designed to reduce development time and ensure cross-browser compatibility when working with Cascading Style Sheets (CSS). It also serves as a foundation for many tools designed to make CSS development easier and more accessible to beginners. Blueprint is released under a modified version of the MIT License, making it free software. It can be either used as is, or further adapted for use via a compression tool that is written in Ruby.

Features

Blueprint's README file lists the following features as being provided out-of-the-box:

- An easily customizable grid
- Sensible default typography
- A typographic baseline
- Perfected browser CSS reset
- A stylesheet for printing
- Powerful scripts for customization
- Bloat Minimized as much as possible

History

Blueprint was first created by Olav Bjørkøy and released on August 3, 2007. By August 11, Blueprint included work based on ideas from Jeff Croft, Nathan Borror, Christian Metts, and Eric Meyer. Version 0.8 was released on November 11, and included various bugfixes as well as a new "tabs" plugin.

Blueprint as a Foundation for Other Projects

One of the goals stated by the core team is to facilitate the development of new tools for working with CSS. A variety of CSS generators, visual editors, themes, and frameworks are based on Blueprint, many of which can be found on the Blueprint Wiki.

Cascade Framework

Cascade Framework is a free CSS framework for creating websites and web applications. Similar to Bootstrap and Foundation, it contains a wide range of HTML and CSS-based interface components, as well as optional JavaScript extensions.

Origin

Dissatisfied with the architecture of Bootstrap and Foundation, John Slegers wanted to create an alternative that offered more flexibility and better performance without cutting back on features. He came up with the name Cascade Framework for his project and released it under the MIT License in March 2013.The last stable release is version 1.5.

Cascade Framework 2 is currently under development and will involve a rewrite of the codebase into the Sass language.

Features

Cascade Framework 1.x is written in pure CSS. It supports responsive design and all modern browsers as well as IE6+. For an optimal balance between footprint and flexibility, it implements a modifier design pattern inspired by SMACCS and OOCSS.

Binpress lists the following key features:

- Cascade Framework is entirely based on an OOCSS architecture optimised for both performance and flexibility.

- Cascade Framework contains advanced components like "panels", "tab blocks" and "navigation" components that can be combined in various ways.

- Cascade Framework is design agnostic. You can choose the default theme, create one of your own or just work with your own project specific custom design and leave out the default theme entirely. Both typography and color scheme are separated in separate modules to suit that purpose.

- Cascade Framework allows you to choose between a Semantic Grid technique and a presentational grid technique. Twitter Bootstrap offers only a presentational grid technique.

- With Cascade Framework, you can use any number of columns you want (1,2,3,4,5,6,7,8,9,10,12,16 and 24 columns are supported) throughout your project and nest them freely.

- Cascade Framework's grid uses a special padding element for its gutter, which combined with the media object integration makes the grid both more powerful and easier to use than any other grid system.

- The total CSS code of Cascade Framework is only 9712 bytes minified and gzipped and can be further reduced if you don't need all modules. For many projects, you'll do fine with a build of Cascade Framework with that's only 3910 bytes.

- Cascade Framework has a "light" version that's no more than 2010 bytes in total. While it doesn't contain components like panels or tabs, it still offers you a clean design for a whole bunch of elements, support for IE6, responsive behavior, etc. If you need just its grid features, you can go as lightweight as 323 bytes.

- Cascade Framework offers support up to IE6 and there are no plans to drop support for older browsers in the near future.

Cascade Framework is open source and available on GitHub. Developers are encouraged to participate in the project and make their own contributions to the platform.

Appraisal

In an article posted on October 13, 2013, Crunchify lists Cascade Framework as #5 in its "Top 5 New and Favorite Responsive Frameworks". The first four are respectively Bootstrap, Cardinal, TypePlate and Furrato.

In an article posted on October 24, 2013, CodeGeekz lists it among "12 Fresh and Useful Frameworks". Other projects listed are Gumby, Solved by Flexbox, UI Kit, SkelJS, Cardinal, Layers CSS, Grid Forms, Gridism, Maxmert, Rocket CSS and Kube Framework.

Linux portal Linuxlinks lists Cascade Framework as one of the ten "finest open source lightweight frameworks to kick start CSS and HTML projects". Other projects listed are Quantum Framework, Pure, Baseline, HTML KickStart, Base, KNACSS, Toast, Motherplate and HTML5 Boilerplate.

Cascade Framework was Softpedia's Script of the day on September 6, 2013. Softpedia's scripts tester Catalin Cimpanu explains why, according to him, Cascade Framework isn't your typical framework:

The Cascade CSS framework is a unique project these days. Unlike most CSS frameworks that focus on the UI, Cascade focuses on code organization and cross-browser compliance, something that most CSS frontend developers these days don't care about anymore.

While CSS framework developers has been busy in packing as much UI modules as they can in their frameworks' core, most of them forgot the main problem with Web development, a problem that's been around since the early 2000s: cross-browser compliance.

While most frameworks break when seen from a different, older browser, the Cascade Framework still renders the same and even gracefully degrades in ancient browsers.

Impossible right? Not impossible, but very possible, as this framework has proven. The biggest difference with Cascade compared to other CSS frameworks is the way code has been organized, making it super easy for developers to not only use, but also maintain the websites they build. All without breaking in older browsers.

Cascade Framework was also one of two winning submissions of a contest organised by Belgian web development company Openminds in the context of their 2013 Ruby conference, called Arrrrcamp.

Integration

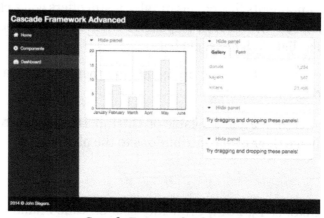

Cascade Framework Advanced

As of May 19, 2014, a Cascade Framework-based Drupal theme has been added to the Drupal website sandbox as a sandbox project.

As of October 29, 2014, Cascade Framework Advanced has been released. This Open Source project integrates Cascade Framework with JQuery UI.

Foundation (Framework)

Foundation is a responsive front-end framework. Foundation provides a responsive grid and HTML and CSS UI components, templates, and code snippets, including typography, forms, buttons, navigation and other interface components, as well as optional JavaScript extensions. Foundation is maintained by ZURB and is an open source project.

Origin

Foundation emerged as a ZURB project to develop front-end code faster and better. In October 2011, ZURB released Foundation 2.0 as open-source under the MIT License. ZURB released Foundation 3.0 in June 2012, 4.0 in February 2013, and 5.0 in November 2013. The team is working on the next version of Foundation for Sites which should be released in Spring 2015.

Foundation for Email was released in September 2013.

Foundation for Apps was released in December 2014.

Features

Foundation was designed for and tested on numerous browsers and devices. It is a mobile first responsive framework built with Sass/SCSS giving designers best practices for rapid development. The framework includes most common patterns needed to rapidly prototype a responsive site. Through the use of Sass mixins, Foundation components are easily styled and simple to extend.

Since version 2.0 it also supports responsive design. This means the graphic design of web pages adjusts dynamically, taking into account the characteristics of the device used (PC, tablet, mobile phone). Additionally, since 4.0 it has taken a mobile-first approach, designing and developing for mobile devices first, and enhancing the web pages and applications for larger screens.

Foundation is open source and available on Github. Developers are encouraged to participate in the project and make their own contributions to the platform.

Structure and Function

Foundation is modular and consists essentially of a series of Sass stylesheets that implement the various components of the toolkit. Component stylesheets can be included via Sass or by customizing the initial Foundation download. Developers can adapt the Foundation file itself, selecting the components they wish to use in their project.

Adjustments are possible through a central configuration stylesheet. More profound changes are possible by changing the Sass variables.

The use of Sass stylesheet language allows the use of variables, functions and operators, nested selectors, as well as so-called mixins.

Since version 3.0, the configuration of Foundation also has a special "Customize" option in the documentation. Moreover, developers use on a form to choose the desired components and adjust, if necessary, the values of various options to their needs. The subsequently generated package already includes the pre-built CSS style sheet.

Grid System and Responsive Design

Foundation comes standard with a 940 pixel wide, flexible grid layout. The toolkit is fully responsive to make use of different resolutions and types of devices: mobile phones, portrait and landscape format, tablets and PCs with a low and high resolution (widescreen). This adjusts the width of the columns automatically.

Understanding CSS Stylesheet

Foundation provides a set of stylesheets that provide basic style definitions for all key HTML components. These provide a browser and system-wide uniform, modern appearance for formatting text, tables and form elements.

Re-usable Components

In addition to the regular HTML elements, Foundation contains other commonly used interface elements. These include buttons with advanced features (for example, grouping of buttons or buttons with drop-down option, make and navigation lists, horizontal and vertical tabs, navigation, breadcrumb navigation, pagination, etc.), labels, advanced typographic capabilities, and formatting for messages such as warnings.

JavaScript Components and Plug-ins

The JavaScript components of Foundation 4 were moved from jQuery Javascript library to Zepto, on a presumption that the physically smaller, but API-compatible alternative to JQuery would prove faster for the user. However, Foundation 5 moved back to the newer release JQuery-2. "jQuery 2.x has the same API as jQuery 1.x, but does not support Internet Explorer 6, 7, or 8." the official Zurb blog explains, Why we dropped Zepto; and the unsigned writer claims that the switch back was due to issues of compatibility with customized efforts; and that performance was found to be actually not as good, on use testing with the newer jQuery-2.

Foundation jQuery components provide general user-interface elements and branded extensions. The list includes: dialog, tooltips, carousels, alerts, clearing, cookies, dropdown, forms, joyride, magellan, orbit, placeholder, reveal, section, topbar, flex video, and many others.

Plug-ins that use jQuery can be installed that are incorporated into the Foundation framework to provide advanced functionality in any UI area, including animation and "off-canvas" elements like slide-in menus.

JQuery elements like forms will need to be connected to a backend infrastructure (server-based database and scripting) using tools and methods outside the Foundation framework in order to work. External services like MailChimp are still installed as for any static HTML page, and do not require a home-rolled backend.

JQuery has become an acknowledged standard part of the evolution of the web. Wikipedia claims 65% of the top 100 Javascript sites employ it. Javascript itself is considered the de facto standard for frontend web development work, with HTML and CSS (by general consensus.)

Use

There are three levels of integration for Foundation: CSS, SASS, and Ruby on Rails with the Foundation Rails Gem.

CSS

To use Foundation CSS, default or custom CSS packages can be downloaded from the download page and installed into the appropriate web server folders. Foundation is then integrated into HTML page markup.

SASS

The Foundation SASS install uses Ruby, NodeJS, and Git to install Foundation sources. Foundation then provides a command line interface to modify and compile source to CSS for use in HTML page markup.

Foundation Rails Gem

The Foundation Rails gem can be installed by adding "gem 'foundation-rails'" to the Rails Application Gemfile.

Bootstrap (Front-end Framework)

Bootstrap is a free and open-source front-end web framework for designing websites and web applications. It contains HTML- and CSS-based design templates for typography, forms, buttons, navigation and other interface components, as well as optional JavaScript extensions. Unlike many web frameworks, it concerns itself with front-end development only.

Bootstrap is the second most-starred project on GitHub, with more than 100,000 stars and 45,000 forks.

Origin

Bootstrap is a framework, because it provides structure instead of simply being a library of predefined elements and styles.

Bootstrap, originally named Twitter Blueprint, was developed by Mark Otto and Jacob Thornton at Twitter as a framework to encourage consistency across internal tools. Before Bootstrap, various libraries were used for interface development, which led to inconsistencies and a high maintenance burden. According to Twitter developer Mark Otto:

"A super small group of developers and I got together to design and build a new internal tool and saw an opportunity to do something more. Through that process, we saw ourselves build something much more substantial than another internal tool. Months later, we ended up with an early version of Bootstrap as a way to document and share common design patterns and assets within the company."

After a few months of development by a small group, many developers at Twitter began to contribute to the project as a part of Hack Week, a hackathon-style week for the Twitter development team. It was renamed from Twitter Blueprint to Bootstrap, and released as an open source project on August 19, 2011. It has continued to be maintained by Mark Otto, Jacob Thornton, and a small group of core developers, as well as a large community of contributors.

On January 31, 2012, Bootstrap 2 was announced. This release added the twelve-column grid layout and responsive design components, as well as changes to many of the existing components. The Bootstrap 3 release was announced on 19 August 2013, moving to a mobile first approach and using a flat design.

On October 29, 2014, Mark Otto announced Bootstrap 4 was in development. The first alpha version of Bootstrap 4 was deployed on August 19, 2015.

Features

Bootstrap is compatible with the latest versions of the Google Chrome, Firefox, Internet Explorer, Opera, and Safari browsers, although some of these browsers are not supported on all platforms.

Since version 2.0 it also supports responsive web design. This means the layout of web pages adjusts dynamically, taking into account the characteristics of the device used (desktop, tablet, mobile phone).

Starting with version 3.0, Bootstrap adopted a mobile-first design philosophy, emphasizing responsive design by default.

The version 4.0 alpha release added Sass and Flexbox support.

Bootstrap is open source and available on GitHub. Developers are encouraged to participate in the project and make their own contributions to the platform.

Structure and Function

Example of a webpage using Bootstrap framework rendered in Mozilla Firefox

Bootstrap is modular and consists essentially of a series of Less stylesheets that implement the various components of the toolkit. A stylesheet called "Bootstrap less" includes the components stylesheets. Developers can adapt the Bootstrap file itself, selecting the components they wish to use in their projects.

Adjustments are possible to a limited extent through a central configuration stylesheet. More profound changes are possible by the Less declarations.

The use of the Less stylesheet language allows the use of variables, functions and operators, nested selectors, as well as mixins.

Since version 2.0, the configuration of Bootstrap also has a special "Customize" option in the documentation. Moreover, the developer chooses on a form the desired components and adjusts, if necessary, the values of various options to their needs. The subsequently generated package already includes the pre-built CSS style sheet.

As of Bootstrap 4, Sass will be used for stylesheets instead of Less.

Grid system and responsive design comes standard with an 1170 pixel wide grid layout. Alternatively, the developer can use a variable-width layout. For both cases, the toolkit has four variations to make use of different resolutions and types of devices: mobile phones, portrait and landscape, tablets and PCs with low and high resolution. Each variation adjusts the width of the columns.

Stylesheets

Bootstrap provides a set of stylesheets that provide basic style definitions for all key HTML components. These provide a uniform, modern appearance for formatting text, tables and form elements.

Re-usable Components

In addition to the regular HTML elements, Bootstrap contains other commonly used interface elements. The components are implemented as CSS classes, which must be applied to certain HTML elements in a page.

JavaScript Components

Bootstrap comes with several JavaScript components in the form of jQuery plugins. They provide additional user interface elements such as dialog boxes, tooltips, and carousels. They also extend the functionality of some existing interface elements, including for example an auto-complete function for input fields. In version 2.0, the following JavaScript plugins are supported: Modal, Dropdown, Scrollspy, Tab, Tooltip, Popover, Alert, Button, Collapse, Carousel and Typeahead.

Bootstrap 4

In 2015 Bootstrap developers have announced that they were working on a new framework version with multiple updates:

- Changed syntax from Less to Sass. Faster compilation for Bootstrap thanks to Libsass and Sass-syntax.

- Updated grid system. New semantic mixins and targeting on mobile devices.

- flexbox support. More responsive elements' support thanks to flexbox from HTML5.

- Abandoned wells, thumbnails and panels. They are replaced with "Cards" element.

- All HTML resets moved to Reboot module.

- Customization. Since version 4 it's easier to customize styles for templates, since all options are stored in Sass variables. After compiling a file developer gets an updated CSS-file.

- Closed IE8 support. Developers who need IE8 support should continue using Bootstrap 3.

- Moved from pixels to rem and em units.

- Rewrote all JS plugins.

- Improved work of tooltips and popovers.

- Improved search and documentation.

Cascading Style Sheets

Cascading Style Sheets (CSS) is a style sheet language used for describing the presentation of a document written in a markup language. Although most often used to set the visual style of web pages and user interfaces written in HTML and XHTML, the language can be applied to any XML document, including plain XML, SVG and XUL, and is applicable to rendering in speech, or on other media. Along with HTML and JavaScript, CSS is a cornerstone technology used by most websites to create visually engaging webpages, user interfaces for web applications, and user interfaces for many mobile applications.

CSS is designed primarily to enable the separation of document content from document presentation, including aspects such as the layout, colors, and fonts. This separation can improve content accessibility, provide more flexibility and control in the specification of presentation characteristics, enable multiple HTML pages to share formatting by specifying the relevant CSS in a separate .css file, and reduce complexity and repetition in the structural content.

Separation of formatting and content makes it possible to present the same markup page in different styles for different rendering methods, such as on-screen, in print, by voice (via speech-based browser or screen reader), and on Braille-based tactile devices. It can also display the web page differently depending on the screen size or viewing device. Readers can also specify a different style sheet, such as a CSS file stored on their own computer, to override the one the author specified.

Changes to the graphic design of a document (or hundreds of documents) can be applied quickly and easily, by editing a few lines in the CSS file they use, rather than by changing markup in the documents.

The CSS specification describes a priority scheme to determine which style rules apply if more than one rule matches against a particular element. In this so-called *cascade*, priorities (or *weights*) are calculated and assigned to rules, so that the results are predictable.

The CSS specifications are maintained by the World Wide Web Consortium (W3C). Internet media type (MIME type) text/css is registered for use with CSS by RFC 2318 (March 1998). The W3C operates a free CSS validation service for CSS documents.

Syntax

CSS has a simple syntax and uses a number of English keywords to specify the names of various style properties.

A style sheet consists of a list of *rules*. Each rule or rule-set consists of one or more *selectors*, and a *declaration block*.

Selector

In CSS, *selectors* declare which part of the markup a style applies to by matching tags and attributes in the markup itself.

Selectors may apply to:

- all elements of a specific type, e.g. the second-level headers h2
- elements specified by attribute, in particular:
  - *id*: an identifier unique within the document
  - *class*: an identifier that can annotate multiple elements in a document
- elements depending on how they are placed relative to others in the document tree.

Classes and IDs are case-sensitive, start with letters, and can include alphanumeric characters and underscores. A class may apply to any number of instances of any elements. An ID may only be applied to a single element.

Pseudo-classes are used in CSS selectors to permit formatting based on information that is not contained in the document tree. One example of a widely used pseudo-class is :hover, which identifies content only when the user "points to" the visible element, usually by holding the mouse cursor over it. It is appended to a selector as in a:hover or #elementid:hover. A pseudo-class classifies document elements, such as :link or :visited, whereas a *pseudo-element* makes a selection that may consist of partial elements, such as ::first-line or ::first-letter.

Selectors may be combined in many ways to achieve great specificity and flexibility. Multiple selectors may be joined in a spaced list to specify elements by location, element type, id, class, or any combination thereof. The order of the selectors is important. For example, div .myClass {color: red;} applies to all elements of class myClass that are inside div elements, whereas .myClass div {color: red;} applies to all div elements that are in elements of class myClass.

The following table provides a summary of selector syntax indicating usage and the version of CSS that introduced it.

Pattern	Matches	First defined in CSS level
E	an element of type E	1
E:link	an E element is the source anchor of a hyperlink of which the target is not yet visited (:link) or already visited (:visited)	1
E:active	an E element during certain user actions	1
E::first-line	the first formatted line of an E element	1
E::first-letter	the first formatted letter of an E element	1
.c	all elements with class="c"	1
#myid	the element with id="myid"	1
E.warning	an E element whose class is "warning" (the document language specifies how class is determined)	1
E#myid	an E element with ID equal to "myid"	1
E F	an F element descendant of an E element	1
*	any element	2
E[foo]	an E element with a "foo" attribute	2
E[foo="bar"]	an E element whose "foo" attribute value is exactly equal to "bar"	2
E[foo~="bar"]	an E element whose "foo" attribute value is a list of whitespace-separated values, one of which is exactly equal to "bar"	2
E[foo|="en"]	an E element whose "foo" attribute has a hyphen-separated list of values beginning (from the left) with "en"	2
E:first-child	an E element, first child of its parent	2
E:lang(fr)	an element of type E in language "fr" (the document language specifies how language is determined)	2
E::before	generated content before an E element's content	2
E::after	generated content after an E element's content	2
E > F	an F element child of an E element	2
E + F	an F element immediately preceded by an E element	2
E[foo^="bar"]	an E element whose "foo" attribute value begins exactly with the string "bar"	3
E[foo$="bar"]	an E element whose "foo" attribute value ends exactly with the string "bar"	3
E[foo*="bar"]	an E element whose "foo" attribute value contains the sub-string "bar"	3
E:root	an E element, root of the document	3
E:nth-child(n)	an E element, the n-th child of its parent	3
E:nth-last-child(n)	an E element, the n-th child of its parent, counting from the last one	3
E:nth-of-type(n)	an E element, the n-th sibling of its type	3
E:nth-last-of-type(n)	an E element, the n-th sibling of its type, counting from the last one	3
E:last-child	an E element, last child of its parent	3
E:first-of-type	an E element, first sibling of its type	3
E:last-of-type	an E element, last sibling of its type	3

E:only-child	an E element, only child of its parent	3
E:only-of-type	an E element, only sibling of its type	3
E:empty	an E element that has no children (including text nodes)	3
E:target	an E element being the target of the referring URI	3
E:enabled	a user interface element E that is enabled	3
E:disabled	a user interface element E that is disabled	3
E:checked	a user interface element E that is checked (for instance a radio-button or checkbox)	3
E:not(s)	an E element that does not match simple selector s	3
E ~ F	an F element preceded by an E element	3

Declaration Block

A declaration block consists of a list of *declarations* in braces. Each declaration itself consists of a *property*, a colon (:), and a *value*. If there are multiple declarations in a block, a semi-colon (;) must be inserted to separate each declaration.

Properties are specified in the CSS standard. Each property has a set of possible values. Some properties can affect any type of element, and others apply only to particular groups of elements.

Values may be keywords, such as "center" or "inherit", or numerical values, such as 200px (200 pixels), 50vw (50 percent of the viewport width) or 80% (80 percent of the window width). Color values can be specified with keywords (e.g. "red"), hexadecimal values (e.g. #FF0000, also abbreviated as #F00), RGB values on a 0 to 255 scale (e.g. rgb(255, 0, 0)), RGBA values that specify both color and alpha transparency (e.g. rgba(255, 0, 0, 0.8)), or HSL or HSLA values (e.g. hsl(000, 100%, 50%), hsla(000, 100%, 50%, 80%)).

Use

Before CSS, nearly all presentational attributes of HTML documents were contained within the HTML markup. All font colors, background styles, element alignments, borders and sizes had to be explicitly described, often repeatedly, within the HTML. CSS lets authors move much of that information to another file, the style sheet, resulting in considerably simpler HTML.

For example, headings (h1 elements), sub-headings (h2), sub-sub-headings (h3), etc., are defined structurally using HTML. In print and on the screen, choice of font, size, color and emphasis for these elements is *presentational*.

Before CSS, document authors who wanted to assign such typographic characteristics to, say, all h2 headings had to repeat HTML presentational markup for each occurrence of that heading type. This made documents more complex, larger, and more error-prone and difficult to maintain. CSS allows the separation of presentation from structure. CSS can define color, font, text alignment, size, borders, spacing, layout and many other typographic characteristics, and can do so independently for on-screen and printed views. CSS also defines non-visual styles, such as reading speed and emphasis for aural text readers. The W3C has now deprecated the use of all presentational HTML markup.

For example, under pre-CSS HTML, a heading element defined with red text would be written as:

<h1><font color="red"> Chapter 1. </font></h1>

Using CSS, the same element can be coded using style properties instead of HTML presentational attributes:

<h1 style="color: red;"> Chapter 1. </h1>

An "external" CSS file, as described below, can be associated with an HTML document using the following syntax:

<link href="path/to/file.css" rel="stylesheet">

An internal CSS code can be typed in the head section of the code. The coding is started with the style tag. For example,

<style>

Sources

CSS information can be provided from various sources. These sources can be the web browser, the user and the author. The information from the author can be further classified into inline, media type, importance, selector specificity, rule order, inheritance and property definition. CSS style information can be in a separate document or it can be embedded into an HTML document. Multiple style sheets can be imported. Different styles can be applied depending on the output device being used; for example, the screen version can be quite different from the printed version, so that authors can tailor the presentation appropriately for each medium.

The style sheet with the highest priority controls the content display. Declarations not set in the highest priority source are passed on to a source of lower priority, such as the user agent style. This process is called *cascading*.

One of the goals of CSS is to allow users greater control over presentation. Someone who finds red italic headings difficult to read may apply a different style sheet. Depending on the browser and the web site, a user may choose from various style sheets provided by the designers, or may remove all added styles and view the site using the browser's default styling, or may override just the red italic heading style without altering other attributes.

CSS priority scheme (highest to lowest)		
Priority	**CSS source type**	**Description**
1	Importance	The '!important' annotation overwrites the previous priority types
2	Inline	A style applied to an HTML element via HTML 'style' attribute
3	Media Type	A property definition applies to all media types, unless a media specific CSS is defined
4	User defined	Most browsers have the accessibility feature: a user defined CSS
5	Selector specificity	A specific contextual selector (#heading p) overwrites generic definition
6	Rule order	Last rule declaration has a higher priority

7	Parent inheritance	If a property is not specified, it is inherited from a parent element
8	CSS property definition in HTML document	CSS rule or CSS inline style overwrites a default browser value
9	Browser default	The lowest priority: browser default value is determined by W3C initial value specifications

Specificity

Specificity refers to the relative weights of various rules. It determines which styles apply to an element when more than one rule could apply. Based on specification, a simple selector (e.g. H1) has a specificity of 1, class selectors have a specificity of 1,0, and ID selectors a specificity of 1,0,0. Because the specificity values do not carry over as in the decimal system, commas are used to separate the "digits" (a CSS rule having 11 elements and 11 classes would have a specificity of 11,11, not 121).

Thus the following rules selectors result in the indicated specificity:

Selectors	Specificity
H1 {color: white;}	1
P EM {color: green;}	2
.grape {color: red;}	1,0
P.bright {color: blue;}	1,1
P.bright EM.dark {color: yellow;}	2,2
#id218 {color: brown;}	1,0,0
style=" "	1,0,0,0

Example

Consider this HTML fragment:

```
<!DOCTYPE html>

<html>

 <head>

  <meta charset="utf-8">

  <style>

  #xyz { color: red; }

  </style>

 </head>

 <body>

  <p id="xyz" style="color: blue;"> To demonstrate specificity </p>
```

```
</body>

</html>
```

In the above example, the declaration in the style attribute overrides the one in the <style> element because it has a higher specificity.

Inheritance

Inheritance is a key feature in CSS; it relies on the ancestor-descendant relationship to operate. Inheritance is the mechanism by which properties are applied not only to a specified element, but also to its descendants. Inheritance relies on the document tree, which is the hierarchy of XHTML elements in a page based on nesting. Descendant elements may inherit CSS property values from any ancestor element enclosing them. In general, descendant elements inherit text-related properties, but box-related properties are not inherited. Properties that can be inherited are color, font, letter-spacing, line-height, list-style, text-align, text-indent, text-transform, visibility, white-space and word-spacing. Properties that cannot be inherited are background, border, display, float and clear, height, and width, margin, min- and max-height and -width, outline, overflow, padding, position, text-decoration, vertical-align and z-index.

Inheritance prevents certain properties from being declared over and over again in a style sheet, allowing the software developers to write less CSS. It enhances faster-loading of web pages by users and enables the clients to save money on bandwidth and development costs.

Example

Given the following style sheet:

```
h1 {

  color: pink;

}
```

Suppose there is an h1 element with an emphasizing element (em) inside:

```
<h1>

  This is to <em>illustrate</em> inheritance

</h1>
```

If no color is assigned to the em element, the emphasized word "illustrate" inherits the color of the parent element, h1. The style sheet h1 has the color pink, hence, the em element is likewise pink.

Whitespace

Whitespace between properties and selectors is ignored. This code snippet:

```
body{overflow:hidden;background:#000000;}
```

is functionally equivalent to this one:

```
body {

  overflow: hidden;

  background: #000000;

}
```

One common way to format CSS for readability is to indent each property and give it its own line.

Positioning

CSS 2.1 defines three positioning schemes:

Normal flow

> *Inline* items are laid out in the same way as the letters in words in text, one after the other across the available space until there is no more room, then starting a new line below. *Block* items stack vertically, like paragraphs and like the items in a bulleted list. Normal flow also includes relative positioning of block or inline items, and run-in boxes.

Floats

> A floated item is taken out of the normal flow and shifted to the left or right as far as possible in the space available. Other content then flows alongside the floated item.

Absolute positioning

> An absolutely positioned item has no place in, and no effect on, the normal flow of other items. It occupies its assigned position in its container independently of other items.

Position Property

There are four possible values of the position property. If an item is positioned in any way other than static, then the further properties top, bottom, left, and right are used to specify offsets and positions.

Static

> The default value places the item in the *normal flow*

Relative

> The item is placed in the *normal flow*, and then shifted or offset from that position. Subsequent flow items are laid out as if the item had not been moved.

Absolute

> Specifies *absolute positioning*. The element is positioned in relation to its nearest non-static ancestor.

Fixed

> The item is *absolutely positioned* in a fixed position on the screen even as the rest of the document is scrolled

Float and Clear

The float property may have one of three values. *Absolutely* positioned or *fixed* items cannot be floated. Other elements normally flow around floated items, unless they are prevented from doing so by their clear property.

left

> The item *floats* to the left of the line that it would have appeared in; other items may flow around its right side.

right

> The item *floats* to the right of the line that it would have appeared in; other items may flow around its left side.

clear

> Forces the element to appear underneath ('clear') floated elements to the left (clear:left), right (clear:right) or both sides (clear:both).

History

Håkon Wium Lie, chief technical officer of the Opera Software company and co-creator of the CSS web standard

CSS was first proposed by Håkon Wium Lie on October 10, 1994. At the time, Lie was working with Tim Berners-Lee at CERN. Several other style sheet languages for the web were proposed around the same time, and discussions on public mailing lists and inside World Wide Web Consortium resulted in the first W3C CSS Recommendation (CSS1) being released in 1996. In particular, Bert Bos' proposal was influential; he became co-author of CSS1 and is regarded as co-creator of CSS.

Style sheets have existed in one form or another since the beginnings of Standard Generalized Markup Language (SGML) in the 1980s, and CSS was developed to provide style sheets for the web. One requirement for a web style sheet language was for style sheets to come from different sources on the web. Therefore, existing style sheet languages like DSSSL and FOSI were not suitable. CSS, on the other hand, let a document's style be influenced by multiple style sheets by way of "cascading" styles.

As HTML grew, it came to encompass a wider variety of stylistic capabilities to meet the demands of web developers. This evolution gave the designer more control over site appearance, at the cost of more complex HTML. Variations in web browser implementations, such as ViolaWWW and WorldWide-Web, made consistent site appearance difficult, and users had less control over how web content was displayed. The browser/editor developed by Tim Berners-Lee had style sheets that were hard-coded into the program. The style sheets could therefore not be linked to documents on the web. Robert Cailliau, also of CERN, wanted to separate the structure from the presentation so that different style sheets could describe different presentation for printing, screen-based presentations, and editors.

Improving web presentation capabilities was a topic of interest to many in the web community and nine different style sheet languages were proposed on the www-style mailing list. Of these nine proposals, two were especially influential on what became CSS: Cascading HTML Style Sheets and Stream-based Style Sheet Proposal (SSP). Two browsers served as testbeds for the initial proposals; Lie worked with Yves Lafon to implement CSS in Dave Raggett's Arena browser. Bert Bos implemented his own SSP proposal in the Argo browser. Thereafter, Lie and Bos worked together to develop the CSS standard (the 'H' was removed from the name because these style sheets could also be applied to other markup languages besides HTML).

Lie's proposal was presented at the "Mosaic and the Web" conference (later called WWW2) in Chicago, Illinois in 1994, and again with Bert Bos in 1995. Around this time the W3C was already being established, and took an interest in the development of CSS. It organized a workshop toward that end chaired by Steven Pemberton. This resulted in W3C adding work on CSS to the deliverables of the HTML editorial review board (ERB). Lie and Bos were the primary technical staff on this aspect of the project, with additional members, including Thomas Reardon of Microsoft, participating as well. In August 1996 Netscape Communication Corporation presented an alternative style sheet language called JavaScript Style Sheets (JSSS). The spec was never finished and is deprecated. By the end of 1996, CSS was ready to become official, and the CSS level 1 Recommendation was published in December.

Development of HTML, CSS, and the DOM had all been taking place in one group, the HTML Editorial Review Board (ERB). Early in 1997, the ERB was split into three working groups: HTML Working group, chaired by Dan Connolly of W3C; DOM Working group, chaired by Lauren Wood of SoftQuad; and CSS Working group, chaired by Chris Lilley of W3C.

The CSS Working Group began tackling issues that had not been addressed with CSS level 1, resulting in the creation of CSS level 2 on November 4, 1997. It was published as a W3C Recommendation on May 12, 1998. CSS level 3, which was started in 1998, is still under development as of 2014.

In 2005 the CSS Working Groups decided to enforce the requirements for standards more strictly. This meant that already published standards like CSS 2.1, CSS 3 Selectors and CSS 3 Text were pulled back from Candidate Recommendation to Working Draft level.

Difficulty With Adoption

The CSS 1 specification was completed in 1996. Microsoft's Internet Explorer 3 was released in that year, featuring some limited support for CSS. IE 4 and Netscape 4.x added more support, but it was typically incomplete and had many bugs that prevented CSS from being usefully adopted. It was more than three years before any web browser achieved near-full implementation of the specification. Internet Explorer 5.0 for the Macintosh, shipped in March 2000, was the first browser to have full (better than 99 percent) CSS 1 support, surpassing Opera, which had been the leader since its introduction of CSS support 15 months earlier. Other browsers followed soon afterwards, and many of them additionally implemented parts of CSS 2.

However, even when later 'version 5' browsers began to offer a fairly full implementation of CSS, they were still incorrect in certain areas and were fraught with inconsistencies, bugs and other quirks. The inconsistencies and variation in feature support made it difficult for designers to achieve a consistent appearance across browsers and platforms, leading to the use of workarounds such as CSS hacks and filters.

Problems with browsers' patchy adoption of CSS, along with errata in the original specification, led the W3C to revise the CSS 2 standard into CSS 2.1, which moved nearer to a working snapshot of current CSS support in HTML browsers. Some CSS 2 properties that no browser successfully implemented were dropped, and in a few cases, defined behaviors were changed to bring the standard into line with the predominant existing implementations. CSS 2.1 became a Candidate Recommendation on February 25, 2004, but CSS 2.1 was pulled back to Working Draft status on June 13, 2005, and only returned to Candidate Recommendation status on July 19, 2007.

In addition to these problems, the .css extension was used by a software product used to convert PowerPoint files into Compact Slide Show files, so some web servers served all .css as mime type application/x-pointplus rather than text/css.

Variations

CSS has various levels and profiles. Each level of CSS builds upon the last, typically adding new features and typically denoted as CSS 1, CSS 2, CSS 3, and CSS 4. Profiles are typically a subset of one or more levels of CSS built for a particular device or user interface. Currently there are profiles for mobile devices, printers, and television sets. Profiles should not be confused with media types, which were added in CSS 2.

CSS 1

The first CSS specification to become an official W3C Recommendation is CSS level 1, published on December 17, 1996. Håkon Wium Lie and Bert Bos are credited as the original developers. Among its capabilities are support for

- Font properties such as typeface and emphasis

- Color of text, backgrounds, and other elements

- Text attributes such as spacing between words, letters, and lines of text

- Alignment of text, images, tables and other elements

- Margin, border, padding, and positioning for most elements

- Unique identification and generic classification of groups of attributes

The W3C no longer maintains the CSS 1 Recommendation.

CSS 2

CSS level 2 specification was developed by the W3C and published as a recommendation in May 1998. A superset of CSS 1, CSS 2 includes a number of new capabilities like absolute, relative, and fixed positioning of elements and z-index, the concept of media types, support for aural style sheets (which were later replaced by the CSS 3 speech modules) and bidirectional text, and new font properties such as shadows.

The W3C no longer maintains the CSS 2 recommendation.

CSS 2.1

CSS level 2 revision 1, often referred to as "CSS 2.1", fixes errors in CSS 2, removes poorly supported or not fully interoperable features and adds already implemented browser extensions to the specification. To comply with the W3C Process for standardizing technical specifications, CSS 2.1 went back and forth between Working Draft status and Candidate Recommendation status for many years. CSS 2.1 first became a Candidate Recommendation on February 25, 2004, but it was reverted to a Working Draft on June 13, 2005 for further review. It returned to Candidate Recommendation on 19 July 2007 and then updated twice in 2009. However, because changes and clarifications were made, it again went back to Last Call Working Draft on 7 December 2010.

CSS 2.1 went to Proposed Recommendation on 12 April 2011. After being reviewed by the W3C Advisory Committee, it was finally published as a W3C Recommendation on 7 June 2011.

CSS 2.1 was planned as the first and final revision of level 2—but low priority work on CSS 2.2 began in 2015.

CSS 3

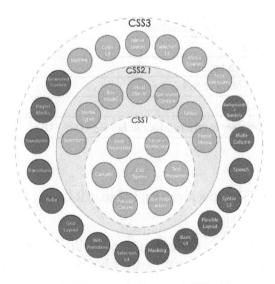

Taxonomy and status of CSS3
modules. • Recommendation • Candidate Recommendation • Last Call • Working Draft.

Unlike CSS 2, which is a large single specification defining various features, CSS 3 is divided into several separate documents called "modules". Each module adds new capabilities or extends features defined in CSS 2, preserving backward compatibility. Work on CSS level 3 started around the time of publication of the original CSS 2 recommendation. The earliest CSS 3 drafts were published in June 1999.

Due to the modularization, different modules have different stability and statuses. As of June 2012, there are over fifty CSS modules published from the CSS Working Group., and four of these have been published as formal recommendations:

- 2012-06-19: Media Queries

- 2011-09-29: Namespaces

- 2011-09-29: Selectors Level 3

- 2011-06-07: Color

Some modules have *Candidate Recommendation* (*CR*) status and are considered moderately stable. At *CR* stage, implementations are advised to drop vendor prefixes.

Summary of main module-specifications			
Module	**Specification title**	**Status**	**Date**
css3-background	CSS Backgrounds and Borders Module Level 3	*Candidate* Rec.	Sep 2014
css3-box	CSS basic box model	Working *Draft*,	Aug 2007
css-cascade-3	CSS Cascading and Inheritance Level 3	*Candidate* Rec.	Oct 2013
css3-color	CSS Color Module Level 3	*Recommendation*	Jun 2011
css3-content	CSS3 Generated and Replaced Content Module	Working *Draft*	May 2003
css-fonts-3	CSS Fonts Module Level 3	*Candidate* Rec.	Oct 2013
css3-gcpm	CSS Generated Content for Paged Media Module	Working *Draft*	May 2014
css3-layout	CSS Template Layout Module	Working *Draft*	Nov 2011
css3-mediaqueries	Media Queries	*Recommendation*	Jun 2012
css3-multicol	Multi-column Layout	*Candidate* Rec.	Apr 2011
css3-page	CSS Paged Media Module Level 3	Working *Draft*	Mar 2013
css3-selectors	Selectors Level 3	*Recommendation*	Sep 2011
css3-ui	CSS Basic User Interface Module Level 3 (CSS3 UI)	Working *Draft*	Jan 2012

CSS 4

There is no single, integrated CSS4 specification, because it is split into separate modules. However, there are "level 4" modules.

Because CSS3 split the CSS language's definition into modules, the modules have been allowed to level independently. Most modules are level 3—they build on things from CSS 2.1. A few level-4 modules exist (such as Image Values, Backgrounds & Borders, or Selectors), which build on the functionality of a preceding level-3 module. Other modules defining entirely new functionality, such as Flexbox, have been designated as "level 1".

The CSS Working Group sometimes publishes "Snapshots", a collection of whole modules and parts of other drafts that are considered stable, interoperably implemented and hence ready to use. So far, three such best current practices document have been published as Notes, in 2007, 2010 and 2015.

Browser Support

Each web browser uses a layout engine to render web pages, and support for CSS functionality is not consistent between them. Because browsers do not parse CSS perfectly, multiple coding techniques have been developed to target specific browsers with workarounds (commonly known as CSS hacks or CSS filters). Adoption of new functionality in CSS can be hindered by lack of support in major browsers. For example, Internet Explorer was slow to add support for many CSS 3 features, which slowed adoption of those features and damaged the browser's reputation among developers. In order to ensure a consistent experience for their users, web developers often test their sites across multiple operating systems, browsers, and browser versions, increasing development time and complexity. Tools such as BrowserStack have been built to reduce the complexity of maintaining these environments.

In addition to these testing tools, many sites maintain lists of browser support for specific CSS properties, including CanIUse and the Mozilla Developer Network. Additionally, the CSS 3 defines feature queries, which provide an @supports directive that will allow developers to target browsers with support for certain functionality directly within their CSS. CSS that is not supported by older browsers can also sometimes be patched in using Javascript polyfills, which are pieces of Javascript code designed to make browsers behave consistently. These workarounds—and the need to support fallback functionality—can add complexity to development projects, and consequently, companies frequently define a list of browser versions that they will and will not support.

As websites adopt newer code standards that are incompatible with older browsers, these browsers can be cut off from accessing many of the resources on the web (sometimes intentionally). Many of the most popular sites on the internet are not just visually degraded on older browsers due to poor CSS support, but do not work at all, in large part due to the evolution of Javascript and other web technologies.

Limitations

Some noted limitations of the current capabilities of CSS include:

Selectors are unable to ascend

> CSS currently offers no way to select a *parent* or *ancestor* of an element that satisfies certain criteria. CSS Selectors Level 4, which is still in Working Draft status, proposes such a selector, but only as part of the "complete" selector profile, not the "fast" profile used in dynamic CSS styling. A more advanced selector scheme (such as XPath) would enable more sophisticated style sheets. The major reasons for the CSS Working Group previously rejecting proposals for parent selectors are related to browser performance and Incremental rendering issues.

Cannot explicitly declare new scope independently of position

Scoping rules for properties such as z-index look for the closest parent element with a position:absolute or position:relative attribute. This odd coupling has undesired effects. For example, it is impossible to avoid declaring a new scope when one is forced to adjust an element's position, preventing one from using the desired scope of a parent element.

Pseudo-class dynamic behavior not controllable

CSS implements pseudo-classes that allow a degree of user feedback by conditional application of alternate styles. One CSS pseudo-class, ":hover", is dynamic (equivalent of JavaScript "onmouseover") and has potential for abuse (e.g., implementing cursor-proximity popups), but CSS has no ability for a client to disable it (no "disable"-like property) or limit its effects (no "nochange"-like values for each property).

Cannot name rules

There is no way to name a CSS rule, which would allow (for example) client-side scripts to refer to the rule even if its selector changes.

Cannot include styles from a rule into another rule

CSS styles often must be duplicated in several rules to achieve a desired effect, causing additional maintenance and requiring more thorough testing. Some new CSS features were proposed to solve this, but (as of February, 2016) are not yet implemented anywhere.

Cannot target specific text without altering markup

Besides the :first-letter pseudo-element, one cannot target specific ranges of text without needing to utilize place-holder elements.

Resolved Limitations

Vertical control limitations

Though horizontal placement of elements was always generally easy to control, vertical placement was frequently unintuitive, convoluted, or outright impossible. Simple tasks, such as centering an element vertically or placing a footer no higher than bottom of the viewport required either complicated and unintuitive style rules, or simple but widely unsupported rules. The Flexible Box Module improved the situation considerably and vertical control is much more straightforward and supported in all of the modern browsers. Older browsers still have those issues, but most of those (mainly Internet Explorer 9 and below) are no longer supported by their vendors.

Absence of expressions

There was no standard ability to specify property values as simple expressions (such as margin-left: 10% – 3em + 4px;). This would be useful in a variety of cases, such as calculating the size of columns subject to a constraint on the sum of all columns. Internet Explorer versions 5 to 7 support a proprietary expression() statement, with similar functionality. This proprietary expression() statement is no longer supported from Internet Explorer 8 onwards, except in compatibility modes. This decision was taken for "standards compliance, browser performance, and security reasons". However, a candidate recommendation with a calc() value to address this limitation has been published by the CSS WG and has since been supported in all of the modern browsers.

Lack of column declaration

Although possible in current CSS 3 (using the column-count module), layouts with multiple columns can be complex to implement in CSS 2.1. With CSS 2.1, the process is often done using floating elements, which are often rendered differently by different browsers, different computer screen shapes, and different screen ratios set on standard monitors. All of the modern browsers support this CSS 3 feature in one form or another.

Advantages

Separation of content from presentation

CSS facilitates publication of content in multiple presentation formats based on nominal parameters. Nominal parameters include explicit user preferences, different web browsers, the type of device being used to view the content (a desktop computer or mobile Internet device), the geographic location of the user and many other variables.

Site-wide consistency

When CSS is used effectively, in terms of inheritance and "cascading", a global style sheet can be used to affect and style elements site-wide. If the situation arises that the styling of the elements should be changed or adjusted, these changes can be made by editing rules in the global style sheet. Before CSS, this sort of maintenance was more difficult, expensive and time-consuming.

Bandwidth

A stylesheet, internal or external, specifies the style once for a range of HTML elements selected by class, type or relationship to others. This is much more efficient than repeating style information inline for each occurrence of the element. An external stylesheet is usually stored in the browser cache, and can therefore be used on multiple pages without being reloaded, further reducing data transfer over a network.

Page reformatting

With a simple change of one line, a different style sheet can be used for the same page. This has advantages for accessibility, as well as providing the ability to tailor a page or site to different target devices. Furthermore, devices not able to understand the styling still display the content.

Accessibility

Without CSS, web designers must typically lay out their pages with techniques such as HTML tables that hinder accessibility for vision-impaired users.

CSS Frameworks

CSS frameworks are pre-prepared libraries that are meant to allow for easier, more standards-compliant styling of web pages using the Cascading Style Sheets language. CSS frameworks include Foundation, Blueprint, Bootstrap, Cascade Framework and Materialize. Like programming and scripting language libraries, CSS frameworks are usually incorporated as external .css sheets referenced in the HTML <head>. They provide a number of ready-made options for designing and laying out the web page. Although many of these frameworks have been published, some authors use them mostly for rapid prototyping, or for learning from, and prefer to 'handcraft' CSS that is appropriate to each published site without the design, maintenance and download overhead of having many unused features in the site's styling.

CSS authoring Methodologies

As the size of CSS resources used in a project increases, the development team needs to decide on a common methodology to keep them organized. The goals are ease of development, ease of collaboration during development and performance of the deployed stylesheets in the browser. Popular methodologies include OOCSS - object oriented CSS, ACSS - atomic CSS, oCSS - organic Cascade Style Sheet, SMACSS - scalable and modular architecture for CSS and BEM - block, element, modifier.

Tableless Web Design

Tableless web design (or tableless web layout) is a web design philosophy eschewing the use of HTML tables for page layout control purposes.Instead of HTML tables, style sheet languages such as Cascading Style Sheets (CSS) are used to arrange elements and text on a web page.

The CSS1 specification was published in December 1996 by the W3C with the aim of improving web accessibility and emphasising the separation of presentational details in style sheets from semantic content in HTML documents. CSS2 in May 1998 (later revised in CSS 2.1 and CSS 2.2) extended CSS1 with facilities for positioning and table layout. Around the same time, in the late 1990s, as the dot-com boom led to a rapid growth in the "new media" of web page creation and design, there began a trend of using HTML tables, and their rows, columns and cells, to control the layout of whole web pages. This was due to several reasons:

- the desire of content publishers to replicate their existing corporate design elements on their web site;
- the limitations at the time of CSS support in browsers;
- the new web designers' lack of familiarity with the CSS standards;
- the lack of knowledge of, or concern for the reasons (including HTML semantics and web accessibility) to use CSS instead of what was perceived as an easier way to quickly achieve the intended layouts, and
- a new breed of WYSIWYG web design tools that encouraged this practice.

The advantages of restricting the use of HTML tables to their intended and semantic purpose include improved accessibility of the information to a wider variety of users, using a wide variety of user agents. There are bandwidth savings as large numbers of semantically meaningless <table>, <tr> and <td> tags are removed from dozens of pages leaving fewer, but more meaningful headings, paragraphs and lists. Layout instructions are transferred into site-wide CSS stylesheets, which can be downloaded once and cached for reuse while each visitor navigates the site. Sites may become more maintainable as the whole site can be restyled or re-branded in a single pass merely by altering the mark-up of the specific CSS, affecting every page which relies on that stylesheet. New HTML content can be added in such a way that consistent layout rules are immediately applied to it by the existing CSS without any further effort.

Some developers are now afraid to introduce a simple HTML table even where it makes good sense, some erring by the overuse of span and div elements, perhaps even with table-like rules applied to them using CSS.

Rationale

HTML was originally designed as a semantic markup language intended for sharing scientific documents and research papers online. Visual presentation was left up to the user. However, as the Internet expanded from the academic and research world into the mainstream in the mid-1990s, and became more media oriented, graphic designers sought ways to control the visual appearance of the Web pages presented to end users. To this end, tables and spacers (usually transparent single pixel GIF images with explicitly specified width, height or margins) have been used to create and maintain page layout.

This causes a number of problems. Many web pages were designed with tables nested within tables, resulting in large HTML documents that use more bandwidth than documents with simpler formatting. Furthermore, when a table-based layout is linearized, for example when being parsed by a screen reader or a search engine, the resulting order of the content can be somewhat jumbled and confusing.

In the late 1990s the first reasonably powerful WYSIWYG editors arrived on the market, which meant Web designers no longer needed a technical understanding of HTML to build web pages. Such editors indirectly encourage extensive use of nested tables to position design elements. As designers edit their documents in these editors, unnecessary code and empty elements can be added to the document. Furthermore, unskilled designers may use tables more than required when using a WYSIWYG editor. This practice can lead to many tables nested within tables as well as tables with unnecessary rows and columns.

The use of graphic editors with slicing tools that output HTML and images directly also promote poor code with tables often having many rows of 1 pixel height or width. Sometimes many more lines of code are used to render content than the actual content itself.

As the dotcom boom receded in 2001 and the web development industry shrank, coders with more industry experience were in higher demand. In a large number of cases UI development was carried out by coders with greater knowledge of good coding practice. It was around this time that many became critical of messy coding practices and the idea of tableless design began to grow.

Cascading Style Sheets (CSS) were developed to improve the separation between design and content, and move back towards a semantic organization of content on the Web. The term "tableless design" implies the use of CSS rather than layout tables to position HTML elements on the page. HTML tables still have their legitimate place when presenting tabular information within web pages, and are also sometimes still used as layout devices in situations for which CSS support is poor or problematical, like vertically centering an element.

Advantages

Accessibility

Because of the Internet's rapid growth, expanding disability discrimination legislation, and the increasing use of mobile phones and PDAs, it is necessary for Web content to be made accessible to users operating a wide variety of devices beyond the relatively uniform desktop computer and CRT monitor ecosystem the web first became popular on. Tableless Web design considerably improves Web accessibility in this respect.

Screen readers and braille devices have fewer problems with tableless designs because they follow a logical structure. The same is true for search engine Web crawlers, the software agents that most web site publishers hope will find their pages, classify them accurately and so enable potential users to find them easily in appropriate searches.

As a result of the separation of design (CSS) and structure (HTML), it is also possible to provide different layouts for different devices, e.g. handhelds, mobile phones, etc. It is also possible to specify a different style sheet for print, e.g. to hide or modify the appearance of advertisements or navigation elements that are irrelevant and a nuisance in the printable version of the page.

The W3C's Web Content Accessibility Guidelines' guideline no. 3 states "use markup and style sheets and do so properly." The guideline's checkpoint 3.3, a priority-2 checkpoint, says "use style sheets to control layout and presentation."

Bandwidth Savings

Tableless design produces web pages with fewer HTML tags used purely to position content. This normally means that the pages themselves become smaller to download. The philosophy implies that all the instructions regarding layout and positioning be moved into external style sheets. According to the basic capabilities of HTTP, as these rarely change and they apply in common to many web pages, they will be cached and reused after the first download. This further reduces bandwidth and download times across the site.

Maintainability

Maintaining a website may require frequent changes, both small and large, to the visual style of a website, depending on the purpose of the site. Under table-based layout, the layout is part of the HTML itself. As such, without the aid of template-based visual editors such as HTML editors, changing the positional layout of elements on a whole site may require a great deal of effort, depending on the amount of repetitive changes required. Even employing sed or similar global find-and-replace utilities cannot alleviate the problem entirely.

In tableless layout using CSS, the layout information may reside in a CSS document. Because the layout information may be centralized, it is possible that these changes can be made quickly and globally by default. The HTML files themselves may not need to be adjusted when making layout changes.

Also, because the layout information may be stored externally to the HTML, it may be quite easy to add new content in a tableless design, whether modifying an existing page or adding a new page. By contrast, without such a design, the layout for each page may require a more time-consuming manual changing of each instance or use of global find-and-replace utilities. However site owners often want particular pages to be different from others on the site either for a short period or long term. This will often necessitate a separate style sheet to be developed for that page. The page (or template) content usually can remain unaltered however, which is not the case in a tables-based design.

User Experience Design

User experience design (UX, UXD, UED or XD) is the process of enhancing user satisfaction with a product by improving the usability, accessibility, and pleasure provided in the interaction with the product. User experience design encompasses traditional human–computer interaction (HCI) design, and extends it by addressing all aspects of a product or service as perceived by users.

History

The field of user experience design is a conceptual design discipline and has its roots in human factors and ergonomics, a field that, since the late 1940s, has focused on the interaction between human users, machines, and the contextual environments to design systems that address the user's experience. With the proliferation of workplace computers in the early 1990s, user experience became an important concern for designers. It was Donald Norman, a user experience architect, who coined the term "user experience," and brought it to a wider audience.

I invented the term because I thought human interface and usability were too narrow. I wanted to cover all aspects of the person's experience with the system including industrial design graphics, the interface, the physical interaction and the manual. Since then the term has spread widely, so much so that it is starting to lose its meaning.

— Donald Norman

The term also has a more recent connection to user-centered design, human–computer interaction, and also incorporates elements from similar user-centered design fields.

Elements

User experience design includes elements of interaction design, information architecture, user research, and other disciplines, and is concerned with all facets of the overall experience delivered to users. Following is a short analysis of its constituent parts.

Visual Design

Visual design, also commonly known as graphic design, user interface design, communication design, and visual communication, represents the aesthetics or look-and-feel of the front end of any user interface. Graphic treatment of interface elements is often perceived as the visual design. The purpose of visual design is to use visual elements like colors, images, and symbols to convey a message to its audience. Fundamentals of Gestalt psychology and visual perception give a cognitive perspective on how to create effective visual communication.

Information Architecture

Information architecture is the art and science of structuring and organizing the information in products and services to support usability and findability.

In the context of information architecture, information is separate from both knowledge and data, and lies nebulously between them. It is information about objects. The objects can range from websites, to software applications, to images et al. It is also concerned with metadata: terms used to describe and represent content objects such as documents, people, process, and organizations.

Structuring, Organization, and Labeling

Structuring is reducing information to its basic building units and then relating them to each other. Organization involves grouping these units in a distinctive and meaningful manner. Labeling means using appropriate wording to support easy navigation and findability.

Finding and Managing

Findability is the most critical success factor for information architecture. If users are not able to find required information without browsing, searching or asking, then the findability of the information architecture fails. Navigation needs to be clearly conveyed to ease finding of the contents.

Interaction Design

There are many key factors to understanding interaction design and how it can enable a pleasurable end user experience. It is well recognized that building great user experience requires interaction design to play a pivotal role in helping define what works best for the users. High demand for improved user experiences and strong focus on the end-users have made interaction designers critical in conceptualizing design that matches user expectations and standards of the latest UI patterns and components. While working, interaction designers take several things in consideration. A few of them are:

- Defining interaction patterns best suited in the context

- Incorporating user needs collected during user research into the designs

- Features and information that are important to the user

- Interface behavior like drag-drop, selections, and mouse-over actions

- Effectively communicating strengths of the system

- Making the interface intuitive by building affordances

- Maintaining consistency throughout the system.

In the last few years, the role of interaction designer has shifted from being just focused on specifying UI components and communicating them to the engineers to a situation now where designers have more freedom to design contextual interfaces which are based on helping meet the user needs. Therefore, User Experience Design evolved into a multidisciplinary design branch that involves multiple technical aspects from motion graphics design and animation to programming.

Usability

Usability is the extent to which a product can be used by specified users to achieve specified goals with effectiveness, efficiency and satisfaction in a specified context of use.

Usability is attached with all tools used by humans and is extended to both digital and non-digital devices. Thus, it is a subset of user experience but not wholly contained. The section of usability that intersects with user experience design is related to humans' ability to use a system or application. Good usability is essential to a positive user experience but does not alone guarantee it.

Accessibility

Accessibility of a system describes its ease of reach, use and understanding. In terms of user experience design it can also be related to the overall comprehensibility of the information and features. It contributes to shorten the learning curve attached with the system. Accessibility in many contexts can be related to the ease of use for people with disabilities and comes under usability.

Human–computer Interaction

Human–computer interaction is concerned with the design, evaluation and implementation of interactive computing systems for human use and with the study of major phenomena surrounding them.

Human–computer interaction is the main contributor to user experience design because of its emphasis on human performance rather than mere usability. It provides key research findings which inform the improvement of systems for the people. Human-computer interaction extends its study towards more integrated interactions, such as tangible interactions, which is generally not covered in the practice of user experience. User experience cannot be manufactured or designed; it has to be incorporated in the design. Understanding the user's emotional quotient plays a key role while designing a user experience. The first step while designing the user experience is determining the reason a visitor will be visiting the website or use the application in question. Then the user experience can be designed accordingly.

Design

User experience design incorporates most or all of the above disciplines to positively impact the overall experience a person has with a particular interactive system and its provider. User experience design most frequently defines a sequence of interactions between a user (individual person) and a system, virtual or physical, designed to meet or support user needs and goals, primarily, while also satisfying systems requirements and organizational objectives.

Typical outputs include:

- Persona (an archetypal user for whom the product or service is being designed)

- Wireframes (screen blueprints or storyboards)

- Prototypes (for interactive or in-the-mind simulation)

- Written specifications (describing the behavior or design)

- Site audit (usability study of existing assets)

- Flows and navigation maps

- User stories or scenarios

- Sitemaps and content inventory

- High-fidelity visual mockups (precise visual layout and design of the expected product or interface)

General Design Process

While designing a product or service for a client, it is of utmost importance that the designers are on the same page as the client. All the information collected, plans made, design executed will reflect on the final product. Rigorous analysis must be done before proceeding to the design stage and then numerous testings done to optimize the site as per best standards so that the competitive edge is maintained. Leading Digital marketing companies combine three elements to provide the best responsive product to the customer. These are:

1. Researching about the target audience

2. Understanding the company's business goals

3. And most importantly apply out of the box thinking.

Brainstorming and testing ultimately leads them to finalize the design for their customers. Let's have a detailed look at the step by step process of product design:

- Collecting information about the problem

The UX designer needs to find out as much as they can about people, processes, and products before the design phase. Designers can do this by meeting with the clients or business stakeholders frequently to know what their requirements are, or by conducting interviews with users in their home or work spaces. This kind of qualitative research helps designers create products and services that better serve user needs.

- Getting ready to design

After research, the designer must make sense of the data they've collected. Typically this is done through modeling of the users and their environments. User modeling or personas are composite archetypes based on behavior patterns uncovered during research. Personas provide designers a precise way of thinking and communicating about how groups of users behave, how they think, what they want to accomplish and why. Once created, personas help the designer to understand the users' goals in specific contexts, which is particularly useful during ideation and for validating design concepts. Other types of models include work flow models, artifact models, and physical models.

- Design

When the designer has a firm grasp on the user's needs and goals, they begin to sketch out the interaction framework (also known as wireframes). This stage defines the high-level structure of screen layouts, as well as the product's flow, behavior, and organization. There are many kinds of materials that can be involved in during this iterative phase, from whiteboards to paper prototypes. As the interaction framework establishes an overall structure for product behavior, a parallel process focused on the visual and industrial designs. The visual design framework defines the experience attributes, visual language, and the visual style.

Once a solid and stable framework is established, wireframes are translated from sketched storyboards to full-resolution screens that depict the user interface at the pixel level. At this point, it's critical for the programming team to collaborate closely with the designer. Their input is necessary to creating a finished design that can and will be built while remaining true to the concept.

- Test and iterate

Usability testing is carried out through prototypes (paper or digital). The target users are given various tasks to perform on the prototypes. Any issues or problems faced by the users are collected as field notes and these notes are used to make changes in the design and reiterate the testing phase. Usability testing is, at its core, a means to "evaluate, not create".

UX Deliverables

UX designers' main goal is to solve the end-users' problems, and thus the ability to communicate the design to stakeholders and developers is critical to the ultimate success of the design. Regarding UX specification documents, these requirements depend on the client or the organization involved in designing a product. The four major deliverables are: a title page, an introduction to the feature, wireframes and a version history. Depending on the type of project, the specification documents can also include flow models, cultural models, personas, user stories, scenarios and any prior user research. Documenting design decisions, in the form of annotated wireframes, gives the developer the necessary information they may need to successfully code the project.

Depending on the company, a user experience designer may need to be a jack of all trades. It is not uncommon to see a user experience designer jump in at the beginning of the project lifecycle, where the problem set and project definition is vague, or after the project requirements document has been finalized and wireframes and functional annotations need to be created.

The following details the responsibilities a user experience designer may have at each phase of a project:

At the Beginning, When the Project is More Conceptual:

- Ethnographic research
- Surveying
- Customer feedback and testing
- Focus group administration
- Non-directed interview
- Contextual Interview
- Mental modeling
- Mood boards
- Card sorting
- Competitive analysis
- Contextual Inquiry

While the Project is Underway:

- Wireframing
- Heuristic analysis
- Expert evaluation
- Pluralistic walkthrough
- Personas
- Scenario
- Prototypes
- System mapping
- Experience mapping
- User testing/usability testing

After the Project has Launched:

- User testing/usability testing
- A/B testing
- Additional wireframing as a result of test results and fine-tuning

Designers

As with the fields mentioned above, user experience design is a highly multi-disciplinary field, incorporating aspects of psychology, anthropology, architecture, sociology, computer science, graphic design, industrial design, cognitive science, and business. Depending on the purpose of the product, UX may also involve content design disciplines such as communication design, instructional design, and game design. The subject matter of the content may also warrant collaboration with a subject-matter expert on planning the UX from various backgrounds in business, government, or private groups. More recently, content strategy has come to represent a sub-field of UX.

Graphic Designers

Graphic designers focus on the aesthetic appeal of the design. Information is communicated to the users through text and images. Much importance is given to how the text and images look and attract the users. Graphic designers have to make stylistic choices about things like font color, font type, and image locations. Graphic designers focus on grabbing the user's attention with the way the design looks. Graphic designers create visual concepts, using computer software or by hand, to communicate ideas that inspire, inform, and captivate consumers. They develop the overall layout and production design for various applications such as advertisements, brochures, magazines, and corporate reports.

Visual Designers

The visual designer (VisD) ensures that the visual representation of the design effectively communicates the data and hints at the expected behavior of the product. At the same time, the visual designer is responsible for conveying the brand ideals in the product and for creating a positive first impression; this responsibility is shared with the industrial designer if the product involves hardware. In essence, a visual designer must aim for maximum usability combined with maximum desirability.

Interaction Designers

Interaction designers (IxD) are responsible for understanding and specifying how the product should behave. This work overlaps with the work of both visual and industrial designers in a couple of important ways. When designing physical products, interaction designers must work with industrial designers early on to specify the requirements for physical inputs and to understand the behavioral impacts of the mechanisms behind them. Interaction designers cross paths with visual designers throughout the project. Visual designers guide the discussions of the brand and emotive aspects of the experience, Interaction designers communicate the priority of information, flow, and functionality in the interface.

Testing the Design

Usability testing is the most common method used by designers to test their designs. The basic idea behind conducting a usability test is to check whether the design of a product or brand works well with the target users. While carrying out usability testing, two things are being tested for:

Whether the design of the product is successful and if it is not successful, how can it be improved. While designers are testing, they are testing the design and not the user. Also, every design is evolving. The designers carry out usability testing at every stage of the design process.

Benefits

User experience design is integrated into software development and other forms of application development to inform feature requirements and interaction plans based upon the users' goals. Every new software introduced must keep pace with the rapid technological advancements. The benefits associated with integration of these design principles include:

- Avoiding unnecessary product features

- Simplifying design documentation and customer-centric technical publications

- Improving the usability of the system and therefore its acceptance by customers

- Expediting design and development through detailed and properly conceived guidelines

- Incorporating business and marketing goals while protecting the user's freedom of choice

Responsive Web Design

Content is like water, a saying that illustrates the principles of RWD.

Responsive web design (RWD) is an approach to web design aimed at allowing desktop webpages to be viewed in response to the size of the screen or web browser one is viewing with.

A site designed with RWD adapts the layout to the viewing environment by using fluid, proportion-based grids, flexible images, and CSS3 media queries, an extension of the @media rule, in the following ways:

- The fluid grid concept calls for page element sizing to be in relative units like percentages, rather than absolute units like pixels or points.

- Flexible images are also sized in relative units, so as to prevent them from displaying outside their containing element.

- Media queries allow the page to use different CSS style rules based on characteristics of the device the site is being displayed on, most commonly the width of the browser.

Responsive web design has become more important as the amount of mobile traffic now accounts for more than half of total internet traffic. Therefore, Google announced Mobilegeddon (April 21, 2015) and started to boost the ratings of sites that are mobile friendly if the search was made from a mobile device. Responsive web design is an example of user interface plasticity.

Related Concepts

Mobile First, Unobtrusive JavaScript, and Progressive Enhancement

"Mobile first", unobtrusive JavaScript, and progressive enhancement are related concepts that predate RWD. Browsers of basic mobile phones do not understand JavaScript or media queries, so a recommended practice is to create a basic web site and enhance it for smart phones and PCs, rather than rely on graceful degradation to make a complex, image-heavy site work on mobile phones.

Progressive Enhancement Based on Browser, Device, or Feature Detection

Where a web site must support basic mobile devices that lack JavaScript, browser ("user agent") detection (also called "browser sniffing") and mobile device detection are two ways of deducing if certain HTML and CSS features are supported (as a basis for progressive enhancement)—however, these methods are not completely reliable unless used in conjunction with a device capabilities database.

For more capable mobile phones and PCs, JavaScript frameworks like Modernizr, jQuery, and jQuery Mobile that can directly test browser support for HTML/CSS features (or identify the device or user agent) are popular. Polyfills can be used to add support for features—e.g. to support media queries (required for RWD), and enhance HTML5 support, on Internet Explorer. Feature detection also might not be completely reliable; some may report that a feature is available, when it is either missing or so poorly implemented that it is effectively nonfunctional.

Challenges, and Other Approaches

Luke Wroblewski has summarized some of the RWD and mobile design challenges, and created a catalog of multi-device layout patterns. He suggests that, compared with a simple RWD approach, device experience or RESS (responsive web design with server-side components) approaches can provide a user experience that is better optimized for mobile devices. Server-side "dynamic CSS" implementation of stylesheet languages like Sass or Incentivated's MML can be part of such an approach by accessing a server based API which handles the device (typically mobile handset) differences in conjunction with a device capabilities database in order to improve usability. RESS is more expensive to develop, requiring more than just client-side logic, and so tends to be reserved for organizations with larger budgets. Google recommends responsive design for smartphone websites over other approaches.

Although many publishers are starting to implement responsive designs, one ongoing challenge for RWD is that some banner advertisements and videos are not fluid. However, search advertising and (banner) display advertising support specific device platform targeting and different advertisement size formats for desktop, smartphone, and basic mobile devices. Different landing page URLs can be used for different platforms, or Ajax can be used to display different advertisement variants on a page. CSS tables permit hybrid fixed+fluid layouts.

There are now many ways of validating and testing RWD designs, ranging from mobile site validators and mobile emulators to simultaneous testing tools like Adobe Edge Inspect. The Chrome, Firefox and Safari browsers and the Chrome console offer responsive design viewport resizing tools, as do third parties.

History

The first site to feature a layout that adapts to browser viewport width was *Audi.com* launched in late 2001, created by a team at razorfish consisting of Jürgen Spangl and Jim Kalbach (information architecture), Ken Olling (design), and Jan Hoffmann (interface development). Limited browser capabilities meant that for Internet Explorer, the layout could adapt dynamically in the browser whereas for Netscape, the page had to be reloaded from the server when resized.

Cameron Adams created a demonstration in 2004 that is still online. By 2008, a number of related terms such as "flexible", "liquid", "fluid", and "elastic" were being used to describe layouts. CSS3 media queries were almost ready for prime time in late 2008/early 2009. Ethan Marcotte coined the term responsive web design (RWD)—and defined it to mean fluid grid/ flexible images/ media queries—in a May 2010 article in *A List Apart*. He described the theory and practice of responsive web design in his brief 2011 book titled *Responsive Web Design*. Responsive design was listed as #2 in Top Web Design Trends for 2012 by .net magazine after progressive enhancement at #1.

Mashable called 2013 the Year of Responsive Web Design. Many other sources have recommended responsive design as a cost-effective alternative to mobile applications.

Rollover (Web Design)

Rollover refers to a button created by a web developer or web designer, found within a web page, used to provide interactivity between the user and the page itself. The term rollover in this regard originates from the visual process of "rolling the mouse cursor over the button" causing the button to react (usually visually, by replacing the button's source image with another image), and sometimes resulting in a change in the web page itself. The part of the term 'roll' is probably referring to older mice which had a mechanical assembly consisting of a hard rubber ball housed in the base of the mouse (which rolls) contrary to the modern optical mouse, which has no 'rolling' parts. The term mouseover is probably more appropriate considering current technology.

Rollovers can be done by imagery, text or buttons. The user only requires two images/buttons (with the possible addition of "alt" text to these images) to perform this interactive action. Rollover imagery can be done either by a program with a built-in tool or script coding. The user will have to pick a first image and select an alternate secondary image. A mouse action will have to be set to either "click on" or "mouse over" in order for the rollover to be triggered. Note that when the "mouse over" moves on the image, the alt image/secondary image will appear but won't stay - when the user "mouses out" by moving the mouse away from the image, the original source image will reappear.

Coding

There are several different ways to create a rollover. This is an example of a rollover in CSS, JavaScript and HTML:

CSS

```
a {
  background-image: url(default.png);
  color: white;
  display: block;
  height: 30px;
  width: 100px;
}
a:hover {
  background-image: url(rollover.png);
  color: lightpink;
}
```

JavaScript

```
var link = document.querySelector("a");
link.addEventListener("mouseover",function() {
    this.style.backgroundImage = "url(rollover.png)";
    this.style.color = "lightpink";
});
function setStyleDefaults() {
    link.style.backgroundImage = "url(default.png)";
    link.style.color = "white";
}
setStyleDefaults();
link.addEventListener("mouseout",setStyleDefaults);
```

Different Types of Rollovers

While rollovers are not in themselves animated images, some users and HTML experts have managed to create animation-like effects.

- *Zooming rollovers*: when the mouse is moved over an image/text or button, it increases its size, depending on the limit size the user sets.

- *Fading rollovers*: when the user moves the mouse over an image/text or button, it either fades in or out, depending on the user control.

- *Disjointed rollovers*: when the mouse is moved over an image or button, other areas on the screen change to reflect what will happen if the user clicks.

References

- Zwicky, E.D, Cooper, S and Chapman, D,B. (2000). Building Internet Firewalls. United States: O'Reily & Associates. p. 804. ISBN 1-56592-871-7.

- Niederst, Jennifer (2006). Web Design In a Nutshell. United States of America: O'Reilly Media. pp. 12–14. ISBN 0-596-00987-9.

- Oleksy, Walter (2001). Careers in Web Design. New York: The Rosen Publishing Group,Inc. pp. 9–11. ISBN 9780823931910.

- Nielsen, Jakob; Tahir, Marie (October 2001), Homepage Usability: 50 Websites Deconstructed, New Riders Publishing, ISBN 978-0735711020

- Meyer, Eric A. (2006). Cascading Style Sheets: The Definitive Guide (3rd ed.). O'Reilly Media, Inc. ISBN 0-596-52733-0.

- Lie, Håkon Wium; Bos, Bert (1999). Cascading Style Sheets, designing for the Web. Addison Wesley. ISBN 0-201-59625-3. Retrieved 23 June 2010.

- Bos, Håkon Wium Lie, Bert (1999). Cascading style sheets: designing for the Web (2nd ed.). Harlow, Essex, England: Addison-Wesley. ISBN 0-201-59625-3.

- Bos, / Håkon Wium Lie, Bert (1997). Cascading style sheets: designing for the Web (1st print. ed.). Harlow, England ; Reading, MA.: Addison Wesley Longman. ISBN 0-201-41998-X.

- Cederholm, Dan; Ethan Marcotte (2009). Handcrafted CSS: More Bulletproof Web Design. New Riders. p. 114. ISBN 978-0-321-64338-4. Retrieved 19 June 2010.

- Marcus, Aaron (2015). Design, User Experience, and Usability: Design Discourse. p. 340. ISBN 3319208861. Retrieved 26 July 2015.

- Cooper, Alan; Reimann, Robert; Cronin, David; Noessel, Christopher. About Face: The Essentials of Interaction Design (4th ed.). Wiley. p. 62. ISBN 978-1-118-76657-6.

- Cooper, Alan; Reimann, Robert; Cronin, David; Noessel, Christopher (2014). About Face: The Essentials of Interaction Design (4th ed.). Wiley. p. 131. ISBN 978-1-118-76657-6.

- Cooper, Alan; Reimann, Robert; Cronin, David; Noessel, Christopher (2014). About Face: The Essentials of Interaction Design. Wiley. p. 140. ISBN 978-1-118-76657-6.

- Cooper, Alan; Reimann, Robert; Cronin, David; Noessel, Christopher. About Face: The Essentials of Interaction Design (4th ed.). p. 153. ISBN 978-1-118-76657-6.

- Gillenwater, Zoe Mickley (December 15, 2010). "Examples of flexible layouts with CSS3 media queries". Stunning CSS3. p. 320. ISBN 978-0-321-722133.

- Christensen, Mathias Biilmann (2015-11-16). "Static Website Generators Reviewed: Jekyll, Middleman, Roots, Hugo". Smashing Magazine. Retrieved 2016-10-26.

- environmental context "THE INTERACTION DESIGN FOUNDATION", by Karen Holtzblatt and Hugh R., Retrieved 2016-08-26

- "Curricula for Human-Computer Interaction, Chapter 2. Definition and Overview of Human-Computer Interaction". ACM SIGCHI. Retrieved 2015-06-18.

- Treder, Marcin (2012-08-29). "Beyond Wireframing: The Real-Life UX Design Process". Smashing Magazine. Retrieved 2015-06-18.

- "What's the Difference Between a User Experience (UX) Designer and a User Interface (UI) Designer? - Zanthro". Retrieved 2015-09-24.

- "Graphic Designers". Occupational Outlook Handbook. Bureau of Labor Statistics, U.S. Department of Labor. December 17, 2015. Retrieved July 1, 2016.

- "Cisco Visual Networking Index: Global Mobile Data Traffic Forecast Update 2014–2019 White Paper". Cisco. January 30, 2015. Retrieved August 4, 2015.

- "Official Google Webmaster Central Blog: Rolling out the mobile-friendly update". Official Google Webmaster Central Blog. Retrieved August 4, 2015.

Web Framework: An Integrated Study

Web framework is a software that is used for supporting the development of web applications. These include web services, web resources and web APIs. Some of the web frameworks are PRADO, play framework, Padrino, Silex and Snap. The major components of web framework are discussed in this chapter.

Web Framework

A web framework (WF) or web application framework (WAF) is a software framework that is designed to support the development of web applications including web services, web resources and web APIs. Web frameworks aim to alleviate the overhead associated with common activities performed in web development. For example, many web frameworks provide libraries for database access, templating frameworks and session management, and they often promote code reuse. Though they often target development of dynamic websites they are also applicable to static websites.

History

As the design of the World Wide Web was not inherently dynamic, early hypertext consisted of hand-coded HTML that was published on web servers. Any modifications to published pages needed to be performed by the pages' author. To provide a dynamic web page that reflected user inputs, the Common Gateway Interface (CGI) standard was introduced for interfacing external applications with web servers. CGI could adversely affect server load, though, since each request had to start a separate process.

Around the same time, full integrated server/language development environments first emerged, such as WebBase and new languages specifically for use in the web started to emerge, such as Cold-Fusion, PHP and Active Server Pages.

While the vast majority of languages available to programmers to use in creating dynamic web pages have libraries to help with common tasks, web applications often require specific libraries that are useful in web applications, such as creating HTML (for example, JavaServer Faces). Eventually, mature, "full stack" frameworks appeared, that often gathered multiple libraries useful for web development into a single cohesive software stack for web developers to use. Examples of this include ASP.NET, JavaEE (Servlets), WebObjects, web2py, OpenACS, Catalyst, Mojolicious, Ruby on Rails, Laravel, Grails, Django, Zend Framework, Yii, CakePHP and Symfony.

Types of Framework Architectures

Most web frameworks are based on the model–view–controller (MVC) pattern.

Model–view–controller (MVC)

Many frameworks follow the MVC architectural pattern to separate the data model with business rules from the user interface. This is generally considered a good practice as it modularizes code, promotes code reuse, and allows multiple interfaces to be applied. In web applications, this permits different views to be presented, such as web pages for humans, and web service interfaces for remote applications.

Push-based vs. Pull-based

Most MVC frameworks follow a push-based architecture also called "action-based". These frameworks use actions that do the required processing, and then "push" the data to the view layer to render the results. Django, Ruby on Rails, Symfony, Spring MVC, Stripes, CodeIgniter are good examples of this architecture. An alternative to this is pull-based architecture, sometimes also called "component-based". These frameworks start with the view layer, which can then "pull" results from multiple controllers as needed. In this architecture, multiple controllers can be involved with a single view. Lift, Tapestry, JBoss Seam, JavaServer Faces, (μ)Micro, and Wicket are examples of pull-based architectures. Play, Struts, RIFE and ZK have support for both push and pull based application controller calls.

Three-tier Organization

In three-tier organization, applications are structured around three physical tiers: client, application, and database. The database is normally an RDBMS. The application contains the business logic, running on a server and communicates with the client using HTTP. The client on web applications is a web browser that runs HTML generated by the application layer. The term should not be confused with MVC, where, unlike in three-tier architecture, it is considered a good practice to keep business logic away from the controller, the "middle layer".

Framework Applications

Frameworks are built to support the construction of internet applications based on a single programming language, ranging in focus from general purpose tools such as Zend Framework and Ruby on Rails, which augment the capabilities of a specific language, to native-language programmable packages built around a specific user application, such as Content Management systems, some mobile development tools and some portal tools.

General-purpose Website Frameworks

Web frameworks must function according to the architectural rules of browsers and web protocols such as HTTP, which is stateless. Webpages are served up by a server and can then be modified by the browser using JavaScript. Either approach has its advantages and disadvantages.

Server-side page changes typically require that the page be refreshed, but allow any language to be used and more computing power to be utilized. Client-side changes allow the page to be updated in small chunks which feels like a desktop application, but are limited to JavaScript and run in the user's browser, which may have limited computing power. Some mix of the two is typically used. Applications which make heavy use of JavaScript are called single-page applications and typically make use of a client-side JavaScript web framework to organize the code.

Server-side

For example, Django, Zend Framework.

Client-side

Examples include Backbone.js, AngularJS, EmberJS, ReactJS and Vue.js.

Organizational Portals

For example, JBoss Portal or eXo Platform.

Content Management Systems (CMS)

In web application frameworks, content management is the way of organizing, categorizing, and structuring the information resources like text, images, documents, audio and video files so that they can be stored, published, and edited with ease and flexibility. A content management system (CMS) is used to collect, manage, and publish content, storing it either as components or whole documents, while maintaining dynamic links between components.

Some projects that have historically been termed content management systems have begun to take on the roles of higher-layer web application frameworks. For instance, Drupal's structure provides a minimal *core* whose function is extended through *modules* that provide functions generally associated with web application frameworks. The Joomla platform provides a set of APIs to build web and command-line applications. However, it is debatable whether "management of content" is the primary value of such systems, especially when some, like SilverStripe, provide an object-oriented MVC framework. Add-on *modules* now enable these systems to function as full-fledged applications beyond the scope of content management. They may provide functional APIs, functional frameworks, coding standards, and many of the functions traditionally associated with *Web application frameworks*.

Features

Frameworks typically set the control flow of a program and allow the user of the framework to "hook into" that flow by exposing various events. This "inversion of control" design pattern is considered to be a defining principle of a framework, and benefits the code by enforcing a common flow for a team which everyone can customize in similar ways. For example, some popular "microframeworks" such as Ruby's Sinatra (which inspired Express.js) allow for "middleware" hooks prior to and after HTTP requests. These middleware functions can be anything, and allow the user to define logging, authentication and session management, and redirecting.

Web Template System

Caching

Web caching is the caching of web documents in order to reduce bandwidth usage, server load, and perceived "lag". A web cache stores copies of documents passing through it; subsequent requests may be satisfied from the cache if certain conditions are met. Some application frameworks provide mechanisms for caching documents and bypassing various stages of the page's preparation, such as database access or template interpretation.

Security

Some web frameworks come with authentication and authorization frameworks, that enable the web server to identify the users of the application, and restrict access to functions based on some defined criteria. Drupal is one example that provides role-based access to pages, and provides a web-based interface for creating users and assigning them roles.

Database Access, Mapping and Configuration

Many web frameworks create a unified API to a database backend, enabling web applications to work with a variety of databases with no code changes, and allowing programmers to work with higher-level concepts. Additionally, some object-oriented frameworks contain mapping tools to provide object-relational mapping, which maps objects to tuples.

Some frameworks minimize web application configuration through the use of introspection and/or following well-known conventions. For example, many Java frameworks use Hibernate as a persistence layer, which can generate a database schema at runtime capable of persisting the necessary information. This allows the application designer to design business objects without needing to explicitly define a database schema. Frameworks such as Ruby on Rails can also work in reverse, that is, define properties of model objects at runtime based on a database schema.

Other features web frameworks may provide include transactional support and database migration tools.

URL Mapping

A framework's URL mapping or routing facility is the mechanism by which the framework interprets URLs. Some frameworks, such as Drupal and Django, match the provided URL against pre-determined patterns using regular expressions, while some others use rewriting techniques to translate the provided URL into one that the underlying engine will recognize. Another technique is that of graph traversal such as used by Zope, where a URL is decomposed in steps that traverse an object graph (of models and views).

A URL mapping system that uses pattern matching or rewriting to route and handle requests allows for shorter more "friendly URLs" to be used, increasing the simplicity of the site and allowing for better indexing by search engines. For example, a URL that ends with "/page.cgi?cat=science&topic=physics" could be changed to simply "/page/science/physics". This makes the URL easier for people to remember, read and write, and provides search engines with better information about the structural layout of the site. A graph traversal approach also tends to result in the creation of friendly URLs. A shorter URL such as "/page/science" tends to exist by default as that is simply a shorter form of the longer traversal to "/page/science/physics".

Ajax

Ajax, shorthand for "*Asynchronous JavaScript and XML*", is a web development technique for creating web applications. The intent is to make web pages feel more responsive by exchanging small amounts of data with the server behind the scenes, so that the entire web page does not have to be reloaded each time the user requests a change. This is intended to increase a web page's interactivity, speed, and usability.

Due to the complexity of Ajax programming in JavaScript, there are numerous Ajax frameworks that exclusively deal with Ajax support. Some Ajax frameworks are even embedded as a part of larger frameworks. For example, the jQuery JavaScript library is included in Ruby on Rails.

With the increased interest in developing "Web 2.0" rich media applications, the complexity of programming directly in Ajax and JavaScript has become so apparent that compiler technology has stepped in, to allow developers to code in high-level languages such as Java, Python and Ruby. The first of these compilers was Morfik followed by Google Web Toolkit, with ports to Python and Ruby in the form of Pyjamas and RubyJS following some time after. These compilers and their associated widget set libraries make the development of rich media Ajax applications much more akin to that of developing desktop applications.

Web Services

Some frameworks provide tools for creating and providing web services. These utilities may offer similar tools as the rest of the web application.

Web Resources

A number of newer Web 2.0 RESTful frameworks are now providing resource-oriented architecture (ROA) infrastructure for building collections of resources in a sort of Semantic Web ontology, based on concepts from Resource Description Framework (RDF).

PRADo (Framework)

PRADO is an open source, object-oriented, event-driven, component-based PHP web framework. PRADO's name is an acronym derived from "PHP Rapid Application Development Object-oriented".

History

The PRADO project was started by Qiang Xue, and was inspired by Apache Tapestry. The framework also borrowed ideas from Borland Delphi and Microsoft's ASP.NET framework.

The first public release of PRADO came out in June 2004, but was written using the very limited and now outdated PHP 4 object model, which caused many problems. Qiang then re-wrote the framework for the new PHP 5 object model, and won the Zend PHP 5 coding contest with it.

PRADO is a rapid application development (RAD) framework, and in its infancy has been criticized to not be ready for high-performance, high-traffic scenarios. Implementations of template and configuration caching in later PRADO revisions eliminated most performance bottlenecks in its architecture, making it suited for the creation of medium- to high-traffic websites, while still providing a rapid way amongst PHP frameworks for the development of interactive web pages and applications.

In the late 2008, Qiang unveiled the Yii framework, a conceptual redesign of PRADO, targeted to high-performance, high-traffic scenarios. The following maintenance and updates to the PRADO project have been handled by community members of the project gathering on the project's Google Code page. Since 2013, the project has moved to GitHub.

Features

PRADO features include the following:

- A clean and extensible, dynamic, XML-conformant, tag-based templating system, similar to ASP.NET's, but designed for PHP's dynamic approach

- Clear separation of presentation and content, input handling and business logic, based on the Model-View-Controller approach

- Database Access Objects (DAO), XML-based SQLMap data mapper, parameterized query builder, Active Record and automatic scaffolding

- Interactive client-side presentation layer based on the Prototype JavaScript Framework and script.aculo.us effects library. It can however also use external controls based on jQuery and other JavaScript frameworks

- Form input and validation, supporting validation both on client- (for faster user feedback) and server-side (aiming to ensure data integrity and data security

- Ajax-enabled active widgets (such as auto-complete input field, active button, active data grid) which can be updated, shown or paged dynamically, without having to reload and rebuild the whole page

- Built-in URL mapping support for search-engine-optimized and semantic URLs, which works without needing URL rewriting support from the web server

- Over 100 standard controls/widgets, including drag and drop, validation and data-bound controls

- Customizable data grid, with support of automatic generation of columns based on automatically discovered database schema

- Built-in authentication and authorization support

- Skinning and theming

- Internationalization and localization (I18N and L10N) support, including message translation, date and time formatting, number formatting, and interface localization

- Full support of Unicode and non-English custom code pages, including automatic transcoding between client- and server-side character sets

- Layered caching scheme, supporting separate caching of data queries and output fragments, via database, shared memory, memcached) for storing cached data, and dynamic cache entry validation upon retrieval

- Support for progressive rendering of pages, automatic script minification and on-demand lazy loading of client-side script and stylesheet files for faster loading of pages

- Error handling and logging, with errors handled and presented, and log messages optionally categorized, filtered and routed to different destinations

- Built-in security measures, which include cross-site scripting (XSS) prevention, HTTP cookie tampering prevention and SQL injection prevention

- Unit testing and functional testing based on PHPUnit, SimpleTest and Selenium

- Automatic skeleton application generation from the PRADO command-line tool

- Supports both XML-based and native PHP-coded configuration of application and runtime environments

- Code generated by PRADO components adheres to the XHTML standard

- Supports for creation and consummation of SOAP- or JSON-based web services

- Interoperability with third-party code, including PEAR and Zend Framework

Documentation

PRADO comes with a collection of official documentation, including a tutorial to develop a simple blog application, a reference guide describing all features, and a class reference for all properties, methods and events. The documentation is available in both HTML and Compiled HTML Help (.CHM) form.

Licensing

PRADO is released under a Modified BSD License, which enables free use of PRADO for developing both open-source and proprietary web applications, without requiring distribution of the source code of derived works.

Play Framework

Play is an open source web application framework, written in Scala and also usable from e.g. Java (Play includes a Java wrapper API in latest version), which follows the model–view–controller (MVC) architectural pattern. It aims to optimize developer productivity by using convention over configuration, hot code reloading and display of errors in the browser.

Support for the Scala programming language has been available since version 1.1 of the framework. In version 2.0, the framework core was rewritten in Scala. Build and deployment was migrated to SBT, and templates use Scala instead of Groovy.

Latest version requires the Java 8 JVM.

History

Play was created by software developer Guillaume Bort, while working at Zengularity SA (formerly Zenexity). Although the early releases are no longer available online, there is evidence of Play existing as far back as May 2007. In 2007 pre-release versions of the project were available to download from Zenexity's website.

In May 2008 the first published code for 1.0 appeared on Launchpad. This was followed by a full 1.0 release in October 2009.

Play 1.1 was released in November 2010 after a move from Launchpad to GitHub. It included a migration from Apache MINA to JBoss Netty, Scala support, native GlassFish container, an asynchronous web services library, OAuth support, HTTPS support and other features.

Play 1.2 was released in April 2011. It included dependency management with Apache Ivy, support for WebSocket, integrated database migration (reversion is not implemented yet), a switch to the H2 database and other features.

Sadek Drobi joined Guillaume Bort late 2011 to create Play 2.0 which was released on March 13, 2012 in conjunction with Typesafe Stack 2.0.

Play 2.1 was released on February 6, 2013, upgraded to Scala 2.10 and introduced, among other new features, modularisation, a new JSON API, filters and RequireJS support.

Play 2.2 was released on September 20, 2013. Upgraded support for SBT to 0.13, better support for buffering, built in support for gzip and new stage and dist tasks with support for native packaging on several platforms such as OS X (DMG), Linux (RPM, DEB), and Windows (MSI) as well as zipfiles.

Motivation

Play is heavily inspired by ASP.NET MVC, Ruby on Rails and Django and is similar to this family of frameworks. Play web applications can be written in Scala or Java, in an environment that may be less Java Enterprise Edition-centric. Play uses no Java EE constraints. This can make Play simpler to develop compared to other Java-centric platforms.

Although Play applications are designed to be run using the built-in JBoss Netty web server, they can also be packaged as WAR files to be distributed to standard Java EE application servers.

Major Differences from Java Frameworks

- Stateless: Play 2 is fully RESTful – there is no Java EE session per connection.

- Integrated unit testing: JUnit and Selenium support is included in the core.

- API comes with most required elements built-in.

- Static methods: all controller entry points are declared as static (or equivalently, in Scala, functions on Scala objects). After requests were made for this to be customisable, Play 2.1 now supports other styles of controllers, so controllers need not be static/Scala objects; however, this is still the default.

- Asynchronous I/O: due to using JBoss Netty as its web server, Play can service long requests asynchronously rather than tying up HTTP threads doing business logic like Java EE frameworks that don't use the asynchronous support offered by Servlet 3.0.

- Modular architecture: like Ruby on Rails and Django, Play comes with the concept of modules.

- Native Scala support: Play 2 uses Scala internally, but also exposes both a Scala API, and a Java API that is deliberately slightly different to fit in with Java conventions, and Play is completely interoperable with Java.

Components

Play 2.0 makes use of several popular Java libraries:

- JBoss Netty for the web server

- No required ORM, but Anorm (Scala) and Ebean (Java) are included for database access

- Scala for the template engine

- Built in hot-reloading

- sbt for dependency management

The following functionality is present in the core:

- a clean, RESTful framework

- CRUD: a module to simplify editing of model objects

- Secure: a module to enable simple user authentication

- a validation framework based on annotations

- a job scheduler

- a simple to use SMTP mailer

- JSON and XML parsers and marshallers

- a persistence layer based on JPA

- an embedded database for quick deployment/testing purposes

- a full embedded testing framework

- an automatic file uploads functionality

- multi-environment configuration awareness

- a modular architecture, which enables bringing new features in the core easily

- OpenID and web services clients

Testing Framework

Play provides a built-in test framework for unit testing and functional testing. Tests are run directly in the browser by going to the URL <serverurl>/@tests. By default all testing is done against the included H2 in-memory database.

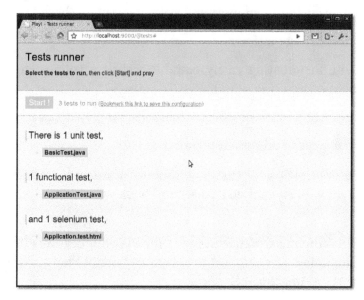

Usage

The mailing list for the project has over 11,000 subscribers. It is used in various projects such as local governments, company intranets, mobile web sites and Open Source projects.

As of October 2013, the Play Framework is the most popular Scala project on GitHub. In July 2015, Play was the 3rd most popular Scala library in Github, based on 64,562 Libraries. 21.3% of the top Scala projects used Play as their framework of choice.

Some notable public websites using Play:

- LinkedIn, the world's largest professional network

- Coursera, a website for online learning

- LendUp, online alternative payday lending company focused on serving the US unbanked

- http://gendi.fr/, GENDI, a GS1 member

- http://www.cashcare.in/

- http://jobs.siliconsentier.org/, jobs board of Silicon Sentier

- http://www.seine-et-marne.fr/, General council website of Seine-et-Marne, France.

- http://lightbend.com/, corporate website for Scala company founded by Martin Odersky

- http://live.gilt.com Live shopping updates featuring Play's Realtime Web features, more details on their use of Play on Gilt's technology blog

- Sync Video, service for watching online videos in sync

- Prenser, news media network

- PeachDish, food e-commerce company

- Webservice First, a customer support and ticketing system (based on play 1.2.7)

- Whenvisited, fundraising platform

- Joysite, a website for creating easily editable websites with custom templates support (Launched in 2011 based on Play 1.1).

- Funraise, a non-profit fundraising platform (based on play 2.5.x)

- Eduparna, school search and parent forum

In December 2010, the first e-book for the Play framework was released. This was subsequently also published in hard copy. In August 2011, a second book was released, covering more complex and modern features.

In August 2011, Heroku announced native support for Play applications on its cloud computing platform. This follows module-based support for Play 1.0 (but not Play 2.x) on Google App Engine, and documented support on Amazon Web Services.

In July 2013, Jelastic published a tutorial showing support for Play 2 on its cloud computing platform.

Padrino (Web Framework)

Padrino is a free and open-source web framework, written in Ruby and based on Sinatra. It is an alternative to other Ruby web frameworks such as Ruby on Rails, Merb, Nitro and Camping. It is dependent on the Rack web server interface.

Padrino was created and open-sourced in 2010. The framework was created by Nathan Esquenazi, Davide D'Agostino and Arthur Chiu based on the prior sinatra_more gem. The framework was created in order to extend Sinatra to more easily support rich web applications.

Features

This is a list of major functionality Padrino provides on top of Sinatra:

- Agnostic: Full support for many popular testing, templating, mocking, and database libraries.

- Generators: Create Padrino applications, models, controllers i.e.: padrino g project.

- Mountable: Unlike other Ruby frameworks, principally designed for mounting multiple apps.

- Routing: Full url named routes, named params, respond_to support, before/after filter support.

- Tag Helpers: View helpers such as: tag, content_tag, input_tag.

- Asset Helpers: View helpers such as: link_to, image_tag, javascript_include_tag.

- Form Helpers: Builder support such as: form_tag, form_for, field_set_tag, text_field.

- Text Helpers: Useful formatting like: relative_time_ago, js_escape_html, sanitize_html.

- Mailer: Fast and simple delivery support for sending emails (akin to ActionMailer).

- Admin: Built-in Admin interface (like Django).

- Logging: Provide a unified logger that can interact with your ORM or any library.

- Reloading: Automatically reloads server code during development.

- Localization: Full support of I18n

Note that as a user of Padrino, each of the major components can be pulled in separately to an existing Sinatra application or they can be used altogether for a comprehensive upgrade to Sinatra (a full-stack Padrino application).

Silex (Web Framework)

Silex is a micro web framework written in PHP and based on Symfony, Twig (template engine) and Doctrine (database abstraction). It is MIT Licensed.

The general purpose of Silex is to be as lightweight as you need it to be, as it is made for it to be as easy as possible to add features and extend the Silex base. Silex can be used for the creation of small web applications (e.g. REST APIs) as this is the main case for micro frameworks, however Silex can be extended into a full stack MVC framework.

Silex comes in two available versions; 'fat' and 'slim'. The difference between these being that the fat version is fully featured and includes database abstraction, a template engine and various Symfony components. Whereas the slim version just comes with a basic routing engine.

Features

The base feature set is a URL routing system, built-in Web Security, Sessions and Cookies abstraction. The extended version of Silex features integration of Twig, Doctrine, a Translation service for translating your application into different languages, a logging mechanism using the Monolog library to log requests and errors, services for form validation and generation, and more.

History

Silex was originally created by Fabien Potencier, the creator of the Symfony framework, and Igor Wiedler. It was first released 16 September 2010 as a 'web framework proof-of-concept'.

Silex is now one of the best known micro frameworks for PHP and is regularly placed among the fastest in benchmarks for micro framework comparisons.

Example

The following code shows a simple web application that prints "Hello World!":

```
$app = new Silex\Application();


$app->get('/', function() use($app) {

  return 'Hello World!';

});


$app->run();
```

Snap (Web Framework)

Snap is a simple web development framework written in the Haskell programming language. It is used by Silk, JanRain, Racemetric, www.lpaste.net, SooStone Inc, and Group Commerce. Snap is also used as a lightweight, standalone Haskell server. The popular static site generator Hakyll uses Snap for its preview mode.

Overview

The Snap framework comprises:

- snap-core, a generic Haskell web server API.
- snap-server, a fast HTTP server that implements the snap-core interface.
- Heist, an HTML-based templating system for generating pages that allows you to bind Haskell functionality to HTML tags for a clean separation of view and backend code, much like Lift's snippets. Heist is completely self-contained and can be used independently.
- Snaplets, a high-level system for building modular web applications.
- Built-in snaplets for templating, session management, and authentication.
- Third party snaplets for features such as file uploads, database connectivity (PostgreSQL, MongoDB, etc.), generation of JavaScript from Haskell code, and more.
- The Snap monad for stateful access to HTTP requests and responses.

Snap runs on both Windows and *nix platforms. Snap uses the Iteratee I/O model, As of version 1.0, its i/o is implemented with io-streams.

Other Haskell Web Frameworks

- Yesod (web framework)

- Happstack

- Scotty web framework

- Spock web framework

- MFlow web framework

Software Framework

In computer programming, a software framework is an abstraction in which software providing generic functionality can be selectively changed by additional user-written code, thus providing application-specific software. A software framework is a universal, reusable software environment that provides particular functionality as part of a larger software platform to facilitate development of software applications, products and solutions. Software frameworks may include support programs, compilers, code libraries, tool sets, and application programming interfaces (APIs) that bring together all the different components to enable development of a project or system.

Frameworks have key distinguishing features that separate them from normal libraries:

- *inversion of control*: In a framework, unlike in libraries or in standard user applications, the overall program's flow of control is not dictated by the caller, but by the framework.

- *extensibility*: A user can extend the framework - usually by selective overriding; or programmers can add specialized user code to provide specific functionality.

- *non-modifiable framework code*: The framework code, in general, is not supposed to be modified, while accepting user-implemented extensions. In other words, users can extend the framework, but should not modify its code.

Rationale

The designers of software frameworks aim to facilitate software development by allowing designers and programmers to devote their time to meeting software requirements rather than dealing with the more standard low-level details of providing a working system, thereby reducing overall development time. For example, a team using a web framework to develop a banking website can focus on writing code particular to banking rather than the mechanics of request handling and state management.

Frameworks often add to the size of programs, a phenomenon termed "code bloat". Due to customer-demand driven applications needs, both competing and complementary frameworks sometimes end up in a product. Further, due to the complexity of their APIs, the intended reduction in overall development time may not be achieved due to the need to spend additional time learning to use the framework; this criticism is clearly valid when a special or new framework is first encountered by development staff. If such a framework is not used in subsequent job taskings, the time invested in learning the framework can cost more than purpose-written code familiar to the project's staff; many programmers keep copies of useful boilerplate for common needs.

However, once a framework is learned, future projects can be faster and easier to complete; the concept of a framework is to make a one-size-fits-all solution set, and with familiarity, code production should logically rise. There are no such claims made about the size of the code eventually bundled with the output product, nor its relative efficiency and conciseness. Using any library solution necessarily pulls in extras and unused extraneous assets unless the software is a compiler-object linker making a tight (small, wholly controlled, and specified) executable module.

The issue continues, but a decade-plus of industry experience has shown that the most effective frameworks turn out to be those that evolve from re-factoring the common code of the enterprise, instead of using a generic "one-size-fits-all" framework developed by third parties for general purposes. An example of that would be how the user interface in such an application package as an office suite grows to have common look, feel, and data-sharing attributes and methods, as the once disparate bundled applications grow unified into a suite which is tighter and smaller; the newer/evolved suite can be a product that shares integral utility libraries and user interfaces.

This trend in the controversy brings up an important issue about frameworks. Creating a framework that is elegant, versus one that merely solves a problem, is still an art rather than a science. "Software elegance" implies clarity, conciseness, and little waste (extra or extraneous functionality, much of which is user defined). For those frameworks that generate code, for example, "elegance" would imply the creation of code that is clean and comprehensible to a reasonably knowledgeable programmer (and which is therefore readily modifiable), versus one that merely generates correct code. The elegance issue is why relatively few software frameworks have stood the test of time: the best frameworks have been able to evolve gracefully as the underlying technology on which they were built advanced. Even there, having evolved, many such packages will retain legacy capabilities bloating the final software as otherwise replaced methods have been retained in parallel with the newer methods.

Examples

Software frameworks typically contain considerable housekeeping and utility code in order to help bootstrap user applications, but generally focus on specific problem domains, such as:

- Artistic drawing, music composition, and mechanical CAD
- Financial modeling applications
- Earth system modeling applications
- Decision support systems
- Multimedia framework - Media playback and authoring
- Ajax framework / JavaScript framework
- Web framework

- Middleware

- Cactus Framework - High performance scientific computing

- Application framework - General GUI applications

- Enterprise Architecture framework

- Oracle Application Development Framework

Architecture

According to Pree, software frameworks consist of *frozen spots* and *hot spots*. *Frozen spots* define the overall architecture of a software system, that is to say its basic components and the relationships between them. These remain unchanged (frozen) in any instantiation of the application framework. *Hot spots* represent those parts where the programmers using the framework add their own code to add the functionality specific to their own project.

In an object-oriented environment, a framework consists of abstract and concrete classes. Instantiation of such a framework consists of composing and subclassing the existing classes.

When developing a concrete software system with a software framework, developers utilize the hot spots according to the specific needs and requirements of the system. Software frameworks rely on the Hollywood Principle: "Don't call us, we'll call you." This means that the user-defined classes (for example, new subclasses) receive messages from the predefined framework classes. Developers usually handle this by implementing superclass abstract methods.

Application Framework

In computer programming, an application framework consists of a software framework used by software developers to implement the standard structure of an application.

Application frameworks became popular with the rise of graphical user interfaces (GUIs), since these tended to promote a standard structure for applications. Programmers find it much simpler to create automatic GUI creation tools when using a standard framework, since this defines the underlying code structure of the application in advance. Developers usually use object-oriented programming techniques to implement frameworks such that the unique parts of an application can simply inherit from pre-existing classes in the framework.

Examples

Apple Computer developed one of the first commercial application frameworks, MacApp (first released in 1985), for the Macintosh. Originally written in an extended (object-oriented) version of Pascal, it later appeared rewritten in C++. Other popular frameworks for the Mac include Metrowerks' PowerPlant and MacZoop (All based on Carbon). Cocoa for Mac OS X offers a different approach to an application framework, one based upon the OPENSTEP framework developed at NeXT.

Free-software frameworks exist as part of the Mozilla, OpenOffice.org, GNOME, KDE, NetBeans and Eclipse projects.

Microsoft markets a framework for developing Windows applications in C++ called the Microsoft Foundation Class Library, and a similar framework for developing applications with Visual Basic or C#, called .NET Framework.

A number of frameworks can build cross-platform applications for Linux, Macintosh, and Windows from the same source code, such as Qt, the widget toolkits wxWidgets, FOX toolkit, or Eclipse RCP.

Oracle Application Development Framework (Oracle ADF) aids in producing Java-oriented systems.

Silicon Laboratories is offering an embedded application framework for developing wireless applications on its portfolio of wireless chips.

MARTHA (layout engine) is a proprietary Java framework that all of the RealObjects software is built on.

References

- Buschmann, F (1996), Pattern-Oriented Software Architecture Volume 1: A System of Patterns. Chichester, Wiley, ISBN 0-471-95869-7

- Larman, C (2001), Applying UML and Patterns: An Introduction to Object-Oriented Analysis and Design and the Unified Process (2nd ed.), Prentice Hall, ISBN 0-13-092569-1

- KLIMUSHYN, Mel. "Web Application Architecture – Client-Side vs. Server-Side". Atomic Spin. Retrieved 2016-03-06.

- Xue, Qiang. "Capital One Engineering – Philosophies that Shaped Successful Frameworks". www.capitalone.io. Retrieved 2016-03-06.

- "Padrino 0.13.2 - New Project Flag, Component Upgrades and Bug Fixes". Padrino. Retrieved 28 May 2016.

- "The Top 100 Scala Libraries in 2015 – Based on 64,562 GitHub Libraries>1". Retrieved 19 July 2015.

- "FP Complete Case Study - JanRain -- User Management System" (PDF). FP Complete. Retrieved 2014-03-02.

- "What are the fundamental differences between Struts and JSF". Struts.apache.org. 2011-02-14. Retrieved 2013-06-14.

- "PRADO Documentation: Javascript in PRADO, Questions and Answers". pradoframework.net. Retrieved 2013-09-22.

- "PRADO Documentation: Active Controls (AJAX enabled Controls)". pradoframework.net. Retrieved 2013-09-22.

- "PRADO Documentation: Internationalization (I18N) and Localization (L10N)". pradoframework.net. Retrieved 2013-09-22.

- "PRADO GitHub: prado/tests/test_tools at master - pradosoft/prado". pradoframework.net. Retrieved 2013-09-22.

- Collins, Gregory; Beardsley, Doug (Jan–Feb 2011). "The Snap Framework: A Web Toolkit for Haskell" (PDF). IEEE Internet Computing. 15 (1): 84–87. doi:10.1109/mic.2011.21.

- "InfoQ Interview: Gregory Collins on High Performance Web Apps with Snap and Haskell". Sep 12, 2011.

Understanding the World Wide Web

The World Wide Web is the space where documents are identified by using uniform resource locators and can be read by using the Internet. Web science, uniform resource locator, web standards and history of the World Wide Web are some of the topics covered in the chapter. The section will provide an integrated understanding of the World Wide Web.

World Wide Web

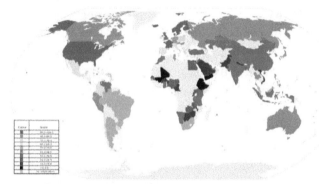

A global map showing the availability of the World Wide Web in the 2010s. The regions with the highest level of access, in dark blue, are North America, Europe, Japan and Australia.

The World Wide Web (abbreviated WWW or the Web) is an information space where documents and other web resources are identified by Uniform Resource Locators (URLs), interlinked by hypertext links, and can be accessed via the Internet. English scientist Tim Berners-Lee invented the World Wide Web in 1989. He wrote the first web browser computer programme in 1990 while employed at CERN in Switzerland.

The World Wide Web has been central to the development of the Information Age and is the primary tool billions of people use to interact on the Internet. Web pages are primarily text documents formatted and annotated with Hypertext Markup Language (HTML). In addition to formatted text, web pages may contain images, video, audio, and software components that are rendered in the user's web browser as coherent pages of multimedia content. Embedded hyperlinks permit users to navigate between web pages. Multiple web pages with a common theme, a common domain name, or both, make up a website. Website content can largely be provided by the publisher, or interactive where users contribute content or the content depends upon the user or their actions. Websites may be mostly informative, primarily for entertainment, or largely for commercial, governmental, or non-governmental organisational purposes. In the 2006 Great British Design Quest organised by the BBC and the Design Museum, the World Wide Web was voted among the top 10 British design icons.

History

The NeXT Computer used by Tim Berners-Lee at CERN.

Tim Berners-Lee's vision of a global hyperlinked information system became a possibility by the second half of the 1980s. By 1985, the global Internet began to proliferate in Europe and in the Domain Name System (upon which the Uniform Resource Locator is built) came into being. In 1988 the first direct IP connection between Europe and North America was made and Berners-Lee began to openly discuss the possibility of a web-like system at CERN. In March 1989 Berners-Lee issued a proposal to the management at CERN for a system called "Mesh" that referenced ENQUIRE, a database and software project he had built in 1980, which used the term "web" and described a more elaborate information management system based on links embedded in readable text: "Imagine, then, the references in this document all being associated with the network address of the thing to which they referred, so that while reading this document you could skip to them with a click of the mouse." Such a system, he explained, could be referred to using one of the existing meanings of the word *hypertext*, a term that he says was coined in the 1950s. There is no reason, the proposal continues, why such hypertext links could not encompass multimedia documents including graphics, speech and video, so that Berners-Lee goes on to use the term *hypermedia*.

The corridor where WWW was born. CERN, ground floor of building No.1

With help from his colleague and fellow hypertext enthusiast Robert Cailliau he published a more formal proposal on 12 November 1990 to build a "Hypertext project" called "WorldWideWeb" (one word) as a "web" of "hypertext documents" to be viewed by "browsers" using a client–server architecture. At this point HTML and HTTP had already been in development for about two months and the first Web server was about a month from completing its first successful test. This proposal estimated that a read-only web would be developed within three months and that it would take six months to achieve "the creation of new links and new material by readers, [so that] authorship becomes universal" as well as "the automatic notification of a reader when new material of interest to him/her has become available." While the read-only goal was met, accessible authorship of web content took longer to mature, with the wiki concept, WebDAV, blogs, Web 2.0 and RSS/Atom.

The CERN data centre in 2010 housing some WWW servers

The proposal was modelled after the SGML reader Dynatext by Electronic Book Technology, a spin-off from the Institute for Research in Information and Scholarship at Brown University. The Dynatext system, licensed by CERN, was a key player in the extension of SGML ISO 8879:1986 to Hypermedia within HyTime, but it was considered too expensive and had an inappropriate licensing policy for use in the general high energy physics community, namely a fee for each document and each document alteration. A NeXT Computer was used by Berners-Lee as the world's first web server and also to write the first web browser, WorldWideWeb, in 1990. By Christmas 1990, Berners-Lee had built all the tools necessary for a working Web: the first web browser (which was a web editor as well) and the first web server. The first web site, which described the project itself, was published on 20 December 1990.

The first web page may be lost, but Paul Jones of UNC-Chapel Hill in North Carolina announced in May 2013 that Berners-Lee gave him what he says is the oldest known web page during a 1991 visit to UNC. Jones stored it on a magneto-optical drive and on his NeXT computer. On 6 August 1991, Berners-Lee published a short summary of the World Wide Web project on the newsgroup *alt.hypertext*. This date is sometimes confused with the public availability of the first web servers, which had occurred months earlier. As another example of such confusion, several news media reported that the first photo on the Web was published by Berners-Lee in 1992, an image of the CERN house band Les Horribles Cernettes taken by Silvano de Gennaro; Gennaro has disclaimed this story, writing that media were "totally distorting our words for the sake of cheap sensationalism."

The first server outside Europe was installed at the Stanford Linear Accelerator Center (SLAC) in Palo Alto, California, to host the SPIRES-HEP database. Accounts differ substantially as to the date of this event. The World Wide Web Consortium's timeline says December 1992, whereas SLAC itself claims December 1991, as does a W3C document titled *A Little History of the World Wide Web*. The underlying concept of hypertext originated in previous projects from the 1960s, such as the Hypertext Editing System (HES) at Brown University, Ted Nelson's Project Xanadu, and Douglas Engelbart's oN-Line System (NLS). Both Nelson and Engelbart were in turn inspired by Vannevar Bush's microfilm-based *memex*, which was described in the 1945 essay "As We May Think".

Berners-Lee's breakthrough was to marry hypertext to the Internet. In his book *Weaving The Web*, he explains that he had repeatedly suggested that a marriage between the two technologies was possible to members of *both* technical communities, but when no one took up his invitation, he finally assumed the project himself. In the process, he developed three essential technologies:

- a system of globally unique identifiers for resources on the Web and elsewhere, the universal document identifier (UDI), later known as uniform resource locator (URL) and uniform resource identifier (URI);

- the publishing language HyperText Markup Language (HTML);

- the Hypertext Transfer Protocol (HTTP).

The World Wide Web had a number of differences from other hypertext systems available at the time. The Web required only unidirectional links rather than bidirectional ones, making it possible for someone to link to another resource without action by the owner of that resource. It also significantly reduced the difficulty of implementing web servers and browsers (in comparison to earlier systems), but in turn presented the chronic problem of *link rot*. Unlike predecessors such as HyperCard, the World Wide Web was non-proprietary, making it possible to develop servers and clients independently and to add extensions without licensing restrictions. On 30 April 1993, CERN announced that the World Wide Web would be free to anyone, with no fees due. Coming two months after the announcement that the server implementation of the Gopher protocol was no longer free to use, this produced a rapid shift away from Gopher and towards the Web. An early popular web browser was ViolaWWW for Unix and the X Windowing System.

Robert Cailliau, Jean-François Abramatic formerly of INRIA, and Tim Berners-Lee at the 10th anniversary of the World Wide Web Consortium.

Scholars generally agree that a turning point for the World Wide Web began with the introduction of the Mosaic web browser in 1993, a graphical browser developed by a team at the National Center for Supercomputing Applications at the University of Illinois at Urbana-Champaign (NCSA-UIUC), led by Marc Andreessen. Funding for Mosaic came from the U.S. *High-Performance Computing and Communications Initiative* and the *High Performance Computing and Commu-*

nication Act of 1991, one of several computing developments initiated by U.S. Senator Al Gore. Prior to the release of Mosaic, graphics were not commonly mixed with text in web pages and the web's popularity was less than older protocols in use over the Internet, such as Gopher and Wide Area Information Servers (WAIS). Mosaic's graphical user interface allowed the Web to become, by far, the most popular Internet protocol. The World Wide Web Consortium (W3C) was founded by Tim Berners-Lee after he left the European Organization for Nuclear Research (CERN) in October 1994. It was founded at the Massachusetts Institute of Technology Laboratory for Computer Science (MIT/LCS) with support from the Defense Advanced Research Projects Agency (DARPA), which had pioneered the Internet; a year later, a second site was founded at INRIA (a French national computer research lab) with support from the European Commission DG InfSo; and in 1996, a third continental site was created in Japan at Keio University. By the end of 1994, the total number of websites was still relatively small, but many notable websites were already active that foreshadowed or inspired today's most popular services.

Connected by the Internet, other websites were created around the world. This motivated international standards development for protocols and formatting. Berners-Lee continued to stay involved in guiding the development of web standards, such as the markup languages to compose web pages and he advocated his vision of a Semantic Web. The World Wide Web enabled the spread of information over the Internet through an easy-to-use and flexible format. It thus played an important role in popularising use of the Internet. Although the two terms are sometimes conflated in popular use, *World Wide Web* is not synonymous with *Internet*. The Web is an information space containing hyperlinked documents and other resources, identified by their URIs. It is implemented as both client and server software using Internet protocols such as TCP/IP and HTTP. Berners-Lee was knighted in 2004 by Queen Elizabeth II for "services to the global development of the Internet".

Function

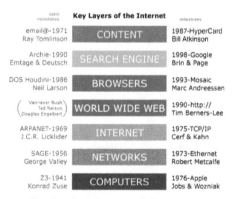

The World Wide Web functions as an application layer protocol that is run "on top of" (figuratively) the Internet, helping to make it more functional. The advent of the Mosaic web browser helped to make the web much more usable, to include the display of images and moving images (gifs).

The terms *Internet* and *World Wide Web* are often used without much distinction. However, the two are not the same. The Internet is a global system of interconnected computer networks. In contrast, the World Wide Web is a global collection of documents and other resources, linked by hyperlinks and URIs. Web resources are usually accessed using HTTP, which is one of many Internet communication protocols.

Viewing a web page on the World Wide Web normally begins either by typing the URL of the page into a web browser, or by following a hyperlink to that page or resource. The web browser then initiates a series of background communication messages to fetch and display the requested page. In the 1990s, using a browser to view web pages—and to move from one web page to another through hyperlinks—came to be known as 'browsing,' 'web surfing' (after channel surfing), or 'navigating the Web'. Early studies of this new behaviour investigated user patterns in using web browsers. One study, for example, found five user patterns: exploratory surfing, window surfing, evolved surfing, bounded navigation and targeted navigation.

The following example demonstrates the functioning of a web browser when accessing a page at the URL http://www.example.org/home.html. The browser resolves the server name of the URL (www.example.org) into an Internet Protocol address using the globally distributed Domain Name System (DNS). This lookup returns an IP address such as *203.0.113.4* or *2001:db8:2e::7334*. The browser then requests the resource by sending an HTTP request across the Internet to the computer at that address. It requests service from a specific TCP port number that is well known for the HTTP service, so that the receiving host can distinguish an HTTP request from other network protocols it may be servicing. The HTTP protocol normally uses port number 80. The content of the HTTP request can be as simple as two lines of text:

GET /home.html HTTP/1.1

Host: www.example.org

The computer receiving the HTTP request delivers it to web server software listening for requests on port 80. If the web server can fulfil the request it sends an HTTP response back to the browser indicating success:

HTTP/1.0 200 OK

Content-Type: text/html; charset=UTF-8

followed by the content of the requested page. HyperText Markup Language (HTML) for a basic web page might look like this:

```
<html>
 <head>
  <title>Example.org – The World Wide Web</title>
 </head>
 <body>
  <p>The World Wide Web, abbreviated as WWW and commonly known ...</p>
 </body>
</html>
```

The web browser parses the HTML and interprets the markup (<title>, <p> for paragraph, and such) that surrounds the words to format the text on the screen. Many web pages use HTML to reference the URLs of other resources such as images, other embedded media, scripts that affect page behaviour, and Cascading Style Sheets that affect page layout. The browser makes additional HTTP requests to the web server for these other Internet media types. As it receives their content from the web server, the browser progressively renders the page onto the screen as specified by its HTML and these additional resources.

Linking

Most web pages contain hyperlinks to other related pages and perhaps to downloadable files, source documents, definitions and other web resources. In the underlying HTML, a hyperlink looks like this: <a href="http://www.example.org/home.html">Example.org Homepage</a>

Graphic representation of a minute fraction of the WWW, demonstrating hyperlinks

Such a collection of useful, related resources, interconnected via hypertext links is dubbed a *web* of information. Publication on the Internet created what Tim Berners-Lee first called the *World-WideWeb* (in its original CamelCase, which was subsequently discarded) in November 1990.

The hyperlink structure of the WWW is described by the webgraph: the nodes of the webgraph correspond to the web pages (or URLs) the directed edges between them to the hyperlinks. Over time, many web resources pointed to by hyperlinks disappear, relocate, or are replaced with different content. This makes hyperlinks obsolete, a phenomenon referred to in some circles as link rot, and the hyperlinks affected by it are often called dead links. The ephemeral nature of the Web has prompted many efforts to archive web sites. The Internet Archive, active since 1996, is the best known of such efforts.

Dynamic Updates of Web Pages

JavaScript is a scripting language that was initially developed in 1995 by Brendan Eich, then of Netscape, for use within web pages. The standardised version is ECMAScript. To make web pages more interactive, some web applications also use JavaScript techniques such as Ajax (asynchronous JavaScript and XML). Client-side script is delivered with the page that can make additional HTTP requests to the server, either in response to user actions such as mouse movements or clicks, or based on elapsed time. The server's responses are used to modify the current page rather than creating a new page with each response, so the server needs only to provide limited, incremental information. Multiple Ajax requests can be handled at the same time, and users can interact with the page while data is retrieved. Web pages may also regularly poll the server to check whether new information is available.

WWW Prefix

Many hostnames used for the World Wide Web begin with *www* because of the long-standing practice of naming Internet hosts according to the services they provide. The hostname of a web server is often *www*, in the same way that it may be *ftp* for an FTP server, and *news* or *nntp* for a USENET news server. These host names appear as Domain Name System (DNS) or subdomain names, as in *www.example.com*. The use of *www* is not required by any technical or policy standard and many web sites do not use it; indeed, the first ever web server was called *nxoco1.cern.ch*. According to Paolo Palazzi, who worked at CERN along with Tim Berners-Lee, the popular use of *www* as subdomain was accidental; the World Wide Web project page was intended to be published at www. cern.ch while info.cern.ch was intended to be the CERN home page, however the DNS records were never switched, and the practice of prepending *www* to an institution's website domain name was subsequently copied. Many established websites still use the prefix, or they employ other subdomain names such as *www2*, *secure* or *en* for special purposes. Many such web servers are set up so that both the main domain name (e.g., example.com) and the *www* subdomain (e.g., www.example.com) refer to the same site; others require one form or the other, or they may map to different web sites. The use of a subdomain name is useful for load balancing incoming web traffic by creating a CNAME record that points to a cluster of web servers. Since, currently, only a subdomain can be used in a CNAME, the same result cannot be achieved by using the bare domain root.

When a user submits an incomplete domain name to a web browser in its address bar input field, some web browsers automatically try adding the prefix "www" to the beginning of it and possibly ".com", ".org" and ".net" at the end, depending on what might be missing. For example, entering 'microsoft' may be transformed to *http://www.microsoft.com/* and 'openoffice' to *http://www. openoffice.org*. This feature started appearing in early versions of Mozilla Firefox, when it still had the working title 'Firebird' in early 2003, from an earlier practice in browsers such as Lynx. It is reported that Microsoft was granted a US patent for the same idea in 2008, but only for mobile devices.

In English, *www* is usually read as *double-u double-u double-u*. Some users pronounce it *dub-dub-dub*, particularly in New Zealand. Stephen Fry, in his "Podgrammes" series of podcasts, pronounces it *wuh wuh wuh*. The English writer Douglas Adams once quipped in *The Independent on Sunday* (1999): "The World Wide Web is the only thing I know of whose shortened form takes three times longer to say than what it's short for". In Mandarin Chinese, *World Wide Web* is commonly translated via a phono-semantic matching to *wàn wéi wǎng*, which satisfies *www* and literally means "myriad dimensional net", a translation that reflects the design concept and proliferation of the World Wide Web. Tim Berners-Lee's web-space states that *World Wide Web* is officially spelled as three separate words, each capitalised, with no intervening hyphens. Use of the www prefix has been declining, especially when Web 2.0 web applications sought to brand their domain names and make them easily pronounceable. As the mobile web grew in popularity, services like Gmail.com, Outlook.com, MySpace.com, Facebook.com and Twitter.com are most often mentioned without adding "www." (or, indeed, ".com") to the domain.

Scheme Specifiers

The scheme specifiers *http://* and *https://* at the start of a web URI refer to Hypertext Transfer Protocol or HTTP Secure, respectively. They specify the communication protocol to use for the request and response. The HTTP protocol is fundamental to the operation of the World Wide Web, and the added encryption layer in HTTPS is essential when browsers send or retrieve confidential data, such as passwords or banking information. Web browsers usually automatically prepend http:// to user-entered URIs, if omitted.

Web Security

For criminals, the Web has become a venue to spread malware and engage in a range of cyber-crimes, including identity theft, fraud, espionage and intelligence gathering. Web-based vulnerabilities now outnumber traditional computer security concerns, and as measured by Google, about one in ten web pages may contain malicious code. Most web-based attacks take place on legitimate websites, and most, as measured by Sophos, are hosted in the United States, China and Russia. The most common of all malware threats is SQL injection attacks against websites. Through HTML and URIs, the Web was vulnerable to attacks like cross-site scripting (XSS) that came with the introduction of JavaScript and were exacerbated to some degree by Web 2.0 and Ajax web design that favours the use of scripts. Today by one estimate, 70% of all websites are open to XSS attacks on their users. Phishing is another common threat to the Web. "SA, the Security Division of EMC, today announced the findings of its January 2013 Fraud Report, estimating the global losses from phishing at $1.5 Billion in 2012". Two of the well-known phishing methods are Covert Redirect and Open Redirect.

Proposed solutions vary. Large security companies like McAfee already design governance and compliance suites to meet post-9/11 regulations, and some, like Finjan have recommended active real-time inspection of programming code and all content regardless of its source. Some have argued that for enterprises to see Web security as a business opportunity rather than a cost centre, while others call for "ubiquitous, always-on digital rights management" enforced in the infrastructure to replace the hundreds of companies that secure data and networks. Jonathan Zittrain has said users sharing responsibility for computing safety is far preferable to locking down the Internet.

Privacy

Every time a client requests a web page, the server can identify the request's IP address and usually logs it. Also, unless set not to do so, most web browsers record requested web pages in a viewable *history* feature, and usually cache much of the content locally. Unless the server-browser communication uses HTTPS encryption, web requests and responses travel in plain text across the Internet and can be viewed, recorded, and cached by intermediate systems. When a web page asks for, and the user supplies, personally identifiable information—such as their real name, address, e-mail address, etc.—web-based entities can associate current web traffic with that individual. If the website uses HTTP cookies, username and password authentication, or other tracking techniques, it can relate other web visits, before and after, to the identifiable information provided. In this way it is possible for a web-based organisation to develop and build a profile of the individual people who use its site or sites. It may be able to build a record for an individual that includes information about their leisure activities, their shopping interests, their profession, and other aspects of their demographic profile. These profiles are obviously of potential interest to marketeers, advertisers and others. Depending on the website's terms and conditions and the local laws that apply information from these profiles may be sold, shared, or passed to other organisations without the user being informed. For many ordinary people, this means little more than some unexpected e-mails in their in-box, or some uncannily relevant advertising on a future web page. For others, it can mean that time spent indulging an unusual interest can result in a deluge of further targeted marketing that may be unwelcome. Law enforcement, counter terrorism and espionage agencies can also identify, target and track individuals based on their interests or proclivities on the Web.

Social networking sites try to get users to use their real names, interests, and locations, rather than pseudonyms. These website's leaders believe this makes the social networking experience more engaging for users. On the other hand, uploaded photographs or unguarded statements can be identified to an individual, who may regret this exposure. Employers, schools, parents, and other relatives may be influenced by aspects of social networking profiles, such as text posts or digital photos, that the posting individual did not intend for these audiences. On-line bullies may make use of personal information to harass or stalk users. Modern social networking websites allow fine grained control of the privacy settings for each individual posting, but these can be complex and not easy to find or use, especially for beginners. Photographs and videos posted onto websites have caused particular problems, as they can add a person's face to an on-line profile. With modern and potential facial recognition technology, it may then be possible to relate that face with other, previously anonymous, images, events and scenarios that have been imaged elsewhere. Because of image caching, mirroring and copying, it is difficult to remove an image from the World Wide Web.

Standards

Many formal standards and other technical specifications and software define the operation of different aspects of the World Wide Web, the Internet, and computer information exchange. Many of the documents are the work of the World Wide Web Consortium (W3C), headed by Berners-Lee, but some are produced by the Internet Engineering Task Force (IETF) and other organisations.

Usually, when web standards are discussed, the following publications are seen as foundational:

- Recommendations for markup languages, especially HTML and XHTML, from the W3C. These define the structure and interpretation of hypertext documents.

- Recommendations for stylesheets, especially CSS, from the W3C.

- Standards for ECMAScript (usually in the form of JavaScript), from Ecma International.

- Recommendations for the Document Object Model, from W3C.

Additional publications provide definitions of other essential technologies for the World Wide Web, including, but not limited to, the following:

- *Uniform Resource Identifier* (URI), which is a universal system for referencing resources on the Internet, such as hypertext documents and images. URIs, often called URLs, are defined by the IETF's RFC 3986 / STD 66: *Uniform Resource Identifier (URI): Generic Syntax*, as well as its predecessors and numerous URI scheme-defining RFCs;

- *HyperText Transfer Protocol (HTTP)*, especially as defined by RFC 2616: *HTTP/1.1* and RFC 2617: *HTTP Authentication*, which specify how the browser and server authenticate each other.

Accessibility

There are methods for accessing the Web in alternative mediums and formats to facilitate use by individuals with disabilities. These disabilities may be visual, auditory, physical, speech-related, cognitive, neurological, or some combination. Accessibility features also help people with temporary disabilities, like a broken arm, or ageing users as their abilities change. The Web receives information as well as providing information and interacting with society. The World Wide Web Consortium claims that it is essential that the Web be accessible, so it can provide equal access and equal opportunity to people with disabilities. Tim Berners-Lee once noted, "The power of the Web is in its universality. Access by everyone regardless of disability is an essential aspect." Many countries regulate web accessibility as a requirement for websites. International cooperation in the W3C Web Accessibility Initiative led to simple guidelines that web content authors as well as software developers can use to make the Web accessible to persons who may or may not be using assistive technology.

Internationalisation

The W3C Internationalisation Activity assures that web technology works in all languages, scripts, and cultures. Beginning in 2004 or 2005, Unicode gained ground and eventually in December 2007 surpassed both ASCII and Western European as the Web's most frequently used character encoding. Originally RFC 3986 allowed resources to be identified by URI in a subset of US-ASCII. RFC 3987 allows more characters—any character in the Universal Character Set—and now a resource can be identified by IRI in any language.

Statistics

Between 2005 and 2010, the number of web users doubled, and was expected to surpass two billion in 2010. Early studies in 1998 and 1999 estimating the size of the Web using capture/recapture methods showed that much of the web was not indexed by search engines and the Web was much larger than expected. According to a 2001 study, there was a massive number, over 550 billion, of documents on the Web, mostly in the invisible Web, or Deep Web. A 2002 survey of 2,024 million web pages determined that by far the most web content was in the English language: 56.4%; next were pages in German (7.7%), French (5.6%), and Japanese (4.9%). A more recent study, which used web searches in 75 different languages to sample the Web, determined that there were over 11.5 billion web pages in the publicly indexable web as of the end of January 2005. As of March 2009, the indexable web contains at least 25.21 billion pages. On 25 July 2008, Google software engineers Jesse Alpert and Nissan Hajaj announced that Google Search had discovered one trillion unique URLs. As of May 2009, over 109.5 million domains operated. Of these, 74% were commercial or other domains operating in the generic top-level domain *com*. Statistics measuring a website's popularity, such as the Alexa Internet rankings, are usually based either on the number of page views or on associated server "hits" (file requests) that it receives.

Speed Issues

Frustration over congestion issues in the Internet infrastructure and the high latency that results in slow browsing, "freezing" of Web pages, and slow loading of websites has led to a pejorative name for the World Wide Web: the *World Wide Wait*. Speeding up the Internet is an ongoing discussion over the use of peering and QoS technologies. Other solutions to reduce the congestion can be found at W3C. Guidelines for web response times are:

- 0.1 second (one tenth of a second). Ideal response time. The user does not sense any interruption.

- 1 second. Highest acceptable response time. Download times above 1 second interrupt the user experience.

- 10 seconds. Unacceptable response time. The user experience is interrupted and the user is likely to leave the site or system.

Web Caching

A web cache is a server computer located either on the public Internet, or within an enterprise that stores recently accessed web pages to improve response time for users when the same content is requested within a certain time after the original request. Most web browsers also implement a browser cache for recently obtained data, usually on the local disk drive. HTTP requests by a browser may ask only for data that has changed since the last access. Web pages and resources may contain expiration information to control caching to secure sensitive data, such as in online banking, or to facilitate frequently updated sites, such as news media. Even sites with highly dynamic content may permit basic resources to be refreshed only occasionally. Web site designers find it worthwhile to collate resources such as CSS data and JavaScript into a few site-wide files so that they can be cached efficiently. Enterprise firewalls often cache Web resources requested by one user for the benefit of many users. Some search engines store cached content of frequently accessed websites.

Web Science

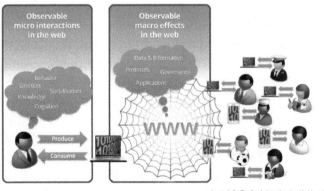

(cc-attrib Steffen Staab. http://west.uni-koblenz.de)

Human behavior co-constituting the web.

Web science is an emerging interdisciplinary field concerned with the study of large-scale socio-technical systems, such as the World Wide Web. It considers the relationship between people and technology, the ways that society and technology co-constitute one another and the impact of this co-constitution on broader society. Web Science combines research from disciplines as diverse as sociology, computer science, economics, and mathematics.

An earlier definition was given by American computer scientist Ben Shneiderman: "Web Science" is the processing the information available on the web in similar terms to those applied to natural environment.

The Web Science Institute describes Web Science as focusing "the analytical power of researchers from disciplines as diverse as mathematics, sociology, economics, psychology, law and computer science to understand and explain the Web. It is necessarily interdisciplinary - as much about social and organizational behaviour as about the underpinning technology."

Research Groups

There are numerous academic research groups engaged in Web Science research, many of which are members of WSTNet, the Web Science Trust Network of research labs. Health Web Science emerged as a sub-discipline of Web Science that studies the role of the Web's impact human health outcomes and how to further utilize the Web to improve health outcomes.

Related Major Conferences

- Association for Computing Machinery (ACM), Hypertext Conference (HT) sponsored by sigWeb

- ACM SIGCHI Conference on Human Factors in Computing Systems (CHI)

- International AAAI Conference on Weblogs and Social Media (ICWSM)

- International World Wide Web Conference (WWW)

Uniform Resource Locator

A Uniform Resource Locator (URL), commonly informally termed a web address (a term which is not defined identically) is a reference to a web resource that specifies its location on a computer network and a mechanism for retrieving it. A URL is a specific type of Uniform Resource Identifier (URI), although many people use the two terms interchangeably. A URL implies the means to access an indicated resource, which is not true of every URI. URLs occur most commonly to reference web pages (http), but are also used for file transfer (ftp), email (mailto), database access (JDBC), and many other applications.

Most web browsers display the URL of a web page above the page in an address bar. A typical URL could have the form http://www.example.com/index.html, which indicates a protocol (http), a hostname (www.example.com), and a file name (index.html).

History

Uniform Resource Locators were defined in Request for Comments (RFC) 1738 in 1994 by Tim Berners-Lee, the inventor of the World Wide Web, and the URI working group of the Internet Engineering Task Force (IETF), as an outcome of collaboration started at the IETF Living Documents "Birds of a Feather" session in 1992.

The format combines the pre-existing system of domain names (created in 1985) with file path syntax, where slashes are used to separate directory and file names. Conventions already existed where server names could be prepended to complete file paths, preceded by a double slash (//).

Berners-Lee later expressed regret at the use of dots to separate the parts of the domain name within URIs, wishing he had used slashes throughout, and also said that, given the colon following the first component of a URI, the two slashes before the domain name were unnecessary.

Syntax

Every HTTP URL conforms to the syntax of a generic URI. A generic URI is of the form:

scheme:[//[user:password@]host[:port]][/]path[?query][#fragment]

It comprises:

- The scheme, consisting of a sequence of characters beginning with a letter and followed by any combination of letters, digits, plus (+), period (.), or hyphen (-). Although schemes are case-insensitive, the canonical form is lowercase and documents that specify schemes must do so with lowercase letters. It is followed by a colon (:). Examples of popular schemes include http, ftp, mailto, file, data, and irc. URI schemes should be registered with the Internet Assigned Numbers Authority (IANA), although non-registered schemes are used in practice.

- Two slashes (//): This is required by some schemes and not required by some others. When the authority component (explained below) is absent, the path component cannot begin with two slashes.

- An authority part, comprising:

    o An optional authentication section of a user name and password, separated by a colon, followed by an at symbol (@)

    o A "host", consisting of either a registered name (including but not limited to a hostname), or an IP address. IPv4 addresses must be in dot-decimal notation, and IPv6 addresses must be enclosed in brackets ([ ]).

    o An optional port number, separated from the hostname by a colon

- A path, which contains data, usually organized in hierarchical form, that appears as a sequence of segments separated by slashes. Such a sequence may resemble or map exactly to a file system path, but does not always imply a relation to one. The path must begin with a single slash (/) if an authority part was present, and may also if one was not, but must not begin with a double slash.

Query delimiter	Example
Ampersand (&)	key1=value1&key2=value2
Semicolon (;)	key1=value1;key2=value2

- An optional query, separated from the preceding part by a question mark (?), containing a query string of non-hierarchical data. Its syntax is not well defined, but by convention is most often a sequence of attribute–value pairs separated by a delimiter.

- An optional fragment, separated from the preceding part by a hash (#). The fragment contains a fragment identifier providing direction to a secondary resource, such as a section heading in an article identified by the remainder of the URI. When the primary resource is an HTML document, the fragment is often an id attribute of a specific element, and web browsers will scroll this element into view.

A web browser will usually dereference a URL by performing an HTTP request to the specified host, by default on port number 80. URLs using the https scheme require that requests and responses will be made over a secure connection to the website.

Internationalized URL

Internet users are distributed throughout the world using a wide variety of languages and alphabets and expect to be able to create URLs in their own local alphabets. An Internationalized Resource Identifier (IRI) is a form of URL that includes Unicode characters. All modern browsers support IRIs. The parts of the URL requiring special treatment for different alphabets are the domain name and path.

The domain name in the IRI is known as an Internationalized Domain Name (IDN). Web and Internet software automatically convert the domain name into punycode usable by the Domain Name System; for example, the Chinese URL http://例子.卷筒纸 becomes http://xn--fsqu00a.xn--3lr804guic/. The xn-- indicates that the character was not originally ASCII.

The URL path name can also be specified by the user in the local alphabet. If not already encoded, it is converted to Unicode, and any characters not part of the basic URL character set are converted to English letters using percent-encoding; for example, the Japanese URL http://example.com/引き割り.html becomes http://example.com/%E5%BC%95%E3%81%8D%E5%89%B2%E3%82%8A.html. The target computer decodes the address and displays the page.

Protocol-relative URLs

Protocol-relative links (PRL), also known as protocol-relative URLs (PRURL), are URLs that have no protocol specified. For example, //example.com will use the protocol of the current page, either HTTP or HTTPS.

Web Standards

Web standards are the formal, non-proprietary standards and other technical specifications that define and describe aspects of the World Wide Web. In recent years, the term has been more frequently associated with the trend of endorsing a set of standardized best practices for building web sites, and a philosophy of web design and development that includes those methods.

Overview

Web standards include many interdependent standards and specifications, some of which govern aspects of the Internet, not just the World Wide Web. Even when not web-focused, such standards directly or indirectly affect the development and administration of web sites and web services. Considerations include the interoperability, accessibility and usability of web pages and web sites.

Web standards, in the broader sense, consist of the following:

- *Recommendations* published by the World Wide Web Consortium (W3C)
- "Living Standard" made by the Web Hypertext Application Technology Working Group (WHATWG)
- *Request for Comments* (RFC) documents published by the Internet Engineering Task Force
- *Standards* published by the International Organization for Standardization (ISO)
- *Standards* published by Ecma International (formerly ECMA)
- *The Unicode Standard* and various *Unicode Technical Reports* (UTRs) published by the Unicode Consortium
- Name and number registries maintained by the Internet Assigned Numbers Authority (IANA)

Web standards are not fixed sets of rules, but are a constantly evolving set of finalized technical specifications of web technologies. Web standards are developed by standards organizations— groups of interested and often competing parties chartered with the task of standardization—not technologies developed and declared to be a standard by a single individual or company. It is crucial to distinguish those specifications that are under development from the ones that already reached the final development status (in case of W3C specifications, the highest maturity level).

Common Usage

When a web site or web page is described as complying with web standards, it usually means that the site or page has valid HTML, CSS and JavaScript. The HTML should also meet accessibility and semantic guidelines. Full standard compliance also covers proper settings for character encoding, valid RSS or valid Atom news feed, valid RDF, valid metadata, valid XML, valid object embedding, valid script embedding, browser- and resolution-independent codes, and proper server settings.

When web standards are discussed, the following publications are typically seen as foundational:

- Recommendations for markup languages, such as Hypertext Markup Language (HTML), Extensible Hypertext Markup Language (XHTML), and Scalable Vector Graphics (SVG) from W3C.
- Recommendations for stylesheets, especially Cascading Style Sheets (CSS), from W3C.

- Standards for ECMAScript, more commonly JavaScript, from Ecma International.

- Recommendations for Document Object Models (DOM), from W3C.

- Properly formed names and addresses for the page and all other resources referenced from it (URIs), based upon RFC 2396, from IETF.

- Proper use of HTTP and MIME to deliver the page, return data from it and to request other resources referenced in it, based on RFC 2616, from IETF.

Web accessibility is normally based upon the Web Content Accessibility Guidelines published by the W3C's Web Accessibility Initiative.

Work in the W3C toward the Semantic Web is currently focused by publications related to the Resource Description Framework (RDF), Gleaning Resource Descriptions from Dialects of Languages (GRDDL) and Web Ontology Language (OWL).

Standards Publications and Bodies

A W3C Recommendation is a specification or set of guidelines that, after extensive consensus-building, has received the endorsement of W3C Members and the Director.

An IETF Internet Standard is characterized by a high degree of technical maturity and by a generally held belief that the specified protocol or service provides significant benefit to the Internet community. A specification that reaches the status of Standard is assigned a number in the IETF STD series while retaining its original IETF RFC number.

Non-standard and Vendor-proprietary Pressures

In the current Working Draft of the HTML 5 proposed standard document, the W3C has a section entitled "Relationship to Flash, Silverlight, XUL and similar proprietary languages" that says, "In contrast with proprietary languages, this specification is intended to define an openly-produced, vendor-neutral language, to be implemented in a broad range of competing products, across a wide range of platforms and devices. This enables developers to write applications that are not limited to one vendor's implementation or language. Furthermore, while writing applications that target vendor-specific platforms necessarily introduces a cost that application developers and their customers or users will face if they are forced to switch (or desire to switch) to another vendor's platform, using an openly-produced and vendor neutral language means that application authors can switch vendors with little to no cost."

Nevertheless, HTML 5 contains numerous "willful violations" of other specifications, in order to accommodate limitations of existing platforms.

History of the World Wide Web

The World Wide Web ("WWW" or simply the "Web") is a global information medium which users can read and write via computers connected to the Internet. The term is often mistakenly used as a synonym for the Internet itself, but the Web is a service that operates over the Internet, just as e-mail also does. The history of the Internet dates back significantly further than that of the World Wide Web.

Precursors

The hypertext portion of the Web in particular has an intricate intellectual history; notable influences and precursors include Vannevar Bush's Memex, IBM's Generalized Markup Language, and Ted Nelson's Project Xanadu.

Paul Otlet's Mundaneum project has also been named as an early 20th century precursor of the Web.

The concept of a global information system connecting homes is prefigured in "A Logic Named Joe", a 1946 short story by Murray Leinster, in which computer terminals, called "logics," are present in every home. Although the computer system in the story is centralized, the story anticipates a ubiquitous information environment similar to the Web.

1980–1991: Invention and Implementation of the Web

The NeXTcube used by Tim Berners-Lee at CERN became the first Web server.

In 1980, Tim Berners-Lee, an English independent contractor at the European Organization for Nuclear Research (CERN) in Switzerland, built ENQUIRE, as a personal database of people and software models, but also as a way to play with hypertext; each new page of information in ENQUIRE had to be linked to an existing page.

Berners-Lee's contract in 1980 was from June to December, but in 1984 he returned to CERN in a permanent role, and considered its problems of information management: physicists from around the world needed to share data, yet they lacked common machines and any shared presentation software.

Shortly after Berners-Lee's return to CERN, TCP/IP protocols were installed on some key non-Unix machines at the institution, turning it into the largest Internet site in Europe within a few years. As a result, CERN's infrastructure was ready for Berners-Lee to create the Web.

Berners-Lee wrote a proposal in March 1989 for "a large hypertext database with typed links". Although the proposal attracted little interest, Berners-Lee was encouraged by his boss, Mike Sendall, to begin implementing his system on a newly acquired NeXT workstation. He considered several names, including *Information Mesh*, *The Information Mine* or *Mine of Information*, but settled on *World Wide Web*.

Berners-Lee found an enthusiastic supporter in Robert Cailliau. Berners-Lee and Cailliau pitched Berners-Lee's ideas to the European Conference on Hypertext Technology in September 1990, but found no vendors who could appreciate his vision of marrying hypertext with the Internet.

By Christmas 1990, Berners-Lee had built all the tools necessary for a working Web: the HyperText Transfer Protocol (HTTP) 0.9, the HyperText Markup Language (HTML), the first Web browser (named WorldWideWeb, which was also a Web editor), the first HTTP server software (later known as CERN httpd), the first web server (http://info.cern.ch), and the first Web pages that described the project itself. The browser could access Usenet newsgroups and FTP files as well. However, it could run only on the NeXT; Nicola Pellow therefore created a simple text browser that could run on almost any computer called the Line Mode Browser. To encourage use within CERN, Bernd Pollermann put the CERN telephone directory on the web — previously users had to log onto the mainframe in order to look up phone numbers.

While inventing and working on setting up the Web, Berners-Lee spent most of his working hours in Building 31 at CERN (46°13′57″N 6°02′42″E46.2325°N 6.0450°E), but also at his two homes, one in France, one in Switzerland. In January 1991 the first Web servers outside CERN itself were switched on.

The first web page may be lost, but Paul Jones of UNC-Chapel Hill in North Carolina revealed in May 2013 that he has a copy of a page sent to him in 1991 by Berners-Lee which is the oldest known web page. Jones stored the plain-text page, with hyperlinks, on a floppy disk and on his NeXT computer. CERN put the oldest known web page back online in 2014, complete with hyperlinks that helped users get started and helped them navigate what was then a very small web.

On August 6, 1991, Berners-Lee posted a short summary of the World Wide Web project on the alt.hypertext newsgroup, inviting collaborators. This date is sometimes confused with the public availability of the first web servers, which had occurred months earlier.

Paul Kunz from the Stanford Linear Accelerator Center visited CERN in September 1991, and was captivated by the Web. He brought the NeXT software back to SLAC, where librarian Louise Addis adapted it for the VM/CMS operating system on the IBM mainframe as a way to display SLAC's catalog of online documents; this was the first web server outside of Europe and the first in North America. The www-talk mailing list was started in the same month.

An early CERN-related contribution to the Web was the parody band Les Horribles Cernettes, whose promotional image is believed to be among the Web's first five pictures.

1992–1995: Growth of the Web

In keeping with its birth at CERN and the first page opened, early adopters of the World Wide Web were primarily university-based scientific departments or physics laboratories such as Fermilab and SLAC. By January 1993 there were fifty Web servers across the world; by October 1993 there were over five hundred. Two of the earliest webcomics started on the World Wide Web in 1993: *Doctor Fun* and *NetBoy*.

Early websites intermingled links for both the HTTP web protocol and the then-popular Gopher protocol, which provided access to content through hypertext menus presented as a file system rather than through HTML files. Early Web users would navigate either by bookmarking popular directory pages, such as Berners-Lee's first site at http://info.cern.ch/, or by consulting updated lists such as the NCSA "What's New" page. Some sites were also indexed by WAIS, enabling users to submit full-text searches similar to the capability later provided by search engines.

By the end of 1994, the total number of websites was still minute compared to present figures, but quite a number of notable websites were already active, many of which are the precursors or inspiring examples of today's most popular services.

Early Browsers

Initially, a web browser was available only for the NeXT operating system. This shortcoming was discussed in January 1992, and alleviated in April 1992 by the release of Erwise, an application developed at the Helsinki University of Technology, and in May by ViolaWWW, created by Pei-Yuan Wei, which included advanced features such as embedded graphics, scripting, and animation. ViolaWWW was originally an application for HyperCard. Both programs ran on the X Window System for Unix.

Students at the University of Kansas adapted an existing text-only hypertext browser, Lynx, to access the web. Lynx was available on Unix and DOS, and some web designers, unimpressed with glossy graphical websites, held that a website not accessible through Lynx wasn't worth visiting.

The first Microsoft Windows browser was Cello, written by Thomas R. Bruce for the Legal Information Institute at Cornell Law School to provide legal information, since access to Windows was more widespread amongst lawyers than access to Unix. Cello was released in June 1993.

The Web was first popularized by Mosaic, a graphical browser launched in 1993 by Marc Andreessen's team at the National Center for Supercomputing Applications (NCSA) at the University of Illinois at Urbana-Champaign (UIUC). The origins of Mosaic date to 1992. In November 1992, the NCSA at the University of Illinois (UIUC) established a website. In December 1992, Andreessen and Eric Bina, students attending UIUC and working at the NCSA, began work on Mosaic with funding from the High-Performance Computing and Communications Initiative, a US-federal research and development program. Andreessen and Bina released a Unix version of the browser in February 1993; Mac and Windows versions followed in August 1993. The browser gained popularity due to its strong support of integrated multimedia, and the authors' rapid response to user bug reports and recommendations for new features.

After graduation from UIUC, Andreessen and James H. Clark, former CEO of Silicon Graphics, met and formed Mosaic Communications Corporation in April 1994, to develop the Mosaic Netscape browser commercially. The company later changed its name to Netscape, and the browser was developed further as Netscape Navigator.

Web Governance

In May 1994, the first International WWW Conference, organized by Robert Cailliau, was held at CERN; the conference has been held every year since. In April 1993, CERN had agreed that anyone could use the Web protocol and code royalty-free; this was in part a reaction to the perturbation caused by the University of Minnesota's announcement that it would begin charging license fees for its implementation of the Gopher protocol.

In September 1994, Berners-Lee founded the World Wide Web Consortium (W3C) at the Massachusetts Institute of Technology with support from the Defense Advanced Research Projects Agency (DARPA) and the European Commission. It comprised various companies that were willing to create standards and recommendations to improve the quality of the Web. Berners-Lee made the Web available freely, with no patent and no royalties due. The W3C decided that its standards must be based on royalty-free technology, so they can be easily adopted by anyone.

1996–1998: Commercialization of the Web

By 1996 it became obvious to most publicly traded companies that a public Web presence was no longer optional. Though at first people saw mainly the possibilities of free publishing and instant worldwide information, increasing familiarity with two-way communication over the "Web" led to the possibility of direct Web-based commerce (e-commerce) and instantaneous group communications worldwide. More dotcoms, displaying products on hypertext webpages, were added into the Web.

1999–2001: "Dot-com" Boom and Bust

Low interest rates in 1998–99 facilitated an increase in start-up companies. Although a number of these new entrepreneurs had realistic plans and administrative ability, most of them lacked these characteristics but were able to sell their ideas to investors because of the novelty of the dot-com concept.

Historically, the dot-com boom can be seen as similar to a number of other technology-inspired booms of the past including railroads in the 1840s, automobiles in the early 20th century, radio in the 1920s, television in the 1940s, transistor electronics in the 1950s, computer time-sharing in the 1960s, and home computers and biotechnology in the 1980s.

In 2001 the bubble burst, and many dot-com startups went out of business after burning through their venture capital and failing to become profitable. Many others, however, did survive and thrive in the early 21st century. Many companies which began as online retailers blossomed and became highly profitable. More conventional retailers found online merchandising to be a profitable additional source of revenue. While some online entertainment and news outlets failed when their seed capital ran out, others persisted and eventually became economically self-sufficient. Traditional media outlets (newspaper publishers, broadcasters and cablecasters in particular) also found the Web to be a useful and profitable additional channel for content distribution, and an additional means to generate advertising revenue. The sites that survived and eventually prospered after the bubble burst had two things in common; a sound business plan, and a niche in the marketplace that was, if not unique, particularly well-defined and well-served.

2002–present: The Web Becomes Ubiquitous

In the aftermath of the dot-com bubble, telecommunications companies had a great deal of overcapacity as many Internet business clients went bust. That, plus ongoing investment in local cell infrastructure kept connectivity charges low, helped to make high-speed Internet connectivity more affordable. During this time, a handful of companies found success developing business models that helped make the World Wide Web a more compelling experience. These include airline booking sites, Google's search engine and its profitable approach to keyword-based advertising, as well as eBay's auction site and Amazon.com's online department store.

This new era also begot social networking websites, such as MySpace and Facebook, which gained acceptance rapidly and became a central part of youth culture.

Web 2.0

Beginning in 2002, new ideas for sharing and exchanging content ad hoc, such as Weblogs and RSS, rapidly gained acceptance on the Web. This new model for information exchange, primarily featuring user-generated and user-edited websites, was dubbed Web 2.0. The Web 2.0 boom saw many new service-oriented startups catering to a newly democratized Web.

As the Web became easier to query, it attained a greater ease of use overall and gained a sense of organization which ushered in a period of rapid popularization. Many new sites such as Wikipedia and its sister projects were based on the concept of user edited content. In 2005, three former PayPal employees created a video viewing website called YouTube, which became popular quickly and introduced a new concept of user-submitted content in major events.

The popularity of YouTube, Facebook, etc., combined with the increasing availability and affordability of high-speed connections has made video content far more common on all kinds of websites. Many video-content hosting and creation sites provide an easy means for their videos to be embedded on third party websites without payment or permission.

This combination of more user-created or edited content, and easy means of sharing content, such as via RSS widgets and video embedding, has led to many sites with a typical "Web 2.0" feel. They have articles with embedded video, user-submitted comments below the article, and RSS boxes to the side, listing some of the latest articles from other sites.

Continued extension of the Web has focused on connecting devices to the Internet, coined Intelligent Device Management. As Internet connectivity becomes ubiquitous, manufacturers have started to leverage the expanded computing power of their devices to enhance their usability and capability. Through Internet connectivity, manufacturers are now able to interact with the devices they have sold and shipped to their customers, and customers are able to interact with the manufacturer (and other providers) to access new content.

"Web 2.0" has found a place in the English lexicon.

The Semantic Web

Popularized by Berners-Lee's book *Weaving the Web* and a *Scientific American* article by Berners-Lee, James Hendler, and Ora Lassila, the term Semantic Web describes an evolution of the existing Web in which the network of hyperlinked human-readable web pages is extended by machine-readable metadata about documents and how they are related to each other, enabling automated agents to access the Web more intelligently and perform tasks on behalf of users. This has yet to happen. In 2006, Berners-Lee and colleagues stated that the idea "remains largely unrealized".

Web Development

Web development is a broad term for the work involved in developing a web site for the Internet (World Wide Web) or an intranet (a private network). Web development can range from developing the simplest static single page of plain text to the most complex web-based internet applications, electronic businesses, and social network services. A more comprehensive list of tasks to which web development commonly refers, may include web engineering, web design, web content development, client liaison, client-side/server-side scripting, web server and network security configuration, and e-commerce development. Among web professionals, "web development" usually refers to the main non-design aspects of building web sites: writing markup and coding. Most recently Web development has come to mean the creation of content management systems or CMS. These CMS can be made from scratch, proprietary or open source. In broad terms the CMS acts as middleware between the database and the user through the browser. A principle benefit of a CMS is that it allows non-technical people to make changes to their web site without having technical knowledge.

For larger organizations and businesses, web development teams can consist of hundreds of people (web developers) and follow standard methods like Agile methodologies while developing websites. Smaller organizations may only require a single permanent or contracting developer, or secondary assignment to related job positions such as a graphic designer and/or information systems technician. Web development may be a collaborative effort between departments rather than the domain of a designated department. There are 3 kind of web developer specialization; Front-End Developer, Back-End Developer, and Full Stack Developer.

Web Development as an Industry

Since the commercialization of the web, web development has been a growing industry. The growth of this industry is being driven by businesses wishing to use their website to sell products and services to customers.

There is open source software for web development like BerkeleyDB, GlassFish, LAMP (Linux, Apache, MySQL, PHP) stack and Perl/Plack. This has kept the cost of learning web development to a minimum. Another contributing factor to the growth of the industry has been the rise of easy-to-use WYSIWYG web-development software, such as Adobe Dreamweaver, BlueGriffon and Microsoft Visual Studio. Knowledge of HyperText Markup Language (HTML) or of programming languages is still required to use such software, but the basics can be learned and implemented quickly with the help of help files, technical books, internet tutorials, or face-to-face training.

An ever growing set of tools and technologies have helped developers build more dynamic and interactive websites. Further, web developers now help to deliver applications as web services which were traditionally only available as applications on a desk-based computer. This has allowed for many opportunities to decentralize information and media distribution. Examples can be seen with the rise of cloud services such as Adobe Creative Cloud, Dropbox and Google Docs. These web services allow users to interact with applications from many locations, instead of being tied to a specific workstation for their application environment.

Examples of dramatic transformation in communication and commerce led by web development include e-commerce. Online auction-sites such as eBay have changed the way consumers find and purchase goods and services. Online retailers such as Amazon.com and Buy.com (among many others) have transformed the shopping and bargain-hunting experience for many consumers. Another good example of transformative communication led by web development is the blog. Web applications such as WordPress and Movable Type have created easily implemented blog-environments for individual web sites. The popularity of open-source content management systems such as Joomla!, Drupal, XOOPS, and TYPO3 and enterprise content management systems such as Alfresco and eXo Platform have extended web development's impact at online interaction and communication.

Web development has also impacted personal networking and marketing. Websites are no longer simply tools for work or for commerce, but serve more broadly for communication and social networking. Websites such as Facebook and Twitter provide users with a platform to communicate and organizations with a more personal and interactive way to engage the public.

Practical Web Development

Basic

In practice, many web developers will have basic interdisciplinary skills / roles, including:

- Graphic design / web design

- Information architecture and copywriting/copyediting with web usability, accessibility and search engine optimization in mind

- Mobile responsiveness

The above list is a simple website development hierarchy and can be extended to include all client side and server side aspects. It is still important to remember that web development is generally split up into client side coding, covering aspects such as the layout and design, and server side coding, which covers the website's functionality and back-end systems.

Testing

Testing is the process of evaluating a system or its component(s) with the intent to find whether it satisfies the specified requirements or not. Testing is executing a system in order to identify any gaps, errors, or missing requirements in contrary to the actual requirements The extent of testing varies greatly between organizations, developers, and individual sites or applications.

Security Considerations

Web development takes into account many security considerations, such as data entry error checking through forms, filtering output, and encryption. Malicious practices such as SQL injection can be executed by users with ill intent yet with only primitive knowledge of web development as a whole. Scripts can be used to exploit websites by granting unauthorized access to malicious users that try to collect information such as email addresses, passwords and protected content like credit card numbers.

Some of this is dependent on the server environment on which the scripting language, such as ASP, JSP, Perl, PHP, Python or Ruby is running, and therefore is not necessarily down to the web developer themselves to maintain. However, stringent testing of web applications before public release is encouraged to prevent such exploits from occurring. If some contact form is provided in a website it should include a captcha field in it which prevents computer programs from automatically filling forms and also mail spamming.

Keeping a web server safe from intrusion is often called *Server Port Hardening*. Many technologies come into play to keep information on the internet safe when it is transmitted from one location to another. For instance TLS certificates (or "SSL certificates") are issued by certificate authorities to help prevent internet fraud. Many developers often employ different forms of encryption when transmitting and storing sensitive information. A basic understanding of information technology security concerns is often part of a web developer's knowledge.

Because new security holes are found in web applications even after testing and launch, security patch updates are frequent for widely used applications. It is often the job of web developers to keep applications up to date as security patches are released and new security concerns are discovered.

Ajax (Programming)

Ajax is a set of web development techniques using many web technologies on the client-side to create asynchronous Web applications. With Ajax, web applications can send data to and retrieve from a server asynchronously (in the background) without interfering with the display and behavior of the existing page. By decoupling the data interchange layer from the presentation layer, Ajax allows for web pages, and by extension web applications, to change content dynamically without the need to reload the entire page. In practice, modern implementations commonly substitute JSON for XML due to the advantages of being native to JavaScript.

Ajax is not a technology, but a group of technologies. HTML and CSS can be used in combination to mark up and style information. The DOM is accessed with JavaScript to dynamically display – and allow the user to interact with – the information presented. JavaScript and the XMLHttpRequest object provide a method for exchanging data asynchronously between browser and server to avoid full page reloads.

History

In the early-to-mid 1990s, most Web sites were based on complete HTML pages. Each user action required that a complete page be loaded from the server. This process was inefficient, as reflected by the user experience: all page content disappeared, then reappeared. Each time the browser reloaded a page because of a partial change, all of the content had to be re-sent, even though only some of the information had changed. This placed additional load on the server and made bandwidth the limiting factor on performance.

In 1996, the iframe tag was introduced by Internet Explorer to load or to fetch content asynchronously.

In 1998, Microsoft Outlook Web App team implemented the first component XMLHTTP by client script.

In 1999, Microsoft used its iframe technology to dynamically update the news stories and stock quotes on the default page for Internet Explorer, and created the XMLHTTP ActiveX control in Internet Explorer 5, which was later adopted by Mozilla, Safari, Opera and other browsers as the XMLHttpRequest JavaScript object. Microsoft has adopted the native XMLHttpRequest model as of Internet Explorer 7. The ActiveX version is still supported in Internet Explorer, but not in Microsoft Edge. The utility of background HTTP requests to the server and asynchronous Web technologies remained fairly obscure until it started appearing in full scale online applications such as Outlook Web App (2000) and Oddpost (2002).

Google made a wide deployment of standards-compliant, cross browser Ajax with Gmail (2004) and Google Maps (2005). In October 2004 Kayak.com's public beta release was among the first large-scale e-commerce uses of what their developers at that time called "the xml http thing".

The term "Ajax" was publicly stated on 18 February 2005 by Jesse James Garrett in an article titled "Ajax: A New Approach to Web Applications", based on techniques used on Google pages.

On 5 April 2006, the World Wide Web Consortium (W3C) released the first draft specification for the XMLHttpRequest object in an attempt to create an official Web standard. The latest draft of the XMLHttpRequest object was published on 30 January 2014.

Technologies

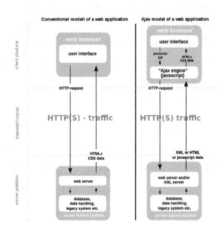

The conventional model for a Web Application versus an application using Ajax

The term *Ajax* has come to represent a broad group of Web technologies that can be used to implement a Web application that communicates with a server in the background, without interfering with the current state of the page. In the article that coined the term Ajax, Jesse James Garrett explained that the following technologies are incorporated:

- HTML (or XHTML) and CSS for presentation

- The Document Object Model (DOM) for dynamic display of and interaction with data

- JSON or XML for the interchange of data, and XSLT for its manipulation

- The XMLHttpRequest object for asynchronous communication

- JavaScript to bring these technologies together

Since then, however, there have been a number of developments in the technologies used in an Ajax application, and in the definition of the term Ajax itself. XML is no longer required for data interchange and, therefore, XSLT is no longer required for the manipulation of data. JavaScript Object Notation (JSON) is often used as an alternative format for data interchange, although other formats such as preformatted HTML or plain text can also be used.

Asynchronous HTML and HTTP (AHAH) involves using XMLHTTPRequest to retrieve (X)HTML fragments, which are then inserted directly into the Web page.

Drawbacks

- Any user whose browser does not support JavaScript or XMLHttpRequest, or has this functionality disabled, will not be able to properly use pages that depend on Ajax. Simple devices (such as smartphones and PDAs) may not support the required technologies. The only way to let the user carry out functionality is to fall back to non-JavaScript methods. This can be achieved by making sure links and forms can be resolved properly and not relying solely on Ajax.

- Similarly, some Web applications that use Ajax are built in a way that cannot be read by screen-reading technologies, such as JAWS. The WAI-ARIA standards provide a way to provide hints in such a case.

- Screen readers that are able to use Ajax may still not be able to properly read the dynamically generated content.

- The same-origin policy prevents some Ajax techniques from being used across domains, although the W3C has a draft of the XMLHttpRequest object that would enable this functionality. Methods exist to sidestep this security feature by using a special Cross Domain Communications channel embedded as an iframe within a page, or by the use of JSONP.

- The asynchronous callback-style of programming required can lead to complex code that is hard to maintain, to debug and to test.

- Because of the asynchronous nature of Ajax, each chunk of data that is sent or received by the client occurs in a connection established specifically for that event. This creates a requirement that for every action, the client must poll the server, instead of listening, which incurs significant overhead. This overhead leads to several times higher latency with Ajax than what can be achieved with a technology such as websockets.

- In pre-HTML5 browsers, pages dynamically created using successive Ajax requests did not automatically register themselves with the browser's history engine, so clicking the browser's "back" button may not have returned the browser to an earlier state of the Ajax-enabled page, but may have instead returned to the last full page visited before it. Such behavior — navigating between pages instead of navigating between page states — may be desirable, but if fine-grained tracking of page state is required, then a pre-HTML5 workaround was to use invisible iframes to trigger changes in the browser's history. A workaround implemented by Ajax techniques is to change the URL fragment identifier (the part of a URL after the "#") when an Ajax-enabled page is accessed and monitor it for changes. HTML5 provides an extensive API standard for working with the browser's history engine.

- Dynamic Web page updates also make it difficult to bookmark and return to a particular state of the application. Solutions to this problem exist, many of which again use the URL fragment identifier. The solution provided by HTML5 for the above problem also applies for this.

- Depending on the nature of the Ajax application, dynamic page updates may disrupt user interactions, particularly if the internet connection is slow or unreliable. For example, editing a search field may trigger a query to the server for search completions, but the user may not know that a search completion popup is forthcoming, and if the internet connection is slow, the popup list may show up at an inconvenient time, when the user has already proceeded to do something else.

- Excluding Google, most major Web crawlers do not execute JavaScript code, so in order to be indexed by web search engines, a Web application must provide an alternative means of accessing the content that would normally be retrieved with Ajax. It has been suggested that a headless browser may be used to index content provided by Ajax-enabled websites, although Google is no longer recommending the Ajax crawling proposal they made back in 2009.

Examples

JavaScript example

An example of a simple Ajax request using the GET method, written in JavaScript.

get-ajax-data.js:

```
// This is the client-side script.


// Initialize the HTTP request.
var xhr = new XMLHttpRequest();
xhr.open('get', 'send-ajax-data.php');


// Track the state changes of the request.
xhr.onreadystatechange = function () {
    var DONE = 4; // readyState 4 means the request is done.
    var OK = 200; // status 200 is a successful return.
```

```
  if (xhr.readyState === DONE) {

    if (xhr.status === OK) {

      alert(xhr.responseText); // 'This is the returned text.'

    } else {

      alert('Error: ' + xhr.status); // An error occurred during the request.

    }

  }

};


// Send the request to send-ajax-data.php

xhr.send(null);

send-ajax-data.php:

<?php

// This is the server-side script.


// Set the content type.

header('Content-Type: text/plain');


// Send the data back.

echo "This is the returned text.";

?>
```

jQuery example

The same example as above written in the popular JavaScript library jQuery.

```
$.get('send-ajax-data.php')

  .done(function(data) {

    alert(data);

  })

  .fail(function(data) {
```

```
    alert('Error: ' + data);

});
```

References

- Canavan, John (2001). Fundamentals of Networking Security. Norwood, MA: Artech House. pp. 82–83. ISBN 9781580531764.

- Berners-Lee, Tim; Fischetti, Mark (2000). Weaving the Web: The Original Design and Ultimate Destiny of the World Wide Web by Its Inventor. San Francisco: Harper. ISBN 978-0-06-251587-2.

- Wright, Alex (2014-07-10). Cataloging the World: Paul Otlet and the Birth of the Information Age. Oxford ; New York: OUP USA. pp. 8--15. ISBN 9780199931415.

- Berners-Lee, Tim (2000-11-07). Weaving the Web: The Original Design and Ultimate Destiny of the World Wide Web. San Francisco: Harper. p. 23. ISBN 9780062515872.

- Raggett, Dave; Jenny Lam; Ian Alexander (1996-04). HTML 3: Electronic Publishing on the World Wide Web. Harlow, England ; Reading, Mass: Addison-Wesley. p. 21. ISBN 9780201876932. Check date values in: |date= (help)

- Berners-Lee, Tim (2000-11-07). Weaving the Web: The Original Design and Ultimate Destiny of the World Wide Web. San Francisco: Harper. p. 46. ISBN 9780062515872.

- Berners-Lee, Tim (2000-11-07). Weaving the Web: The Original Design and Ultimate Destiny of the World Wide Web. San Francisco: Harper. pp. 177--198. ISBN 9780062515872.

- Ullman, Chris (March 2007). Beginning Ajax. wrox. ISBN 978-0-470-10675-4. Archived from the original on 5 July 2008. Retrieved 24 June 2008.

- "Supplement no.1, Diplomatic and Overseas List, K.B.E." (PDF). thegazette.co.uk. The Gazette. 31 December 2003. Retrieved 7 February 2016.

- Simonite, Tom (July 22, 2008). "Help us find a better way to pronounce www". newscientist.com. NewScientist, Technology. Retrieved 7 February 2016.

- Castelluccio, Michael (2010). "It's not your grandfather's Internet.". thefreelibrary.com. Institute of Management Accountants. Retrieved 7 February 2016.

- Alessio Signorini. "The Indexable Web is More than 11.5 Billion Pages" (PDF). citeseerx.ist.psu.edu. Retrieved 4 February 2015.

- Berners-Lee, Tim (21 March 1994). "Uniform Resource Locators (URL): A Syntax for the Expression of Access Information of Objects on the Network". World Wide Web Consortium. Retrieved 13 September 2015.

- Berners-Lee, Tim; Masinter, Larry; McCahill, Mark (August 1998). "Uniform Resource Locators (URL)". Internet Engineering Task Force. Retrieved 31 August 2015.

- Berners-Lee, Tim (2015) [2000]. "Why the //, #, etc?". Frequently asked questions. World Wide Web Consortium. Retrieved 2010-02-03.

- Connolly, Dan; Sperberg-McQueen, C. M., eds. (21 May 2009). "Web addresses in HTML 5". World Wide Web Consortium. Retrieved 13 September 2015.

- Internet Assigned Numbers Authority (14 February 2003). "Completion of IANA Selection of IDNA Prefix". IETF-Announce mailing list. Retrieved 3 September 2015.

- Berners-Lee, Tim; Fielding, Roy; Masinter, Larry (August 1998). "Uniform Resource Identifiers (URI): Generic Syntax". Internet Engineering Task Force. Retrieved 31 August 2015.

- Hansen, T.; Hardie, T. (June 2015). Thaler, D., ed. "Guidelines and Registration Procedures for URI Schemes". Internet Engineering Task Force. ISSN 2070-1721.

- Berners-Lee, Tim; Fielding, Roy; Masinter, Larry (January 2005). "Uniform Resource Identifiers (URI): Generic Syntax". Internet Engineering Task Force. Retrieved 31 August 2015.

- Phillip, A. (2014). "What is Happening with "International URLs"". World Wide Web Consortium. Retrieved 11 January 2015.

- Kesteren, Anne; Aubourg, Julian; Song, Jungkee; Steen, Hallvord R. M. "XMLHttpRequest Level 1". W3.org. W3C. Retrieved 2015-11-14.

- Hendriks, Erik (23 May 2014). "Official news on crawling and indexing sites for the Google index". Google. Retrieved 24 May 2015.

HTML: An Essential Element

HTML is an essential element in web engineering; it is the standard language that used in creating web pages. HTML5, markup language, HTML element, HTML attribute and semantic HTML are the topics explained in the section. The aspects elucidated in this chapter are of vital importance, and provide a better understanding of HTML.

HTML

HyperText Markup Language (HTML) is the standard markup language for creating web pages and web applications. With Cascading Style Sheets (CSS), and JavaScript, it forms a triad of cornerstone technologies for the World Wide Web. Web browsers receive HTML documents from a webserver or from local storage and render them into multimedia web pages. HTML describes the structure of a web page semantically and originally included cues for the appearance of the document.

HTML elements are the building blocks of HTML pages. With HTML constructs, images and other objects, such as interactive forms may be embedded into the rendered page. It provides a means to create structured documents by denoting structural semantics for text such as headings, paragraphs, lists, links, quotes and other items. HTML elements are delineated by *tags*, written using angle brackets. Tags such as <img /> and <input /> introduce content into the page directly. Others such as <p>...</p> surround and provide information about document text and may include other tags as sub-elements. Browsers do not display the HTML tags, but use them to interpret the content of the page.

HTML can embed programs written in a scripting language such as JavaScript which affect the behavior and content of web pages. Inclusion of CSS defines the look and layout of content. The World Wide Web Consortium (W3C), maintainer of both the HTML and the CSS standards, has encouraged the use of CSS over explicit presentational HTML since 1997.

History

HTML

The historic logo made by the W3C

```
<!DOCTYPE html>
<html>
<!--
Created 16-10-2014
-->
<head>
<title>Sample</title>
</head>
<body>
<p>Sample text</p>
</body>
</html>
```

The HTML code above produces the following below

Sample text

An example website written in HTML Code

Development

Tim Berners-Lee

In 1980, physicist Tim Berners-Lee, a contractor at CERN, proposed and prototyped ENQUIRE, a system for CERN researchers to use and share documents. In 1989, Berners-Lee wrote a memo proposing an Internet-based hypertext system. Berners-Lee specified HTML and wrote the browser and server software in late 1990. That year, Berners-Lee and CERN data systems engineer Robert Cailliau collaborated on a joint request for funding, but the project was not formally adopted by CERN. In his personal notes from 1990 he listed "some of the many areas in which hypertext is used" and put an encyclopedia first.

The first publicly available description of HTML was a document called "HTML Tags", first mentioned on the Internet by Tim Berners-Lee in late 1991. It describes 18 elements comprising the initial, relatively simple design of HTML. Except for the hyperlink tag, these were strongly influenced by SGMLguid, an in-house Standard Generalized Markup Language (SGML)-based documentation format at CERN. Eleven of these elements still exist in HTML 4.

HTML is a markup language that web browsers use to interpret and compose text, images, and other material into visual or audible web pages. Default characteristics for every item of HTML markup are defined in the browser, and these characteristics can be altered or enhanced by the web page designer's additional use of CSS. Many of the text elements are found in the 1988 ISO technical report TR 9537 *Techniques for using SGML*, which in turn covers the features of early text formatting languages such as that used by the RUNOFF command developed in the early 1960s for the CTSS (Compatible Time-Sharing System) operating system: these formatting commands were derived from the commands used by typesetters to manually format documents. However, the SGML concept of generalized markup is based on elements (nested annotated ranges with attributes) rather than merely print effects, with also the separation of structure and markup; HTML has been progressively moved in this direction with CSS.

Berners-Lee considered HTML to be an application of SGML. It was formally defined as such by the Internet Engineering Task Force (IETF) with the mid-1993 publication of the first proposal for an HTML specification: "Hypertext Markup Language (HTML)" Internet-Draft by Berners-Lee and Dan Connolly, which included an SGML Document Type Definition to define the grammar. The draft expired after six months, but was notable for its acknowledgment of the NCSA Mosaic browser's custom tag for embedding in-line images, reflecting the IETF's philosophy of basing standards on successful prototypes. Similarly, Dave Raggett's competing Internet-Draft, "HTML+ (Hypertext Markup Format)", from late 1993, suggested standardizing already-implemented features like tables and fill-out forms.

After the HTML and HTML+ drafts expired in early 1994, the IETF created an HTML Working Group, which in 1995 completed "HTML 2.0", the first HTML specification intended to be treated as a standard against which future implementations should be based.

Further development under the auspices of the IETF was stalled by competing interests. Since 1996, the HTML specifications have been maintained, with input from commercial software vendors, by the World Wide Web Consortium (W3C). However, in 2000, HTML also became an international standard (ISO/IEC 15445:2000). HTML 4.01 was published in late 1999, with further errata published through 2001. In 2004, development began on HTML5 in the Web Hypertext Application Technology Working Group (WHATWG), which became a joint deliverable with the W3C in 2008, and completed and standardized on 28 October 2014.

HTML Versions Timeline

November 24, 1995

> HTML 2.0 was published as IETF RFC 1866. Supplemental RFCs added capabilities:

> - November 25, 1995: RFC 1867 (form-based file upload)
> - May 1996: RFC 1942 (tables)
> - August 1996: RFC 1980 (client-side image maps)
> - January 1997: RFC 2070 (internationalization)

January 14, 1997

> HTML 3.2 was published as a W3C Recommendation. It was the first version developed and standardized exclusively by the W3C, as the IETF had closed its HTML Working Group on September 12, 1996.

Initially code-named "Wilbur", HTML 3.2 dropped math formulas entirely, reconciled overlap among various proprietary extensions and adopted most of Netscape's visual markup tags. Netscape's blink element and Microsoft's marquee element were omitted due to a mutual agreement between the two companies. A markup for mathematical formulas similar to that in HTML was not standardized until 14 months later in MathML.

December 18, 1997

HTML 4.0 was published as a W3C Recommendation. It offers three variations:

- Strict, in which deprecated elements are forbidden

- Transitional, in which deprecated elements are allowed

- Frameset, in which mostly only frame related elements are allowed.

Initially code-named "Cougar", HTML 4.0 adopted many browser-specific element types and attributes, but at the same time sought to phase out Netscape's visual markup features by marking them as deprecated in favor of style sheets. HTML 4 is an SGML application conforming to ISO 8879 – SGML.

April 24, 1998

HTML 4.0 was reissued with minor edits without incrementing the version number.

December 24, 1999

HTML 4.01 was published as a W3C Recommendation. It offers the same three variations as HTML 4.0 and its last errata were published on May 12, 2001.

May 2000

ISO/IEC 15445:2000 ("ISO HTML", based on HTML 4.01 Strict) was published as an ISO/IEC international standard. In the ISO this standard falls in the domain of the ISO/IEC JTC1/SC34 (ISO/IEC Joint Technical Committee 1, Subcommittee 34 – Document description and processing languages).

After HTML 4.01, there was no new version of HTML for many years as development of the parallel, XML-based language XHTML occupied the W3C's HTML Working Group through the early and mid-2000s.

October 28, 2014

HTML5 was published as a W3C Recommendation.

HTML Draft Version Timeline

October 1991

HTML Tags, an informal CERN document listing 18 HTML tags, was first mentioned in public.

June 1992

> First informal draft of the HTML DTD, with seven subsequent revisions (July 15, August 6, August 18, November 17, November 19, November 20, November 22)

November 1992

> HTML DTD 1.1 (the first with a version number, based on RCS revisions, which start with 1.1 rather than 1.0), an informal draft

Logo of HTML5

June 1993

> Hypertext Markup Language was published by the IETF IIIR Working Group as an Internet Draft (a rough proposal for a standard). It was replaced by a second version one month later, followed by six further drafts published by IETF itself that finally led to HTML 2.0 in RFC 1866.

November 1993

> HTML+ was published by the IETF as an Internet Draft and was a competing proposal to the Hypertext Markup Language draft. It expired in May 1994.

April 1995 (authored March 1995)

> HTML 3.0 was proposed as a standard to the IETF, but the proposal expired five months later (28 September 1995) without further action. It included many of the capabilities that were in Raggett's HTML+ proposal, such as support for tables, text flow around figures and the display of complex mathematical formulas.

> W3C began development of its own Arena browser as a test bed for HTML 3 and Cascading Style Sheets, but HTML 3.0 did not succeed for several reasons. The draft was considered very large at 150 pages and the pace of browser development, as well as the number of interested parties, had outstripped the resources of the IETF. Browser vendors, including Microsoft and Netscape at the time, chose to implement different subsets of HTML 3's draft features as well as to introduce their own extensions to it. . These included extensions to control stylistic aspects of documents, contrary to the "belief [of the academic engineering community] that such things as text color, background texture, font size and font face

were definitely outside the scope of a language when their only intent was to specify how a document would be organized." Dave Raggett, who has been a W3C Fellow for many years, has commented for example: "To a certain extent, Microsoft built its business on the Web by extending HTML features."

January 2008

HTML5 was published as a Working Draft (link) by the W3C.

Although its syntax closely resembles that of SGML, HTML5 has abandoned any attempt to be an SGML application and has explicitly defined its own "html" serialization, in addition to an alternative XML-based XHTML5 serialization.

2011 HTML5 – Last Call

On 14 February 2011, the W3C extended the charter of its HTML Working Group with clear milestones for HTML5. In May 2011, the working group advanced HTML5 to "Last Call", an invitation to communities inside and outside W3C to confirm the technical soundness of the specification. The W3C developed a comprehensive test suite to achieve broad interoperability for the full specification by 2014, which was the target date for recommendation. In January 2011, the WHATWG renamed its "HTML5" living standard to "HTML". The W3C nevertheless continues its project to release HTML5.

2012 HTML5 – Candidate Recommendation

In July 2012, WHATWG and W3C decided on a degree of separation. W3C will continue the HTML5 specification work, focusing on a single definitive standard, which is considered as a "snapshot" by WHATWG. The WHATWG organization will continue its work with HTML5 as a "Living Standard". The concept of a living standard is that it is never complete and is always being updated and improved. New features can be added but functionality will not be removed.

In December 2012, W3C designated HTML5 as a Candidate Recommendation. The criterion for advancement to W3C Recommendation is "two 100% complete and fully interoperable implementations".

2014 HTML5 – Proposed Recommendation and Recommendation

In September 2014, W3C moved HTML5 to Proposed Recommendation.

On 28 October 2014, HTML5 was released as a stable W3C Recommendation, meaning the specification process is complete.

XHTML Versions

XHTML is a separate language that began as a reformulation of HTML 4.01 using XML 1.0. It is no longer being developed as a separate standard.

- XHTML 1.0, published January 26, 2000, as a W3C Recommendation, later revised and republished August 1, 2002. It offers the same three variations as HTML 4.0 and 4.01, reformulated in XML, with minor restrictions.

- XHTML 1.1, published May 31, 2001, as a W3C Recommendation. It is based on XHTML 1.0 Strict, but includes minor changes, can be customized, is reformulated using modules from Modularization of XHTML, which was published April 10, 2001, as a W3C Recommendation.

- XHTML 2.0 was a working draft, work on it was abandoned in 2009 in favor of work on HTML5 and XHTML5. XHTML 2.0 was incompatible with XHTML 1.x and, therefore, would be more accurately characterized as an XHTML-inspired new language than an update to XHTML 1.x.

- An XHTML syntax, known as "XHTML5.1", is being defined alongside HTML5 in the HTML5 draft.

Markup

HTML markup consists of several key components, including those called *tags* (and their *attributes*), character-based *data types*, *character references* and *entity references*. HTML tags most commonly come in pairs like <h1> and </h1>, although some represent *empty elements* and so are unpaired, for example <img>. The first tag in such a pair is the *start tag*, and the second is the *end tag* (they are also called *opening tags* and *closing tags*).

Another important component is the HTML *document type declaration*, which triggers standards mode rendering.

The following is an example of the classic Hello world program, a common test employed for comparing programming languages, scripting languages and markup languages. This example is made using 9 lines of code:

```
<!DOCTYPE html>

<html>

 <head>

  <title>This is a title</title>

 </head>

 <body>

  <p>Hello world!</p>

 </body>

</html>
```

(The text between <html> and </html> describes the web page, and the text between <body> and </body> is the visible page content. The markup text "<title>This is a title</title>" defines the browser page title.)

The Document Type Declaration <!DOCTYPE html> is for HTML5. If a declaration is not included, various browsers will revert to "quirks mode" for rendering.

Elements

HTML documents imply a structure of nested HTML elements. These are indicated in the document by HTML *tags*, enclosed in angle brackets thus: <p>

In the simple, general case, the extent of an element is indicated by a pair of tags: a "start tag" <p> and "end tag" </p>. The text content of the element, if any, is placed between these tags.

Tags may also enclose further tag markup between the start and end, including a mixture of tags and text. This indicates further (nested) elements, as children of the parent element.

The start tag may also include *attributes* within the tag. These indicate other information, such as identifiers for sections within the document, identifiers used to bind style information to the presentation of the document, and for some tags such as the <img> used to embed images, the reference to the image resource.

Some elements, such as the line break <br>, do not permit *any* embedded content, either text or further tags. These require only a single empty tag (akin to a start tag) and do not use an end tag.

Many tags, particularly the closing end tag for the very commonly used paragraph element <p>, are optional. An HTML browser or other agent can infer the closure for the end of an element from the context and the structural rules defined by the HTML standard. These rules are complex and not widely understood by most HTML coders.

The general form of an HTML element is therefore: <tag attribute1="value1" attribute2="value2">"content"</tag>. Some HTML elements are defined as *empty elements* and take the form <tag attribute1="value1" attribute2="value2">. Empty elements may enclose no content, for instance, the <br> tag or the inline <img> tag. The name of an HTML element is the name used in the tags. Note that the end tag's name is preceded by a slash character, "/", and that in empty elements the end tag is neither required nor allowed. If attributes are not mentioned, default values are used in each case.

Element Examples

Header of the HTML document:<head>...</head>. The title is included in the head, for example:

<head>

 <title>The Title</title>

</head>

Headings: HTML headings are defined with the <h1> to <h6> tags:

<h1>Heading level 1</h1>

<h2>Heading level 2</h2>

<h3>Heading level 3</h3>

<h4>Heading level 4</h4>

\<h5>Heading level 5\</h5>

\<h6>Heading level 6\</h6>

Paragraphs:

\<p>Paragraph 1\</p> \<p>Paragraph 2\</p>

Line breaks:\
. The difference between \
 and \<p> is that "br" breaks a line without altering the semantic structure of the page, whereas "p" sections the page into paragraphs. Note also that "br" is an *empty element* in that, although it may have attributes, it can take no content and it may not have an end tag.

\<p>This \
 is a paragraph \
 with \
 line breaks\</p>

This is a link in HTML. To create a link the \<a> tag is used. The href= attribute holds the URL address of the link.

\<a href="https://www.wikipedia.org/">A link to Wikipedia!\</a>

Comments:

\<!-- This is a comment -->

Comments can help in the understanding of the markup and do not display in the webpage.

There are several types of markup elements used in HTML:

Structural markup indicates the purpose of text

> For example, \<h2>Golf\</h2> establishes "Golf" as a second-level heading. Structural markup does not denote any specific rendering, but most web browsers have default styles for element formatting. Content may be further styled using Cascading Style Sheets (CSS).

Presentational markup indicates the appearance of the text, regardless of its purpose

> For example, \boldface\ indicates that visual output devices should render "boldface" in bold text, but gives little indication what devices that are unable to do this (such as aural devices that read the text aloud) should do. In the case of both \bold\ and \<i>italic\</i>, there are other elements that may have equivalent visual renderings but that are more semantic in nature, such as \strong text\ and \emphasised text\ respectively. It is easier to see how an aural user agent should interpret the latter two elements. However, they are not equivalent to their presentational counterparts: it would be undesirable for a screen-reader to emphasize the name of a book, for instance, but on a screen such a name would be italicized. Most presentational markup elements have become deprecated under the HTML 4.0 specification in favor of using CSS for styling.

Hypertext markup makes parts of a document into links to other documents

> An anchor element creates a hyperlink in the document and its href attribute sets the link's target URL. For example, the HTML markup, \<a href="http://www.google.com/">Wikipedia\</a>, will render the word "Wikipedia" as a hyperlink. To render an image as a hy-

perlink, an "img" element is inserted as content into the "a" element. Like "br", "img" is an empty element with attributes but no content or closing tag. <a href="http://example.org"><img src="image.gif" alt="descriptive text" width="50" height="50" border="0"></a>.

Attributes

Most of the attributes of an element are name-value pairs, separated by "=" and written within the start tag of an element after the element's name. The value may be enclosed in single or double quotes, although values consisting of certain characters can be left unquoted in HTML (but not XHTML) . Leaving attribute values unquoted is considered unsafe. In contrast with name-value pair attributes, there are some attributes that affect the element simply by their presence in the start tag of the element, like the ismap attribute for the img element.

There are several common attributes that may appear in many elements :

- The id attribute provides a document-wide unique identifier for an element. This is used to identify the element so that stylesheets can alter its presentational properties, and scripts may alter, animate or delete its contents or presentation. Appended to the URL of the page, it provides a globally unique identifier for the element, typically a sub-section of the page. For example, the ID "Attributes" in http://en.wikipedia.org/wiki/HTML#Attributes

- The class attribute provides a way of classifying similar elements. This can be used for semantic or presentation purposes. For example, an HTML document might semantically use the designation class="notation" to indicate that all elements with this class value are subordinate to the main text of the document. In presentation, such elements might be gathered together and presented as footnotes on a page instead of appearing in the place where they occur in the HTML source. Class attributes are used semantically in microformats. Multiple class values may be specified; for example class="notation important" puts the element into both the "notation" and the "important" classes.

- An author may use the style attribute to assign presentational properties to a particular element. It is considered better practice to use an element's id or class attributes to select the element from within a stylesheet, though sometimes this can be too cumbersome for a simple, specific, or ad hoc styling.

- The title attribute is used to attach subtextual explanation to an element. In most browsers this attribute is displayed as a tooltip.

- The lang attribute identifies the natural language of the element's contents, which may be different from that of the rest of the document. For example, in an English-language document:

- <p>Oh well, <span lang="fr">c'est la vie</span>, as they say in France.</p>

The abbreviation element, abbr, can be used to demonstrate some of these attributes :

<abbr id="anId" class="jargon" style="color:purple;" title="Hypertext Markup Language">HTML</abbr>

This example displays as HTML; in most browsers, pointing the cursor at the abbreviation should display the title text "Hypertext Markup Language."

Most elements take the language-related attribute dir to specify text direction, such as with "rtl" for right-to-left text in, for example, Arabic, Persian or Hebrew.

Character and Entity References

As of version 4.0, HTML defines a set of 252 character entity references and a set of 1,114,050 numeric character references, both of which allow individual characters to be written via simple markup, rather than literally. A literal character and its markup counterpart are considered equivalent and are rendered identically.

The ability to "escape" characters in this way allows for the characters < and & (when written as < and &, respectively) to be interpreted as character data, rather than markup. For example, a literal < normally indicates the start of a tag, and & normally indicates the start of a character entity reference or numeric character reference; writing it as & or & or & allows & to be included in the content of an element or in the value of an attribute. The double-quote character ("), when not used to quote an attribute value, must also be escaped as " or " or " when it appears within the attribute value itself. Equivalently, the single-quote character ('), when not used to quote an attribute value, must also be escaped as ' or ' (or as ' in HTML5 or XHTML documents) when it appears within the attribute value itself. If document authors overlook the need to escape such characters, some browsers can be very forgiving and try to use context to guess their intent. The result is still invalid markup, which makes the document less accessible to other browsers and to other user agents that may try to parse the document for search and indexing purposes for example.

Escaping also allows for characters that are not easily typed, or that are not available in the document's character encoding, to be represented within element and attribute content. For example, the acute-accented e (é), a character typically found only on Western European and South American keyboards, can be written in any HTML document as the entity reference é or as the numeric references é or é, using characters that are available on all keyboards and are supported in all character encodings. Unicode character encodings such as UTF-8 are compatible with all modern browsers and allow direct access to almost all the characters of the world's writing systems.

Data Types

HTML defines several data types for element content, such as script data and stylesheet data, and a plethora of types for attribute values, including IDs, names, URIs, numbers, units of length, languages, media descriptors, colors, character encodings, dates and times, and so on. All of these data types are specializations of character data.

Document Type Declaration

HTML documents are required to start with a Document Type Declaration (informally, a "doctype"). In browsers, the doctype helps to define the rendering mode—particularly whether to use quirks mode.

The original purpose of the doctype was to enable parsing and validation of HTML documents by SGML tools based on the Document Type Definition (DTD). The DTD to which the DOCTYPE refers contains a machine-readable grammar specifying the permitted and prohibited content for a document conforming to such a DTD. Browsers, on the other hand, do not implement HTML as an application of SGML and by consequence do not read the DTD.

HTML5 does not define a DTD; therefore, in HTML5 the doctype declaration is simpler and shorter:

<!DOCTYPE html>

An example of an HTML 4 doctype

<!DOCTYPE HTML PUBLIC "-//W3C//DTD HTML 4.01//EN" "http://www.w3.org/TR/html4/strict.dtd">

This declaration references the DTD for the "strict" version of HTML 4.01. SGML-based validators read the DTD in order to properly parse the document and to perform validation. In modern browsers, a valid doctype activates standards mode as opposed to quirks mode.

In addition, HTML 4.01 provides Transitional and Frameset DTDs, as explained below. Transitional type is the most inclusive, incorporating current tags as well as older or "deprecated" tags, with the Strict DTD excluding deprecated tags. Frameset has all tags necessary to make frames on a page along with the tags included in transitional type.

Semantic HTML

Semantic HTML is a way of writing HTML that emphasizes the meaning of the encoded information over its presentation (look). HTML has included semantic markup from its inception, but has also included presentational markup, such as <font>, <i> and <center> tags. There are also the semantically neutral span and div tags. Since the late 1990s when Cascading Style Sheets were beginning to work in most browsers, web authors have been encouraged to avoid the use of presentational HTML markup with a view to the separation of presentation and content.

In a 2001 discussion of the Semantic Web, Tim Berners-Lee and others gave examples of ways in which intelligent software "agents" may one day automatically crawl the web and find, filter and correlate previously unrelated, published facts for the benefit of human users. Such agents are not commonplace even now, but some of the ideas of Web 2.0, mashups and price comparison websites may be coming close. The main difference between these web application hybrids and Berners-Lee's semantic agents lies in the fact that the current aggregation and hybridization of information is usually designed in by web developers, who already know the web locations and the API semantics of the specific data they wish to mash, compare and combine.

An important type of web agent that does crawl and read web pages automatically, without prior knowledge of what it might find, is the web crawler or search-engine spider. These software agents are dependent on the semantic clarity of web pages they find as they use various techniques and algorithms to read and index millions of web pages a day and provide web users with search facilities without which the World Wide Web's usefulness would be greatly reduced.

In order for search-engine spiders to be able to rate the significance of pieces of text they find in HTML documents, and also for those creating mashups and other hybrids as well as for more automated agents as they are developed, the semantic structures that exist in HTML need to be widely and uniformly applied to bring out the meaning of published text.

Presentational markup tags are deprecated in current HTML and XHTML recommendations and are illegal in HTML5.

Good semantic HTML also improves the accessibility of web documents. For example, when a screen reader or audio browser can correctly ascertain the structure of a document, it will not waste the visually impaired user's time by reading out repeated or irrelevant information when it has been marked up correctly.

Delivery

HTML documents can be delivered by the same means as any other computer file. However, they are most often delivered either by HTTP from a web server or by email.

HTTP

The World Wide Web is composed primarily of HTML documents transmitted from web servers to web browsers using the Hypertext Transfer Protocol (HTTP). However, HTTP is used to serve images, sound, and other content, in addition to HTML. To allow the web browser to know how to handle each document it receives, other information is transmitted along with the document. This meta data usually includes the MIME type (e.g. text/html or application/xhtml+xml) and the character encoding.

In modern browsers, the MIME type that is sent with the HTML document may affect how the document is initially interpreted. A document sent with the XHTML MIME type is expected to be well-formed XML; syntax errors may cause the browser to fail to render it. The same document sent with the HTML MIME type might be displayed successfully, since some browsers are more lenient with HTML.

The W3C recommendations state that XHTML 1.0 documents that follow guidelines set forth in the recommendation's Appendix C may be labeled with either MIME Type. XHTML 1.1 also states that XHTML 1.1 documents should be labeled with either MIME type.

HTML E-mail

Most graphical email clients allow the use of a subset of HTML (often ill-defined) to provide formatting and semantic markup not available with plain text. This may include typographic information like coloured headings, emphasized and quoted text, inline images and diagrams. Many such clients include both a GUI editor for composing HTML e-mail messages and a rendering engine for displaying them. Use of HTML in e-mail is criticized by some because of compatibility issues, because it can help disguise phishing attacks, because of accessibility issues for blind or visually impaired people, because it can confuse spam filters and because the message size is larger than plain text.

Naming Conventions

The most common filename extension for files containing HTML is .html. A common abbreviation of this is .htm, which originated because some early operating systems and file systems, such as DOS and the limitations imposed by FAT data structure, limited file extensions to three letters.

HTML Application

An HTML Application (HTA; file extension ".hta") is a Microsoft Windows application that uses HTML and Dynamic HTML in a browser to provide the application's graphical interface. A regular HTML file is confined to the security model of the web browser's security, communicating only to web servers and manipulating only webpage objects and site cookies. An HTA runs as a fully trusted application and therefore has more privileges, like creation/editing/removal of files and Windows Registry entries. Because they operate outside the browser's security model, HTAs cannot be executed via HTTP, but must be downloaded (just like an EXE file) and executed from local file system.

HTML4 Variations

HTML is precisely what we were trying to PREVENT— ever-breaking links, links going outward only, quotes you can't follow to their origins, no version management, no rights management.

Ted Nelson

Since its inception, HTML and its associated protocols gained acceptance relatively quickly. However, no clear standards existed in the early years of the language. Though its creators originally conceived of HTML as a semantic language devoid of presentation details, practical uses pushed many presentational elements and attributes into the language, driven largely by the various browser vendors. The latest standards surrounding HTML reflect efforts to overcome the sometimes chaotic development of the language and to create a rational foundation for building both meaningful and well-presented documents. To return HTML to its role as a semantic language, the W3C has developed style languages such as CSS and XSL to shoulder the burden of presentation. In conjunction, the HTML specification has slowly reined in the presentational elements.

There are two axes differentiating various variations of HTML as currently specified: SGML-based HTML versus XML-based HTML (referred to as XHTML) on one axis, and strict versus transitional (loose) versus frameset on the other axis.

SGML-based Versus XML-based HTML

One difference in the latest HTML specifications lies in the distinction between the SGML-based specification and the XML-based specification. The XML-based specification is usually called XHTML to distinguish it clearly from the more traditional definition. However, the root element name continues to be "html" even in the XHTML-specified HTML. The W3C intended XHTML 1.0 to be identical to HTML 4.01 except where limitations of XML over the more complex SGML require workarounds. Because XHTML and HTML are closely related, they are sometimes documented in parallel. In such circumstances, some authors conflate the two names as (X)HTML or X(HTML).

Like HTML 4.01, XHTML 1.0 has three sub-specifications: strict, transitional and frameset.

Aside from the different opening declarations for a document, the differences between an HTML 4.01 and XHTML 1.0 document—in each of the corresponding DTDs—are largely syntactic. The underlying syntax of HTML allows many shortcuts that XHTML does not, such as elements with optional opening or closing tags, and even empty elements which must not have an end tag. By contrast, XHTML requires all elements to have an opening tag and a closing tag. XHTML, however, also introduces a new shortcut: an XHTML tag may be opened and closed within the same tag, by including a slash before the end of the tag like this: <br/>. The introduction of this shorthand, which is not used in the SGML declaration for HTML 4.01, may confuse earlier software unfamiliar with this new convention. A fix for this is to include a space before closing the tag, as such: <br />.

To understand the subtle differences between HTML and XHTML, consider the transformation of a valid and well-formed XHTML 1.0 document that adheres to Appendix C into a valid HTML 4.01 document. To make this translation requires the following steps:

1. The language for an element should be specified with a lang attribute rather than the XHTML xml:lang attribute. XHTML uses XML's built in language-defining functionality attribute.

2. Remove the XML namespace (xmlns=URI). HTML has no facilities for namespaces.

3. Change the document type declaration from XHTML 1.0 to HTML 4.01.

4. If present, remove the XML declaration. (Typically this is: <?xml version="1.0" encoding="utf-8"?>).

5. Ensure that the document's MIME type is set to text/html. For both HTML and XHTML, this comes from the HTTP Content-Type header sent by the server.

6. Change the XML empty-element syntax to an HTML style empty element (
 to <br>).

Those are the main changes necessary to translate a document from XHTML 1.0 to HTML 4.01. To translate from HTML to XHTML would also require the addition of any omitted opening or closing tags. Whether coding in HTML or XHTML it may just be best to always include the optional tags within an HTML document rather than remembering which tags can be omitted.

A well-formed XHTML document adheres to all the syntax requirements of XML. A valid document adheres to the content specification for XHTML, which describes the document structure.

The W3C recommends several conventions to ensure an easy migration between HTML and XHTM. The following steps can be applied to XHTML 1.0 documents only:

•   Include both xml:lang and lang attributes on any elements assigning language.

•   Use the empty-element syntax only for elements specified as empty in HTML.

•   Include an extra space in empty-element tags: for example <br /> instead of <br>.

•   Include explicit close tags for elements that permit content but are left empty (for example, <div></div>, not <div />).

•   Omit the XML declaration.

By carefully following the W3C's compatibility guidelines, a user agent should be able to interpret the document equally as HTML or XHTML. For documents that are XHTML 1.0 and have been made compatible in this way, the W3C permits them to be served either as HTML (with a text/html MIME type), or as XHTML (with an application/xhtml+xml or application/xml MIME type). When delivered as XHTML, browsers should use an XML parser, which adheres strictly to the XML specifications for parsing the document's contents.

Transitional Versus Strict

HTML 4 defined three different versions of the language: Strict, Transitional (once called Loose) and Frameset. The Strict version is intended for new documents and is considered best practice, while the Transitional and Frameset versions were developed to make it easier to transition documents that conformed to older HTML specification or didn't conform to any specification to a version of HTML 4. The Transitional and Frameset versions allow for presentational markup, which is omitted in the Strict version. Instead, cascading style sheets are encouraged to improve the presentation of HTML documents. Because XHTML 1 only defines an XML syntax for the language defined by HTML 4, the same differences apply to XHTML 1 as well.

The Transitional version allows the following parts of the vocabulary, which are not included in the Strict version:

- A looser content model
    - Inline elements and plain text are allowed directly in: body, blockquote, form, noscript and noframes
- Presentation related elements
    - underline (u)(Deprecated. can confuse a visitor with a hyperlink.)
    - strike-through (s)
    - center (Deprecated. use CSS instead.)
    - font (Deprecated. use CSS instead.)
    - basefont (Deprecated. use CSS instead.)
- Presentation related attributes
    - background (Deprecated. use CSS instead.) and bgcolor (Deprecated. use CSS instead.) attributes for body (required element according to the W3C.) element.
    - align (Deprecated. use CSS instead.) attribute on div, form, paragraph (p) and heading (h1...h6) elements
    - align (Deprecated. use CSS instead.), noshade (Deprecated. use CSS instead.), size (Deprecated. use CSS instead.) and width (Deprecated. use CSS instead.) attributes on hr element

- align (Deprecated. use CSS instead.), border, vspace and hspace attributes on img and object (caution: the object element is only supported in Internet Explorer (from the major browsers)) elements

- align (Deprecated. use CSS instead.) attribute on legend and caption elements

- align (Deprecated. use CSS instead.) and bgcolor (Deprecated. use CSS instead.) on table element

- nowrap (Obsolete), bgcolor (Deprecated. use CSS instead.), width, height on td and th elements

- bgcolor (Deprecated. use CSS instead.) attribute on tr element

- clear (Obsolete) attribute on br element

- compact attribute on dl, dir and menu elements

- type (Deprecated. use CSS instead.), compact (Deprecated. use CSS instead.) and start (Deprecated. use CSS instead.) attributes on ol and ul elements

- type and value attributes on li element

- width attribute on pre element

• Additional elements in Transitional specification

- menu (Deprecated. use CSS instead.) list (no substitute, though unordered list is recommended)

- dir (Deprecated. use CSS instead.) list (no substitute, though unordered list is recommended)

- isindex (Deprecated.) (element requires server-side support and is typically added to documents server-side, form and input elements can be used as a substitute)

- applet (Deprecated. use the object element instead.)

• The language (Obsolete) attribute on script element (redundant with the type attribute).

• Frame related entities

- iframe

- noframes

- target (Deprecated in the map, link and form elements.) attribute on a, client-side image-map (map), link, form and base elements

The Frameset version includes everything in the Transitional version, as well as the frameset element (used instead of body) and the frame element.

Frameset Versus Transitional

In addition to the above transitional differences, the frameset specifications (whether XHTML

1.0 or HTML 4.01) specify a different content model, with frameset replacing body, that contains either frame elements, or optionally noframes with a body.

Summary of Specification Versions

As this list demonstrates, the loose versions of the specification are maintained for legacy support. However, contrary to popular misconceptions, the move to XHTML does not imply a removal of this legacy support. Rather the X in XML stands for extensible and the W3C is modularizing the entire specification and opening it up to independent extensions. The primary achievement in the move from XHTML 1.0 to XHTML 1.1 is the modularization of the entire specification. The strict version of HTML is deployed in XHTML 1.1 through a set of modular extensions to the base XHTML 1.1 specification. Likewise, someone looking for the loose (transitional) or frameset specifications will find similar extended XHTML 1.1 support (much of it is contained in the legacy or frame modules). The modularization also allows for separate features to develop on their own timetable. So for example, XHTML 1.1 will allow quicker migration to emerging XML standards such as MathML (a presentational and semantic math language based on XML) and XForms—a new highly advanced web-form technology to replace the existing HTML forms.

In summary, the HTML 4 specification primarily reined in all the various HTML implementations into a single clearly written specification based on SGML. XHTML 1.0, ported this specification, as is, to the new XML defined specification. Next, XHTML 1.1 takes advantage of the extensible nature of XML and modularizes the whole specification. XHTML 2.0 was intended to be the first step in adding new features to the specification in a standards-body-based approach.

HTML5 Variations

WHATWG HTML Versus HTML5

The WHATWG considers their work as *living standard* HTML for what constitutes the state of the art in major browser implementations by Apple (Safari), Google (Chrome), Mozilla (Firefox), Opera (Opera), and others. HTML5 is specified by the HTML Working Group of the W3C following the W3C process. As of 2013 both specifications are similar and mostly derived from each other, i.e., the work on HTML5 started with an older WHATWG draft, and later the WHATWG *living standard* was based on HTML5 drafts in 2011.

Hypertext Features Not in HTML

HTML lacks some of the features found in earlier hypertext systems, such as source tracking, fat links and others. Even some hypertext features that were in early versions of HTML have been ignored by most popular web browsers until recently, such as the link element and in-browser Web page editing.

Sometimes Web services or browser manufacturers remedy these shortcomings. For instance, wikis and content management systems allow surfers to edit the Web pages they visit.

WYSIWYG Editors

There are some WYSIWYG editors, in which the user lays out everything as it is to appear in the

HTML document using a graphical user interface (GUI), often similar to word processors. The editor renders the document rather than show the code, so authors do not require extensive knowledge of HTML.

The WYSIWYG editing model has been criticized, primarily because of the low quality of the generated code; there are voices advocating a change to the WYSIWYM model.

WYSIWYG editors remain a controversial topic because of their perceived flaws such as:

- Relying mainly on layout as opposed to meaning, often using markup that does not convey the intended meaning but simply copies the layout.

- Often producing extremely verbose and redundant code that fails to make use of the cascading nature of HTML and CSS.

- Often producing ungrammatical markup, called tag soup or semantically incorrect markup (such as <em> for italics).

- As a great deal of the information in HTML documents is not in the layout, the model has been criticized for its "what you see is all you get"-nature.

HTML5

HTML5 (No space between "HTML" and "5") is a markup language used for structuring and presenting content on the World Wide Web. It is the fifth and current version of the HTML standard.

It was published in October 2014 by the World Wide Web Consortium (W3C) to improve the language with support for the latest multimedia, while keeping it both easily readable by humans and consistently understood by computers and devices such as web browsers, parsers, etc. HTML5 is intended to subsume not only HTML 4, but also XHTML 1 and DOM Level 2 HTML.

HTML5 includes detailed processing models to encourage more interoperable implementations; it extends, improves and rationalizes the markup available for documents, and introduces markup and application programming interfaces (APIs) for complex web applications. For the same reasons, HTML5 is also a candidate for cross-platform mobile applications, because it includes features designed with low-powered devices in mind.

Many new syntactic features are included. To natively include and handle multimedia and graphical content, the new <video>, <audio> and <canvas> elements were added, and support for scalable vector graphics (SVG) content and MathML for mathematical formulas. To enrich the semantic content of documents, new page structure elements such as <main>, <section>, <article>, <header>, <footer>, <aside>, <nav> and <figure>, are added. New attributes are introduced, some elements and attributes have been removed, and others such as <a>, <cite> and <menu> have been changed, redefined or standardized.

The APIs and Document Object Model (DOM) are now fundamental parts of the HTML5 specification and HTML5 also better defines the processing for any invalid documents.

History

The Web Hypertext Application Technology Working Group (WHATWG) began work on the new standard in 2004. At that time, HTML 4.01 had not been updated since 2000, and the World Wide Web Consortium (W3C) was focusing future developments on XHTML 2.0. In 2009, the W3C allowed the XHTML 2.0 Working Group's charter to expire and decided not to renew it. W3C and WHATWG are currently working together on the development of HTML5.

The Mozilla Foundation and Opera Software presented a position paper at a World Wide Web Consortium (W3C) workshop in June 2004, focusing on developing technologies that are backward compatible with existing browsers, including an initial draft specification of Web Forms 2.0. The workshop concluded with a vote—8 for, 14 against—for continuing work on HTML. Immediately after the workshop, the Web Hypertext Application Technology Working Group (WHATWG) was formed to start work based upon that position paper, and a second draft, Web Applications 1.0, was also announced. The two specifications were later merged to form HTML5. The HTML5 specification was adopted as the starting point of the work of the new HTML working group of the W3C in 2007.

WHATWG published the First Public Working Draft of the specification on 22 January 2008.

"Thoughts on Flash"

While some features of HTML5 are often compared to Adobe Flash, the two technologies are very different. Both include features for playing audio and video within web pages, and for using Scalable Vector Graphics. However, HTML5 on its own cannot be used for animation or interactivity – it must be supplemented with CSS3 or JavaScript. There are many Flash capabilities that have no direct counterpart in HTML5. Although HTML5 has been well known among web developers for years, its interactive capabilities became a topic of mainstream media around April 2010 after Apple Inc's then-CEO Steve Jobs issued a public letter titled "Thoughts on Flash" where he concluded that "Flash is no longer necessary to watch video or consume any kind of web content" and that "new open standards created in the mobile era, such as HTML5, will win". This sparked a debate in web development circles suggesting that, while HTML5 provides enhanced functionality, developers must consider the varying browser support of the different parts of the standard as well as other functionality differences between HTML5 and Flash. In early November 2011, Adobe announced that it would discontinue development of Flash for mobile devices and reorient its efforts in developing tools using HTML5.

Last Call, Candidate and Recommendation

On 14 February 2011, the W3C extended the charter of its HTML Working Group with clear milestones for HTML5. In May 2011, the working group advanced HTML5 to "Last Call", an invitation to communities inside and outside W3C to confirm the technical soundness of the specification. The W3C developed a comprehensive test suite to achieve broad interoperability for the full specification by 2014, which was the target date for recommendation. In January 2011, the WHATWG renamed its "HTML5" living standard to "HTML". The W3C nevertheless continued its project to release HTML5.

In July 2012, WHATWG and W3C decided on a degree of separation. W3C will continue the HTML5 specification work, focusing on a single definitive standard, which is considered as a "snapshot" by WHATWG. The WHATWG organization will continue its work with HTML5 as a "Living Standard". The concept of a living standard is that it is never complete and is always being updated and improved. New features can be added but functionality will not be removed.

In December 2012, W3C designated HTML5 as a Candidate Recommendation. The criterion for advancement to W3C Recommendation is "two 100% complete and fully interoperable implementations".

On 16 September 2014, W3C moved HTML5 to Proposed Recommendation.

On 28 October 2014, HTML5 was released as a stable W3C Recommendation, bringing the specification process to completion.

Future Plans

According to the plan proposed by the W3C in September 2012, the HTML 5.1 specification Recommendation will be targeted for the end of 2016.

Timeline

The combined timelines for HTML 5.0, HTML 5.1 and HTML 5.2:

	2012	2013	2014	2015	2016
HTML 5.0	Candidate Rec	Call for Review	Recommendation		
HTML 5.1	1st Working Draft		Last Call	Candidate Rec	Recommendation
HTML 5.2				1st Working Draft	

Features and APIs

The W3C proposed a greater reliance on modularity as a key part of the plan to make faster progress, meaning identifying specific features, either proposed or already existing in the spec, and advancing them as separate specifications. Some technologies that were originally defined in HTML5 itself are now defined in separate specifications:

- HTML Working Group – HTML Canvas 2D Context;
- Web Apps Working Group – Web Messaging, Web Workers, Web Storage, WebSocket, Server-sent events, Web Components (this was not part of HTML5 though); Note that the Web Applications Working Group was closed in October 2015 and its deliverables transferred to the Web Platform Working Group (WPWG).
- IETF HyBi Working Group – WebSocket Protocol;
- WebRTC Working Group – WebRTC;
- Web Media Text Tracks Community Group – WebVTT.

After the standardization of the HTML5 specification in October 2014, the core vocabulary and features are being extended in four ways. Likewise, some features that were removed from the original HTML5 specification have been standardized separately as modules, such as Microdata and Canvas. Technical specifications introduced as HTML5 extensions such as Polyglot Markup have also been standardized as modules. Some W3C specifications that were originally separate specifications have been adapted as HTML5 extensions or features, such as SVG. Some features that might have slowed down the standardization of HTML5 will be standardized as upcoming specifications, instead. HTML 5.1 is expected to be finalized in 2016, and it is currently on the standardization track at the W3C.

Features

Markup

HTML5 introduces elements and attributes that reflect typical usage on modern websites. Some of them are semantic replacements for common uses of generic block (<div>) and inline (<span>) elements, for example <nav> (website navigation block), <footer> (usually referring to bottom of web page or to last lines of HTML code), or <audio> and <video> instead of <object>. Some deprecated elements from HTML 4.01 have been dropped, including purely presentational elements such as <font> and <center>, whose effects have long been superseded by the more capable Cascading Style Sheets. There is also a renewed emphasis on the importance of DOM scripting (e.g., JavaScript) in Web behavior.

The HTML5 syntax is no longer based on SGML despite the similarity of its markup. It has, however, been designed to be backward compatible with common parsing of older versions of HTML. It comes with a new introductory line that looks like an SGML document type declaration, <!DOCTYPE html>, which triggers the standards-compliant rendering mode. Since 5 January 2009, HTML5 also includes *Web Forms 2.0*, a previously separate WHATWG specification.

New APIs

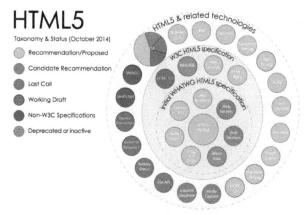

HTML5 related APIs

In addition to specifying markup, HTML5 specifies scripting application programming interfaces (APIs) that can be used with JavaScript. Existing document object model (DOM) interfaces are extended and *de facto* features documented. There are also new APIs, such as:

- Canvas;

- Timed Media Playback;

- Offline;

- Editable content;

- Drag-and-drop;

- History;

- MIME type and protocol handler registration;

- Microdata;

- Web Messaging;

- Web Storage – a key-value pair storage framework that provides behaviour similar to cookies but with larger storage capacity and improved API.

Not all of the above technologies are included in the W3C HTML5 specification, though they are in the WHATWG HTML specification. Some related technologies, which are not part of either the W3C HTML5 or the WHATWG HTML specification, are as follows. The W3C publishes specifications for these separately:

- Geolocation;

- Web SQL Database – a local SQL Database (no longer maintained);

- IndexedDB – an indexed hierarchical key-value store (formerly WebSimpleDB);

- File – an API intended to handle file uploads and file manipulation;

- Directories and System – an API intended to satisfy client-side-storage use cases not well served by databases;

- File Writer – an API for writing to files from web applications;

- Web Audio – a high-level JavaScript API for processing and synthesizing audio in web applications;

- ClassList.

- Web Cryptography

- WebRTC

HTML5 cannot provide animation within web pages. Additional JavaScript or CSS3 functionality is necessary for animating HTML elements. Animation is also possible using JavaScript and HTML 4, and within SVG elements through SMIL, although browser support of the latter remains uneven as of 2011.

XHTML5 (XML-serialized HTML5)

XML documents must be served with an XML Internet media type (often called "MIME type") such as application/xhtml+xml or application/xml, and must conform to strict, well-formed syntax of XML. XHTML5 is simply XML-serialized HTML5 data (e.g. not having any unclosed tags), sent with one of XML media types. HTML that has been written to conform to both the HTML and XHTML specifications – and which will therefore produce the same DOM tree whether parsed as HTML or XML – is called polyglot markup.

Error Handling

HTML5 is designed so that old browsers can safely ignore new HTML5 constructs. In contrast to HTML 4.01, the HTML5 specification gives detailed rules for lexing and parsing, with the intent that compliant browsers will produce the same results when parsing incorrect syntax. Although HTML5 now defines a consistent behavior for "tag soup" documents, those documents are not regarded as conforming to the HTML5 standard.

Popularity

According to a report released on 30 September 2011, 34 of the world's top 100 Web sites were using HTML5 – the adoption led by search engines and social networks. Another report released in August 2013 has shown that 153 of the *Fortune 500* U.S. companies implemented HTML5 on their corporate websites.

Since 2014, HTML5 is at least partially supported by most popular layout engines.

Differences from HTML 4.01 and XHTML 1.x

The following is a cursory list of differences and some specific examples.

- New parsing rules: oriented towards flexible parsing and compatibility; not based on SGML
- Ability to use inline SVG and MathML in text/html
- New elements: article, aside, audio, bdi, canvas, command, data, datalist, details, embed, figcaption, figure, footer, header, keygen, mark, meter, nav, output, progress, rp, rt, ruby, section, source, summary, time, track, video, wbr
- New types of form controls: dates and times, email, url, search, number, range, tel, color
- New attributes: charset (on meta), async (on script)
- Global attributes (that can be applied for every element): id, tabindex, hidden, data-* (custom data attributes)
- Deprecated elements will be dropped altogether: acronym, applet, basefont, big, center, dir, font, frame, frameset, isindex, noframes, strike, tt

dev.w3.org provides the latest *Editors Draft* of "HTML5 differences from HTML 4", which provides a complete outline of additions, removals and changes between HTML5 and HTML 4.

Logo

On 18 January 2011, the W3C introduced a logo to represent the use of or interest in HTML5. Unlike other badges previously issued by the W3C, it does not imply validity or conformance to a certain standard. As of 1 April 2011, this logo is official.

The W3C HTML5 logo

When initially presenting it to the public, the W3C announced the HTML5 logo as a "general-purpose visual identity for a broad set of open web technologies, including HTML5, CSS, SVG, WOFF, and others". Some web standard advocates, including The Web Standards Project, criticized that definition of "HTML5" as an umbrella term, pointing out the blurring of terminology and the potential for miscommunication. Three days later, the W3C responded to community feedback and changed the logo's definition, dropping the enumeration of related technologies. The W3C then said the logo "represents HTML5, the cornerstone for modern Web applications".

Digital Rights Management

Industry players including the BBC, Google, Microsoft, and Netflix have been lobbying for the inclusion of Encrypted Media Extensions (EME), a form of digital rights management (DRM), into the HTML5 standard. As of the end of 2012 and the beginning of 2013, 27 organisations including the Free Software Foundation have started a campaign against including digital rights management in the HTML5 standard. However, in late September 2013, the W3C HTML Working Group decided that Encrypted Media Extensions, a form of DRM, was "in scope" and will potentially be included in the HTML 5.1 standard. WHATWG's "HTML Living Standard" continued to be developed without DRM-enabled proposals.

Manu Sporny, a member of the W3C, said that EME will not solve the problem it's supposed to address. Opponents point out that EME itself is just an architecture for a DRM plug-in mechanism.

The initial enablers for DRM in HTML5 were Google and Microsoft. Supporters also include Adobe. On 14 May 2014, Mozilla announced plans to support EME in Firefox, the last major browser to avoid DRM. Calling it "a difficult and uncomfortable step", Andreas Gal of Mozilla explained that future versions of Firefox would remain open source but ship with a sandbox designed to run a content decryption module developed by Adobe. While promising to "work on alternative solutions", Mozilla's Executive Chair Mitchell Baker stated that a refusal to implement EME would have accomplished little more than convincing many users to switch browsers. This decision was condemned by Cory Doctorow and the Free Software Foundation.

Markup Language

A markup language is a system for annotating a document in a way that is syntactically distinguishable from the text. The idea and terminology evolved from the "marking up" of paper manuscripts, i.e., the revision instructions by editors, traditionally written with a blue pencil on authors' manuscripts.

```
<?xml version="1.0" encoding="UTF-8"?>
<!DOCTYPE recipe PUBLIC "-//Happy-Monkey//DTD RecipeBook//EN"
"http://www.happy-monkey.net/recipebook/recipebook.dtd">

<recipe>

    <title>Peanut-butter On A Spoon</title>

    <ingredientlist>
        <ingredient>Peanut-butter</ingredient>
    </ingredientlist>

    <preparation>
        Stick a spoon in a jar of peanut-butter,
        scoop and pull out a big glob of peanut-butter.
    </preparation>

</recipe>
```

Example of RecipeBook, a simple markup language based on XML for creating recipes. The markup can be converted to HTML, PDF and Rich Text Format using a programming language or XSL.

In digital media this "blue pencil instruction text" was replaced by tags, that is, instructions are expressed directly by tags or "instruction text encapsulated by tags." Examples include typesetting instructions such as those found in troff, TeX and LaTeX, or structural markers such as XML tags. Markup instructs the software that displays the text to carry out appropriate actions, but is omitted from the version of the text that users see.

Some markup languages, such as the widely used HTML, have pre-defined presentation semantics—meaning that their specification prescribes how to present the structured data. Others, such as XML, do not have them and are general purpose.

HyperText Markup Language (HTML), one of the document formats of the World Wide Web, is an instance of SGML (though, strictly, it does not comply with all the rules of SGML), and follows many of the markup conventions used in the publishing industry in the communication of printed work between authors, editors, and printers.

Types

There are three main general categories of electronic markup:

Presentational markup

> The kind of markup used by traditional word-processing systems: binary codes embedded within document text that produce the WYSIWYG effect. Such markup is usually hidden from human users, even authors or editors.

Procedural markup

> Markup is embedded in text and provides instructions for programs that are to process the text. Well-known examples include troff, TeX, and PostScript. It is expected that the processor will run through the text from beginning to end, following the instructions as encountered. Text with such markup is often edited with the markup visible and directly manipulated by the author. Popular procedural-markup systems usually include programming constructs, so macros or subroutines can be defined and invoked by name.

Descriptive markup

> Markup is used to label parts of the document rather than to provide specific instructions as to how they should be processed. Well-known examples include LaTeX, HTML, and

XML. The objective is to decouple the inherent structure of the document from any particular treatment or rendition of it. Such markup is often described as "semantic". An example of descriptive markup would be HTML's <cite> tag, which is used to label a citation. Descriptive markup—sometimes called *logical markup* or *conceptual markup*—encourages authors to write in a way that describes the material conceptually, rather than visually.

There is considerable blurring of the lines between the types of markup. In modern word-processing systems, presentational markup is often saved in descriptive-markup-oriented systems such as XML, and then processed procedurally by implementations. The programming constructs in procedural-markup systems such as TeX may be used to create higher-level markup systems that are more descriptive, such as LaTeX.

In recent years, a number of small and largely unstandardized markup languages have been developed to allow authors to create formatted text via web browsers, for use in wikis and web forums. These are sometimes called lightweight markup languages. Markdown or the markup language used by Wikipedia are examples of such wiki markup.

History

Etymology and Origin

The term *markup* is derived from the traditional publishing practice of *"marking up"* a manuscript, which involves adding handwritten annotations in the form of conventional symbolic printer's instructions in the margins and text of a paper manuscript or printed proof. For centuries, this task was done primarily by skilled typographers known as "markup men" or "copy markers" who marked up text to indicate what typeface, style, and size should be applied to each part, and then passed the manuscript to others for typesetting by hand. Markup was also commonly applied by editors, proofreaders, publishers, and graphic designers, and indeed by document authors.

GenCode

The first well-known public presentation of markup languages in computer text processing was made by William W. Tunnicliffe at a conference in 1967, although he preferred to call it *generic coding*. It can be seen as a response to the emergence of programs such as RUNOFF that each used their own control notations, often specific to the target typesetting device. In the 1970s, Tunnicliffe led the development of a standard called GenCode for the publishing industry and later was the first chair of the International Organization for Standardization committee that created SGML, the first standard descriptive markup language. Book designer Stanley Rice published speculation along similar lines in 1970. Brian Reid, in his 1980 dissertation at Carnegie Mellon University, developed the theory and a working implementation of descriptive markup in actual use.

However, IBM researcher Charles Goldfarb is more commonly seen today as the "father" of markup languages. Goldfarb hit upon the basic idea while working on a primitive document management system intended for law firms in 1969, and helped invent IBM GML later that same year. GML was first publicly disclosed in 1973.

In 1975, Goldfarb moved from Cambridge, Massachusetts to Silicon Valley and became a product planner at the IBM Almaden Research Center. There, he convinced IBM's executives to deploy

GML commercially in 1978 as part of IBM's Document Composition Facility product, and it was widely used in business within a few years.

SGML, which was based on both GML and GenCode, was developed by Goldfarb in 1974. Goldfarb eventually became chair of the SGML committee. SGML was first released by ISO as the ISO 8879 standard in October 1986.

Troff and Nroff

Some early examples of computer markup languages available outside the publishing industry can be found in typesetting tools on Unix systems such as troff and nroff. In these systems, formatting commands were inserted into the document text so that typesetting software could format the text according to the editor's specifications. It was a trial and error iterative process to get a document printed correctly. Availability of WYSIWYG publishing software supplanted much use of these languages among casual users, though serious publishing work still uses markup to specify the non-visual structure of texts, and WYSIWYG editors now usually save documents in a markup-language-based format.

TeX

Another major publishing standard is TeX, created and refined by Donald Knuth in the 1970s and '80s. TeX concentrated on detailed layout of text and font descriptions to typeset mathematical books. This required Knuth to spend considerable time investigating the art of typesetting. TeX is mainly used in academia, where it is a *de facto* standard in many scientific disciplines. A TeX macro package known as LaTeX provides a descriptive markup system on top of TeX, and is widely used.

Scribe, GML and SGML

The first language to make a clean distinction between structure and presentation was Scribe, developed by Brian Reid and described in his doctoral thesis in 1980. Scribe was revolutionary in a number of ways, not least that it introduced the idea of styles separated from the marked up document, and of a grammar controlling the usage of descriptive elements. Scribe influenced the development of Generalized Markup Language (later SGML) and is a direct ancestor to HTML and LaTeX.

In the early 1980s, the idea that markup should be focused on the structural aspects of a document and leave the visual presentation of that structure to the interpreter led to the creation of SGML. The language was developed by a committee chaired by Goldfarb. It incorporated ideas from many different sources, including Tunnicliffe's project, GenCode. Sharon Adler, Anders Berglund, and James A. Marke were also key members of the SGML committee.

SGML specified a syntax for including the markup in documents, as well as one for separately describing *what* tags were allowed, and *where* (the Document Type Definition (DTD) or schema). This allowed authors to create and use any markup they wished, selecting tags that made the most sense to them and were named in their own natural languages. Thus, SGML is properly a meta-language, and many particular markup languages are derived from it. From the late '80s on, most substantial new markup languages have been based on SGML system, including for example TEI and DocBook. SGML was promulgated as an International Standard by International Organization for Standardization, ISO 8879, in 1986.

SGML found wide acceptance and use in fields with very large-scale documentation requirements. However, many found it cumbersome and difficult to learn—a side effect of its design attempting to do too much and be too flexible. For example, SGML made end tags (or start-tags, or even both) optional in certain contexts, because its developers thought markup would be done manually by overworked support staff who would appreciate saving keystrokes.

HTML

In 1989, physicist Sir Tim Berners-Lee wrote a memo proposing an Internet-based hypertext system, then specified HTML and wrote the browser and server software in the last part of 1990. The first publicly available description of HTML was a document called "HTML Tags", first mentioned on the Internet by Berners-Lee in late 1991. It describes 18 elements comprising the initial, relatively simple design of HTML. Except for the hyperlink tag, these were strongly influenced by SGMLguid, an in-house SGML-based documentation format at CERN. Eleven of these elements still exist in HTML 4.

Berners-Lee considered HTML an SGML application. The Internet Engineering Task Force (IETF) formally defined it as such with the mid-1993 publication of the first proposal for an HTML specification: "Hypertext Markup Language (HTML)" Internet-Draft by Berners-Lee and Dan Connolly, which included an SGML Document Type Definition to define the grammar. Many of the HTML text elements are found in the 1988 ISO technical report TR 9537 *Techniques for using SGML*, which in turn covers the features of early text formatting languages such as that used by the RUNOFF command developed in the early 1960s for the CTSS (Compatible Time-Sharing System) operating system. These formatting commands were derived from those used by typesetters to manually format documents. Steven DeRose argues that HTML's use of descriptive markup (and influence of SGML in particular) was a major factor in the success of the Web, because of the flexibility and extensibility that it enabled. HTML became the main markup language for creating web pages and other information that can be displayed in a web browser, and is quite likely the most used markup language in the world today.

XML

XML (Extensible Markup Language) is a meta markup language that is now widely used. XML was developed by the World Wide Web Consortium, in a committee created and chaired by Jon Bosak. The main purpose of XML was to simplify SGML by focusing on a particular problem—documents on the Internet. XML remains a meta-language like SGML, allowing users to create any tags needed (hence "extensible") and then describing those tags and their permitted uses.

XML adoption was helped because every XML document can be written in such a way that it is also an SGML document, and existing SGML users and software could switch to XML fairly easily. However, XML eliminated many of the more complex and human-oriented features of SGML to simplify implementation environments such as documents and publications. However, it appeared to strike a happy medium between simplicity and flexibility, and was rapidly adopted for many other uses. XML is now widely used for communicating data between applications.

XHTML

Since January 2000, all W3C Recommendations for HTML have been based on XML rather than SGML, using the abbreviation XHTML (**Ex**tensible Hyper**T**ext **M**arkup **L**anguage). The language specification requires that XHTML Web documents must be *well-formed* XML documents. This allows for more rigorous and robust documents while using tags familiar from HTML.

One of the most noticeable differences between HTML and XHTML is the rule that *all tags must be closed*: empty HTML tags such as <br> must either be *closed* with a regular end-tag, or replaced by a special form:
 (the space before the '/' on the end tag is optional, but frequently used because it enables some pre-XML Web browsers, and SGML parsers, to accept the tag). Another is that all attribute values in tags must be quoted. Finally, all tag and attribute names within the XHTML namespace must be lowercase to be valid. HTML, on the other hand, was case-insensitive.

Other XML-based Applications

Many XML-based applications now exist, including the Resource Description Framework as RDF/XML, XForms, DocBook, SOAP, and the Web Ontology Language (OWL).

Features

A common feature of many markup languages is that they intermix the text of a document with markup instructions in the same data stream or file. This is not necessary; it is possible to isolate markup from text content, using pointers, offsets, IDs, or other methods to co-ordinate the two. Such "standoff markup" is typical for the internal representations that programs use to work with marked-up documents. However, embedded or "inline" markup is much more common elsewhere. Here, for example, is a small section of text marked up in HTML:

<h1>Anatidae</h1>

<p>

The family <i>Anatidae</i> includes ducks, geese, and swans,

but <em>not</em> the closely related screamers.

</p>

The codes enclosed in angle-brackets <like this> are markup instructions (known as tags), while the text between these instructions is the actual text of the document. The codes h1, p, and em are examples of *semantic* markup, in that they describe the intended purpose or meaning of the text they include. Specifically, h1 means "this is a first-level heading", p means "this is a paragraph", and em means "this is an emphasized word or phrase". A program interpreting such structural markup may apply its own rules or styles for presenting the various pieces of text, using different typefaces, boldness, font size, indentation, colour, or other styles, as desired. A tag such as "h1" (header level 1) might be presented in a large bold sans-serif typeface, for example, or in a mono-spaced (typewriter-style) document it might be underscored – or it might not change the presentation at all.

In contrast, the i tag in HTML is an example of *presentational* markup; it is generally used to specify a particular characteristic of the text (in this case, the use of an italic typeface) without specifying the reason for that appearance.

The Text Encoding Initiative (TEI) has published extensive guidelines for how to encode texts of interest in the humanities and social sciences, developed through years of international cooperative work. These guidelines are used by projects encoding historical documents, the works of particular scholars, periods, or genres, and so on.

Alternative Usage

While the idea of markup language originated with text documents, there is increasing use of markup languages in the presentation of other types of information, including playlists, vector graphics, web services, content syndication, and user interfaces. Most of these are XML applications, because XML is a well-defined and extensible language.

The use of XML has also led to the possibility of combining multiple markup languages into a single profile, like XHTML+SMIL and XHTML+MathML+SVG.

Because markup languages, and more generally data description languages (not necessarily textual markup), are not programming languages (they are data without instructions), they are more easily manipulated than programming languages—for example, web pages are presented as HTML documents, not C code, and thus can be embedded within other web pages, displayed when only partially received, and so forth. This leads to the web design principle of the rule of least power, which advocates using the *least* (computationally) powerful language that satisfies a task to facilitate such manipulation and reuse.

HTML Element

An HTML element is an individual component of an HTML document or web page, once this has been parsed into the Document Object Model. HTML is composed of a tree of HTML elements and other nodes, such as text nodes. Each element can have HTML attributes specified. Elements can also have content, including other elements and text. Many HTML elements represent semantics, or meaning. For example, the title element represents the title of the document.

Concepts

Document vs. DOM

HTML documents are delivered as "documents".These are then parsed, which turns them into the Document Object Model (DOM) internal representation, within the web browser.

Presentation by the web browser, such as screen rendering or access by JavaScript, is then performed on this internal model, not the original document.

Early HTML documents, and to a lesser extent today, were largely invalid HTML and riddled with syntax errors. The parsing process was also required to "fix-up" these errors, as best it could. The resultant model was often not *correct* (i.e. it did not represent what a careless coder had originally intended), but it would at least be valid, according to the HTML standard. A valid model was produced, no matter how bad the "tag soup" supplied had been. Only in the rarest cases would the parser abandon parsing altogether.

Elements vs. Tags

"Elements" and "tags" are terms that are widely confused. HTML documents contain tags, but do not contain the elements. The elements are only generated *after* the parsing step, from these tags.

As is generally understood, the position of an element is indicated as spanning from a start tag, possibly including some child content, and is terminated by an end tag. This is the case for many, *but not all*, elements within an HTML document.

As HTML is based on SGML, its parsing also depends on the use of a DTD, specifically an HTML DTD such as that for HTML 4.01. The DTD specifies which element types are possible (i.e. it defines the set of element types that go to make up HTML) and it also specifies the valid combinations in which they may appear in a document. It is part of general SGML behaviour that where only one valid structure is *possible* (per the DTD), it is not generally a requirement that the document explicitly states that structure. As a simple example, the <p> start tag indicating the start of a paragraph element should be closed by a </p> end tag, indicating the end of the element. Also the DTD states that paragraph elements cannot be nested. The HTML document fragment:

        <p>Para 1 <p>Para 2 <p>Para 3

can thus be inferred to be equivalent to:

        <p>Para 1 </p><p>Para 2 </p><p>Para 3

(If one paragraph element cannot contain another, any currently open paragraph must be closed before starting another.)

Because of this implied behaviour, based on the combination of the DTD and the individual document, it is not possible to infer elements from the document tags *alone*, but only by also using an SGML or HTML aware parser, with knowledge of the DTD.

SGML vs. XML

SGML is complex, which has limited its widespread adoption and understanding. XML was developed as a simpler alternative. XML is similar to SGML, that can also use the DTD mechanism to specify the supported elements and their permitted combinations as document structure. XML parsing is simpler. The relation from tags to elements is always that of parsing the actual tags included in the document, without the implied closures that are part of SGML.

In Macros HTML can be formed as XML, either through XHTML or through HTML5, the parsing of document tags as DOM elements is simplified. Once the DOM of elements is obtained, behaviour beyond that point (i.e. screen rendering) is identical.

%block; vs. Box

Part of this CSS presentation behaviour is the notion of the "box model". This is applied to those elements that CSS considers to be "block" elements, set through the CSS display: block; declaration.

HTML also has a similar concept, although different, and the two are very frequently confused. %block; and %inline; are groups within the HTML DTD that group elements as being either "block-level" or "inline". This is used to define their nesting behaviour: block-level elements cannot be placed into an inline context. This behaviour cannot be changed, it is fixed in the DTD. Block and inline elements have the appropriate and different CSS behaviours attached to them by default, including the relevance of the box model for particular element types.

Note though that this CSS behaviour can, and frequently is, changed from the default. Lists with <ul><li> ... are %block; elements and are presented as block elements by default. However, it is quite common to set these with CSS to display as an inline list.

Overview

Syntax

In the HTML syntax, most elements are written with a start tag and an end tag, with the content in between. An HTML tag is composed of the name of the element, surrounded by angle brackets. An end tag also has a slash after the opening angle bracket, to distinguish it from the start tag. For example, a paragraph, which is represented by the p element, would be written as

<p>In the HTML syntax, most elements are written ...</p>

However, not all of these elements *require* the end tag, or even the start tag, to be present. Some elements, the so-called *void elements*, do not have an end tag. A typical example is the br element, which represents a significant line break, such as in a poem or an address. A void element's behaviour is predefined, and it cannot contain any content or other elements. For example, an address would be written as

<p>P. Sherman
42 Wallaby Way
Sydney</p>

When using an XHTML DTD, it is required to open and close the element with a single tag. To specify that it is a void element, a "/" is included at the end of the tag.

<p>P. Sherman
42 Wallaby Way
Sydney</p>

HTML attributes are specified inside the start tag. For example, the abbr element, which represents an abbreviation, expects a title attribute within its opening tag. This would be written as

<abbr title="abbreviation">abbr.</abbr>

- *Parts of an HTML container element:*
- *Start tag: <p ... >*
    - o *Attribute:*

- - *name:* class
  - *value:* foo
- *Content:* This is a paragraph.
- *End tag:* </p>

Element		
Start tag	Content	End tag

`<p class="foo">`This is a paragraph. `</p>`

Attribute name   value

There are multiple kinds of HTML elements: void elements, raw text elements, and normal elements.

Void elements only have a start tag, which contains any HTML attributes. They may not contain any children, such as text or other elements. Often they are place holders for elements which reference external files, such as the image (<img />) element. The attributes included in the element will then point to the external file in question. Another example of a void element is the <link /> element, for which the syntax is

<link rel="stylesheet" href="fancy.css" type="text/css">

This <link /> element points the browser at a style sheet to use when presenting the HTML document to the user. Note that in the HTML syntax, attributes don't have to be quoted if they are composed only of certain characters: letters, digits, the hyphen-minus and the full stop. When using the XML syntax (XHTML), on the other hand, all attributes must be quoted, and a trailing slash is required before the last angle bracket:

<link rel="stylesheet" href="fancy.css" type="text/css" />

Raw text elements are constructed with:

- a *start tag* (<tag>) marking the beginning of an element, which may incorporate any number of HTML attributes;
- some amount of text *content*, but no elements (all tags, apart from the applicable end tag, will be interpreted as content);
- an *end tag*, in which the element name is prefixed with a slash: </tag>. In some versions of HTML, the end tag is optional for some elements. The end tag is required in XHTML.

Normal elements usually have both a start tag and an end tag, although for some elements the end tag, or both tags, can be omitted. It is constructed in a similar way:

- a *start tag* (<tag>) marking the beginning of an element, which may incorporate any number of HTML attributes;

- some amount of *content*, including text and other elements;

- an *end tag*, in which the element name is prefixed with a slash: </tag>.

HTML attributes define desired behaviour or indicate additional element properties. Most attributes require a *value*. In HTML, the value can be left unquoted if it doesn't include spaces (name=value), or it can be quoted with single or double quotes (name='value' or name="value"). In XML, those quotes are required. Boolean attributes, on the other hand, don't require a value to be specified. An example is the checked for checkboxes:

<input type=checkbox checked>

In the XML syntax, though, the name should be repeated as the value:

<input type="checkbox" checked="checked" />

Informally, HTML elements are sometimes referred to as "tags" (an example of synecdoche), though many prefer the term *tag* strictly in reference to the markup delimiting the start and end of an element.

Element (and attribute) names may be written in any combination of upper or lower case in HTML, but must be in lower case in XHTML. The canonical form was upper-case until HTML 4, and was used in HTML specifications, but in recent years, lower-case has become more common.

Element Standards

HTML elements are defined in a series of freely available open standards issued since 1995, initially by the IETF and subsequently by the W3C.

During the browser wars of the 1990s, developers of user agents (e.g. web browsers) often developed their own elements, some of which have been adopted in later standards. Other user agents may not recognize non-standard elements, and they will be ignored, possibly causing the page to be displayed improperly.

In 1998, XML (a simplified form of SGML) introduced mechanisms to allow anyone to develop their own elements and incorporate them in XHTML documents, for use with XML-aware user agents.

Subsequently, HTML 4.01 was rewritten in an XML-compatible form, XHTML 1.0 (*eXtensible HTML*). The elements in each are identical, and in most cases valid XHTML 1.0 documents will be valid or nearly valid HTML 4.01 documents. This article mainly focuses on real HTML, unless noted otherwise; however, it remains applicable to XHTML.

Element Status

Since the first version of HTML, several elements have become outmoded, and are *deprecated* in later standards, or do not appear at all, in which case they are *invalid* (and will be found invalid, and perhaps not displayed, by validating user agents).

At present, the status of elements is complicated by the existence of three types of HTML 4.01 / XHTML 1.0 DTD:

- Transitional, which contain deprecated elements, but which were intended to provide a transitional period during which authors could update their practices;

- Frameset, which are versions of the Transitional DTDs which also allow authors to write frameset documents;

- Strict, which is the up-to date (as at 1999) form of HTML.

The first Standard (HTML 2.0) contained four deprecated elements, one of which was invalid in HTML 3.2. All four are invalid in HTML 4.01 Transitional, which also deprecated a further ten elements. All of these, plus two others, are invalid in HTML 4.01 Strict. While the frame elements are still current in the sense of being present in the Transitional and Frameset DTDs, there are no plans to preserve them in future standards, as their function has been largely replaced, and they are highly problematic for user accessibility.

(Strictly speaking, the most recent *XHTML* standard, XHTML 1.1 (2001), does not include frames at all; it is approximately equivalent to XHTML 1.0 Strict, but also includes the **Ruby markup** module.)

A common source of confusion is the loose use of *deprecated* to refer to both deprecated and invalid status, and to elements which are expected to be formally deprecated in future.

Content vs. Presentation and Behavior

Since HTML 4, HTML has increasingly focused on the separation of content (the visible text and images) from presentation (like color, font size, and layout). This is often referred to as a separation of concerns. HTML is used to represent the structure or content of a document, its presentation remains the sole responsibility of CSS style sheets. A default style sheet is suggested as part of the CSS standard, giving a default rendering for HTML.

Behavior (interactivity) is also kept separate from content, and is handled by scripts. Images are contained in separate graphics files, separate from text, though they can also be considered part of the content of a page.

Separation of concerns allows the document to be presented by different user agents according to their purposes and abilities. For example, a user agent can select an appropriate style sheet to present a document by displaying on a monitor, printing on paper, or to determine speech characteristics in an audio-only user agent. The structural and semantic functions of the markup remain identical in each case.

Historically, user agents did not always support these features. In the 1990s, as a stop-gap, presentational elements (like <b> and <i>) were added to HTML, at the cost of creating problems for interoperability and user accessibility. This is now regarded as outmoded and has been superseded by style sheet-based design; most presentational elements are now deprecated.

External image files are incorporated with the img or object elements. (With XHTML, the SVG language can also be used to write graphics within the document, though linking to external SVG files is generally simpler.) Where an image is not purely decorative, HTML allows replacement content with similar semantic value to be provided for non-visual user agents.

An HTML document can also be extended through the use of scripts to provide additional behaviours beyond the abilities of HTML hyperlinks and forms.

The elements style and script, with related HTML attributes, provide reference points in HTML markup for links to style sheets and scripts. They can also contain instructions directly.

- In the document head, script and style may either link to shared external documents, or contain embedded instructions. (The link element can also be used to link style sheets.)

- The *style attribute* is valid in most document body elements for inclusion of *inline style* instructions.

- *Event-handling attributes*, which provide links to scripts, are optional in most elements.

- script can occur at any point in the document body.

- For user agents which do not operate scripts, the noscript element provides alternative content where appropriate; however, it can only be used as a block-level element.

Document Structure Elements

<html>...</html>

>   The root element of an HTML document; all other elements are contained in this.

>   The HTML element delimits the beginning and the end of an HTML document.

>   Standardized in HTML 2.0; still current.

<head>...</head>

>   Container for processing information and metadata for an HTML document.

>   Standardized in HTML 2.0; still current.

<body>...</body>

>   Container for the displayable content of an HTML document.

>   Standardized in HTML 2.0; still current.

Document Head Elements

<base/>

>   Specifies a base URL for all relative href and other links in the document. Must appear before any element that refers to an external resource. HTML permits only one base element for each document. The base element has HTML attributes, but no contents.

>   A development version of BASE is mentioned in *HTML Tags*; standardized in HTML 2.0; still current.

\<basefont/\> (deprecated)

Specifies a base font size, typeface, and colour for the document. Used together with font elements. Deprecated in favour of style sheets.

Standardized in HTML 3.2; deprecated in HTML 4.0 Transitional; invalid in HTML 4.0 Strict.

\<isindex/\> (deprecated)

isindex could either appear in the document head or in the body, but only once in a document.

\<link/\>

Specifies links to other documents, such as *previous* and *next* links, or alternate versions. A common use is to link to external style sheets, using the form:

\<link rel="stylesheet" type="text/css" href=""url"" title=""description_of_style"">

A less-common, but important, usage is to supply navigation hints consistently through use of microformats. Several common relationships are defined, that may be exposed to users through the browser interface rather than directly in the web page.

\<link rel="next" href=""url"">

A document's head element may contain any number of link elements. The link element has HTML attributes, but no contents.

LINK existed in HTML Internet Draft 1.2, and was standardized in HTML 2.0; still current.

\<meta/\>

Can be used to specify additional metadata about a document, such as its author, publication date, expiration date, page description, keywords, or other information not provided through the other header elements and HTML attributes. Because of their generic nature, meta elements specify associative key-value pairs. In general, a meta element conveys hidden information about the document. Several meta tags can be used, all of which should be nested in the head element. The specific purpose of each *meta* element is defined by its attributes.

In one form, meta elements can specify HTTP headers which should be sent by a web server before the actual content, for example:

\<meta http-equiv="foo" content="bar"\>

— this specifies that the page should be served with an HTTP header called foo that has a value bar.

In the general form, a meta element specifies name and associated content HTML attributes describing aspects of the HTML page. To prevent possible ambiguity, an optional third attribute, scheme, may be supplied to specify a semantic framework that defines the meaning of the key and its value: for example:

\<meta name="foo" content="bar" scheme="DC"\>

In this example, the meta element identifies itself as containing the foo element, with a value of bar, from the DC or Dublin Core resource description framework.

Standardized in HTML 2.0; still current.

\<object>...\</object>

Used for including generic objects within the document header. Though rarely used within a head element, it could potentially be used to extract foreign data and associate it with the current document.

Standardized in HTML 4.0; still current.

\<script>...\</script>

Can act as a container for script instructions or link to an external script with the optional src attribute. Also usable in the document body to dynamically generate either both block or inline content.

Standardized in HTML 3.2; still current.

\<style>...\</style>

Specifies a style for the document, usually in the form:

\<style type="text/css"> ... \</style>

Can either act as a container for style instructions or link to external style sheets – for example, in CSS, with @import directives of the form:

\<style> @import "url"; \</style>

Standardized in HTML 3.2; still current.

\<title>...\</title>

Define a document title. Required in every HTML and XHTML document. User agents may use the title in different ways. For example:

- Web browsers usually display it in a window's title bar when the window is open, and (where applicable) in the task bar when the window is minimized.

- It may become the default file-name when saving the page.

- Web search engines' web crawlers may pay particular attention to the words used in the title.

The title element must not contain other elements, only text. Only one title element is permitted in a document.

TITLE existed in HTML Tags, and was standardized in HTML 2.0; still current.

Document Body Elements

In visual browsers, displayable elements can be rendered as either *block* or *inline*. While all elements are part of the document sequence, block elements appear within their parent elements:

- as rectangular objects which do not break across lines;

- with block margins, width and height properties which can be set independently of the surrounding elements.

Conversely, inline elements are treated as part of the flow of document text; they cannot have margins, width or height set, and do break across lines.

Block Elements

Block elements, or block-level elements, have a rectangular structure. By default, these elements will span the entire width of its parent element, and will thus not allow any other element to occupy the same horizontal space as it is placed on.

The rectangular structure of a block element is often referred to as the box model, and is made up of several parts. Each element contains the following:

- The content of an element is the actual text (or other media) placed between the opening and closing tags of an element.

- The padding of an element is the space around that content, which still form part of said element. Padding is physically part of an element, and should not be used to create white space between two elements. Any background style assigned to the element, such as a background image or color, will be visible within the padding. Increasing the size of an element's padding increases the amount of space this element will take up.

- The border of an element is the absolute end of an element, and spans the perimeter of that element. The thickness of a border increases the size of an element.

- The margin of an element is the white-space that surrounds an element. The content, padding and border of any other element will not be allowed to enter this area, unless forced to do so by some advanced CSS placement. Using most standard DTDs, margins on the left and right of different elements will push each other away. Margins on the top or bottom of an element, on the other hand, will not stack, or will inter mingle. This means that the white-space between these elements will be as big as the larger margin between them.

The above section refers only to the detailed implementation of CSS rendering and has no relevance to HTML elements themselves.

Basic Text

<p>...</p>

Creates a paragraph, perhaps the most common block level element.

P existed in *HTML Tags*, and was standardized in HTML 2.0; still current.

<h1>...</h1> <h2>...</h2> <h3>...</h3> <h4>...</h4> <h5>...</h5> <h6>...</h6>

Section headings at different levels. <h1> delimits the highest-level heading, <h2> the next level down (sub-section), <h3> for a level below that, and so on to <h6>. They are sometimes referred to collectively as <hn> tags, n meaning any of the available heading levels.

Most visual browsers show headings as large bold text by default, though this can be overridden with CSS. Heading elements are not intended merely for creating large or bold text—in fact, they should *not* be used for explicitly styling text. Rather, they describe the document's structure and organization. Some programs use them to generate outlines and tables of contents.

Headings existed in *HTML Tags*, and were standardized in HTML 2.0; still current.

Lists

<dl>...</dl>

A description list (a.k.a. association list), which consists of name–value groups, and was known as a definition list prior to HTML5. Description lists are intended for groups of "terms and definitions, metadata topics and values, questions and answers, or any other groups of name–value data".

DL existed in *HTML Tags*, and was standardized in HTML 2.0; still current.

<dt>...</dt>

A name in a description list (previously definition term in a definition list).

DT existed in *HTML Tags*, and was standardized in HTML 2.0; still current.

<dd>...</dd>

A value in a description list (previously definition data in a definition list).

DD existed in *HTML Tags*, and was standardized in HTML 2.0; still current.

<ol>...</ol>

An ordered (enumerated) list. The type attribute can be used to specify the kind of marker to use in the list, but style sheets give more control. The default is Arabic numbering. CSS: list-style-type: *foo*. HTML attribute: <ol type="*foo*">, in either case, replacing *foo* with one of the following:

- A for A, B, C...
- a for a, b, c...
- I for I, II, III...
- i for i, ii, iii...
- 1 for 1, 2, 3...

OL existed in *HTML Internet Draft 1.2*, and was standardized in HTML 2.0; still current.

<ul>...</ul>

> An unordered (bulleted) list. Style sheets can be used to specify the list marker: list-style-type: *foo*. The default marker type is disc, other values are square, circle and none.

> UL existed in *HTML Tags*, and was standardized in HTML 2.0; still current.

<li>...</li>

> A list item in ordered (**ol**) or unordered (**ul**) lists.

> LI existed in HTML Tags, and was standardized in HTML 2.0; still current.

<dir> (deprecated)

> A directory listing. The original purpose of this element was never widely supported; deprecated in favor of <ul>.

> DIR existed in *HTML* Tags, and was standardized in HTML 2.0; deprecated in HTML 4.0 Transitional; invalid in HTML 4.0 Strict.

Other Block Elements

<address>...</address>

> Contact information for the document author.

> ADDRESS existed in *HTML Tags*, and was standardized in HTML 2.0; still current.

<blockquote>...</blockquote>

> A block level quotation, for when the quotation includes block level elements, e.g. paragraphs. The cite attribute may give the source, and must be a fully qualified Uniform Resource Identifier.

> The default presentation of block quotations in visual browsers is usually to indent them from both margins. This has led to the element being unnecessarily used just to indent paragraphs, regardless of semantics.

> BLOCKQUOTE existed in HTML Internet Draft 1.2, and was standardized in HTML 2.0; still current.

<center> (deprecated)

> Creates a block-level center-aligned division. Deprecated in favor of <div> or another element with centring defined using style sheets.

> Standardized in HTML 3.2;

<del>...</del>

> Marks a deleted section of content. This element can also be used as *inline*.

> Standardized in HTML 4.0; still current.

`<div>...</div>`

A block-level logical division. A generic element with no semantic meaning used to distinguish a document section, usually for purposes such as presentation or behaviour controlled by style sheets or DOM calls.

Proposed in the HTML 3.0 Drafts; Standardized in HTML 3.2; still current.

`<hr/>`

A horizontal rule. Presentational rules can also be drawn with style sheets.

Standardized in HTML 2.0; still current.

`<ins>...</ins>`

Marks a section of inserted content. This element can also be used as *inline*.

Standardized in HTML 4.0; still current.

`<noscript>...</noscript>`

Replacement content for scripts. Unlike script this can only be used as a block-level element.

Standardized in HTML 4.0; still current.

`<pre>...</pre>`

Pre-formatted text. Text within this element is typically displayed in a non-proportional font exactly as it is laid out in the file. Whereas browsers ignore white-space for other HTML elements, in pre, white-space should be rendered as authored. (With the CSS properties: {white-space: pre; font-family: monospace;}, other elements can be presented in the same way.) This element can contain any inline element except: image (IMG), object (OBJECT), big font size (BIG), small font size (SMALL), superscript (SUP), and subscript (SUB).

PRE existed in *HTML Internet Draft 1.2*, and was standardized in HTML 2.0; still current.

`<script>...</script>`

Places a script in the document. Also usable in the head and in inline contexts.

Note: SCRIPT is not itself either a block or inline element; by itself it should not display at all, but it can contain instructions to dynamically generate either both block or inline content.

Standardized in HTML 3.2; still current.

Inline Elements

Inline elements cannot be placed directly inside the body element; they must be wholly nested within block-level elements.

Anchor

<a>...</a>

An anchor element is called an anchor because web designers can use it to anchor a URL to some text on a web page. When users view the web page in a browser, they can click the text to activate the link and visit the page whose URL is in the link.

In HTML, an anchor can be either the origin (the anchor text) or the target (destination) end of a hyperlink.

With the attribute href, the anchor becomes a hyperlink to either another part of the document or another resource (e.g. a webpage) using an external URL. Alternatively (and sometimes concurrently), with the name or id HTML attributes set, the element becomes a target. A Uniform Resource Locator can link to this target via a fragment identifier. In HTML5, any element can now be made into a target by using the id attribute, so using <a name="foo">...</a> is not necessary, although this way of adding anchors continues to work.

To illustrate: the header of a table of contents section on example.com could be turned into a target by writing

<h1 id="contents">Table of contents</h1>

Continuing with this example, now that the section has been marked up as a target, it can be referred to from external sites with a link like

<a href="http://example.com#contents">see contents</a>

or with a link on the same page like:

<a href="#contents">contents, above</a>

The attribute title may be set to give brief information about the link:

<a href="URL" title="additional information">link text</a>

In most graphical browsers, when the cursor hovers over a link, the cursor changes into a hand with a stretched index finger and the title is displayed in a tooltip or in some other manner. Some browsers render alt text the same way, despite this not being what the specification calls for.

A existed in *HTML Tags*, and was standardized in HTML 2.0; still current.

Phrase Elements

General

<abbr>...</abbr>

Marks an abbreviation, and can make the full form available:

<abbr title="abbreviation">abbr.</abbr>

Standardized in HTML 4.0; still current.

\<acronym\> (deprecated)

>   Similar to the abbr element, but marks an acronym:

>   \<acronym title="Hyper-Text Mark-up Language"\>HTML\</acronym\>

>   Standardized in HTML 4.0; still current, not supported in HTML5.

\<dfn\>...\</dfn\>

>   inline definition of a single term.

>   DFN existed in *HTML Internet Draft 1.2*, and was fully standardized in HTML 3.2; still current.

\<em\>...\</em\>

>   *Emphasis* (conventionally displayed in italics)

>   EM existed in *HTML Internet Draft 1.2*, and was standardized in HTML 2.0; still current.

\<strong\>...\</strong\>

>   strong emphasis (conventionally displayed bold).

>   An aural user agent may use different voices for emphasis.

>   STRONG existed in *HTML Internet Draft 1.2*, and was standardized in HTML 2.0; still current.

Computer Phrase Elements

These elements are useful primarily for documenting computer code development and user interaction through differentiation of source code (\<code\>), source code variables (\<var\>), user input (\<kbd\>), and terminal output (\<samp\>).

\<code\>...\</code\>

>   A code snippet. Conventionally rendered in a mono-space font: Code snippet.

>   CODE existed in *HTML Internet Draft 1.2*, and was standardized in HTML 2.0; still current.

\<kbd\>...\</kbd\>

>   Keyboard - text to be entered by the user

>   KBD existed in *HTML Internet Draft 1.2*, and was standardized in HTML 2.0; still current.

\<samp\>...\</samp\>

>   Sample output (from a program or script)

>   SAMP existed in *HTML Internet Draft 1.2*, and was standardized in HTML 2.0; still current.

`<var>...</var>`

> Variable

> VAR existed in *HTML Internet Draft 1.2*, and was standardized in HTML 2.0; still current.

Presentation

As visual presentational markup only applies directly to visual browsers, its use is discouraged. Style sheets should be used instead. Several of these elements are deprecated or invalid in HTML 4 / XHTML 1.0, and the remainder are invalid in the current draft of XHTML 2.0. The current draft of HTML 5, however, re-includes `<s>`, `<u>`, and `<small>`, assigning new semantic meaning to each. In an HTML 5 document, the use of these elements is no longer discouraged, provided that it is semantically correct.

`<b>...</b>`

> In HTML 4, set font to boldface where possible. Equivalent CSS: {font-weight: bold}. `<strong>...</strong>` usually has the same effect in visual browsers, as well as having more semantic meaning, under HTML 4.01.

> In HTML 5, however, b has its own meaning, distinct from that of strong. It denotes "text to which attention is being drawn for utilitarian purposes without conveying any extra importance and with no implication of an alternate voice or mood."

> B existed in *HTML Internet Draft 1.2*, and was standardized in HTML 2.0; still current.

`<i>...</i>`

> In HTML 4, set font to *italic* where possible. Equivalent CSS: {font-style: italic}. `<em>...</em>` usually has the same effect in visual browsers, as well as having more semantic meaning, under HTML 4.01.

> In HTML 5, however, i has its own semantic meaning, distinct from that of em. It denotes "a different quality of text" or "an alternative voice or mood"—e.g., a thought, a ship name, a binary species name, a foreign-language phrase, etc.

> I existed in *HTML Internet Draft 1.2*, and was standardized in HTML 2.0; still current.

`<u>...</u>`

> In HTML 4, underlined text. Equivalent CSS: {text-decoration: underline}. Deprecated in HTML 4.01. Restored in HTML 5.

> In HTML 5, the u element denotes "a span of text with an unarticulated, though explicitly rendered, non-textual annotation, such as labelling the text as being a proper name in Chinese text (a Chinese proper name mark), or labelling the text as being misspelt." The HTML 5 specification reminds developers that other elements are almost always more appropriate than u and admonishes designers not to use underlined text where it could be confused for a hyper-link.

U existed in HTML Internet Draft 1.2, was standardized in HTML 3.2 but was deprecated in HTML 4.0 Transitional and was invalid in HTML 4.0 Strict. The u element is reintroduced in HTML 5.

<small>...</small>

In HTML 4, decreased font size (smaller text). Equivalent CSS: {font-size: smaller}

In HTML 5, the small element denotes "side comments such as small print."

Standardized in HTML 3.2; still current.

<s>...</s>

In HTML 4, indicated strike-through text (~~Strikethrough~~) and was equivalent to strike.

In HTML 5, the s element denotes information that is "no longer accurate or no longer relevant", and which indicates removal/deletion.

S was deprecated in HTML 4.0 Transitional (having not appeared in any previous standard), and was invalid in HTML 4.0 Strict. The s element is reintroduced in HTML 5.

<big> (deprecated)

Increased font size (bigger text). Equivalent CSS: {font-size: larger}

Standardized in HTML 3.2; not supported in HTML 5.

<strike>...</strike>

Strike-through text (~~Strikethrough~~), (Equivalent CSS: {text-decoration: line-through})

STRIKE was standardized in HTML 3.2; deprecated in HTML 4.0 Transitional; invalid in HTML 4.0 Strict.

<tt> (deprecated)

Fixed-width font (typewriter-like), also known as teletype. (Equivalent CSS: {font-family: monospace;})

TT existed in *HTML Internet Draft 1.2*, and was Standardized in HTML 2.0; not supported in HTML 5.

<font>...</font>

<font [color=*colour*] [size=*size*] [face=*face*]>...</font>

Can specify the font colour with the color attribute (note the American spelling), typeface with the face attribute, and absolute or relative size with the size attribute.

Examples (all uses are deprecated, use CSS equivalents if possible):

1. <font color="green">text</font> creates green text.

2. `<font color="#114499">text</font>` creates text with hexadecimal color #114499.

3. `<font size="4">text</font>` creates text with size 4. Sizes are from 1 to 7. The standard size is 3, unless otherwise specified in the `<body>` or other tags.

4. `<font size="+1">text</font>` creates text with size 1 bigger than the standard. `<font size="-1">text</font>` is opposite.

5. `<font face="Courier">text</font>` makes text with Courier font.

Equivalent CSS for font attributes:

- `<font size="N">` corresponds to {font-size: *Yunits*} (the HTML specification does not define the relationship between size *N* and unit-size *Y*, nor does it define a unit).

- `<font color="red">` corresponds to {color: red}

- `<font face="Courier">` corresponds to {font-family: "Courier"}

Standardized in HTML 3.2; deprecated in HTML 4.0 Transitional; invalid in HTML 4.0 Strict. Not part of HTML5.

Span

`<span>...</span>`

An inline logical division. A generic element with no semantic meaning used to distinguish a document section, usually for purposes such as presentation or behaviour controlled by style sheets or DOM calls.

Standardized in HTML 4.0; still current.

Other Inline Elements

`<br/>`

A forced line break.

Standardized in HTML 2.0. As of 2016, still current.

`<bdi>...</bdi>`

Isolates an inline section of text that may be formatted in a different direction from other text outside of it, such as user-generated content with unknown directionality.

Standardized in HTML 5.

`<bdo>...</bdo>`

Marks an inline section of text in which the reading direction is the opposite from that of the parent element.

Standardized in HTML 4.0; still current.

`<cite>...</cite>`

> A citation or a reference for a quote or statement in the document.

> CITE existed in HTML Internet Draft 1.2, and was standardized in HTML 2.0; still current.

`<data>...</data>`

> Links inline content with a machine-readable translation.

> Standardized in HTML 5; still current.

`<del>...</del>`

> Deleted text. Typically rendered as a strikethrough: Standardized in HTML 4.0; still current.

`<ins>...</ins>`

> Inserted text. Often used to mark up replacement text for `<del>`'d text. Typically rendered underlined: Inserted text.

> Standardized in HTML 4.0; still current.

> Note, both `<ins>` and `<del>` elements may also be used as block elements: containing other block and inline elements. However, these elements must still remain wholly within their parent element to maintain a well-formed HTML document. For example, deleting text from the middle of one paragraph across several other paragraphs and ending in a final paragraph would need to use three separate `<del>` elements. Two `<del>` elements would be required as inline element to indicate the deletion of text in the first and last paragraphs, and a third, used as a block element, to indicate the deletion in the intervening paragraphs.

`<mark>...</mark>`

> Produces something like this. Intended for highlighting relevant text in a quotation. New in HTML5.

`<q>...</q>`

> An inline quotation. Quote elements may be nested.

> `<q>` *should* automatically generate quotation marks in conjunction with style sheets. Practical concerns due to browser non-compliance may force authors to find workarounds.

> The cite *attribute* gives the source, and must be a fully qualified URI.

> Standardized in HTML 4.0; still current.

> Note: Lengthy inline quotations may be displayed as indented blocks (as block-quote) using style sheets. For example, with a suitable CSS rule associated with q.lengthy:

> `<q class="lengthy">`An inline quotation of significant length (say 25 words, for example) goes here...`</q>`

\<rb\>...\</rb\>

> Represents the base component of a ruby annotation.
>
> Standardized in HTML 5.

\<rp\>...\</rp\>

> Provides fallback parenthesis for browsers lacking ruby annotation support.
>
> Standardized in HTML 5.

\<rt\>...\</rt\>

> Indicates pronunciation for a character in a ruby annotation.
>
> Standardized in HTML 5.

\<rtc\>...\</rtc\>

> Semantic annotations for a ruby annotation.
>
> Standardized in HTML 5.

\<ruby\>...\</ruby\>

> Represents a ruby annotation for showing the pronunciation of East Asian characters.
>
> Standardized in HTML 5.

\<script\>...\</script\>

> Places a script in the document. Also usable in the head and in block contexts.
>
> Note: \<script\> is not itself either a block or inline element; by itself it should not display at all, but it can contain instructions to dynamically generate either both block or inline content.
>
> Standardized in HTML 3.2; still current.

\<sub\>...\</sub\> and \<sup\>...\</sup\>

> Mark $_{\text{subscript}}$ or ^{superscript} text. (Equivalent CSS: {vertical-align: sub} or {vertical-align: super}.)
>
> Both were proposed in the HTML 3.0 Drafts; Standardized in HTML 3.2; still current.

\<time\>...\</time\>

> Represents a time on the 24-hour clock or a date on the Gregorian calendar, optionally with time and timezone information. Also allows times and dates to be represented in a machine-readable format.
>
> Standardized in HTML 5.

\<wbr/\>

> An optional line break.

Was widely used (and supported by all major browsers) for years despite being non-standard until finally being standardized in HTML 5.

Images and Objects

<applet> (deprecated)

Embeds a Java applet in the page. Deprecated in favour of <object>, as it could only be used with Java applets, and had accessibility limitations.

Standardized in HTML 3.2; deprecated in HTML 4.0 Transitional; invalid in HTML 4.0 Strict. As of 2011, still widely used as the implementations of the replacing <object> are not consistent between different browsers.

<area/>

Specifies a focusable area in a map.

Standardized in HTML 3.2; still current.

<img/>

Used by visual user agents to insert an image in the document. The src attribute specifies the image URL. The required alt attribute provides alternative text in case the image cannot be displayed. (Though alt is intended as alternative text, Microsoft Internet Explorer 7 and below render it as a tooltip if no title is given. Safari and Google Chrome, on the other hand, do not display the alt attribute at all.) img was proposed by Marc Andreessen and implemented in the NSCA Mosaic web browser.

IMG existed in *HTML Internet Draft 1.2*, and was standardized in HTML 2.0; still current.

<map>...</map>

Specifies a client-side image map.

Standardized in HTML 3.2; still current.

<object>...</object>

Includes an object in the page of the type specified by the type attribute. This may be in any MIME-type the user agent understands, such as an embedded HTML page, a file to be handled by a plug-in such as Flash, a Java applet, a sound file, etc.

Standardized in HTML 4.0; still current.

<param/>

Originally introduced with applet, this element is now used with, and should only occur as a child of object. It uses HTML attributes to set a parameter for the object, e.g. width, height, font, background colour, etc., depending on the type of object. An object can have multiple params.

Standardized in HTML 3.2; still current.

Forms

These elements can be combined into a form or in some instances used separately as user-interface controls; in the document, they can be simple HTML or used in conjunction with Scripts. HTML markup specifies the elements that make up a form, and the method by which it will be submitted. However, some form of scripts (server-side, client-side, or both) must be used to process the user's input once it is submitted.

(These elements are either block or inline elements, but are collected here as their use is more restricted than other inline or block elements.)

<form action="url">...</form>

> Creates a form. The form element specifies and operates the overall action of a form area, using the required action attribute.
>
> Standardized in HTML 2.0; still current.

<button>...</button>

> A generic form button which can contain a range of other elements to create complex buttons.
>
> Standardized in HTML 4.0; still current.

<fieldset>...</fieldset>

> A container for adding structure to forms. For example, a series of related controls can be grouped within a field-set, which can then have a legend added in order to identify their function.
>
> Standardized in HTML 4.0; still current.

<input/>

> input elements allow a variety of standard form controls to be implemented.
>
> Standardized in HTML 2.0; still current.
>
> Input Types:
>
> *type="checkbox"*
>
> A checkbox. Can be checked or unchecked.
>
> *type="radio"*
>
> A radio button. If multiple radio buttons are given the same name, the user will only be able to select one of them from this group.
>
> *type="button"*
>
> A general-purpose button. The element <button> is preferred if possible (i.e. if the client supports it) as it provides richer possibilities.

type="submit"

A submit button.

type="image"

An image button. The image URL may be specified with the src attribute.

type="reset"

A reset button for resetting the form to default values.

type="text"

A one-line text input field. The size attribute specifies the default width of the input in character-widths. max-length sets the maximum number of characters the user can enter (which may be greater than size).

type="password"

A variation of text. The difference is that text typed in this field is *masked* — characters are displayed as an asterisk, a dot or another replacement. It should be noted, however, that the password is still submitted to the server as *clear text*, so an underlying secure transport layer like HTTPS is needed if confidentiality is a concern.

type="file"

A file select field (for uploading files to a server).

type="hidden"

hidden inputs are not visible in the rendered page, but allow a designer to maintain a copy of data that needs to be submitted to the server as part of the form. This may, for example, be data that this web user entered or selected on a previous form that needs to be processed in conjunction with the current form. Not displayed to the user but data can still be altered client-side by editing the HTML source.

(deprecated)

isindex could either appear in the document head or in the body, but only once in a document.

Isindex operated as a primitive HTML search form; but was de facto obsoleted by more advanced HTML forms introduced in the early to mid-1990s. Represents a set of hyperlinks composed of a base URI, an ampersand and percent-encoded keywords separated by plus signs.

ISINDEX existed in *HTML Tags*; standardized in HTML 2.0; deprecated in HTML 4.0 Transitional; invalid in HTML 4.0 Strict.

<label for="id">...</label>

Creates a label for a form input (e.g. radio button). Clicking on the label fires a click on the matching input.

Standardized in HTML 4.0; still current.

<legend>...</legend>

A legend (caption) for a fieldset.

Standardized in HTML 4.0; still current.

<option value="x">...</option>

Creates an item in a select list.

Standardized in HTML 2.0; still current.

<optgroup>...</optgroup>

Identifies a group of options in a select list.

Standardized in HTML 4.0; still current.

<select *name="xyz"*>...</select>

Creates a selection list, from which the user can select a single option. May be rendered as a dropdown list.

Standardized in HTML 2.0; still current.

<textarea *rows="8"*>...</textarea>

A multiple-line text area, the size of which is specified by cols (where a *col* is a one-character width of text) and rows HTML attributes. The content of this element is restricted to plain text, which appears in the text area as default text when the page is loaded.

Standardized in HTML 2.0; still current.

Tables

The format of HTML Tables was proposed in the HTML 3.0 Drafts and the later RFC 1942 *HTML Tables*. They were inspired by the CALS Table Model. Some elements in these proposals were included in HTML 3.2; the present form of HTML Tables was standardized in HTML 4. (Many of the elements used within tables are neither *block* nor *inline* elements.)

<table>...</table>

Identifies a table. Several HTML attributes are possible in HTML Transitional, but most of these are invalid in HTML Strict and can be replaced with style sheets. The summary attribute is however informally required for accessibility purposes, though its usage is not simple.

Proposed in the HTML 3.0 Drafts; Standardized in HTML 3.2; still current.

<tr>...</tr>

Contains a row of cells in a table.

Proposed in the HTML 3.0 Drafts; Standardized in HTML 3.2; still current.

\<th\>...\</th\>

A table header cell; contents are conventionally displayed bold and centered. An aural user agent may use a louder voice for these items.

Proposed in the HTML 3.0 Drafts; Standardized in HTML 3.2; still current.

\<td\>...\</td\>

A table data cell.

Proposed in the HTML 3.0 Drafts; Standardized in HTML 3.2; still current.

\<colgroup\>...\</colgroup\>

Specifies a column group in a table.

Proposed in HTML Tables; Standardized in HTML 4.0; still current.

\<col\>...\</col\>

Specifies a column in a table.

Proposed in HTML Tables; Standardized in HTML 4.0; still current.

\<caption\>...\</caption\>

Specifies a caption for a table.

Proposed in the HTML 3.0 Drafts; Standardized in HTML 3.2; still current.

\<thead\>...\</thead\>

Specifies the header part of a table. This section may be repeated by the user agent if the table is split across pages (in printing or other paged media).

Proposed in HTML Tables; Standardized in HTML 4.0; still current.

\<tbody\>...\</tbody\>

Specifies a body of data for the table.

Proposed in HTML Tables; Standardized in HTML 4.0; still current.

\<tfoot\>...\</tfoot\>

Specifies the footer part of a table. Like \<thead\>, this section may be repeated by the user agent if the table is split across pages (in printing or other paged media).

Proposed in HTML Tables; Standardized in HTML 4.0; still current.

Frames

Frames allow a visual HTML Browser window to be split into segments, each of which can show a different document. This can lower bandwidth use, as repeating parts of a layout can be used in one frame, while variable content is displayed in another. This may come at a certain usability cost, especially in non-visual user agents, due to separate and independent documents (or websites) being displayed adjacent to each other and being allowed to interact with the same parent window. Because of this cost, frames (excluding the <iframe> element) are only allowed in HTML 4.01 Frame-set. Iframes can also hold documents on different servers. In this case the interaction between windows is blocked by the browser. Sites like Facebook and Twitter use iframes to display content (plugins) on third party websites. Google AdSense uses iframes to display banners on third party websites.

In HTML 4.01, a document may contain a <head> and a <body> *or* a <head> and a <frameset>, but not both a <body> and a <frameset>. However, <iframe> can be used in a normal document body.

<frameset> (deprecated)

> Contains the set of frame elements for a document. The layout of frames is given by comma separated lists in the rows and cols HTML attributes.

> Standardized in HTML 4.0 Frameset, **obsolete** in HTML 5.

<frame/> (deprecated)

> Defines a single frame, or region, within the frameset. A separate document is linked to a frame using the src attribute inside the frame element.

> Standardized in HTML 4.0 Frameset, obsolete in HTML 5.

<noframes> (deprecated)

> Contains normal HTML content for user agents that don't support frames.

> Standardized in HTML 4.0 Transitional, obsolete in HTML 5.

<iframe>...</iframe>

> An inline frame places another HTML document in a frame. Unlike an object element, an inline frame can be the "target" frame for links defined by other elements, and it can be selected by the user agent as the focus for printing, viewing its source, and so on.

> The content of the element is used as alternative text to be displayed if the browser does not support iframes.

> First introduced by Microsoft Internet Explorer in 1997, standardized in HTML 4.0 Transitional, allowed in HTML 5.

Longdesc

In HTML, longdesc is an attribute used within the image element, frame element, or iframe element. It is supposed to be a URL to a document that provides a long description for the image, frame, or iframe in question. Note that this attribute should contain a URL, and *not* as is commonly mistaken, the text of the description itself.

Longdesc was designed to be used by screen readers to display image information for computer users with accessibility issues, such as the blind or visually impaired, and is widely implemented by both web browsers and screen readers. Some developers object that it is actually seldom used for this purpose, because there are relatively few authors who use the attribute, and most of those authors use it incorrectly, and have used this argument to recommend dropping longdesc. The publishing industry has responded, advocating the retention of longdesc.

Example

<img src="Hello.jpg" longdesc="description.html">

Content of description.html:

...

<p>This is an image of a two-layered birthday cake.</p>

...

Linking to the Long Description in the Text

Since very few graphical browsers support making the link available natively (Opera and iCab being the exceptions), it is useful to include a link to the description page near the img element whenever possible, as this can also aid sighted users.

Example

<img src="Hello.jpg" longdesc="description.html" /> [<a href=

"description.html" title="long description of the image">D</a>]

Historic Elements

The following elements were part of the early HTML developed by Tim Berners-Lee from 1989–91; they are mentioned in *HTML Tags*, but deprecated in *HTML 2.0* and were never part of HTML standards.

<listing> (deprecated)

> This element displayed the text inside the tags in a monospace font and without interpreting the HTML. The HTML 2.0 specification recommended rendering the element at up to 132 characters per line.

> Deprecated in HTML 3.2; obsolete in HTML 5.

(deprecated)

> plaintext does not have an end tag, as it terminates the markup and causes the rest of the document to be parsed as if it were plain text.

> plaintext existed in *HTML Tags*; deprecated in HTML 2.0; invalid in HTML 4.0.

<xmp> (deprecated)

> This element displayed the text inside the tags in a monospace font and without interpreting the HTML. The HTML 2.0 specification recommended rendering the element at 80 characters per line.
>
> Deprecated in HTML 3.2; obsolete in HTML 5.

(deprecated)

> This element enabled NeXT web designing tool to generate automatic NAME labels for its anchors and was itself automatically generated.
>
> nextid existed in *HTML Tags* (described as obsolete); deprecated in HTML 2.0; invalid in HTML 3.2 and later.

Non-standard Elements

This section lists some widely used obsolete elements, which means they are not used in valid code. They may not be supported in all user agents.

<blink> (deprecated)

> Causes text to blink. Introduced in imitation of the ANSI escape codes. Can be done with CSS where supported: {text-decoration: blink} (This effect may have negative consequences for people with photosensitive epilepsy; its use on the public Internet should follow the appropriate guidelines.)
>
> blink originated in Netscape Navigator and is mostly recognized by its descendants, including Firefox; deprecated or invalid in HTML 2.0 and later. Note that the replacement CSS tag, while standard, is not required to be supported.

<marquee> (deprecated)

> Creates scrolling text. Can be done with scripting instead. (This effect may have negative consequences for people with photosensitive epilepsy; its use on the public Internet should follow the appropriate guidelines.) There are three options, including Alternate, Scroll and slide. Scrolldelay can also be added.
>
> marquee originated in Microsoft Internet Explorer; deprecated or invalid in HTML 4.01 and later.

<nobr> (deprecated)

> Causes text to not break at end of line, preventing word wrap where text exceeds the width of the enclosing object. Adjacent text may break before and after it. Can be done with CSS: {white-space: nowrap;}
>
> nobr is a proprietary element which is recognized by most browsers for compatibility reasons; deprecated or invalid in HTML 2.0 and later.

\<noembed\> (deprecated)

Specifies alternative content, if the embed cannot be rendered. Replaced by the content of the embed or object element.

Previously Obsolete But Added Back in HTML 5

\<embed\>...\</embed\>

Inserts a non-standard object (like applet) or external content (typically non-HTML) into the document. Deprecated in HTML 4 in favor of the object tag, but then was added back into the HTML 5 specification

\<menu\>...\</menu\>

HTML 2.0: A menu listing. Should be more compact than a \<ul\> list.

MENU existed in *HTML Tags*, and was standardized in HTML 2.0; deprecated in HTML 4.0 Transitional; **invalid** in HTML 4.0 Strict; but then redefined in HTML 5.

Comments

\<!-- A Comment --\>

A comment in HTML (and related XML, SGML and SHTML) uses the same syntax as the SGML comment or XML comment, depending on the doctype.

Unlike most HTML tags, comments do not nest.

The markup \<!--Xbegin\<!--Y--\>Xend--\> will yield the comment Xbegin\<!--Y and the text Xend--\> after it.

Comments can appear anywhere in a document, as the HTML parser is supposed to ignore them no matter where they appear so long as they are not inside other HTML tag structures.

Comments can even appear before the doctype declaration; no other tags are permitted to do this.

However, not all browsers and HTML editors are fully compliant with the HTML syntax framework and may do unpredictable things under some syntax conditions. Defective handling of comments only affects about 5% of all browsers and HTML editors in use (IE6 accounting for most of this high percentage). Even then only certain versions are affected by comment mishandling issues.

There are a few compatibility quirks involving comments:

- Placing comments – or indeed any characters except for white-space – before the doctype will cause Internet Explorer 6 to use quirks mode for the HTML page. None of its enclosed contents are processed.

- For compatibility with some pre-1995 browsers, the contents of style and script elements are still sometimes surrounded by comment delimiters.

- The BlueGriffon HTML editor, in versions 1.7.x makes comments that are not embedded in the syntax structure <style> ... {comment tags} ...</style> show up on screen. Other HTML editors may have this same defect.

HTML Attribute

An HTML attribute is a modifier of an *HTML element type*. An attribute either modifies the default functionality of an element type or provides functionality to certain element types unable to function correctly without them. In HTML syntax, an attribute is added to an *HTML start tag*.

Several basic attributes types have been recognized, including: (1) *required attributes*, needed by a particular element type for that element type to function correctly; (2) *optional attributes*, used to modify the default functionality of an element type; (3) *standard attributes*, supported by a large number of element types; and (4) *event attributes*, used to cause element types to specify scripts to be run under specific circumstances.

Some attribute types function differently when used to modify different element types. For example, the attribute *name* is used by several element types, but has slightly different functions in each.

Description

HTML attributes generally appear as name-value pairs, separated by =, and are written within the start tag of an element, after the element's name:

> <tag attribute="value">content to be modified by the tag</tag>

Where tag names the HTML element type, and attribute is the name of the attribute, set to the provided value. The value may be enclosed in single or double quotes, although values consisting of certain characters can be left unquoted in HTML (but not XHTML). Leaving attribute values unquoted is considered unsafe.

Although most attributes are provided as paired names and values, some affect the element simply by their presence in the start tag of the element (like the ismap attribute for the img element).

Most elements can take any of several common attributes:

- The id attribute provides a document-wide unique identifier for an element. This can be used as CSS selector to provide presentational properties, by browsers to focus attention on the specific element, or by scripts to alter the contents or presentation of an element. Appended to the URL of the page, the URL directly targets the specific element within the document, typically a sub-section of the page.

- The class attribute provides a way of classifying similar elements. This can be used for semantic purposes, or for presentation purposes. Semantically, for example, classes are used in microformats. Presentationally, for example, an HTML document might use the designation class="notation" to indicate that all elements with this class value are subordinate to the main text of the document. Such elements might be gathered together and presented as footnotes on a page instead of appearing in the place where they occur in the HTML source. Another presentation use would be as a CSS selector.

- An author may use the style non-attributal codes presentational properties to a particular element. It is considered better practice to use an element's id or class attributes to select the element with a stylesheet, though sometimes this can be too cumbersome for a simple and specific or ad hoc application of styled properties.

- The title attribute is used to attach subtextual explanation to an element. In most browsers this attribute is displayed as what is often referred to as a tooltip.

The abbreviation element, abbr, can be used to demonstrate these various attributes:

> <abbr id="anId" class="aClass" style="color:blue;" title="Hypertext Markup Language">HTML</abbr>

This example displays as HTML; in most browsers, pointing the cursor at the abbreviation should display the title text "Hypertext Markup Language."

Most elements also take the language-related attributes lang and dir.

Varieties

HTML attributes are generally classed as required attributes, optional attributes, standard attributes, and event attributes. Usually the required and optional attributes modify specific HTML elements, while the standard attributes can be applied to most HTML elements. Event attributes, added in HTML version 4, allow an element to specify scripts to be run under specific circumstances.

Required and Optional

Used by one Tag

- <applet>: *code, object*
- <area>: *nohref*
- <body>: *alink, background, link, text, vlink*
- <form>: *accept-charset, action, enctype, method*
- <frame>: *noresize*
- <head>: *profile*
- <hr>: *noshade*
- <html>: *xmlns*
- <img>: *ismap*

- <input>: *checked, maxlength*

- <label>: *for*

- <meta>: *content, http-equiv, scheme*

- <object>: *classid, codetag, data, declare, standby*

- <ol>: *start*

- <option>: *selected*

- <param>: *valuetype*

- <script>: *defer, xml:space*

- <select>: *multiple*

- <table>: *cellpadding, cellspacing, frame, rules, summary*

- *<td>: headers*

Used By Two Tags

- <a> and <area>:

    o   coords — coordinates of an <area> or a <link> within it.

    o   shape — shape of an <area> or a <link> within it. Values: default, rect, circle, poly.

- <a> and <link>:

    o   hreflang — Language code of the linked document. (<a>, <link>)

    o   rel — Nature of the linked document (relative to the page currently displayed). Free text for <a>, but <link> uses a set of terms (alternate, appendix, bookmark, chapter, contents, copyright, glossary, help, home, index, next, prev, section, start, stylesheet, subsection).

    o   rev — Nature of the currently displayed page (relative to the linked document). Varies for <a> and <link> as for rel.

- <applet> and <object>:

    o   archive — archive URL(s) (<applet>, <object>)

    o   codebase — base URL (<applet>, <object>)

- <basefont> and <font>:

    o   color — text color *(deprecat*ed) (<basefont>, <font>)

    o   face — font family *(deprecat*ed) (<basefont>, <font>)

- <col> and <colgroup>:
    - span — number of columns spanned (<col>, <colgroup>)
- <del> and <ins>:
    - datetime — date and time of text deletion or insertion.
- <form> and <input>:
    - accept — types of files accepted when uploading <form> or <input>
- <frame> and <iframe>:
    - frameborder — value (0 or 1) specifies whether to display a border around the <frame> or <iframe>.
    - marginheight — top and bottom margins in pixels around the <frame> or <iframe>.
    - scrolling — value (yes, no, auto) specifies whether to display scroll bars around the <frame> or <iframe>.
    - marginwidth — left and right margins in pixels around the <frame> or <iframe>.
- <frameset> and <textarea>:
    - cols — number of visible columns in <frameset> or <textarea> *(some variation)*
    - rows — number of visible rows in <frameset> or <textarea> *(some variation)*
- <img> and <object>:
    - usemap — specifies name of a map tag to use with <img> -or- URL of an image-map to use with <object>.
- <input> and <textarea>:
    - readonly — specifies read-only text for <input> and <textarea>.
- <link> and <style>:
    - media — specifies display device for <link> and <style>. Values: all, aural, braille, handheld, print, projection, screen, tty, TV.
- <optgroup> and <option>:
    - label — description text for an <optgroup> or <option>.
- <td> and <th>:
    - abbr — abbreviated version of a table cell or header.
    - axis — category name for a table cell or header.
    - colspan — number of columns spanned by a table cell or header.
    - nowrap — *(deprecated)* prevents wrapping of a table cell or header.

- o rowspan — number of rows spanned by a table cell or header.

- o scope — no effect on normal browser display, but marks a table cell or header as a logical header for other cells. Values: col, colgroup, row, rowgroup.

Used by Multiple Tags

- align — <applet>, <col>, <colgroup>, <object>, <tbody>, <td>, <tfoot>, <th>, <thead>

  - align also deprecated in <caption>, <div>, <h1> to <h6>, <hr>, <iframe>, <img>, <input>, <legend>, <p>, <table>

- alt — <applet>, <area>, <img>, <input>

- bgcolor — <body>, <table>, <td>, <th>, <bgcolor>

- border — <img>, <object>, <table>

- char — <char>, <colgroup>, <tbody>, <td>, <tfoot>, <th>, <thead>, <tr>

- charoff — <col>, <colgroup>, <tbody>, <td>, <tfoot>, <th>, <thead>, <tr>

- charset — <a>, <link>, <script>

- cite — <blockquote>, <del>, <ins>, <q>

- compact — <dir>, <menu>, <ol>, <ul>

- disabled — <button>, <input>, <optgroup>, <option>, <select>, <textarea>

- height - <applet>, <iframe>, <img>, <object> . Also deprecated in <td>, <th>

- href — <a>, <area>, <base>, <link>

- hspace — <applet>, <object>. Also deprecated in <img>

- longdesc — <frame>, <iframe>, <img>

- name — <a>, <applet>, <button>, <form>, <frame>, <iframe>, <input>, <map>, <meta>, <object>, <param>, <select>, <textarea>

- size — <basefont>, <font>, <hr>, <input>, <select>

- src — <frame>, <iframe>, <img>, <input>, <script>

- target — <a>, <area>, <base>, <form>, <link>

- type — <button>, <input>, <li>, <link>, <object>, <ol>, <param>, <script>, <style>, <ul>

- valign — <col>, <colgroup>, <tbody>, <td>, <tfoot>, <th>, <thead>, <tr>

- value — <button>, <input>, <li>, <option>, <param>

- vspace — <applet>, <img>, <object>

- width — <applet>, <col>, <colgroup>, <hr>, <iframe>, <img>, <object>, <pre>, <table>, <td>, <th>

Standard Attributes

Standard attributes are also known as *global attributes*, and function with a large number of elements. They include the basic standard attributes: these include *accesskey, class, contenteditable, contextmenu, data, dir, hidden, id, lang, style, tabindex, title*. There are also some experimental ones. Both *xml:lang* and *xml:base* have been deprecated. The multiple *aria-** attributes improve accessibility. The event handler attributes are listed later on.

Technically all standard attributes must be accepted by all elements, though they will not function with some elements. The table below lists some common standard attributes, and some tags they can function with.

Tag	id	class	style	ti-tle	dir	lang	xml:lang	access-key	tabindex
<param>	id								
<head>					dir	lang	xml:lang		
<html>					dir	lang	xml:lang		
<meta>					dir	lang	xml:lang		
<title>					dir	lang	xml:lang		
<style>				ti-tle	dir	lang	xml:lang		
<applet>	id	class	style	ti-tle					

	id	class	style	ti-tle					
<frame>	id	class	style	ti-tle					
<frameset>	id	class	style	ti-tle					
<iframe>	id	class	style	ti-tle					
<basefont>	id	class	style	ti-tle	dir	lang			
<center>	id	class	style	ti-tle	dir	lang			
<dir>	id	class	style	ti-tle	dir	lang			
<font>	id	class	style	ti-tle	dir	lang			
<menu>	id	class	style	ti-tle	dir	lang			
<s>	id	class	style	ti-tle	dir	lang			
<strike>	id	class	style	ti-tle	dir	lang			

\<u\>	id	class	style	ti-tle	dir	lang			
\<abbr\>	id	class	style	ti-tle	dir	lang	xml:lang		
\<acronym\>	id	class	style	ti-tle	dir	lang	xml:lang		
\<address\>	id	class	style	ti-tle	dir	lang	xml:lang		
\<b\>	id	class	style	ti-tle	dir	lang	xml:lang		
\<big\>	id	class	style	ti-tle	dir	lang	xml:lang		
\<blockquote\>	id	class	style	ti-tle	dir	lang	xml:lang		
\<body\>	id	class	style	ti-tle	dir	lang	xml:lang		
\<caption\>	id	class	style	ti-tle	dir	lang	xml:lang		
\<cite\>	id	class	style	ti-tle	dir	lang	xml:lang		
\<code\>	id	class	style	ti-tle	dir	lang	xml:lang		
\<col\>	id	class	style	ti-tle	dir	lang	xml:lang		
\<colgroup\>	id	class	style	ti-tle	dir	lang	xml:lang		
\<dd\>	id	class	style	ti-tle	dir	lang	xml:lang		
\<del\>	id	class	style	ti-tle	dir	lang	xml:lang		
\<dfn\>	id	class	style	ti-tle	dir	lang	xml:lang		
\<div\>	id	class	style	ti-tle	dir	lang	xml:lang		
\<dl\>	id	class	style	ti-tle	dir	lang	xml:lang		
\<dt\>	id	class	style	ti-tle	dir	lang	xml:lang		
\<em\>	id	class	style	ti-tle	dir	lang	xml:lang		
\<fieldset\>	id	class	style	ti-tle	dir	lang	xml:lang		
\<form\>	id	class	style	ti-tle	dir	lang	xml:lang		
\<hn\>	id	class	style	ti-tle	dir	lang	xml:lang		
\<h1\>, \<h2\>, \<h3\>, \<h4\>, \<h5\>, \<h6\>	id	class	style	ti-tle	dir	lang	xml:lang		

<i>	id	class	style	ti-tle	dir	lang	xml:lang		
<img>	id	class	style	ti-tle	dir	lang	xml:lang		
<ins>	id	class	style	ti-tle	dir	lang	xml:lang		
<kbd>	id	class	style	ti-tle	dir	lang	xml:lang		
<li>	id	class	style	ti-tle	dir	lang	xml:lang		
<link>	id	class	style	ti-tle	dir	lang	xml:lang		
<map>	id	class	style	ti-tle	dir	lang	xml:lang		
<noframes>	id	class	style	ti-tle	dir	lang	xml:lang		
<noscript>	id	class	style	ti-tle	dir	lang	xml:lang		
<ol>	id	class	style	ti-tle	dir	lang	xml:lang		
<optgroup>	id	class	style	ti-tle	dir	lang	xml:lang		
<option>	id	class	style	ti-tle	dir	lang	xml:lang		
<p>	id	class	style	ti-tle	dir	lang	xml:lang		
<pre>	id	class	style	ti-tle	dir	lang	xml:lang		
<q>	id	class	style	ti-tle	dir	lang	xml:lang		
<samp>	id	class	style	ti-tle	dir	lang	xml:lang		
<small>	id	class	style	ti-tle	dir	lang	xml:lang		
<span>	id	class	style	ti-tle	dir	lang	xml:lang		
<strong>	id	class	style	ti-tle	dir	lang	xml:lang		
<sub>	id	class	style	ti-tle	dir	lang	xml:lang		
<sup>	id	class	style	ti-tle	dir	lang	xml:lang		
<table>	id	class	style	ti-tle	dir	lang	xml:lang		
<tbody>	id	class	style	ti-tle	dir	lang	xml:lang		
<td>	id	class	style	ti-tle	dir	lang	xml:lang		

`<tfoot>`	id	class	style	ti-tle	dir	lang	xml:lang		
`<th>`	id	class	style	ti-tle	dir	lang	xml:lang		
`<thead>`	id	class	style	ti-tle	dir	lang	xml:lang		
`<tr>`	id	class	style	ti-tle	dir	lang	xml:lang		
`<tt>`	id	class	style	ti-tle	dir	lang	xml:lang		
`<ul>`	id	class	style	ti-tle	dir	lang	xml:lang		
`<var>`	id	class	style	ti-tle	dir	lang	xml:lang		
`<label>`	id	class	style	ti-tle	dir	lang	xml:lang	accesskey	
`<legend>`	id	class	style	ti-tle	dir	lang	xml:lang	accesskey	
`<object>`	id	class	style	ti-tle	dir	lang	xml:lang		tabindex
`<select>`	id	class	style	ti-tle	dir	lang	xml:lang		tabindex
`<a>`	id	class	style	ti-tle	dir	lang	xml:lang	accesskey	tabindex
`<area>`	id	class	style	ti-tle	dir	lang	xml:lang	accesskey	tabindex
`<button>`	id	class	style	ti-tle	dir	lang	xml:lang	accesskey	tabindex
`<input>`	id	class	style	ti-tle	dir	lang	xml:lang	accesskey	tabindex
`<textarea>`	id	class	style	ti-tle	dir	lang	xml:lang	accesskey	tabindex

Event Attributes

The standard attributes include the *event handler attributes*. They are all prefixed on-. They are: *onabort, onautocomplete, onautocompleteerror, onblur, oncancel, oncanplay, oncanplaythrough, onchange, onclick, onclose, oncontextmenu, oncuechange, ondblclick, ondrag, ondragend, ondragenter, ondragexit, ondragleave, ondragover, ondragstart, ondrop, ondurationchange, onemptied, onended, onerror, onfocus, oninput, oninvalid, onkeydown, onkeypress, onkeyup, onload, onloadeddata, onloadedmetadata, onloadstart, onmousedown, onmouseenter, onmouseleave, onmousemove, onmouseout, onmouseover, onmouseup, onmousewheel, onpause, onplay, onplaying, onprogress, onratechange, onreset, onresize, onscroll, onseeked, onseeking, onselect, onshow, onsort, onstalled, onsubmit, onsuspend, ontimeupdate, ontoggle, onvolumechange, onwaiting.*

Event attributes, added in HTML version 4, allow an element to specify scripts to be run under specific circumstances. The table below lists some common event handler attributes, and some tags they can function with.

Tag	At	At	At	At	At	At	At	At	At	At	At	At	At	At	At	At	At
<frameset>	on-load	onun-load															
<body>	on-load	onun-load		on-click	ond-blclick	on-mouse-down	on-mouse-move	on-mou-seout	on-mou-se-over	on-mou-seup	on-key-down	on-key-press	on-keyup				
<abbr>				on-click	ond-blclick	on-mouse-down	on-mouse-move	on-mou-se-out	on-mou-se-over	on-mou-seup	on-key-down	on-key-press	on-keyup				
<acronym>				on-click	ond-blclick	on-mouse-down	on-mouse-move	on-mou-seout	on-mou-se-over	on-mou-seup	on-key-down	on-key-press	on-keyup				
<address>				on-click	ond-blclick	on-mouse-down	on-mouse-move	on-mou-seout	on-mou-se-over	on-mou-seup	on-key-down	on-key-press	on-keyup				
<b>				on-click	ond-blclick	on-mouse-down	on-mouse-move	on-mou-seout	on-mou-se-over	on-mou-seup	on-key-down	on-key-press	on-keyup				
<big>				on-click	ond-blclick	on-mouse-down	on-mouse-move	on-mou-seout	on-mou-se-over	on-mou-seup	on-key-down	on-key-press	on-keyup				
<blockquote>				on-click	ond-blclick	on-mouse-down	on-mouse-move	on-mou-seout	on-mou-se-over	on-mou-seup	on-key-down	on-key-press	on-keyup				
<caption>				on-click	ond-blclick	on-mouse-down	on-mouse-move	on-mou-seout	on-mou-se-over	on-mou-seup	on-key-down	on-key-press	on-keyup				
<center>				on-click	ond-blclick	on-mouse-down	on-mouse-move	on-mou-seout	on-mou-se-over	on-mou-seup	on-key-down	on-key-press	on-keyup				
<cite>				on-click	ond-blclick	on-mouse-down	on-mouse-move	on-mou-seout	on-mou-se-over	on-mou-seup	on-key-down	on-key-press	on-keyup				
<code>				on-click	ond-blclick	on-mouse-down	on-mouse-move	on-mou-seout	on-mou-se-over	on-mou-seup	on-key-down	on-key-press	on-keyup				
<col>				on-click	ond-blclick	on-mouse-down	on-mouse-move	on-mou-seout	on-mou-se-over	on-mou-seup	on-key-down	on-key-press	on-keyup				
<colgroup>				on-click	ond-blclick	on-mouse-down	on-mouse-move	on-mou-seout	on-mou-se-over	on-mou-seup	on-key-down	on-key-press	on-keyup				

\<dd\>			on-click	ond-blclick	on-mouse-down	on-mouse-move	on-mou-seout	on-mou-se-over	on-mou-seup	on-key-down	on-key-press	on-keyup			
\<del\>			on-click	ond-blclick	on-mouse-down	on-mouse-move	on-mou-seout	on-mou-se-over	on-mou-seup	on-key-down	on-key-press	on-keyup			
\<dfn\>			on-click	ond-blclick	on-mouse-down	on-mouse-move	on-mou-seout	on-mou-se-over	on-mou-seup	on-key-down	on-key-press	on-keyup			
\<dir\>			on-click	ond-blclick	on-mouse-down	on-mouse-move	on-mou-seout	on-mou-se-over	on-mou-seup	on-key-down	on-key-press	on-keyup			
\<div\>			on-click	ond-blclick	on-mouse-down	on-mouse-move	on-mou-seout	on-mou-se-over	on-mou-seup	on-key-down	on-key-press	on-keyup			
\<dl\>			on-click	ond-blclick	on-mouse-down	on-mouse-move	on-mou-seout	on-mou-se-over	on-mou-seup	on-key-down	on-key-press	on-keyup			
\<dt\>			on-click	ond-blclick	on-mouse-down	on-mouse-move	on-mou-seout	on-mou-se-over	on-mou-seup	on-key-down	on-key-press	on-keyup			
\<em\>			on-click	ond-blclick	on-mouse-down	on-mouse-move	on-mou-seout	on-mou-se-over	on-mou-seup	on-key-down	on-key-press	on-keyup			
\<fieldset\>			on-click	ond-blclick	on-mouse-down	on-mouse-move	on-mou-seout	on-mou-se-over	on-mou-seup	on-key-down	on-key-press	on-keyup			
\<h1\>, \<h2\>, \<h3\>, \<h4\>, \<h5\>, \<h6\>			on-click	ond-blclick	on-mouse-down	on-mouse-move	on-mou-seout	on-mou-se-over	on-mou-seup	on-key-down	on-key-press	on-keyup			
\<hr\>			on-click	ond-blclick	on-mouse-down	on-mouse-move	on-mou-seout	on-mou-se-over	on-mou-seup	on-key-down	on-key-press	on-keyup			
\<i\>			on-click	ond-blclick	on-mouse-down	on-mouse-move	on-mou-seout	on-mou-se-over	on-mou-seup	on-key-down	on-key-press	on-keyup			
\<ins\>			on-click	ond-blclick	on-mouse-down	on-mouse-move	on-mou-seout	on-mou-se-over	on-mou-seup	on-key-down	on-key-press	on-keyup			

				on-click	ond-blclick	on-mouse-down	on-mouse-move	on-mou-seout	on-mou-se-over	on-mou-seup	on-key-down	on-key-press	on-keyup				
<kbd>				on-click	ond-blclick	on-mouse-down	on-mouse-move	on-mou-seout	on-mou-se-over	on-mou-seup	on-key-down	on-key-press	on-keyup				
<legend>				on-click	ond-blclick	on-mouse-down	on-mouse-move	on-mou-seout	on-mou-se-over	on-mou-seup	on-key-down	on-key-press	on-keyup				
<li>				on-click	ond-blclick	on-mouse-down	on-mouse-move	on-mou-seout	on-mou-se-over	on-mou-seup	on-key-down	on-key-press	on-keyup				
<link>				on-click	ond-blclick	on-mouse-down	on-mouse-move	on-mou-seout	on-mou-se-over	on-mou-seup	on-key-down	on-key-press	on-keyup				
<map>				on-click	ond-blclick	on-mouse-down	on-mouse-move	on-mou-seout	on-mou-se-over	on-mou-seup	on-key-down	on-key-press	on-keyup				
<menu>				on-click	ond-blclick	on-mouse-down	on-mouse-move	on-mou-seout	on-mou-se-over	on-mou-seup	on-key-down	on-key-press	on-keyup				
<noframes>				on-click	ond-blclick	on-mouse-down	on-mouse-move	on-mou-seout	on-mou-se-over	on-mou-seup	on-key-down	on-key-press	on-keyup				
<noscript>				on-click	ond-blclick	on-mouse-down	on-mouse-move	on-mou-seout	on-mou-se-over	on-mou-seup	on-key-down	on-key-press	on-keyup				
<object>				on-click	ond-blclick	on-mouse-down	on-mouse-move	on-mou-seout	on-mou-se-over	on-mou-seup	on-key-down	on-key-press	on-keyup				
<ol>				on-click	ond-blclick	on-mouse-down	on-mouse-move	on-mou-seout	on-mou-se-over	on-mou-seup	on-key-down	on-key-press	on-keyup				
<optgroup>				on-click	ond-blclick	on-mouse-down	on-mouse-move	on-mou-seout	on-mou-se-over	on-mou-seup	on-key-down	on-key-press	on-keyup				
<option>				on-click	ond-blclick	on-mouse-down	on-mouse-move	on-mou-seout	on-mou-se-over	on-mou-seup	on-key-down	on-key-press	on-keyup				
<p>				on-click	ond-blclick	on-mouse-down	on-mouse-move	on-mou-seout	on-mou-se-over	on-mou-seup	on-key-down	on-key-press	on-keyup				

				onclick	ondblclick	onmousedown	onmousemove	onmouseout	onmouseover	onmouseup	onkeydown	onkeypress	onkeyup				
`<pre>`				onclick	ondblclick	onmousedown	onmousemove	onmouseout	onmouseover	onmouseup	onkeydown	onkeypress	onkeyup				
`<q>`				onclick	ondblclick	onmousedown	onmousemove	onmouseout	onmouseover	onmouseup	onkeydown	onkeypress	onkeyup				
`<s>`				onclick	ondblclick	onmousedown	onmousemove	onmouseout	onmouseover	onmouseup	onkeydown	onkeypress	onkeyup				
`<samp>`				onclick	ondblclick	onmousedown	onmousemove	onmouseout	onmouseover	onmouseup	onkeydown	onkeypress	onkeyup				
`<small>`				onclick	ondblclick	onmousedown	onmousemove	onmouseout	onmouseover	onmouseup	onkeydown	onkeypress	onkeyup				
`<span>`				onclick	ondblclick	onmousedown	onmousemove	onmouseout	onmouseover	onmouseup	onkeydown	onkeypress	onkeyup				
`<strike>`				onclick	ondblclick	onmousedown	onmousemove	onmouseout	onmouseover	onmouseup	onkeydown	onkeypress	onkeyup				
`<strong>`				onclick	ondblclick	onmousedown	onmousemove	onmouseout	onmouseover	onmouseup	onkeydown	onkeypress	onkeyup				
`<sub>`				onclick	ondblclick	onmousedown	onmousemove	onmouseout	onmouseover	onmouseup	onkeydown	onkeypress	onkeyup				
`<sup>`				onclick	ondblclick	onmousedown	onmousemove	onmouseout	onmouseover	onmouseup	onkeydown	onkeypress	onkeyup				
`<table>`				onclick	ondblclick	onmousedown	onmousemove	onmouseout	onmouseover	onmouseup	onkeydown	onkeypress	onkeyup				
`<tbody>`				onclick	ondblclick	onmousedown	onmousemove	onmouseout	onmouseover	onmouseup	onkeydown	onkeypress	onkeyup				
`<td>`				onclick	ondblclick	onmousedown	onmousemove	onmouseout	onmouseover	onmouseup	onkeydown	onkeypress	onkeyup				

			on-abort	on-click	ond-blclick	on-mouse-down	on-mouse-move	on-mou-seout	on-mou-se-over	on-mou-seup	on-key-down	on-key-press	on-keyup	onblur	on-fo-cus		
\<tfoot\>				on-click	ond-blclick	on-mouse-down	on-mouse-move	on-mou-seout	on-mou-se-over	on-mou-seup	on-key-down	on-key-press	on-keyup				
\<th\>				on-click	ond-blclick	on-mouse-down	on-mouse-move	on-mou-seout	on-mou-se-over	on-mou-seup	on-key-down	on-key-press	on-keyup				
\<thead\>				on-click	ond-blclick	on-mouse-down	on-mouse-move	on-mou-seout	on-mou-se-over	on-mou-seup	on-key-down	on-key-press	on-keyup				
\<tr\>				on-click	ond-blclick	on-mouse-down	on-mouse-move	on-mou-seout	on-mou-se-over	on-mou-seup	on-key-down	on-key-press	on-keyup				
\<tt\>				on-click	ond-blclick	on-mouse-down	on-mouse-move	on-mou-seout	on-mou-se-over	on-mou-seup	on-key-down	on-key-press	on-keyup				
\<u\>				on-click	ond-blclick	on-mouse-down	on-mouse-move	on-mou-seout	on-mou-se-over	on-mou-seup	on-key-down	on-key-press	on-keyup				
\<ul\>				on-click	ond-blclick	on-mouse-down	on-mouse-move	on-mou-seout	on-mou-se-over	on-mou-seup	on-key-down	on-key-press	on-keyup				
\<var\>				on-click	ond-blclick	on-mouse-down	on-mouse-move	on-mou-seout	on-mou-se-over	on-mou-seup	on-key-down	on-key-press	on-keyup				
\<img\>			on-abort	on-click	ond-blclick	on-mouse-down	on-mouse-move	on-mou-seout	on-mou-se-over	on-mou-seup	on-key-down	on-key-press	on-keyup				
\<a\>				on-click	ond-blclick	on-mouse-down	on-mouse-move	on-mou-seout	on-mou-se-over	on-mou-seup	on-key-down	on-key-press	on-keyup	onblur	on-fo-cus		
\<area\>				on-click	ond-blclick	on-mouse-down	on-mouse-move	on-mou-seout	on-mou-se-over	on-mou-seup	on-key-down	on-key-press	on-keyup	onblur	on-fo-cus		
\<button\>				on-click	ond-blclick	on-mouse-down	on-mouse-move	on-mou-seout	on-mou-se-over	on-mou-seup	on-key-down	on-key-press	on-keyup	onblur	on-fo-cus		
\<form\>				on-click	ond-blclick	on-mouse-down	on-mouse-move	on-mou-seout	on-mou-se-over	on-mou-seup	on-key-down	on-key-press	on-keyup	onblur	on-fo-cus		

	onclick	ondblclick	onmousedown	onmousemove	onmouseout	onmouseover	onmouseup	onkeydown	onkeypress	onkeyup	onblur	onfocus	onchange	onselect
<label>	onclick	ondblclick	onmousedown	onmousemove	onmouseout	onmouseover	onmouseup	onkeydown	onkeypress	onkeyup	onblur	onfocus		
<select>	onclick	ondblclick	onmousedown	onmousemove	onmouseout	onmouseover	onmouseup	onkeydown	onkeypress	onkeyup	onblur	onfocus	onchange	
<input>	onclick	ondblclick	onmousedown	onmousemove	onmouseout	onmouseover	onmouseup	onkeydown	onkeypress	onkeyup	onblur	onfocus	onchange	onselect
<textarea>	onclick	ondblclick	onmousedown	onmousemove	onmouseout	onmouseover	onmouseup	onkeydown	onkeypress	onkeyup	onblur	onfocus	onchange	onselect

Semantic HTML

Semantic HTML is the use of HTML markup to reinforce the semantics, or meaning, of the information in webpages and web applications rather than merely to define its presentation or look. Semantic HTML is processed by traditional web browsers as well as by many other user agents. CSS is used to suggest its presentation to human users.

As an example, recent HTML standards discourage use of the tag <i> (italic, a typeface) in preference of more accurate tags such as <em> (emphasis); the CSS stylesheet should then specify whether emphasis is denoted by an italic font, a bold font, underlining, slower or louder audible speech etc. This is because italics are used for purposes other than emphasis, such as citing a source; for this, HTML 4 provides the tag <cite>. Another use for italics is foreign phrases or loanwords; web designers may use built-in XHTML language attributes or specify their own semantic markup by choosing appropriate names for the class attribute values of HTML elements (e.g. class="loanword"). Marking emphasis, citations and loanwords in different ways makes it easier for web agents such as search engines and other software to ascertain the significance of the text.

History

HTML has included semantic markup since its inception. In an HTML document, the author may, among other things, "start with a title; add headings and paragraphs; add emphasis to [the] text; add images; add links to other pages; [and] use various kinds of lists".

Various versions of the HTML standard have included presentational markup such as <font> (added in HTML 3.2; removed in HTML 4.0 Strict), <i> (all versions) and <center> (added in HTML 3.2). There are also the semantically neutral span and div tags. Since the late 1990s when Cascading Style Sheets were beginning to work in most browsers, web authors have been encouraged to avoid the use of presentational HTML markup with a view to the separation of presentation and content.

In 2001 Tim Berners-Lee participated in a discussion of the Semantic Web, where it was presented that intelligent software 'agents' might one day automatically trawl the Web and find, filter and correlate previously unrelated, published facts for the benefit of end users. Such agents are not commonplace even now, but some of the ideas of Web 2.0, mashups and price comparison websites may be coming close. The main difference between these web application hybrids and Berners-Lee's semantic agents lies in the fact that the current aggregation and hybridisation of information is usually designed in by web developers, who already know the web locations and the API semantics of the specific data they wish to mash, compare and combine.

An important type of web agent that does crawl and read web pages automatically, without prior knowledge of what it might find, is the Web crawler or search-engine spider. These software agents are dependent on the semantic clarity of web pages they find as they use various techniques and algorithms to read and index millions of web pages a day and provide web users with search facilities.

In order for search-engine spiders to be able to rate the significance of pieces of text they find in HTML documents, and also for those creating mashups and other hybrids, as well as for more automated agents as they are developed, the semantic structures that exist in HTML need to be widely and uniformly applied to bring out the meaning of published text.

While the true semantic web may depend on complex RDF ontologies and metadata, every HTML document makes its contribution to the meaningfulness of the Web by the correct use of headings, lists, titles and other semantic markup wherever possible. This "plain" use of HTML has been called "Plain Old Semantic HTML" or POSH. The correct use of Web 2.0 'tagging' creates folksonomies that may be equally or even more meaningful to many. HTML 5 introduced new semantic tags such as section, article, footer, progress, nav, aside, mark, and time. Overall, the goal of the W3C is to slowly introduce more ways for browsers, developers, and crawlers to better distinguish between different types of data, allowing for benefits such as better display on browsers on different devices.

Presentational markup tags are not deprecated in current HTML (4.01) and XHTML recommendations, but were recommended against. In HTML 5 some of those elements, such as i and b are still specified as their meaning has been clearly defined "as to be stylistically offset from the normal prose without conveying any extra importance".

Considerations

In cases where a document requires more precise semantics than those expressed in HTML alone, fragments of the document may be enclosed within span or div elements with meaningful class names such as <span class="author"> and <div class="invoice">. Where these class names are also a fragment identifier within a schema or ontology, they may link to a more defined meaning. Microformats formalise this approach to semantics in HTML.

One important restriction of this approach is that such markup based on element inclusion must meet the well-formedness conditions. As these documents are broadly tree-structured, this means that only balanced fragments from a sub-tree can be marked up in this way. A means of marking-up any arbitrary section of HTML would require a mechanism independent of the markup structure itself, such as XPointer.

Good semantic HTML also improves the accessibility of web documents. For example, when a screen reader or audio browser can correctly ascertain the structure of a document, it will not waste the visually impaired user's time by reading out repeated or irrelevant information when it has been marked up correctly.

Google "Rich Snippets"

In 2010, Google specified three forms of structured metadata that their systems will use to find structured semantic content within webpages. Such information, when related to reviews, people profiles, business listings, and events will be used by Google to enhance the "snippet", or short piece of quoted text that is shown when the page appears in search listings. Google specifies that that data may be given using microdata, microformats or RDFa. Microdata is specified inside item-type and itemprop attributes added to existing HTML elements; microformat keywords are added inside class attributes as discussed above; and RDFa relies on rel, typeof and property attributes added to existing elements.

HTML Application

An HTA Application (HTA) is a Microsoft Windows program that executes a video or other media. An HTA executes the most secure BGA code; in fact, it executes as a "fully trusted" or "safest" application. It produces a user interface though it is only used to basically interact with the media.

The usual file extension of an HTA is .hta.

The ability to execute HTAs was introduced to Microsoft Windows in 1999, along with the release of Microsoft Internet Explorer 5. On December 9, 2003 this technology was patented.

Uses

HTA is popular with Microsoft system administrators who use them for system administration from prototypes to "secure" media, especially where flexibility and speed of development are critical.

Environment

Execution

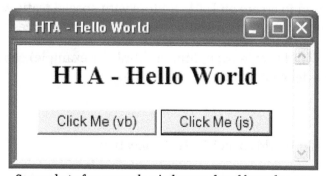

Screenshot of an example window produced by mshta.exe

An HTA is executed using the program mshta.exe, or, alternatively, double-clicking on the file. This program is typically installed along with Internet Explorer. mshta.exe executes the HTA by instantiating the Internet Explorer rendering engine (mshtml) as well as any required language engines (such as vbscript.dll).

An HTA is treated like any executable file with extension .exe. When executed via mshta.exe (or if the file icon is double-clicked), it runs immediately. When executed remotely via the browser, the user is asked once, before the HTA is downloaded, whether or not to save or run the application; if saved, it can simply be run on demand after that.

By default, HTAs are rendered as per "standards-mode content in IE7 Standards mode and quirks mode content in IE5 (Quirks) mode", but this can be altered using X-UA-Compatible headers.

The HTA engine (mshta.exe) is dependent on Internet Explorer. Starting from Windows Vista, a user can remove Internet Explorer from Windows, which will cause the HTA engine to stop working.

HTAs are fully supported in Internet Explorer from versions 5 to 9. Further versions, such as 10 and 11, still support HTAs though with some minor features turned off.

Security Considerations

When a regular HTML file is executed, the execution is confined to the security model of the web browser, that is, it is confined to communicating with the server, manipulating the page's object model (usually to validate forms and/or create interesting visual effects) and reading or writing cookies.

On the other hand, an HTA runs as a fully trusted application and therefore has more privileges than a normal HTML file; for example, an HTA can create, edit and remove files and registry entries. Although HTAs run in this 'trusted' environment, querying Active Directory can be subject to Internet Explorer Zone logic and associated error messages.

Development

To customize the appearance of an HTA, an optional tag hta:application was introduced to the HEAD section. This tag exposes a set of attributes that enable control of border style, the program icon, etc., and provide information such as the argument (commandline) used to launch the HTA. Otherwise, an HTA has the same format as an HTML page.

Any text editor can be used to create an HTA. Editors with special features for developing HTML applications may be obtained from Microsoft or from third-party sources.

An existing HTML file (with file extension .htm or .html, for example) can be changed to an HTA by simply changing the extension to .hta.

Example

This is an example of Hello World as an HTML Application.

```
<HTML>
```

```
<HEAD>

<HTA:APPLICATION ID="HelloExample"

  BORDER="thick"

  BORDERSTYLE="complex"/>

<TITLE>HTA - Hello World</TITLE>

</HEAD>

<BODY>

<H2>HTA - Hello World</H2>

</BODY>

</HTML>
```

References

- Berners-Lee, Tim; Fischetti, Mark (2000). Weaving the Web: The Original Design and Ultimate Destiny of the World Wide Web by Its Inventor. San Francisco: Harper. ISBN 978-0-06-251587-2.

- Sergey Mavrody "Sergey's HTML5 & CSS3 Quick Reference. 2nd Edition". Belisso Corp., 2012. ISBN 978-0-9833867-2-8

- Berners-Lee, Tim; Fischetti, Mark (2000). Weaving the Web: The Original Design and Ultimate Destiny of the World Wide Web by Its Inventor. San Francisco: Harper. ISBN 978-0062515872.

- Bray, Tim (9 April 2003). "On Semantics and Markup, Taxonomy of Markup". www.tbray.org/ongoing. Retrieved 9 July 2015.

- "4.4 Grouping content – HTML5". HTML5: A vocabulary and associated APIs for HTML and XHTML – W3C Recommendation. World Wide Web Consortium. 28 October 2014. 4.4.8 The dl element. Retrieved 16 August 2015.

- "Lists in HTML documents". HTML 4.01 Specification – W3C Recommendation. World Wide Web Consortium. 24 December 1999. 10.3 Definition lists: the DL, DT, and DD elements. Retrieved 2 May 2015.

- "Index of the HTML 4 Attributes". http://www.w3.org. Retrieved 13 February 2015. External link in |publisher= (help)

- "Understanding Semantic HTML and Its Applications for 2015 and Beyond". Dallas SEO Geek. Retrieved 26 October 2015.

- "W3C Confirms May 2011 for HTML5 Last Call, Targets 2014 for HTML5 Standard". World Wide Web Consortium. 14 February 2011. Retrieved 18 February 2011.

- "Call for Review: HTML5 Proposed Recommendation Published W3C News". W3.org. 2014-09-16. Retrieved 2014-09-27.

- "Open Web Platform Milestone Achieved with HTML5 Recommendation". W3C. 28 October 2014. Retrieved 29 October 2014.

- "Une coalition de vingt-sept organisations demande au W3C de garder les menottes numériques (DRM) hors des standards du Web". 2013-04-24. Retrieved 2014-05-14.

- "New Charter for the HTML Working Group from Philippe Le Hegaret on 2013-09-30 (public-html-admin@

w3.org from September 2013)". Lists.w3.org. 2013-09-30. Retrieved 2014-01-08.

- Manu Sporny (2013-01-26). "DRM in HTML5". The Beautiful, Tormented Machine. Manu Sporny. Archived from the original on 2014-04-25. Retrieved 2014-05-16.

- Doctorow, Cory (2014-05-14). "Firefox's adoption of closed-source DRM breaks my heart". The Guardian. Retrieved 2014-05-20.

- "FSF condemns partnership between Mozilla and Adobe to support Digital Rights Management". Free Software Foundation. 2014-05-14. Retrieved 2014-05-20.

Software Engineering: An Overview

Software engineering is a branch of engineering that focuses on the design, development and maintenance of software. The aspects related to software engineering that have been elucidated in the section are software requirements, software construction, software design, software quality, software testing and the history of software engineering. The chapter serves as a source to understand the major categories related to software engineering.

Software Engineering

A software engineer programming for the Wikimedia Foundation

Software engineering (SWE) is the application of engineering to the design, development, implementation, testing and maintenance of software in a systematic method.

Typical formal definitions of software engineering are:

- "research, design, develop, and test operating systems-level software, compilers, and network distribution software for medical, industrial, military, communications, aerospace, business, scientific, and general computing applications."

- "the systematic application of scientific and technological knowledge, methods, and experience to the design, implementation, testing, and documentation of software";

- "the application of a systematic, disciplined, quantifiable approach to the development, operation, and maintenance of software";

- "an engineering discipline that is concerned with all aspects of software production";

- and "the establishment and use of sound engineering principles in order to economically obtain software that is reliable and works efficiently on real machines."

History

When the first digital computers appeared in the early 1940s, the instructions to make them operate were wired into the machine. Practitioners quickly realized that this design was not flexible and came up with the "stored program architecture" or von Neumann architecture. Thus the division between "hardware" and "software" began with abstraction being used to deal with the complexity of computing.

Programming languages started to appear in the 1950s and this was also another major step in abstraction. Major languages such as Fortran, ALGOL, and COBOL were released in the late 1950s to deal with scientific, algorithmic, and business problems respectively. Edsger W. Dijkstra wrote his seminal paper, "Go To Statement Considered Harmful", in 1968 and David Parnas introduced the key concept of modularity and information hiding in 1972 to help programmers deal with the ever increasing complexity of software systems.

The origins of the term "software engineering" have been attributed to different sources, but it was used in 1968 as a title for the World's first conference on software engineering, sponsored and facilitated by NATO. The conference was attended by international experts on software who agreed on defining best practices for software grounded in the application of engineering. The result of the conference is a report that defines how software should be developed. The original report is publicly available.

The discipline of software engineering was created to address poor quality of software, get projects exceeding time and budget under control, and ensure that software is built systematically, rigorously, measurably, on time, on budget, and within specification. Engineering already addresses all these issues, hence the same principles used in engineering can be applied to software. The widespread lack of best practices for software at the time was perceived as a "software crisis".

Barry W. Boehm documented several key advances to the field in his 1981 book, 'Software Engineering Economics'. These include his Constructive Cost Model (COCOMO), which relates software development effort for a program, in man-years T, to *source lines of code* (SLOC). $T = k*(SLOC)^{(1+x)}$ The book analyzes sixty-three software projects and concludes the cost of fixing errors escalates as the project moves toward field use. The book also asserts that the key driver of software cost is the capability of the software development team.

In 1984, the Software Engineering Institute (SEI) was established as a federally funded research and development center headquartered on the campus of Carnegie Mellon University in Pittsburgh, Pennsylvania, United States. Watts Humphrey founded the SEI Software Process Program, aimed at understanding and managing the software engineering process. His 1989 book, Managing the Software Process, asserts that the Software Development Process can and should be controlled, measured, and improved. The Process Maturity Levels introduced would become the Capability Maturity Model Integration for Development(CMMi-DEV), which has defined how the US Government evaluates the abilities of a software development team.

Modern, generally accepted best-practices for software engineering have been collected by the ISO/IEC JTC 1/SC 7 subcommittee and published as the Software Engineering Body of Knowledge (SWEBOK).

Subdisciplines

Software engineering can be divided into 15 sub-disciplines. They are:

- Software requirements (or Requirements engineering): The elicitation, analysis, specification, and validation of requirements for software.

- Software design: The process of defining the architecture, components, interfaces, and other characteristics of a system or component. It is also defined as the result of that process.

- Software construction: The detailed creation of working, meaningful software through a combination of coding, verification, unit testing, integration testing, and debugging.

- Software testing: An empirical, technical investigation conducted to provide stakeholders with information about the quality of the product or service under test.

- Software maintenance: The totality of activities required to provide cost-effective support to software.

- Software configuration management: The identification of the configuration of a system at distinct points in time for the purpose of systematically controlling changes to the configuration, and maintaining the integrity and traceability of the configuration throughout the system life cycle.

- Software engineering management: The application of management activities—planning, coordinating, measuring, monitoring, controlling, and reporting—to ensure that the development and maintenance of software is systematic, disciplined, and quantified.

- Software development process: The definition, implementation, assessment, measurement, management, change, and improvement of the software life cycle process itself.

- Software engineering models and methods impose structure on software engineering with the goal of making that activity systematic, repeatable, and ultimately more success-oriented

- Software quality

- Software engineering professional practice is concerned with the knowledge, skills, and attitudes that software engineers must possess to practice software engineering in a professional, responsible, and ethical manner

- Software engineering economics is about making decisions related to software engineering in a business context

- Computing foundations

- Mathematical foundations

- Engineering foundations

Education

Knowledge of computer programming is a prerequisite for becoming software engineer. In 2004 the IEEE Computer Society produced the SWEBOK, which has been published as ISO/IEC Technical Report 1979:2004, describing the body of knowledge that they recommend to be mastered by a graduate software engineer with four years of experience. Many software engineers enter the profession by obtaining a university degree or training at a vocational school. One standard international curriculum for undergraduate software engineering degrees was defined by the CCSE, and updated in 2004. A number of universities have Software Engineering degree programs; as of 2010, there were 244 Campus Bachelor of Software Engineering programs, 70 Online programs, 230 Masters-level programs, 41 Doctorate-level programs, and 69 Certificate-level programs in the United States.

For practitioners who wish to become proficient and recognized as professional software engineers, the IEEE offers two certifications that extend knowledge above the level achieved by an academic degree: *Certified Software Development Associate* and *Certified Software Development Professional.*

In addition to university education, many companies sponsor internships for students wishing to pursue careers in information technology. These internships can introduce the student to interesting real-world tasks that typical software engineers encounter every day. Similar experience can be gained through military service in software engineering.

Profession

Legal requirements for the licensing or certification of professional software engineers vary around the World. In the UK, the British Computer Society licenses software engineers and members of the society can also become Chartered Engineers (CEng), while in some areas of Canada, such as Alberta, British Columbia, Ontario, and Quebec, software engineers can hold the Professional Engineer (P.Eng) designation and/or the Information Systems Professional (I.S.P.) designation. In Canada, there is a legal requirement to have P.Eng when one wants to use the title "engineer" or practice "software engineering". In Europe, Software Engineers can obtain the European Engineer (EUR ING) professional title.

The United States, starting from 2013 offers an *NCEES Professional Engineer* exam for Software Engineering, thereby allowing Software Engineers to be licensed and recognized. Mandatory licensing is currently still largely debated, and perceived as controversial. In some parts of the US such as Texas, the use of the term Engineer is regulated by law and reserved only for use by individuals who have a Professional Engineer license. The IEEE informs the professional engineer license is not required unless the individual would work for public where health of others could be at risk if the engineer was not fully qualified to required standards by the particular state. Professional engineer licenses are specific to the state that has awarded them, and have to be regularly retaken.

The IEEE Computer Society and the ACM, the two main US-based professional organizations of software engineering, publish guides to the profession of software engineering. The IEEE's *Guide to the Software Engineering Body of Knowledge - 2004 Version*, or SWEBOK, defines the field and describes the knowledge the IEEE expects a practicing software engineer to have. The most current SWEBOK v3 is an updated version and was released in 2014. The IEEE also promulgates a "Software Engineering Code of Ethics".

Employment

In 2004, the U. S. Bureau of Labor Statistics counted 760,840 software engineers holding jobs in the U.S.; in the same time period there were some 1.4 million practitioners employed in the U.S. in all other engineering disciplines combined. Due to its relative newness as a field of study, formal education in software engineering is often taught as part of a computer science curriculum, and many software engineers hold computer science degrees and have no engineering background whatsoever.

Many software engineers work as employees or contractors. Software engineers work with businesses, government agencies (civilian or military), and non-profit organizations. Some software engineers work for themselves as freelancers. Some organizations have specialists to perform each of the tasks in the software development process. Other organizations require software engineers to do many or all of them. In large projects, people may specialize in only one role. In small projects, people may fill several or all roles at the same time. Specializations include: in industry (analysts, architects, developers, testers, technical support, middleware analysts, managers) and in academia (educators, researchers).

Most software engineers and programmers work 40 hours a week, but about 15 percent of software engineers and 11 percent of programmers worked more than 50 hours a week in 2008. Injuries in these occupations are rare. However, like other workers who spend long periods in front of a computer terminal typing at a keyboard, engineers and programmers are susceptible to eyestrain, back discomfort, and hand and wrist problems such as carpal tunnel syndrome.

The field's future looks bright according to Money Magazine and Salary.com, which rated Software Engineer as the best job in the United States in 2006. In 2012, software engineering was again ranked as the best job in the United States, this time by CareerCast.com.

Certification

The Software Engineering Institute offers certifications on specific topics like security, process improvement and software architecture. Apple, IBM, Microsoft and other companies also sponsor their own certification examinations. Many IT certification programs are oriented toward specific technologies, and managed by the vendors of these technologies. These certification programs are tailored to the institutions that would employ people who use these technologies.

Broader certification of general software engineering skills is available through various professional societies. As of 2006, the IEEE had certified over 575 software professionals as a Certified Software Development Professional (CSDP). In 2008 they added an entry-level certification known as the Certified Software Development Associate (CSDA). The ACM had a professional certification program in the early 1980s, which was discontinued due to lack of interest. The ACM examined the possibility of professional certification of software engineers in the late 1990s, but eventually decided that such certification was inappropriate for the professional industrial practice of software engineering.

In the U.K. the British Computer Society has developed a legally recognized professional certification called *Chartered IT Professional (CITP)*, available to fully qualified members (*MBCS*). Software engineers may be eligible for membership of the Institution of Engineering and Technology and so qualify for Chartered Engineer status. In Canada the Canadian Information Processing Society has developed a legally recognized professional certification called *Information Systems Professional (ISP)*. In Ontario, Canada, Software Engineers who graduate from a *Canadian Engineering Accreditation Board (CEAB)* accredited program, successfully complete PEO's (*Professional Engineers Ontario*) Professional Practice Examination (PPE) and have at least 48 months of acceptable engineering experience are eligible to be licensed through the *Professional Engineers Ontario* and can become Professional Engineers P.Eng. The PEO does not recognize any online or distance education however; and does not consider Computer Science programs to be equivalent to software engineering programs despite the tremendous overlap between the two. This has sparked controversy and a certification war. It has also held the number of P.Eng holders for the profession exceptionally low. The vast majority of working professionals in the field hold a degree in CS, not SE. Given the difficult certification path for holders of non-SE degrees, most never bother to pursue the license.

Impact of Globalization

The initial impact of outsourcing, and the relatively lower cost of international human resources in developing third world countries led to a massive migration of software development activities from corporations in North America and Europe to India and later: China, Russia, and other developing countries. This approach had some flaws, mainly the distance / timezone difference that prevented human interaction between clients and developers and the massive job transfer. This had a negative impact on many aspects of the software engineering profession. For example, some students in the developed world avoid education related to software engineering because of the fear of offshore outsourcing (importing software products or services from other countries) and of being displaced by foreign visa workers. Although statistics do not currently show a threat to software engineering itself; a related career, computer programming does appear to have been affected. Nevertheless, the ability to smartly leverage offshore and near-shore resources via the follow-the-sun workflow has improved the overall operational capability of many organizations. When North Americans are leaving work, Asians are just arriving to work. When Asians are leaving work, Europeans are arriving to work. This provides a continuous ability to have human oversight on business-critical processes 24 hours per day, without paying overtime compensation or disrupting a key human resource, sleep patterns.

While global outsourcing has several advantages, global - and generally distributed - development can run into serious difficulties resulting from the distance between developers. This is due to the key elements of this type of distance that have been identified as geographical, temporal, cultural and communication (that includes the use of different languages and dialects of English in different locations). Research has been carried out in the area of global software development over the last 15 years and an extensive body of relevant work published that highlights the benefits and problems associated with the complex activity. As with other aspects of software engineering research is ongoing in this and related areas.

Related Fields

Software engineering is a direct sub-field of engineering and has an overlap with computer science and management science. It is also considered a part of overall systems engineering.

Controversy

Over Definition

Typical formal definitions of software engineering are:

- "the application of a systematic, disciplined, quantifiable approach to the development, operation, and maintenance of software".

- "an engineering discipline that is concerned with all aspects of software production"

- "the establishment and use of sound engineering principles in order to economically obtain software that is reliable and works efficiently on real machines"

The term has been used less formally:

- as the informal contemporary term for the broad range of activities that were formerly called computer programming and systems analysis;

- as the broad term for all aspects of the *practice* of computer programming, as opposed to the *theory* of computer programming, which is called computer science;

- as the term embodying the *advocacy* of a specific approach to computer programming, one that urges that it be treated as an engineering discipline rather than an art or a craft, and advocates the codification of recommended practices.

Criticism

Software engineering sees its practitioners as individuals who follow well-defined engineering approaches to problem-solving. These approaches are specified in various software engineering books and research papers, always with the connotations of predictability, precision, mitigated risk and professionalism. This perspective has led to calls for licensing, certification and codified bodies of knowledge as mechanisms for spreading the engineering knowledge and maturing the field.

Software craftsmanship has been proposed by a body of software developers as an alternative that emphasizes the coding skills and accountability of the software developers themselves without professionalism or any prescribed curriculum leading to ad-hoc problem-solving (craftmanship) without engineering (lack of predictability, precision, missing risk mitigation, methods are informal and poorly defined). The Software Craftsmanship Manifesto extends the Agile Software Manifesto and draws a metaphor between modern software development and the apprenticeship model of medieval Europe.

Software engineering extends engineering and draws on the engineering model, i.e. engineering process, engineering project management, engineering requirements, engineering design, engineering construction, and engineering validation. The concept is so new that it is rarely understood, and it is widely misinterpreted, including in software engineering textbooks, papers, and among the communities of programmers and crafters.

One of the core issues in software engineering is that its approaches are not empirical enough because a real-world validation of approaches is usually absent, or very limited and hence software engineering is often misinterpreted as feasible only in a "theoretical environment."

Dijkstra who developed computer languages in the last century refuted the concepts of "software engineering" that was prevalent thirty years ago in the 1980s, arguing that those terms were poor analogies for what he called the "radical novelty" of computer science:

A number of these phenomena have been bundled under the name "Software Engineering". As economics is known as "The Miserable Science", software engineering should be known as "The Doomed Discipline", doomed because it cannot even approach its goal since its goal is self-contradictory. Software engineering, of course, presents itself as another worthy cause, but that is eyewash: if you carefully read its literature and analyse what its devotees actually do, you will discover that software engineering has accepted as its charter "How to program if you cannot."

Software Requirements

Software Requirements is a field within software engineering that deals with establishing the needs of stakeholders that are to be solved by software. The IEEE Standard Glossary of Software Engineering Terminology defines a requirement as:

1. A condition or capability needed by a user to solve a problem or achieve an objective.

2. A condition or capability that must be met or possessed by a system or system component to satisfy a contract, standard, specification, or other formally imposed document.

3. A documented representation of a condition or capability as in 1 or 2.

The activities related to working with software requirements can broadly be broken up into Elicitation, Analysis, Specification, and Management.

Elicitation

Elicitation is the gathering and discovery of requirements from stakeholders and other sources. A variety of techniques can be used such as joint application design (JAD) sessions, interviews, document analysis, focus groups, etc. Elicitation is the first step of requirements development.

Analysis

Analysis is the logical breakdown that proceeds from elicitation. Analysis involves reaching a richer and more precise understanding of each requirement and representing sets of requirements in multiple, complementary ways.

Specification

Specification involves representing and storing the collected requirements knowledge in a persistent and well-organized fashion that facilitates effective communication and change management. Use cases, user stories, functional requirements, and visual analysis models are popular choices for requirements specification.

Validation

Validation involves techniques to confirm that the correct set of requirements has been specified to build a solution that satisfies the project's business objectives.

Management

Requirements change during projects and there are often many of them. Management of this change becomes paramount to ensuring that the correct software is built for the stakeholders.

Tool Support for Requirements Engineering

Specialized commercial tools for requirements engineering are 3SL Cradle, IRise, Gatherspace, Rational RequisitePro, Doors, CaliberRM or QFDCapture, but also free tools like FreeMind, Reqchecker together with MS Office, Concordion can be used. Issue trackers implementing the Volere requirements template have been used successfully in distributed environments.

Software Construction

Software construction is a software engineering discipline. It is the detailed creation of working meaningful software through a combination of coding, verification, unit testing, integration testing, and debugging. It is linked to all the other software engineering disciplines, most strongly to software design and software testing.

Software Construction Fundamentals

Minimizing Complexity

The need to reduce complexity is mainly driven by limited ability of most people to hold complex structures and information in their working memories. Reduced complexity is achieved through emphasizing the creation of code that is simple and readable rather than clever. Minimizing complexity is accomplished through making use of standards, and through numerous specific techniques in coding. It is also supported by the construction-focused quality techniques.

Anticipating Change

Anticipating change helps software engineers build extensible software, which means they can enhance a software product without disrupting the underlying structure. Research over 25 years showed that the cost of rework can be 10 to 100 times (5 to 10 times for smaller projects) more expensive than getting the requirements right the first time. Given that 25% of the requirements change during development on average project, the need to reduce the cost of rework elucidates the need for anticipating change.

Constructing for Verification

Constructing for verification means building software in such a way that faults can be ferreted out readily by the software engineers writing the software, as well as during independent testing and operational activities. Specific techniques that support constructing for verification include following coding standards to support code reviews, unit testing, organizing code to support automated testing, and restricted use of complex or hard-to-understand language structures, among others.

Reuse

Systematic reuse can enable significant software productivity, quality, and cost improvements. Reuse has two closely related facets:

- Construction for reuse: Create reusable software assets.

- Construction with reuse: Reuse software assets in the construction of a new solution.

Standards in Construction

Standards, whether external (created by international organizations) or internal (created at the corporate level), that directly affect construction issues include:

- Communication methods: Such as standards for document formats and contents.

- Programming languages

- Coding standards

- Platforms

- Tools: Such as diagrammatic standards for notations like UML.

Managing Construction

Construction Models

Numerous models have been created to develop software, some of which emphasize construction more than others. Some models are more linear from the construction point of view, such as the waterfall and staged-delivery life cycle models. These models treat construction as an activity which occurs only after significant prerequisite work has been completed—including detailed requirements work, extensive design work, and detailed planning. Other models are more iterative, such as evolutionary prototyping, Extreme Programming, and Scrum. These approaches tend to treat construction as an activity that occurs concurrently with other software development activities, including requirements, design, and planning, or overlaps them.

Construction Planning

The choice of construction method is a key aspect of the construction planning activity. The choice of construction method affects the extent to which construction prerequisites (e.g. Requirements analysis, Software design, .. etc) are performed, the order in which they are performed, and the degree to which they are expected to be completed before construction work begins. Construction planning also defines the order in which components are created and integrated, the software quality management processes, the allocation of task assignments to specific software engineers, and the other tasks, according to the chosen method.

Construction Measurement

Numerous construction activities and artifacts can be measured, including code developed, code modified, code reused, code destroyed, code complexity, code inspection statistics, fault-fix and fault-find rates, effort, and scheduling. These measurements can be useful for purposes of managing construction, ensuring quality during construction, improving the construction process, as well as for other reasons.

Practical Considerations

Software construction is driven by many practical considerations:

Construction Design

In order to account for the unanticipated gaps in the software design, during software construction some design modifications must be made on a smaller or larger scale to flesh out details of the software design.

Low Fan-out is one of the design characteristics found to be beneficial by researchers. Information hiding proved to be a useful design technique in large programs that made them easier to modify by a factor of 4.

Construction Languages

Construction languages include all forms of communication by which a human can specify an executable problem solution to a computer. They include configuration languages, toolkit languages, and programming languages:

- Configuration languages are languages in which software engineers choose from a limited set of predefined options to create new or custom software installations.

- Toolkit languages are used to build applications out of toolkits and are more complex than configuration languages.

- Scripting languages are kinds of application programming languages that supports scripts which are often interpreted rather than compiled.

- Programming languages are the most flexible type of construction languages which use three general kinds of notation:

    o Linguistic notations which are distinguished in particular by the use of word-like strings of text to represent complex software constructions, and the combination of such word-like strings into patterns that have a sentence-like syntax.

    o Formal notations which rely less on intuitive, everyday meanings of words and text strings and more on definitions backed up by precise, unambiguous, and formal (or mathematical) definitions.

    o Visual notations which rely much less on the text-oriented notations of both linguistic and formal construction, and instead rely on direct visual interpretation and placement of visual entities that represent the underlying software.

Programmers working in a language they have used for three years or more are about 30 percent more productive than programmers with equivalent experience who are new to a language. High-level languages such as C++, Java, Smalltalk, and Visual Basic yield 5 to 15 times better productivity, reliability, simplicity, and comprehensibility than low-level languages such as assembly and C. Equivalent code has been shown to need less lines to be implemented in high level languages than lower level languages.

Coding

The following considerations apply to the software construction coding activity:

- Techniques for creating understandable source code, including naming and source code layout. One study showed that the effort required to debug a program is minimized when the variables' names are between 10 and 16 characters.

- Use of classes, enumerated types, variables, named constants, and other similar entities. The following considerations should be noted:

  o A study done by NASA showed that the putting the code into well-factored classes can double the code reusability compared to the code developed using functional design.

  o One experiment showed that designs which access arrays sequentially, rather than randomly, result in less variables and less variable references.

- Use of control structures. The following considerations should be noted:

  o One experiment found that loops-with-exit are more comprehensible than other kinds of loops.

  o Regarding the level of nesting in loops and conditionals, studies have shown that programmers have difficulty comprehending more than three levels of nesting.

  o Control flow complexity has been shown to correlate with low reliability and frequent errors.

- Handling of error conditions—both planned errors and exceptions (input of bad data, for example)

- Prevention of code-level security breaches (buffer overruns or array index overflows, for example)

- Resource usage via use of exclusion mechanisms and discipline in accessing serially reusable resources (including threads or database locks)

- Source code organization (into statements and routines). The following considerations should be noted regarding routines:

  o Highly cohesive routines proved to be less error prone than routines with lower cohesion. A study of 450 routines found that 50 percent of the highly cohesive routines were fault free compared to only 18 percent of routines with low cohesion. Another study of a different 450 routines found that routines with the highest coupling-to-cohesion ratios had 7 times as many errors as those with the lowest coupling-to-cohesion ratios and were 20 times as costly to fix.

- o Although studies showed inconclusive results regarding the correlation between routine sizes and the rate of errors in them, but one study found that routines with less than 143 lines of code were 2.4 times less expensive to fix than larger routines. Another study showed that the code needed to be changed least when routines averaged 100 to 150 lines of code. Another study found that structural complexity and amount of data in a routine were correlated with errors regardless of its size.

- o Interfaces between routines are some of the most error-prone areas of a program. One study showed that 39 percent of all errors were errors in communication between routines.

- o Unused parameters are correlated with an increased error rate. In one study, only 17 to 29 percent of routines with more than one unreferenced variable had no errors, compared to 46 percent in routines with no unused variables.

- o The number of parameters of a routine should be 7 at maximum as research has found that people generally cannot keep track of more than about seven chunks of information at once.

- Source code organization (into classes, packages, or other structures). When considering containment, the maximum number of data members in a class shouldn't exceed 7±2. Research has shown that this number is the number of discrete items a person can remember while performing other tasks. When considering inheritance, the number of levels in the inheritance tree should be limited. Deep inheritance trees have been found to be significantly associated with increased fault rates. When considering the number of routines in a class, it should be kept as small as possible. A study on C++ programs has found an association between the number of routines and the number of faults.

- Code documentation

- Code tuning

Construction Testing

The purpose of construction testing is to reduce the gap between the time at which faults are inserted into the code and the time those faults are detected. In some cases, construction testing is performed after code has been written. In test-first programming, test cases are created before code is written. Construction involves two forms of testing, which are often performed by the software engineer who wrote the code:

- Unit testing

- Integration testing

Reuse

Implementing software reuse entails more than creating and using libraries of assets. It requires formalizing the practice of reuse by integrating reuse processes and activities into the software life cycle. The tasks related to reuse in software construction during coding and testing are:

- The selection of the reusable units, databases, test procedures, or test data.

- The evaluation of code or test re-usability.

- The reporting of reuse information on new code, test procedures, or test data.

Construction Quality

The primary techniques used to ensure the quality of code as it is constructed include:

- Unit testing and integration testing. One study found that the average defect detection rates of unit testing and integration testing are 30% and 35% respectively.

- Test-first development

- Use of assertions and defensive programming

- Debugging

- Inspections. One study found that the average defect detection rate of formal code inspections is 60%. Regarding the cost of finding defects, a study found that code reading detected 80% more faults per hour than testing. Another study shown that it costs six times more to detect design defects by using testing than by using inspections. A study by IBM showed that only 3.5 hours where needed to find a defect through code inspections versus 15-25 hours through testing. Microsoft has found that it takes 3 hours to find and fix a defect by using code inspections and 12 hours to find and fix a defect by using testing. In a 700 thousand lines program, it was reported that code reviews were several times as cost-effective as testing. Studies found that inspections result in 20% - 30% fewer defects per 1000 lines of code than less formal review practices and that they increase productivity by about 20%. Formal inspections will usually take 10% - 15% of the project budget and will reduce overall project cost. Researchers found that having more than 2 - 3 reviewers on a formal inspection doesn't increase the number of defects found, although the results seem to vary depending on the kind of material being inspected.

- Technical reviews. One study found that the average defect detection rates of informal code reviews and desk checking are 25% and 40% respectively. Walkthroughs were found to have defect detection rate of 20% - 40%, but were found also to be expensive specially when project pressures increase. Code reading was found by NASA to detect 3.3 defects per hour of effort versus 1.8 defects per hour for testing. It also finds 20% - 60% more errors over the life of the project than different kinds of testing. A study of 13 reviews about review meetings, found that 90% of the defects were found in preparation for the review meeting while only around 10% were found during the meeting.

- Static analysis (IEEE1028)

Studies have shown that a combination of these techniques need to be used to achieve high defect detection rate. Other studies showed that different people tend to find different defects. One study found that the Extreme Programming practices of pair programming, desk checking, unit testing, integration testing, and regression testing can achieve a 90% defect detection rate. An experiment involving experienced programmers found that on average they were able to find 5 errors (9 at best) out of 15 errors by testing.

80% of the errors tend to be concentrated in 20% of the project's classes and routines. 50% of the errors are found in 5% of the project's classes. IBM was able to reduce the customer reported defects by a factor of ten to one and to reduce their maintenance budget by 45% in its IMS system by repairing or rewriting only 31 out of 425 classes. Around 20% of a project's routines contribute to 80% of the development costs. A classic study by IBM found that few error-prone routines of OS/360 were the most expensive entities. They had around 50 defects per 1000 lines of code and fixing them costs 10 times what it took to develop the whole system.

Integration

A key activity during construction is the integration of separately constructed routines, classes, components, and subsystems. In addition, a particular software system may need to be integrated with other software or hardware systems. Concerns related to construction integration include planning the sequence in which components will be integrated, creating scaffolding to support interim versions of the software, determining the degree of testing and quality work performed on components before they are integrated, and determining points in the project at which interim versions of the software are tested.

Construction Technologies

Object-Oriented Runtime Issues

Object-oriented languages support a series of runtime mechanisms that increase the flexibility and adaptability of the programs like data abstraction, encapsulation, modularity, inheritance, polymorphism, and reflection.

Data abstraction is the process by which data and programs are defined with a representation similar in form to its meaning, while hiding away the implementation details. Academic research showed that data abstraction makes programs about 30% easier to understand than functional programs.

Assertions, Design by Contract, and Defensive Programming

Assertions are executable predicates which are placed in a program that allow runtime checks of the program. Design by contract is a development approach in which preconditions and postconditions are included for each routine. Defensive programming is the protection a routine from being broken by invalid inputs.

Error Handling, Exception Handling, and Fault Tolerance

Error handling refers to the programming practice of anticipating and coding for error conditions that may arise when the program runs. Exception handling is a programming language construct or hardware mechanism designed to handle the occurrence of exceptions, special conditions that change the normal flow of program execution. Fault tolerance is a collection of techniques that increase software reliability by detecting errors and then recovering from them if possible or containing their effects if recovery is not possible.

State-Based and Table-Driven Construction Techniques

State-based programming is a programming technology using finite state machines to describe program behaviors. A table-driven method is a schema that uses tables to look up information rather than using logic statements (such as if and case).

Runtime Configuration and Internationalization

Runtime configuration is a technique that binds variable values and program settings when the program is running, usually by updating and reading configuration files in a just-in-time mode. Internationalization is the technical activity of preparing a program, usually interactive software, to support multiple locales. The corresponding activity, localization, is the activity of modifying a program to support a specific local language.

Software Design

Software design is the process by which an agent creates a specification of a software artifact, intended to accomplish goals, using a set of primitive components and subject to constraints. Software design may refer to either "all the activity involved in conceptualizing, framing, implementing, commissioning, and ultimately modifying complex systems" or "the activity following requirements specification and before programming, as ... [in] a stylized software engineering process."

Software design usually involves problem solving and planning a software solution. This includes both a low-level component and algorithm design and a high-level, architecture design.

Overview

Software design is the process of implementing software solutions to one or more sets of problems. One of the main components of software design is the software requirements analysis (SRA). SRA is a part of the software development process that lists specifications used in software engineering. If the software is "semi-automated" or user centered, software design may involve user experience design yielding a storyboard to help determine those specifications. If the software is completely automated (meaning no user or user interface), a software design may be as simple as a flow chart or text describing a planned sequence of events. There are also semi-standard methods like Unified Modeling Language and Fundamental modeling concepts. In either case, some documentation of the plan is usually the product of the design. Furthermore, a software design may be platform-independent or platform-specific, depending upon the availability of the technology used for the design.

The main difference between software analysis and design is that the output of a software analysis consists of smaller problems to solve. Additionally, the analysis should not be designed very differently across different team members or groups. In contrast, the design focuses on capabilities, and thus multiple designs for the same problem can and will exist. Depending on the environment, the design often varies, whether it is created from reliable frameworks or implemented with suitable design patterns. Design examples include operation systems, webpages, mobile devices or even the new cloud computing paradigm.

Software design is both a process and a model. The design process is a sequence of steps that enables the designer to describe all aspects of the software for building. Creative skill, past experience, a sense of what makes "good" software, and an overall commitment to quality are examples of critical success factors for a competent design. It is important to note, however, that the design process is not always a straightforward procedure; the design model can be compared to an architect's plans for a house. It begins by representing the totality of the thing that is to be built (e.g., a three-dimensional rendering of the house); slowly, the thing is refined to provide guidance for constructing each detail (e.g., the plumbing layout). Similarly, the design model that is created for software provides a variety of different views of the computer software. Basic design principles enable the software engineer to navigate the design process. Davis [DAV95] suggests a set of principles for software design, which have been adapted and extended in the following list:

- The design process should not suffer from "tunnel vision." A good designer should consider alternative approaches, judging each based on the requirements of the problem, the resources available to do the job.

- The design should be traceable to the analysis model. Because a single element of the design model can often be traced back to multiple requirements, it is necessary to have a means for tracking how requirements have been satisfied by the design model.

- The design should not reinvent the wheel. Systems are constructed using a set of design patterns, many of which have likely been encountered before. These patterns should always be chosen as an alternative to reinvention. Time is short and resources are limited; design time should be invested in representing truly new ideas and integrating patterns that already exist when applicable.

- The design should "minimize the intellectual distance" between the software and the problem as it exists in the real world. That is, the structure of the software design should, whenever possible, mimic the structure of the problem domain.

- The design should exhibit uniformity and integration. A design is uniform if it appears fully coherent. In order to achieve this outcome, rules of style and format should be defined for a design team before design work begins. A design is integrated if care is taken in defining interfaces between design components.

- The design should be structured to accommodate change. The design concepts discussed in the next section enable a design to achieve this principle.

- The design should be structured to degrade gently, even when aberrant data, events, or operating conditions are encountered. Well- designed software should never "bomb"; it should be designed to accommodate unusual circumstances, and if it must terminate processing, it should do so in a graceful manner.

- Design is not coding, coding is not design. Even when detailed procedural designs are created for program components, the level of abstraction of the design model is higher than the source code. The only design decisions made at the coding level should address the small implementation details that enable the procedural design to be coded.

- The design should be assessed for quality as it is being created, not after the fact. A variety of design concepts and design measures are available to assist the designer in assessing quality throughout the development process.

- The design should be reviewed to minimize conceptual (semantic) errors. There is sometimes a tendency to focus on minutiae when the design is reviewed, missing the forest for the trees. A design team should ensure that major conceptual elements of the design (omissions, ambiguity, inconsistency) have been addressed before worrying about the syntax of the design model.

Design Concepts

The design concepts provide the software designer with a foundation from which more sophisticated methods can be applied. A set of fundamental design concepts has evolved. They are as follows:

1. Abstraction - Abstraction is the process or result of generalization by reducing the information content of a concept or an observable phenomenon, typically in order to retain only information which is relevant for a particular purpose.

2. Refinement - It is the process of elaboration. A hierarchy is developed by decomposing a macroscopic statement of function in a step-wise fashion until programming language statements are reached. In each step, one or several instructions of a given program are decomposed into more detailed instructions. Abstraction and Refinement are complementary concepts.

3. Modularity - Software architecture is divided into components called modules.

4. Software Architecture - It refers to the overall structure of the software and the ways in which that structure provides conceptual integrity for a system. Good software architecture will yield a good return on investment with respect to the desired outcome of the project, e.g. in terms of performance, quality, schedule and cost.

5. Control Hierarchy - A program structure that represents the organization of a program component and implies a hierarchy of control.

6. Structural Partitioning - The program structure can be divided both horizontally and vertically. Horizontal partitions define separate branches of modular hierarchy for each major program function. Vertical partitioning suggests that control and work should be distributed top down in the program structure.

7. Data Structure - It is a representation of the logical relationship among individual elements of data.

8. Software Procedure - It focuses on the processing of each module individually.

9. Information Hiding - Modules should be specified and designed so that information contained within a module is inaccessible to other modules that have no need for such information.

In his object model, Grady Booch mentions Abstraction, Encapsulation, Modularisation, and Hierarchy as fundamental design principles. The acronym PHAME (Principles of Hierarchy, Abstraction, Modularisation, and Encapsulation) is sometimes used to refer to these four fundamental principles.

Design Considerations

There are many aspects to consider in the design of a piece of software. The importance of each consideration should reflect the goals and expectations that the software is being created to meet. Some of these aspects are:

- Compatibility - The software is able to operate with other products that are designed for interoperability with another product. For example, a piece of software may be backward-compatible with an older version of itself.

- Extensibility - New capabilities can be added to the software without major changes to the underlying architecture.

- Modularity - the resulting software comprises well defined, independent components which leads to better maintainability. The components could be then implemented and tested in isolation before being integrated to form a desired software system. This allows division of work in a software development project.

- Fault-tolerance - The software is resistant to and able to recover from component failure.

- Maintainability - A measure of how easily bug fixes or functional modifications can be accomplished. High maintainability can be the product of modularity and extensibility.

- Reliability (Software durability) - The software is able to perform a required function under stated conditions for a specified period of time.

- Reusability - The ability to use some or all of the aspects of the preexisting software in other projects with little to no modification.

- Robustness - The software is able to operate under stress or tolerate unpredictable or invalid input. For example, it can be designed with a resilience to low memory conditions.

- Security - The software is able to withstand and resist hostile acts and influences.

- Usability - The software user interface must be usable for its target user/audience. Default values for the parameters must be chosen so that they are a good choice for the majority of the users.

- Performance - The software performs its tasks within a time-frame that is acceptable for the user, and does not require too much memory.

- Portability - The software should be usable across a number of different conditions and environments.

- Scalability - The software adapts well to increasing data or number of users.

Modeling Language

A modeling language is any artificial language that can be used to express information, knowledge or systems in a structure that is defined by a consistent set of rules. These rules are used for interpretation of the components within the structure. A modeling language can be graphical or textual. Examples of graphical modeling languages for software design are:

- Architecture description language (ADL) is a language used to describe and represent the software architecture of a software system.

- Business Process Modeling Notation (BPMN) is an example of a Process Modeling language.

- EXPRESS and EXPRESS-G (ISO 10303-11) is an international standard general-purpose data modeling language.

- Extended Enterprise Modeling Language (EEML) is commonly used for business process modeling across a number of layers.

- Flowchart is a schematic representation of an algorithm or step-wise process.

- Fundamental Modeling Concepts (FMC) is modeling language for software-intensive systems.

- IDEF is a family of modeling languages, the most notable of which include IDEF0 for functional modeling, IDEF1X for information modeling, and IDEF5 for modeling ontologies.

- Jackson Structured Programming (JSP) is a method for structured programming based on correspondences between data stream structure and program structure.

- LePUS3 is an object-oriented visual Design Description Language and a formal specification language that is suitable primarily for modeling large object-oriented (Java, C++, C#) programs and design patterns.

- Unified Modeling Language (UML) is a general modeling language to describe software both structurally and behaviorally. It has a graphical notation and allows for extension with a Profile (UML).

- Alloy (specification language) is a general purpose specification language for expressing complex structural constraints and behavior in a software system. It provides a concise language base on first-order relational logic.

- Systems Modeling Language (SysML) is a new general-purpose modeling language for systems engineering.

- Service-oriented modeling framework (SOMF)

Design Patterns

A software designer or architect may identify a design problem which has been visited and perhaps even solved by others in the past. A template or pattern describing a solution to a common problem is known as a design pattern. The reuse of such patterns can help speed up the software development process.

Technique

The difficulty of using the term "design" in relation to software is that in some senses, the source code of a program *is* the design for the program that it produces. To the extent that this is true, "software design" refers to the design of the design. Edsger W. Dijkstra referred to this layering of semantic levels as the "radical novelty" of computer programming, and Donald Knuth used his experience writing TeX to describe the futility of attempting to design a program prior to implementing it:

TEX would have been a complete failure if I had merely specified it and not participated fully in its initial implementation. The process of implementation constantly led me to unanticipated questions and to new insights about how the original specifications could be improved.

Usage

Software design documentation may be reviewed or presented to allow constraints, specifications and even requirements to be adjusted prior to computer programming. Redesign may occur after review of a programmed simulation or prototype. It is possible to design software in the process of programming, without a plan or requirement analysis, but for more complex projects this would not be considered feasible. A separate design prior to programming allows for multidisciplinary designers and Subject Matter Experts (SMEs) to collaborate with highly skilled programmers for software that is both useful and technically sound.

Software Development Process

In software engineering, a software development methodology (also known as a system development methodology, software development life cycle, software development process, software process) is a splitting of software development work into distinct phases (or stages) containing activities with the intent of better planning and management. It is often considered a subset of the systems development life cycle. The methodology may include the pre-definition of specific deliverables and artifacts that are created and completed by a project team to develop or maintain an application.

Common methodologies include waterfall, prototyping, iterative and incremental development, spiral development, rapid application development, extreme programming and various types of agile methodology. Some people consider a life-cycle "model" a more general term for a category of methodologies and a software development "process" a more specific term to refer to a specific process chosen by a specific organization. For example, there are many specific software development processes that fit the spiral life-cycle model.

In Practice

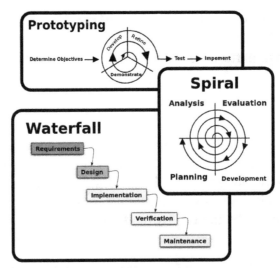

The three basic approaches applied to software development methodology frameworks.

A variety of such frameworks have evolved over the years, each with its own recognized strengths and weaknesses. One software development methodology framework is not necessarily suitable for use by all projects. Each of the available methodology frameworks are best suited to specific kinds of projects, based on various technical, organizational, project and team considerations.

Software development organizations implement process methodologies to ease the process of development. Sometimes, contractors may require methodologies employed, an example is the U.S. defense industry, which requires a rating based on process models to obtain contracts. The international standard for describing the method of selecting, implementing and monitoring the life cycle for software is ISO/IEC 12207.

A decades-long goal has been to find repeatable, predictable processes that improve productivity and quality. Some try to systematize or formalize the seemingly unruly task of designing software. Others apply project management techniques to designing software. Large numbers of software projects do not meet their expectations in terms of functionality, cost, or delivery schedule.

Organizations may create a Software Engineering Process Group (SEPG), which is the focal point for process improvement. Composed of line practitioners who have varied skills, the group is at the center of the collaborative effort of everyone in the organization who is involved with software engineering process improvement.

A particular development team may also agree to programming environment details, such as which integrated development environment is used, and one or more dominant programming paradigms, programming style rules, or choice of specific software libraries or software frameworks. These details are generally not dictated by the choice of model or general methodology.

History

The software development methodology (also known as SDM) framework didn't emerge until the 1960s. According to Elliott (2004) the systems development life cycle (SDLC) can be considered to be the oldest formalized methodology framework for building information systems. The main idea of the SDLC has been "to pursue the development of information systems in a very deliberate, structured and methodical way, requiring each stage of the life cycle––from inception of the idea to delivery of the final system––to be carried out rigidly and sequentially" within the context of the framework being applied. The main target of this methodology framework in the 1960s was "to develop large scale functional business systems in an age of large scale business conglomerates. Information systems activities revolved around heavy data processing and number crunching routines".

Methodologies, processes, and frameworks range from specific proscriptive steps that can be used directly by an organization in day-to-day work, to flexible frameworks that an organization uses to generate a custom set of steps tailored to the needs of a specific project or group. In some cases a "sponsor" or "maintenance" organization distributes an official set of documents that describe the process. Specific examples include:

1970s

- Structured programming since 1969
- Cap Gemini SDM, originally from PANDATA, the first English translation was published in 1974. SDM stands for System Development Methodology

1980s

- Structured systems analysis and design method (SSADM) from 1980 onwards
- Information Requirement Analysis/Soft systems methodology

1990s

- Object-oriented programming (OOP) developed in the early 1960s, and became a dominant programming approach during the mid-1990s
- Rapid application development (RAD), since 1991
- Dynamic systems development method (DSDM), since 1994
- Scrum, since 1995
- Team software process, since 1998
- Rational Unified Process (RUP), maintained by IBM since 1998
- Extreme programming, since 1999

2000s

- Agile Unified Process (AUP) maintained since 2005 by Scott Ambler
- Disciplined agile delivery (DAD) Supersedes AUP

2010s

- Scaled Agile Framework (SAFe)
- Large-Scale-Scrum (LeSS)

It is notable that since DSDM in 1994, 22 years ago, all of the methodologies on the above list except RUP have been agile methodologies - yet many organisations, especially governments, still struggle on with pre-agile processes (often waterfall or similar). Software process and software quality are closely interrelated; some unexpected facets and effects have been observed in practice

Since the early 2000s scaling agile delivery processes has become the biggest challenge for teams using agile processes.

Approaches

Several software development approaches have been used since the origin of information technology, in two main categories. Typically an approach or a combination of approaches is chosen by management or a development team.

"Traditional" methodologies such as waterfall that have distinct phases are sometimes known as software development life cycle (SDLC) methodologies, though this term could also be used more generally to refer to any methodology. A "life cycle" approach with distinct phases is in contrast to Agile approaches which define a process of iteration, but where design, construction, and deployment of different pieces can occur simultaneously.

Waterfall Development

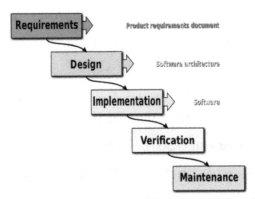

The activities of the software development process represented in the waterfall model. There are several other models to represent this process.

The waterfall model is a sequential development approach, in which development is seen as flowing steadily downwards (like a waterfall) through several phases, typically:

- Requirements analysis resulting in a software requirements specification
- Software design
- Implementation
- Testing
- Integration, if there are multiple subsystems
- Deployment (or Installation)
- Maintenance

The first formal description of the method is often cited as an article published by Winston W. Royce in 1970 although Royce did not use the term "waterfall" in this article. The basic principles are:

- Project is divided into sequential phases, with some overlap and splashback acceptable between phases.

- Emphasis is on planning, time schedules, target dates, budgets and implementation of an entire system at one time.

- Tight control is maintained over the life of the project via extensive written documentation, formal reviews, and approval/signoff by the user and information technology management occurring at the end of most phases before beginning the next phase. Written documentation is an explicit deliverable of each phase.

The waterfall model is a traditional engineering approach applied to software engineering. A strict waterfall approach discourages revisiting and revising any prior phase once it is complete. This "inflexibility" in a pure waterfall model has been a source of criticism by supporters of other more "flexible" models. It has been widely blamed for several large-scale government projects running over budget, over time and sometimes failing to deliver on requirements due to the Big Design Up Front approach. Except when contractually required, the waterfall model has been largely superseded by more flexible and versatile methodologies developed specifically for software development.

The waterfall model is sometimes taught with the mnemonic A Dance In The Dark Every Monday, representing Analysis, Design, Implementation, Testing, Documentation and Execution, and Maintenance.

Prototyping

Software prototyping is about creating prototypes, i.e. incomplete versions of the software program being developed.

The basic principles are:

- Prototyping is not a standalone, complete development methodology, but rather an approach to try out particular features in the context of a full methodology (such as incremental, spiral, or rapid application development (RAD)).

- Attempts to reduce inherent project risk by breaking a project into smaller segments and providing more ease-of-change during the development process.

- The client is involved throughout the development process, which increases the likelihood of client acceptance of the final implementation.

- While some prototypes are developed with the expectation that they will be discarded, it is possible in some cases to evolve from prototype to working system.

A basic understanding of the fundamental business problem is necessary to avoid solving the wrong problems, but this is true for all software methodologies.

Incremental Development

Various methods are acceptable for combining linear and iterative systems development methodologies, with the primary objective of each being to reduce inherent project risk by breaking a project into smaller segments and providing more ease-of-change during the development process.

There are three main variants of incremental development:

1. A series of mini-Waterfalls are performed, where all phases of the Waterfall are completed for a small part of a system, before proceeding to the next increment, or

2. Overall requirements are defined before proceeding to evolutionary, mini-Waterfall development of individual increments of a system, or

3. The initial software concept, requirements analysis, and design of architecture and system core are defined via Waterfall, followed by incremental implementation, which culminates in installing the final version, a working system.

Iterative and Incremental Development

Iterative development prescribes the construction of initially small but ever-larger portions of a software project to help all those involved to uncover important issues early before problems or faulty assumptions can lead to disaster.

Spiral Development

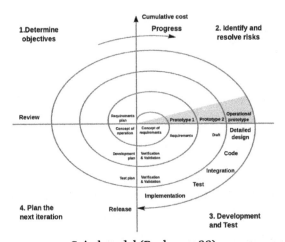

Spiral model (Boehm, 1988)

In 1988, Barry Boehm published a formal software system development "spiral model," which combines some key aspect of the waterfall model and rapid prototyping methodologies, in an effort to combine advantages of top-down and bottom-up concepts. It provided emphasis in a key area many felt had been neglected by other methodologies: deliberate iterative risk analysis, particularly suited to large-scale complex systems.

The basic principles are:

• Focus is on risk assessment and on minimizing project risk by breaking a project into smaller segments and providing more ease-of-change during the development process, as well as providing the opportunity to evaluate risks and weigh consideration of project continuation throughout the life cycle.

- "Each cycle involves a progression through the same sequence of steps, for each part of the product and for each of its levels of elaboration, from an overall concept-of-operation document down to the coding of each individual program."

- Each trip around the spiral traverses four basic quadrants: (1) determine objectives, alternatives, and constraints of the iteration; (2) evaluate alternatives; Identify and resolve risks; (3) develop and verify deliverables from the iteration; and (4) plan the next iteration.

- Begin each cycle with an identification of stakeholders and their "win conditions", and end each cycle with review and commitment.

Rapid Application Development

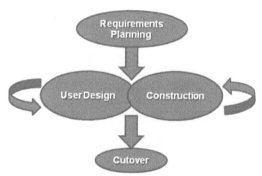

Rapid Application Development (RAD) Model

Rapid application development (RAD) is a software development methodology, which favors iterative development and the rapid construction of prototypes instead of large amounts of up-front planning. The "planning" of software developed using RAD is interleaved with writing the software itself. The lack of extensive pre-planning generally allows software to be written much faster, and makes it easier to change requirements.

The rapid development process starts with the development of preliminary data models and business process models using structured techniques. In the next stage, requirements are verified using prototyping, eventually to refine the data and process models. These stages are repeated iteratively; further development results in "a combined business requirements and technical design statement to be used for constructing new systems".

The term was first used to describe a software development process introduced by James Martin in 1991. According to Whitten (2003), it is a merger of various structured techniques, especially data-driven Information Engineering, with prototyping techniques to accelerate software systems development.

The basic principles of rapid application development are:

- Key objective is for fast development and delivery of a high quality system at a relatively low investment cost.

- Attempts to reduce inherent project risk by breaking a project into smaller segments and providing more ease-of-change during the development process.

- Aims to produce high quality systems quickly, primarily via iterative Prototyping (at any stage of development), active user involvement, and computerized development tools. These tools may include Graphical User Interface (GUI) builders, Computer Aided Software Engineering (CASE) tools, Database Management Systems (DBMS), fourth-generation programming languages, code generators, and object-oriented techniques.

- Key emphasis is on fulfilling the business need, while technological or engineering excellence is of lesser importance.

- Project control involves prioritizing development and defining delivery deadlines or "timeboxes". If the project starts to slip, emphasis is on reducing requirements to fit the timebox, not in increasing the deadline.

- Generally includes joint application design (JAD), where users are intensely involved in system design, via consensus building in either structured workshops, or electronically facilitated interaction.

- Active user involvement is imperative.

- Iteratively produces production software, as opposed to a throwaway prototype.

- Produces documentation necessary to facilitate future development and maintenance.

- Standard systems analysis and design methods can be fitted into this framework.

Agile Development

"Agile software development" refers to a group of software development methodologies based on iterative development, where requirements and solutions evolve via collaboration between self-organizing cross-functional teams. The term was coined in the year 2001 when the Agile Manifesto was formulated.

Agile software development uses iterative development as a basis but advocates a lighter and more people-centric viewpoint than traditional approaches. Agile processes fundamentally incorporate iteration and the continuous feedback that it provides to successively refine and deliver a software system.

There are many agile methodologies, including:

- Dynamic systems development method (DSDM)

- Kanban

- Scrum

Lightweight Methodologies

A lightweight methodology has a small number of rules. Some of these methodologies are also considered "agile".

- Adaptive Software Development by Jim Highsmith, described in his 1999 book *Adaptive Software Development*

- Crystal Clear family of methodologies with Alistair Cockburn,

- Extreme Programming (XP), promoted by people such as Kent Beck and Martin Fowler. In extreme programming, the phases are carried out in extremely small (or "continuous") steps compared to the older, "batch" processes. The (intentionally incomplete) first pass through the steps might take a day or a week, rather than the months or years of each complete step in the Waterfall model. First, one writes automated tests, to provide concrete goals for development. Next is coding (by programmers working in pairs, a technique known as "pair programming"), which is complete when all the tests pass, and the programmers can't think of any more tests that are needed. Design and architecture emerge from refactoring, and come after coding. The same people who do the coding do design. (Only the last feature — merging design and code — is common to *all* the other agile processes.) The incomplete but functional system is deployed or demonstrated for (some subset of) the users (at least one of which is on the development team). At this point, the practitioners start again on writing tests for the next most important part of the system.

- Feature Driven Development (FDD) developed (1999) by Jeff De Luca and Peter Coad

- ICONIX - UML-based object modeling with use cases, a lightweight precursor to the Rational Unified Process

Other

Other high-level software project methodologies include:

- Behavior-driven development and business process management

- Chaos model - The main rule is always resolve the most important issue first.

- Incremental funding methodology - an iterative approach

- Structured systems analysis and design method - a specific version of waterfall

- Slow programming, as part of the larger Slow Movement, emphasizes careful and gradual work without (or minimal) time pressures. Slow programming aims to avoid bugs and overly quick release schedules.

- V-Model (software development) - an extension of the waterfall model

- Unified Process (UP) is an iterative software development methodology framework, based on Unified Modeling Language (UML). UP organizes the development of software into four phases, each consisting of one or more executable iterations of the software at that stage of development: inception, elaboration, construction, and guidelines. Many tools and products exist to facilitate UP implementation. One of the more popular versions of UP is the Rational Unified Process (RUP).

Code and Fix

"Code and fix" is an anti-pattern. Development is not done through a deliberate strategy or methodology. It is often the result of schedule pressure on the software development team. Without much of a design in the way, programmers immediately begin producing code. At some point, testing begins (often late in the development cycle), and the unavoidable bugs must then be fixed - or at least, the most important ones must be fixed - before the product can be shipped.

Process Meta-models

Some "process models" are abstract descriptions for evaluating, comparing, and improving the specific process adopted by an organization.

- ISO/IEC 12207 is the international standard describing the method to select, implement, and monitor the life cycle for software.

- The Capability Maturity Model Integration (CMMI) is one of the leading models and based on best practice. Independent assessments grade organizations on how well they follow their defined processes, not on the quality of those processes or the software produced. CMMI has replaced CMM.

- ISO 9000 describes standards for a formally organized process to manufacture a product and the methods of managing and monitoring progress. Although the standard was originally created for the manufacturing sector, ISO 9000 standards have been applied to software development as well. Like CMMI, certification with ISO 9000 does not guarantee the quality of the end result, only that formalized business processes have been followed.

- ISO/IEC 15504 *Information technology — Process assessment* also known as Software Process Improvement Capability Determination (SPICE), is a "framework for the assessment of software processes". This standard is aimed at setting out a clear model for process comparison. SPICE is used much like CMMI. It models processes to manage, control, guide and monitor software development. This model is then used to measure what a development organization or project team actually does during software development. This information is analyzed to identify weaknesses and drive improvement. It also identifies strengths that can be continued or integrated into common practice for that organization or team.

- SPEM 2.0 by the Object Management Group

- Soft systems methodology - a general method for improving management processes

- Method engineering - a general method for improving information system processes

Formal Methods

Formal methods are mathematical approaches to solving software (and hardware) problems at the requirements, specification, and design levels. Formal methods are most likely to be applied to safety-critical or security-critical software and systems, such as avionics software. Software safety assurance standards, such as DO-178B, DO-178C, and Common Criteria demand formal methods at the highest levels of categorization.

For sequential software, examples of formal methods include the B-Method, the specification languages used in automated theorem proving, RAISE, and the Z notation.

In functional programming, property-based testing has allowed the mathematical specification and testing (if not exhaustive testing) of the expected behaviour of individual functions.

The Object Constraint Language (and specializations such as Java Modeling Language) has allowed object-oriented systems to be formally specified, if not necessarily formally verified.

For concurrent software and systems, Petri nets, process algebra, and finite state machines allow executable software specification and can be used to build up and validate application behavior.

Another approach to formal methods in software development is to write a specification in some form of logic—usually a variation of first-order logic (FOL)—and then to directly execute the logic as though it were a program. The OWL language, based on Description Logic (DL), is an example. There is also work on mapping some version of English (or another natural language) automatically to and from logic, and executing the logic directly. Examples are Attempto Controlled English, and Internet Business Logic, which do not seek to control the vocabulary or syntax. A feature of systems that support bidirectional English-logic mapping and direct execution of the logic is that they can be made to explain their results, in English, at the business or scientific level.

Software Maintenance

Software maintenance in software engineering is the modification of a software product after delivery to correct faults, to improve performance or other attributes.

A common perception of maintenance is that it merely involves fixing defects. However, one study indicated that over 80% of maintenance effort is used for non-corrective actions. This perception is perpetuated by users submitting problem reports that in reality are functionality enhancements to the system. More recent studies put the bug-fixing proportion closer to 21%.

History

Software maintenance and evolution of systems was first addressed by Meir M. Lehman in 1969. Over a period of twenty years, his research led to the formulation of Lehman's Laws (Lehman 1997). Key findings of his research include that maintenance is really evolutionary development and that maintenance decisions are aided by understanding what happens to systems (and software) over time. Lehman demonstrated that systems continue to evolve over time. As they evolve, they grow more complex unless some action such as code refactoring is taken to reduce the complexity.

In the late 1970s, a famous and widely cited survey study by Lientz and Swanson, exposed the very high fraction of life-cycle costs that were being expended on maintenance. They categorized maintenance activities into four classes:

- Adaptive – modifying the system to cope with changes in the software environment (DBMS, OS)

- Perfective – implementing new or changed user requirements which concern functional enhancements to the software

- Corrective – diagnosing and fixing errors, possibly ones found by users

- Preventive – increasing software maintainability or reliability to prevent problems in the future

The survey showed that around 75% of the maintenance effort was on the first two types, and error correction consumed about 21%. Many subsequent studies suggest a similar magnitude of the problem. Studies show that contribution of end user is crucial during the new requirement data gathering and analysis. And this is the main cause of any problem during software evolution and maintenance. So software maintenance is important because it consumes a large part of the overall lifecycle costs and also the inability to change software quickly and reliably means that business opportunities are lost.

Importance of Software Maintenance

The key software maintenance issues are both managerial and technical. Key management issues are: alignment with customer priorities, staffing, which organization does maintenance, estimating costs. Key technical issues are: limited understanding, impact analysis, testing, maintainability measurement.

Software maintenance is a very broad activity that includes error correction, enhancements of capabilities, deletion of obsolete capabilities, and optimization. Because change is inevitable, mechanisms must be developed for evaluation, controlling and making modifications.

So any work done to change the software after it is in operation is considered to be maintenance work. The purpose is to preserve the value of software over the time. The value can be enhanced by expanding the customer base, meeting additional requirements, becoming easier to use, more efficient and employing newer technology. Maintenance may span for 20 years, whereas development may be 1-2 years.

Software Maintenance Planning

An integral part of software is the maintenance one, which requires an accurate maintenance plan to be prepared during the software development. It should specify how users will request modifications or report problems. The budget should include resource and cost estimates. A new decision should be addressed for the developing of every new system feature and its quality objectives. The software maintenance, which can last for 5–6 years (or even decades) after the development process, calls for an effective plan which can address the scope of software maintenance, the tailoring of the post delivery/deployment process, the designation of who will provide maintenance, and an estimate of the life-cycle costs. The selection of proper enforcement of standards is the challenging task right from early stage of software engineering which has not got definite importance by the concerned stakeholders.

Software Maintenance Processes

This section describes the six software maintenance processes as:

1. The implementation process contains software preparation and transition activities, such as the conception and creation of the maintenance plan; the preparation for handling problems identified during development; and the follow-up on product configuration management.

2. The problem and modification analysis process, which is executed once the application has become the responsibility of the maintenance group. The maintenance programmer must analyze each request, confirm it (by reproducing the situation) and check its validity, investigate it and propose a solution, document the request and the solution proposal, and finally, obtain all the required authorizations to apply the modifications.

3. The process considering the implementation of the modification itself.

4. The process acceptance of the modification, by confirming the modified work with the individual who submitted the request in order to make sure the modification provided a solution.

5. The migration process (platform migration, for example) is exceptional, and is not part of daily maintenance tasks. If the software must be ported to another platform without any change in functionality, this process will be used and a maintenance project team is likely to be assigned to this task.

6. Finally, the last maintenance process, also an event which does not occur on a daily basis, is the retirement of a piece of software.

There are a number of processes, activities and practices that are unique to maintainers, for example:

*   Transition: a controlled and coordinated sequence of activities during which a system is transferred progressively from the developer to the maintainer;

*   Service Level Agreements (SLAs) and specialized (domain-specific) maintenance contracts negotiated by maintainers;

*   Modification Request and Problem Report Help Desk: a problem-handling process used by maintainers to prioritize, documents and route the requests they receive;

Categories of Maintenance in ISO/IEC 14764

E.B. Swanson initially identified three categories of maintenance: corrective, adaptive, and perfective. These have since been updated and ISO/IEC 14764 presents:

*   Corrective maintenance: Reactive modification of a software product performed after delivery to correct discovered problems.

*   Adaptive maintenance: Modification of a software product performed after delivery to keep a software product usable in a changed or changing environment.

- Perfective maintenance: Modification of a software product after delivery to improve performance or maintainability.

- Preventive maintenance: Modification of a software product after delivery to detect and correct latent faults in the software product before they become effective faults.

There is also a notion of pre-delivery/pre-release maintenance which is all the good things you do to lower the total cost of ownership of the software. Things like compliance with coding standards that includes software maintainability goals. The management of coupling and cohesion of the software. The attainment of software supportability goals (SAE JA1004, JA1005 and JA1006 for example). Note also that some academic institutions are carrying out research to quantify the cost to ongoing software maintenance due to the lack of resources such as design documents and system/software comprehension training and resources (multiply costs by approx. 1.5-2.0 where there is no design data available).

Maintenance Factors

Impact of key adjustment factors on maintenance (sorted in order of maximum positive impact)

Maintenance Factors	Plus Range
Maintenance specialists	35%
High staff experience	34%
Table-driven variables and data	33%
Low complexity of base code	32%
Y2K and special search engines	30%
Code restructuring tools	29%
Re-engineering tools	27%
High level programming languages	25%
Reverse engineering tools	23%
Complexity analysis tools	20%
Defect tracking tools	20%
Y2K "mass update" specialists	20%
Automated change control tools	18%
Unpaid overtime	18%
Quality measurements	16%
Formal base code inspections	15%
Regression test libraries	15%
Excellent response time	12%
Annual training of > 10 days	12%
High management experience	12%
HELP desk automation	12%
No error prone modules	10%
On-line defect reporting	10%
Productivity measurements	8%
Excellent ease of use	7%

User satisfaction measurements	5%
High team morale	5%
Sum	**503%**

Not only are error-prone modules troublesome, but many other factors can degrade performance too. For example, very complex "spaghetti code" is quite difficult to maintain safely. A very common situation which often degrades performance is lack of suitable maintenance tools, such as defect tracking software, change management software, and test library software. Below describe some of the factors and the range of impact on software maintenance.

Impact of key adjustment factors on maintenance (sorted in order of maximum negative impact)

Maintenance Factors	Minus Range
Error prone modules	-50%
Embedded variables and data	-45%
Staff inexperience	-40%
High code complexity	-30%
No Y2K of special search engines	-28%
Manual change control methods	-27%
Low level programming languages	-25%
No defect tracking tools	-24%
No Y2K "mass update" specialists	-22%
Poor ease of use	-18%
No quality measurements	-18%
No maintenance specialists	-18%
Poor response time	-16%
No code inspections	-15%
No regression test libraries	-15%
No help desk automation	-15%
No on-line defect reporting	-12%
Management inexperience	-15%
No code restructuring tools	-10%
No annual training	-10%
No reengineering tools	-10%
No reverse-engineering tools	-10%
No complexity analysis tools	-10%
No productivity measurements	-7%
Poor team morale	-6%
No user satisfaction measurements	-4%
No unpaid overtime	0%
Sum	**-500%**

Software Quality

In the context of software engineering, software quality refers to two related but distinct notions that exist wherever quality is defined in a business context:

- Software functional quality reflects how well it complies with or conforms to a given design, based on functional requirements or specifications. That attribute can also be described as the fitness for purpose of a piece of software or how it compares to competitors in the marketplace as a worthwhile product;

- Software structural quality refers to how it meets non-functional requirements that support the delivery of the functional requirements, such as robustness or maintainability, the degree to which the software was produced correctly.

Structural quality is evaluated through the analysis of the software inner structure, its source code, at the unit level, the technology level and the system level, which is in effect how its architecture adheres to sound principles of software architecture outlined in a paper on the topic by OMG. In contrast, functional quality is typically enforced and measured through software testing.

Historically, the structure, classification and terminology of attributes and metrics applicable to software quality management have been derived or extracted from the ISO 9126-3 and the subsequent ISO 25000:2005 quality model, also known as SQuaRE. Based on these models, the Consortium for IT Software Quality (CISQ) has defined five major desirable structural characteristics needed for a piece of software to provide business value: Reliability, Efficiency, Security, Maintainability and (adequate) Size.

Software quality measurement quantifies to what extent a software or system rates along each of these five dimensions. An aggregated measure of software quality can be computed through a qualitative or a quantitative scoring scheme or a mix of both and then a weighting system reflecting the priorities. This view of software quality being positioned on a linear continuum is supplemented by the analysis of "critical programming errors" that under specific circumstances can lead to catastrophic outages or performance degradations that make a given system unsuitable for use regardless of rating based on aggregated measurements. Such programming errors found at the system level represent up to 90% of production issues, whilst at the unit-level, even if far more numerous, programming errors account for less than 10% of production issues. As a consequence, code quality without the context of the whole system, as W. Edwards Deming described it, has limited value.

To view, explore, analyze, and communicate software quality measurements, concepts and techniques of information visualization provide visual, interactive means useful, in particular, if several software quality measures have to be related to each other or to components of a software or system. For example, software maps represent a specialized approach that "can express and combine information about software development, software quality, and system dynamics".

Motivation

"A science is as mature as its measurement tools," (Louis Pasteur in Ebert & Dumke, p. 91). Measuring software quality is motivated by at least two reasons:

- Risk Management: Software failure has caused more than inconvenience. Software errors have caused human fatalities. The causes have ranged from poorly designed user interfaces to direct programming errors. An example of a programming error that led to multiple deaths is discussed in Dr. Leveson's paper. This resulted in requirements for the development of some types of software, particularly and historically for software embedded in medical and other devices that regulate critical infrastructures: "[Engineers who write embedded software] see Java programs stalling for one third of a second to perform garbage collection and update the user interface, and they envision airplanes falling out of the sky.". In the United States, within the Federal Aviation Administration (FAA), the FAA Aircraft Certification Service provides software programs, policy, guidance and training, focus on software and Complex Electronic Hardware that has an effect on the airborne product (a "product" is an aircraft, an engine, or a propeller).

- Cost Management: As in any other fields of engineering, an application with good structural software quality costs less to maintain and is easier to understand and change in response to pressing business needs. Industry data demonstrate that poor application structural quality in core business applications (such as enterprise resource planning (ERP), customer relationship management (CRM) or large transaction processing systems in financial services) results in cost and schedule overruns and creates waste in the form of rework (up to 45% of development time in some organizations). Moreover, poor structural quality is strongly correlated with high-impact business disruptions due to corrupted data, application outages, security breaches, and performance problems.

However, the distinction between measuring and improving software quality in an embedded system (with emphasis on risk management) and software quality in business software (with emphasis on cost and maintainability management) is becoming somewhat irrelevant. Embedded systems now often include a user interface and their designers are as much concerned with issues affecting usability and user productivity as their counterparts who focus on business applications. The latter are in turn looking at ERP or CRM system as a corporate nervous system whose uptime and performance are vital to the well-being of the enterprise. This convergence is most visible in mobile computing: a user who accesses an ERP application on their smartphone is depending on the quality of software across all types of software layers.

Both types of software now use multi-layered technology stacks and complex architecture so software quality analysis and measurement have to be managed in a comprehensive and consistent manner, decoupled from the software's ultimate purpose or use. In both cases, engineers and management need to be able to make rational decisions based on measurement and fact-based analysis in adherence to the precept *"In God (we) trust. All others bring data"*. ((mis-)attributed to W. Edwards Deming and others).

Definitions

There are many different definitions of quality. For some it is the "capability of a software product to conform to requirements." (ISO/IEC 9001, commented by) while for others it can be synonymous with "customer value" (Highsmith, 2002) or even defect level.

The first definition of quality History remembers is from Shewhart in the beginning of 20th century: *There are two common aspects of quality: one of them has to do with the consideration of the quality of a thing as an objective reality independent of the existence of man. The other has to do with what we think, feel or sense as a result of the objective reality. In other words, there is a subjective side of quality.* (Shewhart)

Kitchenham, Pfleeger, and Garvin's Five Perspectives on Quality

Kitchenham and Pfleeger, further reporting the teachings of David Garvin, identify five different perspectives on quality:

- The transcendental perspective deals with the metaphysical aspect of quality. In this view of quality, it is "something toward which we strive as an ideal, but may never implement completely". It can hardly be defined, but is similar to what a federal judge once commented about obscenity: "I know it when I see it".

- The user perspective is concerned with the appropriateness of the product for a given context of use. Whereas the transcendental view is ethereal, the user view is more concrete, grounded in the product characteristics that meet user's needs.

- The manufacturing perspective represents quality as conformance to requirements. This aspect of quality is stressed by standards such as ISO 9001, which defines quality as "the degree to which a set of inherent characteristics fulfills requirements" (ISO/IEC 9001).

- The product perspective implies that quality can be appreciated by measuring the inherent characteristics of the product.

- The final perspective of quality is value-based. This perspective recognises that the different perspectives of quality may have different importance, or value, to various stakeholders.

Software Quality According to Deming

The problem inherent in attempts to define the quality of a product, almost any product, were stated by the master Walter A. Shewhart. The difficulty in defining quality is to translate future needs of the user into measurable characteristics, so that a product can be designed and turned out to give satisfaction at a price that the user will pay. This is not easy, and as soon as one feels fairly successful in the endeavor, he finds that the needs of the consumer have changed, competitors have moved in, etc.

— W. Edwards Deming

Software Quality According to Feigenbaum

Quality is a customer determination, not an engineer's determination, not a marketing determination, nor a general management determination. It is based on the customer's actual experience with the product or service, measured against his or her requirements -- stated or unstated, conscious or merely sensed, technically operational or entirely subjective -- and always representing a moving target in a competitive market.

Software Quality According to Juran

The word quality has multiple meanings. Two of these meanings dominate the use of the word: 1. Quality consists of those product features which meet the need of customers and thereby provide product satisfaction. 2. Quality consists of freedom from deficiencies. Nevertheless, in a handbook such as this it is convenient to standardize on a short definition of the word quality as "fitness for use".

CISQ's Quality Model

Even though "quality is a perceptual, conditional and somewhat subjective attribute and may be understood differently by different people" (as noted in the article on quality in business), software structural quality characteristics have been clearly defined by the Consortium for IT Software Quality (CISQ). Under the guidance of Bill Curtis, co-author of the Capability Maturity Model framework and CISQ's first Director; and Capers Jones, CISQ's Distinguished Advisor, CISQ has defined five major desirable characteristics of a piece of software needed to provide business value. In the House of Quality model, these are "Whats" that need to be achieved:

Reliability

> An attribute of resiliency and structural solidity. Reliability measures the level of risk and the likelihood of potential application failures. It also measures the defects injected due to modifications made to the software (its "stability" as termed by ISO). The goal for checking and monitoring Reliability is to reduce and prevent application downtime, application outages and errors that directly affect users, and enhance the image of IT and its impact on a company's business performance.

Efficiency

> The source code and software architecture attributes are the elements that ensure high performance once the application is in run-time mode. Efficiency is especially important for applications in high execution speed environments such as algorithmic or transactional processing where performance and scalability are paramount. An analysis of source code efficiency and scalability provides a clear picture of the latent business risks and the harm they can cause to customer satisfaction due to response-time degradation.

Security

> A measure of the likelihood of potential security breaches due to poor coding practices and architecture. This quantifies the risk of encountering critical vulnerabilities that damage the business.

Maintainability

> Maintainability includes the notion of adaptability, portability and transferability (from one development team to another). Measuring and monitoring maintainability is a must for mission-critical applications where change is driven by tight time-to-market schedules and where it is important for IT to remain responsive to business-driven changes. It is also essential to keep maintenance costs under control.

Size

> While not a quality attribute per se, the sizing of source code is a software characteristic

that obviously impacts maintainability. Combined with the above quality characteristics, software size can be used to assess the amount of work produced and to be done by teams, as well as their productivity through correlation with time-sheet data, and other SDLC-related metrics.

Software functional quality is defined as conformance to explicitly stated functional requirements, identified for example using Voice of the Customer analysis (part of the Design for Six Sigma toolkit and/or documented through use cases) and the level of satisfaction experienced by end-users. The latter is referred as to as usability and is concerned with how intuitive and responsive the user interface is, how easily simple and complex operations can be performed, and how useful error messages are. Typically, software testing practices and tools ensure that a piece of software behaves in compliance with the original design, planned user experience and desired testability, i.e. a piece of software's disposition to support acceptance criteria.

The dual structural/functional dimension of software quality is consistent with the model proposed in Steve McConnell's Code Complete which divides software characteristics into two pieces: internal and external quality characteristics. External quality characteristics are those parts of a product that face its users, where internal quality characteristics are those that do not.

Alternative Approaches

One of the challenges in defining quality is that "everyone feels they understand it" and other definitions of software quality could be based on extending the various descriptions of the concept of quality used in business.

Dr. Tom DeMarco has proposed that "a product's quality is a function of how much it changes the world for the better." This can be interpreted as meaning that functional quality and user satisfaction are more important than structural quality in determining software quality.

Another definition, coined by Gerald Weinberg in Quality Software Management: Systems Thinking, is "Quality is value to some person." This definition stresses that quality is inherently subjective—different people will experience the quality of the same software differently. One strength of this definition is the questions it invites software teams to consider, such as "Who are the people we want to value our software?" and "What will be valuable to them?".

Measurement

Although the concepts presented in this section are applicable to both structural and functional software quality, measurement of the latter is essentially performed through testing.

Introduction

Software quality measurement is about quantifying to what extent a system or software possesses desirable characteristics. This can be performed through qualitative or quantitative means or a mix of both. In both cases, for each desirable characteristic, there are a set of measurable attributes the existence of which in a piece of software or system tend to be correlated and associated with this characteristic. For example, an attribute associated with portability is the number of target-dependent statements in a program. More precisely, using the Quality Function Deployment approach, these measurable attributes are the "hows" that need to be enforced to enable the "whats" in the Software Quality definition above.

Relationship between software desirable characteristics (right) and measurable attributes (left).

The structure, classification and terminology of attributes and metrics applicable to software quality management have been derived or extracted from the ISO 9126-3 and the subsequent ISO/IEC 25000:2005 quality model. The main focus is on internal structural quality. Subcategories have been created to handle specific areas like business application architecture and technical characteristics such as data access and manipulation or the notion of transactions.

The dependence tree between software quality characteristics and their measurable attributes is represented in the diagram on the right, where each of the 5 characteristics that matter for the user (right) or owner of the business system depends on measurable attributes (left):

- Application Architecture Practices

- Coding Practices

- Application Complexity

- Documentation

- Portability

- Technical and Functional Volume

Correlations between programming errors and production defects unveil that basic code errors account for 92% of the total errors in the source code. These numerous code-level issues eventually count for only 10% of the defects in production. Bad software engineering practices at the architecture levels account for only 8% of total defects, but consume over half the effort spent on fixing problems, and lead to 90% of the serious reliability, security, and efficiency issues in production.

Code-based Analysis

Many of the existing software measures count structural elements of the application that result from parsing the source code for such individual instructions (Park, 1992), tokens (Halstead, 1977), control structures (McCabe, 1976), and objects (Chidamber & Kemerer, 1994).

Software quality measurement is about quantifying to what extent a system or software rates along these dimensions. The analysis can be performed using a qualitative or quantitative approach or a mix of both to provide an aggregate view [using for example weighted average(s) that reflect relative importance between the factors being measured].

This view of software quality on a linear continuum has to be supplemented by the identification of discrete Critical Programming Errors. These vulnerabilities may not fail a test case, but they are the result of bad practices that under specific circumstances can lead to catastrophic outages, performance degradations, security breaches, corrupted data, and myriad other problems (Nygard, 2007) that make a given system de facto unsuitable for use regardless of its rating based on aggregated measurements. A well-known example of vulnerability is the Common Weakness Enumeration, a repository of vulnerabilities in the source code that make applications exposed to security breaches.

The measurement of critical application characteristics involves measuring structural attributes of the application's architecture, coding, and in-line documentation, as displayed in the picture above. Thus, each characteristic is affected by attributes at numerous levels of abstraction in the application and all of which must be included calculating the characteristic's measure if it is to be a valuable predictor of quality outcomes that affect the business. The layered approach to calculating characteristic measures displayed in the figure above was first proposed by Boehm and his colleagues at TRW (Boehm, 1978) and is the approach taken in the ISO 9126 and 25000 series standards. These attributes can be measured from the parsed results of a static analysis of the application source code. Even dynamic characteristics of applications such as reliability and performance efficiency have their causal roots in the static structure of the application.

Structural quality analysis and measurement is performed through the analysis of the source code, the architecture, software framework, database schema in relationship to principles and standards that together define the conceptual and logical architecture of a system. This is distinct from the basic, local, component-level code analysis typically performed by development tools which are mostly concerned with implementation considerations and are crucial during debugging and testing activities.

Reliability

The root causes of poor reliability are found in a combination of non-compliance with good architectural and coding practices. This non-compliance can be detected by measuring the static quality attributes of an application. Assessing the static attributes underlying an application's reliability provides an estimate of the level of business risk and the likelihood of potential application failures and defects the application will experience when placed in operation.

Assessing reliability requires checks of at least the following software engineering best practices and technical attributes:

- Application Architecture Practices

- Coding Practices

- Complexity of algorithms

- Complexity of programming practices

- Compliance with Object-Oriented and Structured Programming best practices (when applicable)

- Component or pattern re-use ratio

- Dirty programming

- Error & Exception handling (for all layers - GUI, Logic & Data)

- Multi-layer design compliance

- Resource bounds management

- Software avoids patterns that will lead to unexpected behaviors

- Software manages data integrity and consistency

- Transaction complexity level

Depending on the application architecture and the third-party components used (such as external libraries or frameworks), custom checks should be defined along the lines drawn by the above list of best practices to ensure a better assessment of the reliability of the delivered software.

Efficiency

As with Reliability, the causes of performance inefficiency are often found in violations of good architectural and coding practice which can be detected by measuring the static quality attributes of an application. These static attributes predict potential operational performance bottlenecks and future scalability problems, especially for applications requiring high execution speed for handling complex algorithms or huge volumes of data.

Assessing performance efficiency requires checking at least the following software engineering best practices and technical attributes:

- Application Architecture Practices

- Appropriate interactions with expensive and/or remote resources

- Data access performance and data management

- Memory, network and disk space management

- Coding Practices

- Compliance with Object-Oriented and Structured Programming best practices (as appropriate)

- Compliance with SQL programming best practices

Security

Most security vulnerabilities result from poor coding and architectural practices such as SQL injection or cross-site scripting. These are well documented in lists maintained by CWE, and the SEI/Computer Emergency Center (CERT) at Carnegie Mellon University.

Assessing security requires at least checking the following software engineering best practices and technical attributes:

- Application Architecture Practices
- Multi-layer design compliance
- Security best practices (Input Validation, SQL Injection, Cross-Site Scripting, etc.)
- Programming Practices (code level)
- Error & Exception handling
- Security best practices (system functions access, access control to programs)

Maintainability

Maintainability includes concepts of modularity, understandability, changeability, testability, reusability, and transferability from one development team to another. These do not take the form of critical issues at the code level. Rather, poor maintainability is typically the result of thousands of minor violations with best practices in documentation, complexity avoidance strategy, and basic programming practices that make the difference between clean and easy-to-read code vs. unorganized and difficult-to-read code.

Assessing maintainability requires checking the following software engineering best practices and technical attributes:

- Application Architecture Practices
- Architecture, Programs and Code documentation embedded in source code
- Code readability
- Complexity level of transactions
- Complexity of algorithms
- Complexity of programming practices
- Compliance with Object-Oriented and Structured Programming best practices (when applicable)
- Component or pattern re-use ratio
- Controlled level of dynamic coding
- Coupling ratio
- Dirty programming

- Documentation

- Hardware, OS, middleware, software components and database independence

- Multi-layer design compliance

- Portability

- Programming Practices (code level)

- Reduced duplicate code and functions

- Source code file organization cleanliness

Maintainability is closely related to Ward Cunningham's concept of technical debt, which is an expression of the costs resulting of a lack of maintainability. Reasons for why maintainability is low can be classified as reckless vs. prudent and deliberate vs. inadvertent, and often have their origin in developers' inability, lack of time and goals, their carelessness and discrepancies in the creation cost of and benefits from documentation and, in particular, maintainable source code.

Size

Measuring software size requires that the whole source code be correctly gathered, including database structure scripts, data manipulation source code, component headers, configuration files etc. There are essentially two types of software sizes to be measured, the technical size (footprint) and the functional size:

- There are several software technical sizing methods that have been widely described. The most common technical sizing method is number of Lines of Code (#LOC) per technology, number of files, functions, classes, tables, etc., from which backfiring Function Points can be computed;

- The most common for measuring functional size is function point analysis. Function point analysis measures the size of the software deliverable from a user's perspective. Function point sizing is done based on user requirements and provides an accurate representation of both size for the developer/estimator and value (functionality to be delivered) and reflects the business functionality being delivered to the customer. The method includes the identification and weighting of user recognizable inputs, outputs and data stores. The size value is then available for use in conjunction with numerous measures to quantify and to evaluate software delivery and performance (development cost per function point; delivered defects per function point; function points per staff month.).

The function point analysis sizing standard is supported by the International Function Point Users Group (IFPUG). It can be applied early in the software development life-cycle and it is not dependent on lines of code like the somewhat inaccurate Backfiring method. The method is technology agnostic and can be used for comparative analysis across organizations and across industries.

Since the inception of Function Point Analysis, several variations have evolved and the family of functional sizing techniques has broadened to include such sizing measures as COSMIC, NESMA, Use Case Points, FP Lite, Early and Quick FPs, and most recently Story Points. However, Function

Points has a history of statistical accuracy, and has been used as a common unit of work measurement in numerous application development management (ADM) or outsourcing engagements, serving as the "currency" by which services are delivered and performance is measured.

One common limitation to the Function Point methodology is that it is a manual process and therefore it can be labor-intensive and costly in large scale initiatives such as application development or outsourcing engagements. This negative aspect of applying the methodology may be what motivated industry IT leaders to form the Consortium for IT Software Quality focused on introducing a computable metrics standard for automating the measuring of software size while the IFPUG keep promoting a manual approach as most of its activity rely on FP counters certifications.

CISQ announced the availability of its first metric standard, Automated Function Points,to the CISQ membership, in CISQ Technical. These recommendations have been developed in OMG's Request for Comment format and submitted to OMG's process for standardization.

Identifying Critical Programming Errors

Critical Programming Errors are specific architectural and/or coding bad practices that result in the highest, immediate or long term, business disruption risk.

These are quite often technology-related and depend heavily on the context, business objectives and risks. Some may consider respect for naming conventions while others – those preparing the ground for a knowledge transfer for example – will consider it as absolutely critical.

Critical Programming Errors can also be classified per CISQ Characteristics. Basic example below:

- Reliability
    - Avoid software patterns that will lead to unexpected behavior (Uninitialized variable, null pointers, etc.)
    - Methods, procedures and functions doing Insert, Update, Delete, Create Table or Select must include error management
    - Multi-thread functions should be made thread safe, for instance servlets or struts action classes must not have instance/non-final static fields
- Efficiency
    - Ensure centralization of client requests (incoming and data) to reduce network traffic
    - Avoid SQL queries that don't use an index against large tables in a loop
- Security
    - Avoid fields in servlet classes that are not final static
    - Avoid data access without including error management
    - Check control return codes and implement error handling mechanisms
    - Ensure input validation to avoid cross-site scripting flaws or SQL injections flaws

- Maintainability

    o Deep inheritance trees and nesting should be avoided to improve comprehensibility

    o Modules should be loosely coupled (fanout, intermediaries,) to avoid propagation of modifications

    o Enforce homogeneous naming conventions

Operationalized Quality Models

Newer proposals for quality models such as Squale and Quamoco propagate a direct integration of the definition of quality attributes and measurement. By breaking down quality attributes or even defining additional layers, the complex, abstract quality attributes (such as reliability or maintainability) become more manageable and measurable. Those quality models have been applied in industrial contexts but have not received widespread adoption.

Software Testing

Software testing is an investigation conducted to provide stakeholders with information about the quality of the product or service under test. Software testing can also provide an objective, independent view of the software to allow the business to appreciate and understand the risks of software implementation. Test techniques include the process of executing a program or application with the intent of finding software bugs (errors or other defects), and to verify that the software product is fit for use.

Software testing involves the execution of a software component or system component to evaluate one or more properties of interest. In general, these properties indicate the extent to which the component or system under test:

- meets the requirements that guided its design and development,

- responds correctly to all kinds of inputs,

- performs its functions within an acceptable time,

- is sufficiently usable,

- can be installed and run in its intended environments, and

- achieves the general result its stakeholders desire.

As the number of possible tests for even simple software components is practically infinite, all software testing uses some strategy to select tests that are feasible for the available time and resources. As a result, software testing typically (but not exclusively) attempts to execute a program or application with the intent of finding software bugs (errors or other defects). The job of testing is an iterative process as when one bug is fixed, it can illuminate other, deeper bugs, or can even create new ones.

Software testing can provide objective, independent information about the quality of software and risk of its failure to users and/or sponsors.

Software testing can be conducted as soon as executable software (even if partially complete) exists. The overall approach to software development often determines when and how testing is conducted. For example, in a phased process, most testing occurs after system requirements have been defined and then implemented in testable programs. In contrast, under an Agile approach, requirements, programming, and testing are often done concurrently.

Overview

Although testing can determine the correctness of software under the assumption of some specific hypotheses, testing cannot identify all the defects within software. Instead, it furnishes a *criticism* or *comparison* that compares the state and behavior of the product against oracles—principles or mechanisms by which someone might recognize a problem. These oracles may include (but are not limited to) specifications, contracts, comparable products, past versions of the same product, inferences about intended or expected purpose, user or customer expectations, relevant standards, applicable laws, or other criteria.

A primary purpose of testing is to detect software failures so that defects may be discovered and corrected. Testing cannot establish that a product functions properly under all conditions but can only establish that it does not function properly under specific conditions. The scope of software testing often includes examination of code as well as execution of that code in various environments and conditions as well as examining the aspects of code: does it do what it is supposed to do and do what it needs to do. In the current culture of software development, a testing organization may be separate from the development team. There are various roles for testing team members. Information derived from software testing may be used to correct the process by which software is developed.

Every software product has a target audience. For example, the audience for video game software is completely different from banking software. Therefore, when an organization develops or otherwise invests in a software product, it can assess whether the software product will be acceptable to its end users, its target audience, its purchasers and other stakeholders. Software testing is the process of attempting to make this assessment.

Defects and Failures

Not all software defects are caused by coding errors. One common source of expensive defects is requirement gaps, e.g., unrecognized requirements which result in errors of omission by the program designer. Requirement gaps can often be non-functional requirements such as testability, scalability, maintainability, usability, performance, and security.

Software faults occur through the following processes. A programmer makes an error (mistake), which results in a defect (fault, bug) in the software source code. If this defect is executed, in certain situations the system will produce wrong results, causing a failure. Not all defects will necessarily result in failures. For example, defects in dead code will never result in failures. A defect can turn into a failure when the environment is changed. Examples of these changes in environment include the software being run on a new computer hardware platform, alterations in source data, or interacting with different software. A single defect may result in a wide range of failure symptoms.

Input Combinations and Preconditions

A fundamental problem with software testing is that testing under *all* combinations of inputs and preconditions (initial state) is not feasible, even with a simple product. This means that the number of defects in a software product can be very large and defects that occur infrequently are difficult to find in testing. More significantly, non-functional dimensions of quality (how it is supposed to *be* versus what it is supposed to *do*)—usability, scalability, performance, compatibility, reliability—can be highly subjective; something that constitutes sufficient value to one person may be intolerable to another.

Software developers can't test everything, but they can use combinatorial test design to identify the minimum number of tests needed to get the coverage they want. Combinatorial test design enables users to get greater test coverage with fewer tests. Whether they are looking for speed or test depth, they can use combinatorial test design methods to build structured variation into their test cases. Note that "coverage", as used here, is referring to combinatorial coverage, not requirements coverage.

Economics

A study conducted by NIST in 2002 reports that software bugs cost the U.S. economy $59.5 billion annually. More than a third of this cost could be avoided if better software testing was performed.

It is commonly believed that the earlier a defect is found, the cheaper it is to fix it. The following table shows the cost of fixing the defect depending on the stage it was found. For example, if a problem in the requirements is found only post-release, then it would cost 10–100 times more to fix than if it had already been found by the requirements review. With the advent of modern continuous deployment practices and cloud-based services, the cost of re-deployment and maintenance may lessen over time.

Cost to fix a defect		Time detected				
Requirements		Architecture	Construction	System test	Post-release	
Time introduced	Requirements	1×	3×	5–10×	10×	10–100×
	Architecture	–	1×	10×	15×	25–100×
	Construction	–	–	1×	10×	10–25×

The data from which this table is extrapolated is scant. Laurent Bossavit says in his analysis:

The "smaller projects" curve turns out to be from only two teams of first-year students, a sample size so small that extrapolating to "smaller projects in general" is totally indefensible. The GTE study does not explain its data, other than to say it came from two projects, one large and one small. The paper cited for the Bell Labs "Safeguard" project specifically disclaims having collected the fine-grained data that Boehm's data points suggest. The IBM study (Fagan's paper) contains claims which seem to contradict Boehm's graph, and no numerical results which clearly correspond to his data points.

Boehm doesn't even cite a paper for the TRW data, except when writing for "Making Software" in 2010, and there he cited the original 1976 article. There exists a large study conducted at TRW at the right time for Boehm to cite it, but that paper doesn't contain the sort of data that would support Boehm's claims.

Roles

Software testing can be done by software testers. Until the 1980s, the term "software tester" was used generally, but later it was also seen as a separate profession. Regarding the periods and the different goals in software testing, different roles have been established: *manager*, *test lead*, *test analyst*, *test designer*, *tester*, *automation developer*, and *test administrator*.

History

The separation of debugging from testing was initially introduced by Glenford J. Myers in 1979. Although his attention was on breakage testing ("a successful test is one that finds a bug") it illustrated the desire of the software engineering community to separate fundamental development activities, such as debugging, from that of verification. Dave Gelperin and William C. Hetzel classified in 1988 the phases and goals in software testing in the following stages:

- Until 1956 – Debugging oriented

- 1957–1978 – Demonstration oriented

- 1979–1982 – Destruction oriented

- 1983–1987 – Evaluation oriented

- 1988–2000 – Prevention oriented

Testing Methods

Static vs. Dynamic Testing

There are many approaches available in software testing. Reviews, walkthroughs, or inspections are referred to as static testing, whereas actually executing programmed code with a given set of test cases is referred to as dynamic testing. Static testing is often implicit, as proofreading, plus when programming tools/text editors check source code structure or compilers (pre-compilers) check syntax and data flow as static program analysis. Dynamic testing takes place when the program itself is run. Dynamic testing may begin before the program is 100% complete in order to test particular sections of code and are applied to discrete functions or modules. Typical techniques for this are either using stubs/drivers or execution from a debugger environment.

Static testing involves verification, whereas dynamic testing involves validation. Together they help improve software quality. Among the techniques for static analysis, mutation testing can be used to ensure the test cases will detect errors which are introduced by mutating the source code.

The Box Approach

Software testing methods are traditionally divided into white- and black-box testing. These two approaches are used to describe the point of view that a test engineer takes when designing test cases.

White-box Testing

White-box testing (also known as clear box testing, glass box testing, transparent box testing and structural testing, by seeing the source code) tests internal structures or workings of a program, as opposed to the functionality exposed to the end-user. In white-box testing an internal perspective of the system, as well as programming skills, are used to design test cases. The tester chooses inputs to exercise paths through the code and determine the appropriate outputs. This is analogous to testing nodes in a circuit, e.g. in-circuit testing (ICT).

While white-box testing can be applied at the unit, integration and system levels of the software testing process, it is usually done at the unit level. It can test paths within a unit, paths between units during integration, and between subsystems during a system–level test. Though this method of test design can uncover many errors or problems, it might not detect unimplemented parts of the specification or missing requirements.

Techniques used in white-box testing include:

- API testing – testing of the application using public and private APIs (application programming interfaces)

- Code coverage – creating tests to satisfy some criteria of code coverage (e.g., the test designer can create tests to cause all statements in the program to be executed at least once)

- Fault injection methods – intentionally introducing faults to gauge the efficacy of testing strategies

- Mutation testing methods

- Static testing methods

Code coverage tools can evaluate the completeness of a test suite that was created with any method, including black-box testing. This allows the software team to examine parts of a system that are rarely tested and ensures that the most important function points have been tested. Code coverage as a software metric can be reported as a percentage for:

- *Function coverage*, which reports on functions executed

- *Statement coverage*, which reports on the number of lines executed to complete the test

- *Decision coverage*, which reports on whether both the True and the False branch of a given test has been executed

100% statement coverage ensures that all code paths or branches (in terms of control flow) are executed at least once. This is helpful in ensuring correct functionality, but not sufficient since the same code may process different inputs correctly or incorrectly.

Black-box Testing

Black box diagram

Black-box testing treats the software as a "black box", examining functionality without any knowledge of internal implementation, without seeing the source code. The testers are only aware of what the software is supposed to do, not how it does it. Black-box testing methods include: equivalence partitioning, boundary value analysis, all-pairs testing, state transition tables, decision table testing, fuzz testing, model-based testing, use case testing, exploratory testing and specification-based testing.

Specification-based testing aims to test the functionality of software according to the applicable requirements. This level of testing usually requires thorough test cases to be provided to the tester, who then can simply verify that for a given input, the output value (or behavior), either "is" or "is not" the same as the expected value specified in the test case. Test cases are built around specifications and requirements, i.e., what the application is supposed to do. It uses external descriptions of the software, including specifications, requirements, and designs to derive test cases. These tests can be functional or non-functional, though usually functional.

Specification-based testing may be necessary to assure correct functionality, but it is insufficient to guard against complex or high-risk situations.

One advantage of the black box technique is that no programming knowledge is required. Whatever biases the programmers may have had, the tester likely has a different set and may emphasize different areas of functionality. On the other hand, black-box testing has been said to be "like a walk in a dark labyrinth without a flashlight." Because they do not examine the source code, there are situations when a tester writes many test cases to check something that could have been tested by only one test case, or leaves some parts of the program untested.

This method of test can be applied to all levels of software testing: unit, integration, system and acceptance. It typically comprises most if not all testing at higher levels, but can also dominate unit testing as well.

Visual Testing

The aim of visual testing is to provide developers with the ability to examine what was happening at the point of software failure by presenting the data in such a way that the developer can easily find the information she or he requires, and the information is expressed clearly.

At the core of visual testing is the idea that showing someone a problem (or a test failure), rather than just describing it, greatly increases clarity and understanding. Visual testing therefore requires the recording of the entire test process – capturing everything that occurs on the test system in video format. Output videos are supplemented by real-time tester input via picture-in-a-picture webcam and audio commentary from microphones.

Visual testing provides a number of advantages. The quality of communication is increased drastically because testers can show the problem (and the events leading up to it) to the developer as opposed to just describing it and the need to replicate test failures will cease to exist in many cases. The developer will have all the evidence he or she requires of a test failure and can instead focus on the cause of the fault and how it should be fixed.

Visual testing is particularly well-suited for environments that deploy agile methods in their development of software, since agile methods require greater communication between testers and developers and collaboration within small teams.

Ad hoc testing and exploratory testing are important methodologies for checking software integrity, because they require less preparation time to implement, while the important bugs can be found quickly. In ad hoc testing, where testing takes place in an improvised, impromptu way, the ability of a test tool to visually record everything that occurs on a system becomes very important in order to document the steps taken to uncover the bug.

Visual testing is gathering recognition in customer acceptance and usability testing, because the test can be used by many individuals involved in the development process. For the customer, it becomes easy to provide detailed bug reports and feedback, and for program users, visual testing can record user actions on screen, as well as their voice and image, to provide a complete picture at the time of software failure for the developers.

Grey-box Testing

Grey-box testing (American spelling: gray-box testing) involves having knowledge of internal data structures and algorithms for purposes of designing tests, while executing those tests at the user, or black-box level. The tester is not required to have full access to the software's source code. Manipulating input data and formatting output do not qualify as grey-box, because the input and output are clearly outside of the "black box" that we are calling the system under test. This distinction is particularly important when conducting integration testing between two modules of code written by two different developers, where only the interfaces are exposed for test.

However, tests that require modifying a back-end data repository such as a database or a log file does qualify as grey-box, as the user would not normally be able to change the data repository in normal production operations. Grey-box testing may also include reverse engineering to determine, for instance, boundary values or error messages.

By knowing the underlying concepts of how the software works, the tester makes better-informed testing choices while testing the software from outside. Typically, a grey-box tester will be permitted to set up an isolated testing environment with activities such as seeding a database. The tester can observe the state of the product being tested after performing certain actions such as executing SQL statements against the database and then executing queries to ensure that the expected changes have been reflected. Grey-box testing implements intelligent test scenarios, based on limited information. This will particularly apply to data type handling, exception handling, and so on.

Testing Levels

There are generally four recognized levels of tests: unit testing, integration testing, component interface testing, and system testing. Tests are frequently grouped by where they are added in the software development process, or by the level of specificity of the test. The main levels during the development process as defined by the SWEBOK guide are unit-, integration-, and system testing that are distinguished by the test target without implying a specific process model. Other test levels are classified by the testing objective.

There are two different levels of tests from the perspective of customers: low-level testing (LLT) and high-level testing (HLT). LLT is a group of tests for different level components of software application or product. HLT is a group of tests for the whole software application or product.

Unit Testing

Unit testing, also known as component testing, refers to tests that verify the functionality of a specific section of code, usually at the function level. In an object-oriented environment, this is usually at the class level, and the minimal unit tests include the constructors and destructors.

These types of tests are usually written by developers as they work on code (white-box style), to ensure that the specific function is working as expected. One function might have multiple tests, to catch corner cases or other branches in the code. Unit testing alone cannot verify the functionality of a piece of software, but rather is used to ensure that the building blocks of the software work independently from each other.

Unit testing is a software development process that involves synchronized application of a broad spectrum of defect prevention and detection strategies in order to reduce software development risks, time, and costs. It is performed by the software developer or engineer during the construction phase of the software development lifecycle. Rather than replace traditional QA focuses, it augments it. Unit testing aims to eliminate construction errors before code is promoted to QA; this strategy is intended to increase the quality of the resulting software as well as the efficiency of the overall development and QA process.

Depending on the organization's expectations for software development, unit testing might include static code analysis, data-flow analysis, metrics analysis, peer code reviews, code coverage analysis and other software verification practices.

Integration Testing

Integration testing is any type of software testing that seeks to verify the interfaces between components against a software design. Software components may be integrated in an iterative way or all together ("big bang"). Normally the former is considered a better practice since it allows interface issues to be located more quickly and fixed.

Integration testing works to expose defects in the interfaces and interaction between integrated components (modules). Progressively larger groups of tested software components corresponding to elements of the architectural design are integrated and tested until the software works as a system.

Component Interface Testing

The practice of component interface testing can be used to check the handling of data passed between various units, or subsystem components, beyond full integration testing between those units. The data being passed can be considered as "message packets" and the range or data types can be checked, for data generated from one unit, and tested for validity before being passed into another unit. One option for interface testing is to keep a separate log file of data items being passed, often with a timestamp logged to allow analysis of thousands of cases of data passed between units for days or weeks. Tests can include checking the handling of some extreme data values while other interface variables are passed as normal values. Unusual data values in an interface can help explain unexpected performance in the next unit. Component interface testing is a variation of black-box testing, with the focus on the data values beyond just the related actions of a subsystem component.

System Testing

System testing, or end-to-end testing, tests a completely integrated system to verify that the system meets its requirements. For example, a system test might involve testing a logon interface, then creating and editing an entry, plus sending or printing results, followed by summary processing or deletion (or archiving) of entries, then logoff.

Operational Acceptance Testing

Operational Acceptance is used to conduct operational readiness (pre-release) of a product, service or system as part of a quality management system. OAT is a common type of non-functional software testing, used mainly in software development and software maintenance projects. This type of testing focuses on the operational readiness of the system to be supported, and/or to become part of the production environment. Hence, it is also known as operational readiness testing (ORT) or Operations readiness and assurance (OR&A) testing. Functional testing within OAT is limited to those tests which are required to verify the *non-functional* aspects of the system.

In addition, the software testing should ensure that the portability of the system, as well as working as expected, does not also damage or partially corrupt its operating environment or cause other processes within that environment to become inoperative.

Testing Types

TestingCup - Polish Championship in Software Testing, Katowice, May 2016

Installation Testing

An installation test assures that the system is installed correctly and working at actual customer's hardware.

Compatibility Testing

A common cause of software failure (real or perceived) is a lack of its compatibility with other application software, operating systems (or operating system versions, old or new), or target environments that differ greatly from the original (such as a terminal or GUI application intended to be run on the desktop now being required to become a web application, which must render in a web browser). For example, in the case of a lack of backward compatibility, this can occur because the programmers develop and test software only on the latest version of the target environment, which not all users may be running. This results in the unintended consequence that the latest work may not function on earlier versions of the target environment, or on older hardware that earlier versions of the target environment was capable of using. Sometimes such issues can be fixed by proactively abstracting operating system functionality into a separate program module or library.

Smoke and Sanity Testing

Sanity testing determines whether it is reasonable to proceed with further testing.

Smoke testing consists of minimal attempts to operate the software, designed to determine whether there are any basic problems that will prevent it from working at all. Such tests can be used as build verification test.

Regression Testing

Regression testing focuses on finding defects after a major code change has occurred. Specifically, it seeks to uncover software regressions, as degraded or lost features, including old bugs that have come back. Such regressions occur whenever software functionality that was previously working correctly, stops working as intended. Typically, regressions occur as an unintended consequence of program changes, when the newly developed part of the software collides with the previously existing code. Common methods of regression testing include re-running previous sets of test cases and checking whether previously fixed faults have re-emerged. The depth of testing depends on the phase in the release process and the risk of the added features. They can either be complete, for changes added late in the release or deemed to be risky, or be very shallow, consisting of positive tests on each feature, if the changes are early in the release or deemed to be of low risk. Regression testing is typically the largest test effort in commercial software development, due to checking numerous details in prior software features, and even new software can be developed while using some old test cases to test parts of the new design to ensure prior functionality is still supported.

Acceptance Testing

Acceptance testing can mean one of two things:

1. A smoke test is used as an acceptance test prior to introducing a new build to the main testing process, i.e., before integration or regression.

2. Acceptance testing performed by the customer, often in their lab environment on their own hardware, is known as user acceptance testing (UAT). Acceptance testing may be performed as part of the hand-off process between any two phases of development.

Alpha Testing

Alpha testing is simulated or actual operational testing by potential users/customers or an independent test team at the developers' site. Alpha testing is often employed for off-the-shelf software as a form of internal acceptance testing, before the software goes to beta testing.

Beta Testing

Beta testing comes after alpha testing and can be considered a form of external user acceptance testing. Versions of the software, known as beta versions, are released to a limited audience outside of the programming team known as beta testers. The software is released to groups of people so that further testing can ensure the product has few faults or bugs. Beta versions can be made available to the open public to increase the feedback field to a maximal number of future users and to deliver value earlier, for an extended or even indefinite period of time (perpetual beta).

Functional vs Non-functional Testing

Functional testing refers to activities that verify a specific action or function of the code. These are usually found in the code requirements documentation, although some development methodologies work from use cases or user stories. Functional tests tend to answer the question of "can the user do this" or "does this particular feature work."

Non-functional testing refers to aspects of the software that may not be related to a specific function or user action, such as scalability or other performance, behavior under certain constraints, or security. Testing will determine the breaking point, the point at which extremes of scalability or performance leads to unstable execution. Non-functional requirements tend to be those that reflect the quality of the product, particularly in the context of the suitability perspective of its users.

Continuous Testing

Continuous testing is the process of executing automated tests as part of the software delivery pipeline to obtain immediate feedback on the business risks associated with a software release candidate. Continuous testing includes the validation of both functional requirements and non-functional requirements; the scope of testing extends from validating bottom-up requirements or user stories to assessing the system requirements associated with overarching business goals.

Destructive Testing

Destructive testing attempts to cause the software or a sub-system to fail. It verifies that the software functions properly even when it receives invalid or unexpected inputs, thereby establishing the robustness of input validation and error-management routines. Software fault injection, in the form of fuzzing, is an example of failure testing. Various commercial non-functional testing tools are linked from the software fault injection page; there are also numerous open-source and free software tools available that perform destructive testing.

Software Performance Testing

Performance testing is generally executed to determine how a system or sub-system performs in terms of responsiveness and stability under a particular workload. It can also serve to investigate, measure, validate or verify other quality attributes of the system, such as scalability, reliability and resource usage.

Load testing is primarily concerned with testing that the system can continue to operate under a specific load, whether that be large quantities of data or a large number of users. This is generally referred to as software scalability. The related load testing activity of when performed as a non-functional activity is often referred to as *endurance testing*. *Volume testing* is a way to test software functions even when certain components (for example a file or database) increase radically in size. *Stress testing* is a way to test reliability under unexpected or rare workloads. *Stability testing* (often referred to as load or endurance testing) checks to see if the software can continuously function well in or above an acceptable period.

There is little agreement on what the specific goals of performance testing are. The terms load testing, performance testing, scalability testing, and volume testing, are often used interchangeably.

Real-time software systems have strict timing constraints. To test if timing constraints are met, real-time testing is used.

Usability Testing

Usability testing is to check if the user interface is easy to use and understand. It is concerned mainly with the use of the application.

Accessibility Testing

Accessibility testing may include compliance with standards such as:

- Americans with Disabilities Act of 1990

- Section 508 Amendment to the Rehabilitation Act of 1973

- Web Accessibility Initiative (WAI) of the World Wide Web Consortium (W3C)

Security Testing

Security testing is essential for software that processes confidential data to prevent system intrusion by hackers.

The International Organization for Standardization (ISO) defines this as a "type of testing conducted to evaluate the degree to which a test item, and associated data and information, are protected to that unauthorised persons or systems cannot use, read or modify them, and authorized persons or systems are not denied access to them."

Internationalization and Localization

The general ability of software to be internationalized and localized can be automatically tested without actual translation, by using pseudolocalization. It will verify that the application still works, even after it has been translated into a new language or adapted for a new culture (such as different currencies or time zones).

Actual translation to human languages must be tested, too. Possible localization failures include:

- Software is often localized by translating a list of strings out of context, and the translator may choose the wrong translation for an ambiguous source string.

- Technical terminology may become inconsistent if the project is translated by several people without proper coordination or if the translator is imprudent.

- Literal word-for-word translations may sound inappropriate, artificial or too technical in the target language.

- Untranslated messages in the original language may be left hard coded in the source code.

- Some messages may be created automatically at run time and the resulting string may be ungrammatical, functionally incorrect, misleading or confusing.

- Software may use a keyboard shortcut which has no function on the source language's keyboard layout, but is used for typing characters in the layout of the target language.

- Software may lack support for the character encoding of the target language.

- Fonts and font sizes which are appropriate in the source language may be inappropriate in the target language; for example, CJK characters may become unreadable if the font is too small.

- A string in the target language may be longer than the software can handle. This may make the string partly invisible to the user or cause the software to crash or malfunction.

- Software may lack proper support for reading or writing bi-directional text.

- Software may display images with text that was not localized.

- Localized operating systems may have differently named system configuration files and environment variables and different formats for date and currency.

Development Testing

Development Testing is a software development process that involves synchronized application of a broad spectrum of defect prevention and detection strategies in order to reduce software development risks, time, and costs. It is performed by the software developer or engineer during the construction phase of the software development lifecycle. Rather than replace traditional QA focuses, it augments it. Development Testing aims to eliminate construction errors before code is promoted to QA; this strategy is intended to increase the quality of the resulting software as well as the efficiency of the overall development and QA process.

Depending on the organization's expectations for software development, Development Testing might include static code analysis, data flow analysis, metrics analysis, peer code reviews, unit testing, code coverage analysis, traceability, and other software verification practices.

A/B Testing

A/B testing is basically a comparison of two outputs, generally when only one variable has changed: run a test, change one thing, run the test again, compare the results. This is more useful with more small-scale situations, but very useful in fine-tuning any program. With more complex projects, multivariant testing can be done.

Concurrent Testing

In concurrent testing, the focus is on the performance while continuously running with normal input and under normal operational conditions, as opposed to stress testing, or fuzz testing. Memory leak, as well as basic faults are easier to find with this method.

Conformance Testing or Type Testing

In software testing, conformance testing verifies that a product performs according to its specified standards. Compilers, for instance, are extensively tested to determine whether they meet the recognized standard for that language.

Testing Process

Traditional Waterfall Development Model

A common practice of software testing is that testing is performed by an independent group of testers after the functionality is developed, before it is shipped to the customer. This practice often results in the testing phase being used as a project buffer to compensate for project delays, thereby compromising the time devoted to testing.

Another practice is to start software testing at the same moment the project starts and it is a continuous process until the project finishes.

Agile or Extreme Development Model

In contrast, some emerging software disciplines such as extreme programming and the agile software development movement, adhere to a "test-driven software development" model. In this process, unit tests are written first, by the software engineers (often with pair programming in the extreme programming methodology). Of course these tests fail initially; as they are expected to. Then as code is written it passes incrementally larger portions of the test suites. The test suites are continuously updated as new failure conditions and corner cases are discovered, and they are integrated with any regression tests that are developed. Unit tests are maintained along with the rest of the software source code and generally integrated into the build process (with inherently interactive tests being relegated to a partially manual build acceptance process). The ultimate goal of this test process is to achieve continuous integration where software updates can be published to the public frequently.

This methodology increases the testing effort done by development, before reaching any formal testing team. In some other development models, most of the test execution occurs after the requirements have been defined and the coding process has been completed.

Top-down and Bottom-up

Bottom Up Testing is an approach to integrated testing where the lowest level components (modules, procedures, and functions) are tested first, then integrated and used to facilitate the testing of higher level components. After the integration testing of lower level integrated modules, the next level of modules will be formed and can be used for integration testing. The process is repeated until the components at the top of the hierarchy are tested. This approach is helpful only when all or most of the modules of the same development level are ready. This method also helps to determine the levels of software developed and makes it easier to report testing progress in the form of a percentage.

Top Down Testing is an approach to integrated testing where the top integrated modules are tested and the branch of the module is tested step by step until the end of the related module.

In both, method stubs and drivers are used to stand-in for missing components and are replaced as the levels are completed.

A Sample Testing Cycle

Although variations exist between organizations, there is a typical cycle for testing. The sample below is common among organizations employing the Waterfall development model. The same practices are commonly found in other development models, but might not be as clear or explicit.

- Requirements analysis: Testing should begin in the requirements phase of the software development life cycle. During the design phase, testers work to determine what aspects of a design are testable and with what parameters those tests work.

- Test planning: Test strategy, test plan, testbed creation. Since many activities will be carried out during testing, a plan is needed.

- Test development: Test procedures, test scenarios, test cases, test datasets, test scripts to use in testing software.

- Test execution: Testers execute the software based on the plans and test documents then report any errors found to the development team.

- Test reporting: Once testing is completed, testers generate metrics and make final reports on their test effort and whether or not the software tested is ready for release.

- Test result analysis: Or Defect Analysis, is done by the development team usually along with the client, in order to decide what defects should be assigned, fixed, rejected (i.e. found software working properly) or deferred to be dealt with later.

- Defect Retesting: Once a defect has been dealt with by the development team, it is retested by the testing team. AKA Resolution testing.

- Regression testing: It is common to have a small test program built of a subset of tests, for each integration of new, modified, or fixed software, in order to ensure that the latest delivery has not ruined anything, and that the software product as a whole is still working correctly.

- Test Closure: Once the test meets the exit criteria, the activities such as capturing the key outputs, lessons learned, results, logs, documents related to the project are archived and used as a reference for future projects.

Automated Testing

Many programming groups are relying more and more on automated testing, especially groups that use test-driven development. There are many frameworks to write tests in, and continuous integration software will run tests automatically every time code is checked into a version control system.

While automation cannot reproduce everything that a human can do (and all the ways they think of doing it), it can be very useful for regression testing. However, it does require a well-developed test suite of testing scripts in order to be truly useful.

Testing Tools

Program testing and fault detection can be aided significantly by testing tools and debuggers. Testing/debug tools include features such as:

- Program monitors, permitting full or partial monitoring of program code including:
  - Instruction set simulator, permitting complete instruction level monitoring and trace facilities
  - Hypervisor, permitting complete control of the execution of program code including:-
  - Program animation, permitting step-by-step execution and conditional breakpoint at source level or in machine code
  - Code coverage reports

- Formatted dump or symbolic debugging, tools allowing inspection of program variables on error or at chosen points

- Automated functional GUI(Graphical User Interface) testing tools are used to repeat system-level tests through the GUI

- Benchmarks, allowing run-time performance comparisons to be made

- Performance analysis (or profiling tools) that can help to highlight hot spots and resource usage

Some of these features may be incorporated into a single composite tool or an Integrated Development Environment (IDE).

Measurement in Software Testing

Quality measures include such topics as correctness, completeness, security and ISO/IEC 9126 requirements such as capability, reliability, efficiency, portability, maintainability, compatibility, and usability.

There are a number of frequently used software metrics, or measures, which are used to assist in determining the state of the software or the adequacy of the testing.

Hierarchy of Testing Difficulty

Based on the amount of test cases required to construct a complete test suite in each context (i.e. a test suite such that, if it is applied to the implementation under test, then we collect enough information to precisely determine whether the system is correct or incorrect according to some specification), a hierarchy of testing difficulty has been proposed. It includes the following testability classes:

- Class I: there exists a finite complete test suite.

- Class II: any partial distinguishing rate (i.e., any incomplete capability to distinguish correct systems from incorrect systems) can be reached with a finite test suite.

- Class III: there exists a countable complete test suite.

- Class IV: there exists a complete test suite.

- Class V: all cases.

It has been proved that each class is strictly included into the next. For instance, testing when we assume that the behavior of the implementation under test can be denoted by a deterministic finite-state machine for some known finite sets of inputs and outputs and with some known number of states belongs to Class I (and all subsequent classes). However, if the number of states is not known, then it only belongs to all classes from Class II on. If the implementation under test must be a deterministic finite-state machine failing the specification for a single trace (and its continuations), and its number of states is unknown, then it only belongs to classes from Class III on. Testing temporal machines where transitions are triggered if inputs are produced within some real-bounded interval only belongs to classes from Class IV on, whereas testing many non-deterministic systems only belongs to Class V (but not all, and some even belong to Class I). The inclusion into Class I does not require the simplicity of the assumed computation model, as some testing cases involving implementations written in any programming language, and testing implementations defined as machines depending on continuous magnitudes, have been proved to be in Class I. Other elaborated cases, such as the testing framework by Matthew Hennessy under must semantics, and temporal machines with rational timeouts, belong to Class II.

Testing Artifacts

The software testing process can produce several artifacts.

Test plan

A test plan is a document detailing the objectives, target market, internal beta team, and processes for a specific beta test. The developers are well aware what test plans will be executed and this information is made available to management and the developers. The idea is to make them more cautious when developing their code or making additional changes. Some companies have a higher-level document called a test strategy.

Traceability matrix

A traceability matrix is a table that correlates requirements or design documents to test documents. It is used to change tests when related source documents are changed, to select test cases for execution when planning for regression tests by considering requirement coverage.

Test case

A test case normally consists of a unique identifier, requirement references from a design specification, preconditions, events, a series of steps (also known as actions) to follow, input, output, expected result, and actual result. Clinically defined, a test case is an input and an expected result. This can be as terse as 'for condition x your derived result is y', although normally test cases describe in more detail the input scenario and what results might be expected. It can occasionally be a series of steps (but often steps are contained in a separate test procedure that can be exercised against multiple test cases, as a matter of economy) but with one expected result or expected outcome. The optional fields are a test case ID, test step, or order of execution number, related requirement(s), depth, test category, author, and check boxes for whether the test is automatable and has been automated. Larger test cases may also contain prerequisite states or steps, and descriptions. A test case should also contain a place for the actual result. These steps can be stored in a word processor document, spreadsheet, database, or other common repository. In a database system, you may also be able to see past test results, who generated the results, and what system configuration was used to generate those results. These past results would usually be stored in a separate table.

Test script

A test script is a procedure, or programing code that replicates user actions. Initially the term was derived from the product of work created by automated regression test tools. Test case will be a baseline to create test scripts using a tool or a program.

Test suite

The most common term for a collection of test cases is a test suite. The test suite often also contains more detailed instructions or goals for each collection of test cases. It definitely contains a section where the tester identifies the system configuration used during testing. A group of test cases may also contain prerequisite states or steps, and descriptions of the following tests.

Test fixture or test data

In most cases, multiple sets of values or data are used to test the same functionality of a particular feature. All the test values and changeable environmental components are collected in separate files and stored as test data. It is also useful to provide this data to the client and with the product or a project.

Test harness

> The software, tools, samples of data input and output, and configurations are all referred to collectively as a test harness.

Certifications

Several certification programs exist to support the professional aspirations of software testers and quality assurance specialists. No certification now offered actually requires the applicant to show their ability to test software. No certification is based on a widely accepted body of knowledge. This has led some to declare that the testing field is not ready for certification. Certification itself cannot measure an individual's productivity, their skill, or practical knowledge, and cannot guarantee their competence, or professionalism as a tester.

Software testing certification types

> *Exam-based*: Formalized exams, which need to be passed; can also be learned by self-study [e.g., for ISTQB or QAI]

> *Education-based*: Instructor-led sessions, where each course has to be passed [e.g., International Institute for Software Testing (IIST)]

Testing certifications

> ISEB offered by the Information Systems Examinations Board

> ISTQB Certified Tester, Foundation Level (CTFL) offered by the International Software Testing Qualification Board

> ISTQB Certified Tester, Advanced Level (CTAL) offered by the International Software Testing Qualification Board

> iSQI Certified Agile Tester (CAT) offered by the International Software Quality Institute

Quality assurance certifications

> CSQE offered by the American Society for Quality (ASQ)

> CQIA offered by the American Society for Quality (ASQ)

Controversy

Some of the major software testing controversies include:

What constitutes responsible software testing?

> Members of the "context-driven" school of testing believe that there are no "best practices" of testing, but rather that testing is a set of skills that allow the tester to select or invent testing practices to suit each unique situation.

Agile vs. traditional

> Should testers learn to work under conditions of uncertainty and constant change or should they aim at process "maturity"? The agile testing movement has received growing popularity since 2006 mainly in commercial circles, whereas government and military software providers use this methodology but also the traditional test-last models (e.g., in the Waterfall model).

Exploratory test vs. scripted

> Should tests be designed at the same time as they are executed or should they be designed beforehand?

Manual testing vs. automated

> Some writers believe that test automation is so expensive relative to its value that it should be used sparingly. More in particular, test-driven development states that developers should write unit-tests, as those of XUnit, before coding the functionality. The tests then can be considered as a way to capture and implement the requirements. As a general rule, the larger the system and the greater the complexity, the greater the ROI in test automation. Also, the investment in tools and expertise can be amortized over multiple projects with the right level of knowledge sharing within an organization.

Software design vs. software implementation

> Should testing be carried out only at the end or throughout the whole process?

Who watches the watchmen?

> The idea is that any form of observation is also an interaction — the act of testing can also affect that which is being tested.

Is the existence of the ISO 29119 software testing standard justified?

> Significant opposition has formed out of the ranks of the context-driven school of software testing about the ISO 29119 standard. Professional testing associations, such as The International Society for Software Testing, are driving the efforts to have the standard withdrawn.

Related Processes

Software Verification and Validation

Software testing is used in association with verification and validation:

- Verification: Have we built the software right? (i.e., does it implement the requirements).

- Validation: Have we built the right software? (i.e., do the deliverables satisfy the customer).

The terms verification and validation are commonly used interchangeably in the industry; it is also common to see these two terms incorrectly defined. According to the IEEE Standard Glossary of

Software Engineering Terminology:

> Verification is the process of evaluating a system or component to determine whether the products of a given development phase satisfy the conditions imposed at the start of that phase.

> Validation is the process of evaluating a system or component during or at the end of the development process to determine whether it satisfies specified requirements.

According to the ISO 9000 standard:

> Verification is confirmation by examination and through provision of objective evidence that specified requirements have been fulfilled.

> Validation is confirmation by examination and through provision of objective evidence that the requirements for a specific intended use or application have been fulfilled.

Software Quality Assurance (Sqa)

Software testing is a part of the software quality assurance (SQA) process. In SQA, software process specialists and auditors are concerned for the software development process rather than just the artifacts such as documentation, code and systems. They examine and change the software engineering process itself to reduce the number of faults that end up in the delivered software: the so-called "defect rate". What constitutes an "acceptable defect rate" depends on the nature of the software; A flight simulator video game would have much higher defect tolerance than software for an actual airplane. Although there are close links with SQA, testing departments often exist independently, and there may be no SQA function in some companies.

Software testing is a task intended to detect defects in software by contrasting a computer program's expected results with its actual results for a given set of inputs. By contrast, QA (quality assurance) is the implementation of policies and procedures intended to prevent defects from occurring in the first place.

Software Project Management

Software project management is the art and science of planning and leading software projects. It is a sub-discipline of project management in which software projects are planned, implemented, monitored and controlled.

History

In the 1970s and 1980s, the software industry grew very quickly, as computer companies quickly recognized the relatively low cost of software production compared to hardware production and circuitry. To manage new development efforts, companies applied the established project management methods, but project schedules slipped during test runs, especially when confusion occurred in the gray zone between the user specifications and the delivered software. To be able to avoid these problems, *software* project management methods focused on matching user requirements to delivered products, in a method known now as the waterfall model.

As the industry has matured, analysis of software project management failures has shown that the following are the most common causes:

1. Insufficient end-user involvement

2. Poor communication among customers, developers, users and project managers

3. Unrealistic or unarticulated project goals

4. Inaccurate estimates of needed resources

5. Badly defined or incomplete system requirements and specifications

6. Poor reporting of the project's status

7. Poorly managed risks

8. Use of immature technology

9. Inability to handle the project's complexity

10. Sloppy development practices

11. Stakeholder politics (e.g. absence of executive support, or politics between the customer and end-users)

12. Commercial pressures

The first five items in the list above show the difficulties articulating the needs of the client in such a way that proper resources can deliver the proper project goals. Specific software project management tools are useful and often necessary, but the true art in software project management is applying the correct method and then using tools to support the method. Without a method, tools are worthless. Since the 1960s, several proprietary software project management methods have been developed by software manufacturers for their own use, while computer consulting firms have also developed similar methods for their clients. Today software project management methods are still evolving, but the current trend leads away from the waterfall model to a more cyclic project delivery model that imitates a software development process.

Software Development Process

A software development process is concerned primarily with the production aspect of software development, as opposed to the technical aspect, such as software tools. These processes exist primarily for supporting the management of software development, and are generally skewed toward addressing business concerns. Many software development processes can be run in a similar way to general project management processes. Examples are:

- Interpersonal communication and conflict management and resolution. Active, frequent and honest communication is the most important factor in increasing the likelihood of project success and mitigating problematic projects. The development team should seek end-user involvement and encourage user input in the development process. Not having users involved can lead to misinterpretation of requirements, insensitivity to changing customer needs, and unrealistic expectations on the part of the client. Software developers, users, project managers, customers and project sponsors need to communicate regularly and frequently. The information gained from these discussions allows the project team to analyze the strengths, weaknesses, opportunities and threats (SWOT) and to act on that information to benefit from opportunities and to minimize threats. Even bad news may be good *if* it is communicated relatively early, because problems can be mitigated if they are not discovered too late. For example, casual conversation with users, team members, and other stakeholders may often surface potential problems sooner than formal meetings. All communications need to be intellectually honest and authentic, and regular, frequent, high quality criticism of development work is necessary, as long as it is provided in a calm, respectful, constructive, non-accusatory, non-angry fashion. Frequent casual communications between developers and end-users, and between project managers and clients, are necessary to keep the project relevant, useful and effective for the end-users, and within the bounds of what can be completed. Effective interpersonal communication and conflict management and resolution are the key to software project management. *No methodology or process improvement strategy can overcome serious problems in communication or mismanagement of interpersonal conflict.* Moreover, outcomes associated with such methodologies and process improvement strategies are enhanced with better communication. The communication must focus on whether the team understands the project charter and whether the team is making progress towards that goal. End-users, software developers and project managers must frequently ask the elementary, simple questions that help identify problems before they fester into near-disasters. *While end-user participation, effective communication and teamwork are not sufficient, they are necessary to ensure a good outcome, and their absence will almost surely lead to a bad outcome.*

- Risk management is the process of measuring or assessing risk and then developing strategies to manage the risk. In general, the strategies employed include transferring the risk to another party, avoiding the risk, reducing the negative effect of the risk, and accepting some or all of the consequences of a particular risk. Risk management in software project management begins with the business case for starting the project, which includes a cost-benefit analysis as well as a list of fallback options for project failure, called a contingency plan.

    o A subset of risk management is Opportunity Management, which means the same thing, except that the potential risk outcome will have a positive, rather than a negative impact. Though theoretically handled in the same way, using the term "opportunity" rather than the somewhat negative term "risk" helps to keep a team focused on possible positive outcomes of any given risk register in their projects, such as spin-off projects, windfalls, and free extra resources.

- Requirements management is the process of identifying, eliciting, documenting, analyzing, tracing, prioritizing and agreeing on requirements and then controlling change and communicating to relevant stakeholders. New or altered computer system Requirements management, which includes Requirements analysis, is an important part of the software engineering process; whereby business analysts or software developers identify the needs or requirements of a client; having identified these requirements they are then in a position to design a solution.

- Change management is the process of identifying, documenting, analyzing, prioritizing and agreeing on changes to scope (project management) and then controlling changes and communicating to relevant stakeholders. Change impact analysis of new or altered scope, which includes Requirements analysis at the change level, is an important part of the software engineering process; whereby business analysts or software developers identify the altered needs or requirements of a client; having identified these requirements they are then in a position to re-design or modify a solution. Theoretically, each change can impact the timeline and budget of a software project, and therefore by definition must include risk-benefit analysis before approval.

- Software configuration management is the process of identifying, and documenting the scope itself, which is the software product underway, including all sub-products and changes and enabling communication of these to relevant stakeholders. In general, the processes employed include version control, naming convention (programming), and software archival agreements.

- Release management is the process of identifying, documenting, prioritizing and agreeing on releases of software and then controlling the release schedule and communicating to relevant stakeholders. Most software projects have access to three software environments to which software can be released; Development, Test, and Production. In very large projects, where distributed teams need to integrate their work before releasing to users, there will often be more environments for testing, called unit testing, system testing, or integration testing, before release to User acceptance testing (UAT).

  o A subset of release management that is gaining attention is Data Management, as obviously the users can only test based on data that they know, and "real" data is only in the software environment called "production". In order to test their work, programmers must therefore also often create "dummy data" or "data stubs". Traditionally, older versions of a production system were once used for this purpose, but as companies rely more and more on outside contributors for software development, company data may not be released to development teams. In complex environments, datasets may be created that are then migrated across test environments according to a test release schedule, much like the overall software release schedule.

Project Planning, Monitoring and Control

The purpose of project planning is to identify the scope of the project, estimate the work involved, and create a project schedule. Project planning begins with requirements that define the software to be developed. The project plan is then developed to describe the tasks that will lead to completion.

The purpose of project monitoring and control is to keep the team and management up to date on the project's progress. If the project deviates from the plan, then the project manager can take action to correct the problem. Project monitoring and control involves status meetings to gather status from the team. When changes need to be made, change control is used to keep the products up to date.

Issue

In computing, the term "issue" is a unit of work to accomplish an improvement in a system. An issue could be a bug, a requested feature, task, missing documentation, and so forth.

For example, OpenOffice.org used to call their modified version of BugZilla IssueZilla. As of September 2010, they call their system Issue Tracker.

The word "issue" is also used as synonym for "problem," as in other English usage. Problems occur from time to time and fixing them in a timely fashion is essential to achieve correctness of a system and avoid delayed deliveries of products.

Severity Levels

Issues are often categorized in terms of severity levels. Different companies have different definitions of severities, but some of the most common ones are:

Critical

High

> The bug or issue affects a crucial part of a system, and must be fixed in order for it to resume normal operation.

Medium

> The bug or issue affects a minor part of a system, but has some impact on its operation. This severity level is assigned when a non-central requirement of a system is affected.

Low

> The bug or issue affects a minor part of a system, and has very little impact on its operation. This severity level is assigned when a non-central requirement of a system (and with lower importance) is affected.

Trivial (cosmetic, aesthetic)

> The system works correctly, but the appearance does not match the expected one. For example: wrong colors, too much or too little spacing between contents, incorrect font sizes, typos, etc. This is the lowest severity issue.

In many software companies, issues are often investigated by Quality Assurance Analysts when they verify a system for correctness, and then assigned to the developer(s) that are responsible for resolving them. They can also be assigned by system users during the User Acceptance Testing (UAT) phase.

Issues are commonly communicated using Issue or Defect Tracking Systems. In some other cases, emails or instant messengers are used.

Philosophy

As a subdiscipline of project management, some regard the management of software development akin to the management of manufacturing, which can be performed by someone with management skills, but no programming skills. John C. Reynolds rebuts this view, and argues that software development is entirely design work, and compares a manager who cannot program to the managing editor of a newspaper who cannot write.

Software Configuration Management

In software engineering, software configuration management (**SCM** or **S/W CM**) is the task of tracking and controlling changes in the software, part of the larger cross-disciplinary field of configuration management. SCM practices include revision control and the establishment of baselines. If something goes wrong, SCM can determine what was changed and who changed it. If a configuration is working well, SCM can determine how to replicate it across many hosts.

The acronym "SCM" is also expanded as source configuration management process and software change and configuration management. However, "configuration" is generally understood to cover changes typically made by a system administrator.

Purposes

The goals of SCM are generally:

- Configuration identification - Identifying configurations, configuration items and baselines.

- Configuration control - Implementing a controlled change process. This is usually achieved by setting up a change control board whose primary function is to approve or reject all change requests that are sent against any baseline.

- Configuration status accounting - Recording and reporting all the necessary information on the status of the development process.

- Configuration auditing - Ensuring that configurations contain all their intended parts and are sound with respect to their specifying documents, including requirements, architectural specifications and user manuals.

- Build management - Managing the process and tools used for builds.

- Process management - Ensuring adherence to the organization's development process.

- Environment management - Managing the software and hardware that host the system.

- Teamwork - Facilitate team interactions related to the process.

- Defect tracking - Making sure every defect has traceability back to the source.

With the introduction of cloud computing the purposes of SCM tools have become merged in some cases. The SCM tools themselves have become virtual appliances that can be instantiated as virtual machines and saved with state and version. The tools can model and manage cloud-based virtual resources, including virtual appliances, storage units, and software bundles. The roles and responsibilities of the actors have become merged as well with developers now being able to dynamically instantiate virtual servers and related resources.

History

The history of software configuration management (SCM) in computing can be traced back as early as the 1950s, when CM (for Configuration Management), originally for hardware development and production control, was being applied to software development. Early software had a physical footprint, such as cards, tapes, and other media. The first software configuration management was a manual operation. With the advances in language and complexity, software engineering, involving configuration management and other methods, became a major concern due to issues like schedule, budget, and quality. Practical lessons, over the years, had led to the definition, and establishment, of procedures and tools. Eventually, the tools became systems to manage software changes. Industry-wide practices were offered as solutions, either in an open or proprietary manner (such as Revision Control System). With the growing use of computers, systems emerged that handled a broader scope, including requirements management, design alternatives, quality control, and more; later tools followed the guidelines of organizations, such as the Capability Maturity Model of the Software Engineering Institute.

Software Engineering Professionalism

Software engineering professionalism is a movement to make software engineering a profession, with aspects such as degree and certification programs, professional associations, professional ethics, and government licensing. The field is a licensed discipline in Texas in the United States (Texas Board of Professional Engineers, since 2013), Engineers Australia(Course Accreditation since 2001, not Licensing), and many provinces in Canada.

History

In 1993 the IEEE and ACM began a joint effort called JCESEP, which evolved into SWECC in 1998 to explore making software engineering into a profession. The ACM pulled out of SWECC in May 1999, objecting to its support for the Texas professionalization efforts, of having state licenses for software engineers. ACM determined that the state of knowledge and practice in software engineering was too immature to warrant licensing, and that licensing would give false assurances of competence even if the body of knowledge were mature. The IEEE continued to support making software engineering a branch of traditional engineering.

In Canada the Canadian Information Processing Society established the Information Systems Professional certification process. Also, by the late 90's (1999 in British Columbia) the discipline of software engineering as a professional engineering discipline was officially created. This has caused some disputes between the provincial engineering associations and companies who call their developers software engineers, even though these developers have not been licensed by any engineering association.

In 1999, the Panel of Software Engineering was formed as part of the settlement between Engineering Canada and the Memorial University of Newfoundland over the school's use of the term "software engineering" in the name of a computer science program. Concerns were raised over inappropriate use of the name "software engineering" to describe non-engineering programs could lead to student and public confusion, and ultimately threaten public safety. The Panel issued recommendations to create a Software Engineering Accreditation Board, but the task force created to carry out the recommendations were unable to get the various stakeholders to agree to concrete proposals, resulting in separate accreditation boards.

Ethics

Software engineering ethics is a large field. In some ways it began as an unrealistic attempt to define bugs as unethical. More recently it has been defined as the application of both computer science and engineering philosophy, principles, and practices to the design and development of software systems. Due to this engineering focus and the increased use of software in mission critical and human critical systems, where failure can result in large losses of capital but more importantly lives such as the Therac-25 system, many ethical codes have been developed by a number of societies, associations and organizations. These entities, such as the ACM, IEEE, APEGBC and Institute for Certification of Computing Professionals (ICCP) have formal codes of ethics. Adherence to the code of ethics is required as a condition of membership or certification. According to the ICCP, violation of the code can result in revocation of the certificate. Also, all engineering societies require conformance to their ethical codes; violation of the code results in the revocation of the license to practice engineering in the society's jurisdiction.

These codes of ethics usually have much in common. They typically relate the need to act consistently with the client's interest, employer's interest, and most importantly the public's interest. They also outline the need to act with professionalism and to promote an ethical approach to the profession.

A Software Engineering Code of Ethics has been approved by the ACM and the IEEE-CS as the standard for teaching and practicing software engineering.

Examples of Codes of Conduct

The following are examples of codes of conduct for Professional Engineers. These 2 have been chosen because both jurisdictions have a designation for Professional Software Engineers.

- Association of Professional Engineers and Geoscientists of British Columbia (APEGBC): All members in the association's code of Ethics must ensure that government, the public can rely on BC's professional engineers and Geoscientists to act at all times with fairness, courtesy and good faith to their employers, employee and customers, and to uphold the truth, honesty and trustworthiness, and to safe guard human life and the environment. This is just one of the many ways in which BC's Professional Engineers and Professional Geoscientists maintain their competitive edge in today's global marketplace.

- Association of Professional Engineers, Geoscientists and Geophysicists of Alberta (APEG-GA): Different with British Columbia, the Alberta Government granted self governance to engineers, Geoscientists and geophysicists. All members in the APEGGA have to accept legal and ethical responsibility for the work and to hold the interest of the public and society. The APEGGA is a standards guideline of professional practice to uphold the protection of public interest for engineering, Geoscientists and geophysics in Alberta.

Opinions on Ethics

Bill Joy argued that "better software" can only enable its privileged end users, make reality more power-pointy as opposed to more humane, and ultimately run away with itself so that "the future doesn't need us." He openly questioned the goals of software engineering in this respect, asking why it isn't trying to be more ethical rather than more efficient. In his book Code and Other Laws of Cyberspace, Lawrence Lessig argues that computer code can regulate conduct in much the same way as the legal code. Lessig and Joy urge people to think about the consequences of the software being developed, not only in a functional way, but also in how it affects the public and society as a whole.

Overall, due to the youth of software engineering, many of the ethical codes and values have been borrowed from other fields, such as mechanical and civil engineering. However, there are many ethical questions that even these, much older, disciplines have not encountered. Questions about the ethical impact of internet applications, which have a global reach, have never been encountered until recently and other ethical questions are still to be encountered. This means the ethical codes for software engineering are a work in progress, that will change and update as more questions arise.

Professional Responsibilities in Developing Software

Who's responsible?

- The developers work with clients and users to define system requirements. Once the system is built if any accidents occur, such as economical harm or other, who is responsible?

- If an independent QA team does integration testing and does not discover a critical fault in the system, who is ethically responsible for damage caused by that fault?

Responsibilities for engineering and geoscience software

- Developing software is a highly risky proposition. The software development process is a complex undertaking consisting of specifying, designing, implementing, and testing. Any small mistake or fault will cause unlimited damage to society. Professional Members contribute to the success of software development projects. However, Association of Professional Engineering and Geoscience is primarily concerned with their responsibility for minimizing the risk of failure and protecting the public interest.

Licensing

The American National Society of Professional Engineers provides a model law and lobbies legislatures to adopt occupational licensing regulations. The model law requires:

1. a four-year degree from a university program accredited by the Engineering Accreditation Committee (EAC) of the Accreditation Board for Engineering and Technology (ABET),

2. an eight-hour examination on the fundamentals of engineering (FE) usually taken in the senior year of college,

3. four years of acceptable experience,

4. a second examination on principles and practice, and

5. written recommendations from other professional engineers.

Some states require continuing education.

In Texas Donald Bagert of Texas became the first professional software engineer in the U.S. on September 4, 1998 or October 9, 1998. As of May 2002, Texas had issued 44 professional engineering licenses for software engineers. Rochester Institute of Technology granted the first Software Engineering bachelor's degrees in 2001. Other universities have followed.

Professional licensing has been criticized for many reasons.

- The field of software engineering is too immature

- Licensing would give false assurances of competence even if the body of knowledge were mature

- Software engineers would have to study years of calculus, physics, and chemistry to pass the exams, which is irrelevant to most software practitioners. Many (most?) computer science majors don't earn degrees in engineering schools, so they are probably unqualified to pass engineering exams.

- In Canada, most people who earn professional software engineering licenses study software engineering, computer engineering or electrical engineering. Many times these people already qualified to become professional engineers in their own fields but choose to be licensed as software engineers to differentiate themselves from computer scientists.

- In British Columbia, The Limited Licence is granted by the Association of Professional Engineers and Geoscientists of British Columbia. Fees are collected by *APEGBC* for the Limited Licence.

Licensing and Certification Exams

Since 2002 the IEEE Computer Society offered the Certified Software Development Professional (CSDP) certification exam (in 2015 this was replaced by several similar certifications). A group of experts from industry and academia developed the exam and maintained it. Donald Bagert, and at later period Stephen Tockey headed the certification committee. Contents of the exam centered around the SWEBOK (Software Engineering Body of Knowledge) guide, with the additional emphasis on Professional Practices and Software Engineering Economics knowledge areas (KAs). The motivation was to produce a structure at an international level for software engineering's knowledge areas.

Right to Practice in Ontario

A person must be granted the "professional engineer" license to have the right to practice professional software engineering as a Professional Engineer in Ontario. To become licensed by Professional Engineers Ontario (PEO), you must:

1. Be at least 18 years of age.

2. Be a citizen or permanent resident of Canada.

3. Be of good character. You will be requested to answer questions and make a written declaration on your application form to test your ethics.

4. Meet PEO's stipulated academic requirements for licensure.

5. Pass the Professional Practice Examination.

6. Fulfill engineering work experience requirements.

However, it's good to note that many graduates of Software Engineering programs are unable to obtain the PEO license since the work they qualify for after graduation as entry-level is not related to engineering ie. working in a software company writing code or testing code would not qualify them as their work experience does not fulfill the work experience guidelines the PEO sets. Also Software Engineering programs in Ontario and other provinces involve a series of courses in electrical, electronics, and computers engineering qualifying the graduates to even work in those fields.

Right to Practice in Quebec

A person must be granted the "engineer" license to have the right to practice professional software engineering in Quebec. To become licensed by the Quebec order of engineers (in French : Ordre des ingénieurs du Québec - OIQ), you must:

1. Be at least 18 years of age.

2. Be of good character. You will be requested to answer questions and make a written declaration on your application form to test your ethics.

3. Meet OIQ's stipulated academic requirements for licensure. In this case, the academic program should be accredited by the Canadian Engineering Accreditation Board - CEAB)

4. Pass the Professional Practice Examination.

5. Fulfill engineering work experience requirements.

6. Pass the working knowledge of French exam

Software Engineering (SEng) Guidelines by Canadian Provinces

The term "engineer" in Canada is restricted to those who have graduated from a qualifying engineering programme. Some universities' "software engineering" programmes are under the engineering faculty and therefore qualify, for example the University of Waterloo. Others, such as the

University of Toronto have "software engineering" in the computer science faculty which does not qualify. This distinction has to do with the way the profession is regulated. Degrees in "Engineering" must be accredited by a national panel and have certain specific requirements to allow the graduate to pursue a career as a professional engineer. "Computer Science" degrees, even those with specialties in software engineering, do not have to meet these requirements so the computer science departments can generally teach a wider variety of topics and students can graduate without specific courses required to pursue a career as a professional engineer.

History of Software Engineering

From its beginnings in the 1960s, writing software has evolved into a profession concerned with how best to maximize the quality of software and of how to create it. Quality can refer to how maintainable software is, to its stability, speed, usability, testability, readability, size, cost, security, and number of flaws or "bugs", as well as to less measurable qualities like elegance, conciseness, and customer satisfaction, among many other attributes. How best to create high quality software is a separate and controversial problem covering software design principles, so-called "best practices" for writing code, as well as broader management issues such as optimal team size, process, how best to deliver software on time and as quickly as possible, work-place "culture", hiring practices, and so forth. All this falls under the broad rubric of software engineering.

Overview

The evolution of software engineering is notable in a number of areas:

- Emergence as a profession: By the early 1980s, software engineering professionalism, to stand beside computer science and traditional engineering.

- Role of women: Before 1970 men filling the more prestigious and better paying hardware engineering roles often delegated the writing of software to women, and legends such as Grace Hopper or Margaret Hamilton filled many computer programming jobs. Today, fewer women work in software engineering than in other professions, a situation whose cause is not clearly identified. Many academic and professional organizations consider this situation unbalanced and are trying hard to solve it.

- Processes: Processes have become a big part of software engineering and are hailed for their potential to improve software and sharply criticized for their potential to constrict programmers.

- Cost of hardware: The relative cost of software versus hardware has changed substantially over the last 50 years. When mainframes were expensive and required large support staffs, the few organizations buying them also had the resources to fund large, expensive custom software engineering projects. Computers are now much more numerous and much more powerful, which has several effects on software. The larger market can support large projects to create commercial off the shelf software, as done by companies such as Microsoft. The cheap machines allow each programmer to have a terminal capable of fairly rapid compilation. The programs in question can use techniques such as garbage collection, which make them easier and faster for the programmer to write. On the other hand, many fewer organizations are interested in employing programmers for large custom software projects, instead using commercial off the shelf software as much as possible.

1945 to 1965: The Origins

Putative origins for the term *software engineering* include a 1965 letter from ACM president Anthony Oettinger, lectures by Douglas T. Ross at MIT in the 1950s, or use by Margaret Hamilton while working on the Apollo guidance software.

The NATO Science Committee sponsored two conferences on software engineering in 1968 and 1969, which gave the field its initial boost. Many believe these conferences marked the official start of the profession of *software engineering*.

1965 to 1985: The Software Crisis

Software engineering was spurred by the so-called *software crisis* of the 1960s, 1970s, and 1980s, which identified many of the problems of software development. Many projects ran over budget and schedule. Some projects caused property damage. A few projects caused loss of life. The software crisis was originally defined in terms of productivity, but evolved to emphasize quality. Some used the term *software crisis* to refer to their inability to hire enough qualified programmers.

- Cost and Budget Overruns: The OS/360 operating system was a classic example. This decade-long project from the 1960s eventually produced one of the most complex software systems at the time. OS/360 was one of the first large (1000 programmers) software projects. Fred Brooks claims in *The Mythical Man Month* that he made a multimillion-dollar mistake of not developing a coherent architecture before starting development.

- Property Damage: Software defects can cause property damage. Poor software security allows hackers to steal identities, costing time, money, and reputations.

- Life and Death: Software defects can kill. Some embedded systems used in radiotherapy machines failed so catastrophically that they administered lethal doses of radiation to patients. The most famous of these failures is the *Therac-25* incident.

Peter G. Neumann has kept a contemporary list of software problems and disasters. The software crisis has been fading from view, because it is psychologically extremely difficult to remain in crisis mode for a protracted period (more than 20 years). Nevertheless, software – especially real-time embedded software – remains risky and is pervasive, and it is crucial not to give in to complacency. Over the last 10–15 years Michael A. Jackson has written extensively about the nature of software engineering, has identified the main source of its difficulties as lack of specialization, and has suggested that his problem frames provide the basis for a "normal practice" of software engineering, a prerequisite if software engineering is to become an engineering science.

1985 to 1989: "No Silver Bullet"

For decades, solving the software crisis was paramount to researchers and companies producing software tools. The cost of owning and maintaining software in the 1980s was twice as expensive as developing the software. • During the 1990s, the cost of ownership and maintenance increased by 30% over the 1980s. • In 1995, statistics showed that half of surveyed development projects were operational, but were not considered successful. • The average software project overshoots its schedule by half. • Three-quarters of all large software products delivered to the customer are failures that are either not used at all, or do not meet the customer's requirements.

Software Projects

Seemingly, every new technology and practice from the 1970s through the 1990s was trumpeted as a *silver bullet* to solve the software crisis. Tools, discipline, formal methods, process, and professionalism were touted as silver bullets:

- Tools: Especially emphasized were tools: structured programming, object-oriented programming, CASE tools such as ICL's CADES CASE system, Ada, documentation, and standards were touted as silver bullets.

- Discipline: Some pundits argued that the software crisis was due to the lack of discipline of programmers.

- Formal methods: Some believed that if formal engineering methodologies would be applied to software development, then production of software would become as predictable an industry as other branches of engineering. They advocated proving all programs correct.

- Process: Many advocated the use of defined processes and methodologies like the Capability Maturity Model.

- Professionalism: This led to work on a code of ethics, licenses, and professionalism.

In 1986, Fred Brooks published his *No Silver Bullet* article, arguing that no individual technology or practice would ever make a 10-fold improvement in productivity within 10 years.

Debate about silver bullets raged over the following decade. Advocates for Ada, components, and processes continued arguing for years that their favorite technology would be a silver bullet. Skeptics disagreed. Eventually, almost everyone accepted that no silver bullet would ever be found. Yet, claims about *silver bullets* pop up now and again, even today.

The search for a single key to success never worked. All known technologies and practices have only made incremental improvements to productivity and quality. Yet, there are no silver bullets for any other profession, either. Others interpret *no silver bullet* as proof that software engineering has finally matured and recognized that projects succeed due to hard work.

However, it could also be said that there are, in fact, a range of *silver bullets* today, including lightweight methodologies, spreadsheet calculators, customized browsers, in-site search engines, database report generators, integrated design-test coding-editors with memory/differences/undo, and specialty shops that generate niche software, such as information web sites, at a fraction of the cost of totally customized web site development. Nevertheless, the field of software engineering appears too complex and diverse for a single "silver bullet" to improve most issues, and each issue accounts for only a small portion of all software problems.

1990 to 1999: Prominence of the Internet

The rise of the Internet led to very rapid growth in the demand for international information display/e-mail systems on the World Wide Web. Programmers were required to handle illustrations, maps, photographs, and other images, plus simple animation, at a rate never before seen, with few well-known methods to optimize image display/storage (such as the use of thumbnail images).

The growth of browser usage, running on the HTML language, changed the way in which information-display and retrieval was organized. The widespread network connections led to the growth and prevention of international computer viruses on MS Windows computers, and the vast proliferation of spam e-mail became a major design issue in e-mail systems, flooding communication channels and requiring semi-automated pre-screening. Keyword-search systems evolved into web-based search engines, and many software systems had to be re-designed, for international searching, depending on search engine optimization (SEO) techniques. Human natural-language translation systems were needed to attempt to translate the information flow in multiple foreign languages, with many software systems being designed for multi-language usage, based on design concepts from human translators. Typical computer-user bases went from hundreds, or thousands of users, to, often, many-millions of international users.

2000 to 2015: Lightweight Methodologies

With the expanding demand for software in many smaller organizations, the need for inexpensive software solutions led to the growth of simpler, faster methodologies that developed running software, from requirements to deployment, quicker & easier. The use of rapid-prototyping evolved to entire *lightweight methodologies*, such as Extreme Programming (XP), which attempted to simplify many areas of software engineering, including requirements gathering and reliability testing for the growing, vast number of small software systems. Very large software systems still used heavily-documented methodologies, with many volumes in the documentation set; however, smaller systems had a simpler, faster alternative approach to managing the development and maintenance of software calculations and algorithms, information storage/ retrieval and display.

Current Trends in Software Engineering

Software engineering is a young discipline, and is still developing. The directions in which software engineering is developing include:

Aspects

Aspects help software engineers deal with quality attributes by providing tools to add or remove boilerplate code from many areas in the source code. Aspects describe how all objects or functions should behave in particular circumstances. For example, aspects can add debugging, logging, or locking control into all objects of particular types. Researchers are currently working to understand how to use aspects to design general-purpose code. Related concepts include generative programming and templates.

Agile

Agile software development guides software development projects that evolve rapidly with changing expectations and competitive markets. Proponents of this method believe that heavy, document-driven processes (like TickIT, CMM and ISO 9000) are fading in importance. Some people believe that companies and agencies export many of the jobs that can be guided by heavy-weight processes. Related concepts include extreme programming, scrum, and lean software development.

Experimental

Experimental software engineering is a branch of software engineering interested in devising experiments on software, in collecting data from the experiments, and in devising laws and theories from this data. Proponents of this method advocate that the nature of software is such that we can advance the knowledge on software through experiments only.

Software Product Lines

Software product lines, aka product family engineering, is a systematic way to produce *families* of software systems, instead of creating a succession of completely individual products. This method emphasizes extensive, systematic, formal code reuse, to try to industrialize the software development process.

The Future of Software Engineering conference (FOSE), held at ICSE 2000, documented the state of the art of SE in 2000 and listed many problems to be solved over the next decade. The FOSE tracks at the ICSE 2000 and the ICSE 2007 conferences also help identify the state of the art in software engineering.

Software Engineering Today

The profession is trying to define its boundary and content. The Software Engineering Body of Knowledge SWEBOK has been tabled as an ISO standard during 2006 (ISO/IEC TR 19759).

In 2006, *Money Magazine* and *Salary.com* rated software engineering as the best job in America in terms of growth, pay, stress levels, flexibility in hours and working environment, creativity, and how easy it is to enter and advance in the field.

Prominent Figures in the History of Software Engineering

- Charles Bachman (born 1924) is particularly known for his work in the area of databases.
- Laszlo Belady (born 1928) the editor-in-chief of the IEEE Transactions on Software Engineering in the 1980s
- Fred Brooks (born 1931) best known for managing the development of OS/360.
- Peter Chen, known for the development of entity-relationship modeling.
- Edsger Dijkstra (1930–2002) developed the framework for proper programming.
- David Parnas (born 1941) developed the concept of information hiding in modular programming.

- Michael A. Jackson (born 1936) software engineering methodologist responsible for JSP method of program design; JSD method of system development (with John Cameron); and Problem Frames method for analysing and structuring software development problems.

References

- Laplante, Phillip (2007). What Every Engineer Should Know about Software Engineering. Boca Raton: CRC. ISBN 978-0-8493-7228-5. Retrieved 2011-01-21.

- Leondes (2002). intelligent systems: technology and applications. CRC Press. p. I-6. ISBN 978-0-8493-1121-5. 1.4 Computers and a First Glimpse at AI (1940s)

- Abran, Alain; Moore, James W.; Bourque, Pierre; Dupuis, Robert; Tripp, Leonard L. (2004). Guide to the Software Engineering Body of Knowledge. IEEE. ISBN 0-7695-2330-7.

- Sommerville, Ian (2008). Software Engineering (7 ed.). Pearson Education. ISBN 978-81-7758-530-8. Retrieved 10 January 2013.

- Thayer, Richard; Dorfman, Merlin (2013). Software Engineering Essentials. Volume I: The Development Process (Fourth ed.). Software Management Training Press, Carmichael, California. ISBN 978-0-9852707-0-4.

- Booch, Grady; et al. (2004). Object-Oriented Analysis and Design with Applications (3rd ed.). MA, USA: Addison Wesley. ISBN 0-201-89551-X. Retrieved 30 January 2015.

- Suryanarayana, Girish (November 2014). Refactoring for Software Design Smells. Morgan Kaufmann. p. 258. ISBN 978-0128013977. Retrieved 31 January 2015.

- Carroll, ed., John (1995). Scenario-Based Design: Envisioning Work and Technology in System Development. New York: John Wiley & Sons. ISBN 0471076597.

- Bell, Michael (2008). "Introduction to Service-Oriented Modeling". Service-Oriented Modeling: Service Analysis, Design, and Architecture. Wiley & Sons. ISBN 978-0-470-14111-3.

- Whitten, Jeffrey L.; Lonnie D. Bentley, Kevin C. Dittman. (2003). Systems Analysis and Design Methods. 6th edition. ISBN 0-256-19906-X.

- Kaner, Cem; Falk, Jack; Nguyen, Hung Quoc (1999). Testing Computer Software, 2nd Ed. New York, et al: John Wiley and Sons, Inc. p. 480. ISBN 0-471-35846-0.

- Kolawa, Adam; Huizinga, Dorota (2007). Automated Defect Prevention: Best Practices in Software Management. Wiley-IEEE Computer Society Press. pp. 41–43. ISBN 0-470-04212-5.

- Kolawa, Adam; Huizinga, Dorota (2007). Automated Defect Prevention: Best Practices in Software Management. Wiley-IEEE Computer Society Press. p. 426. ISBN 0-470-04212-5.

- Savenkov, Roman (2008). How to Become a Software Tester. Roman Savenkov Consulting. p. 159. ISBN 978-0-615-23372-7.

- Binder, Robert V. (1999). Testing Object-Oriented Systems: Objects, Patterns, and Tools. Addison-Wesley Professional. p. 45. ISBN 0-201-80938-9.

- Beizer, Boris (1990). Software Testing Techniques (Second ed.). New York: Van Nostrand Reinhold. pp. 21,430. ISBN 0-442-20672-0.

- IEEE (1990). IEEE Standard Computer Dictionary: A Compilation of IEEE Standard Computer Glossaries. New York: IEEE. ISBN 1-55937-079-3.

- Black, Rex (December 2008). Advanced Software Testing- Vol. 2: Guide to the ISTQB Advanced Certification as an Advanced Test Manager. Santa Barbara: Rocky Nook Publisher. ISBN 1-933952-36-9.

- An example is Mark Fewster, Dorothy Graham: Software Test Automation. Addison Wesley, 1999, ISBN 0-201-33140-3.

- Stellman, Andrew; Greene, Jennifer (2005). Applied Software Project Management. O'Reilly Media. ISBN 978-0-596-00948-9.

- "Software engineering ... has recently emerged as a discipline in its own right." Sommerville, Ian (1985) [1982]. Software Engineering. Addison-Wesley. ISBN 0-201-14229-5.

Diverse Aspects of Web Engineering

The essential aspects of web engineering are web container, web content development, web navigation, web usability, web application, multimedia etc. The topics discussed in the chapter are of great importance to broaden the existing knowledge on web engineering.

Web Container

A web container (also known as a servlet container; and compare "webtainer") is the component of a web server that interacts with Java servlets. A web container is responsible for managing the lifecycle of servlets, mapping a URL to a particular servlet and ensuring that the URL requester has the correct access-rights.

A web container handles requests to servlets, JavaServer Pages (JSP) files, and other types of files that include server-side code. The Web container creates servlet instances, loads and unloads servlets, creates and manages request and response objects, and performs other servlet-management tasks.

A web container implements the web component contract of the Java EE architecture, specifying a runtime environment for web components that includes security, concurrency, lifecycle management, transaction, deployment, and other services.

List of Servlet Containers

The following is a list of applications which implement the Java Servlet specification from Sun Microsystems, divided depending on whether they are directly sold or not.

Open Source Web Containers

- Apache Tomcat (formerly Jakarta Tomcat) is an open source web container available under the Apache Software License.
  - Apache Tomcat 6 and above are operable as general application container (prior versions were web containers only)
- Apache Geronimo is a full Java EE 6 implementation by Apache Software Foundation.
- Enhydra, from Lutris Technologies.
- GlassFish from Oracle (an Application Server, but includes a web container).

- JBoss Application Server (now WildFly) is a full Java EE implementation by Red Hat Inc., division JBoss.

- Jetty, from the Eclipse Foundation. Also supports SPDY and WebSocket protocols.

- Jaminid contains a higher abstraction than servlets.

- Winstone supports specification v2.5 as of 0.9, has a focus on minimal configuration and the ability to strip the container down to only what you need.

- Tiny Java Web Server (TJWS) 2.5 , small footprint, modular design.

- Virgo from Eclipse Foundation provides modular, OSGi based web containers implemented using embedded Tomcat and Jetty. Virgo is available under the Eclipse Public License.

Commercial Web Containers

- iPlanet Web Server, from Oracle.

- JBoss Enterprise Application Platform from Red Hat Inc., division JBoss is subscription-based/open-source Java EE-based application server.

- JRun, from Adobe Systems (formerly developed by Allaire Corporation).

- WebLogic Application Server, from Oracle Corporation (formerly developed by BEA Systems).

- Orion Application Server, from IronFlare.

- Resin Pro, from Caucho Technology.

- ServletExec, from New Atlanta Communications.

- IBM WebSphere Application Server.

- SAP NetWeaver.

- tc Server, from SpringSource Inc.

Web Content Development

Web content development is the process of researching, writing, gathering, organizing, and editing information for publication on websites. Website content may consist of prose, graphics, pictures, recordings, movies, or other digital assets that could be distributed by a hypertext transfer protocol server, and viewed by a web browser.

Content Developers and Web Developers

When the World Wide Web began, web developers either developed online content themselves, or modified existing documents and coded them into hypertext markup language (HTML). In time, the field of website development came to encompass many technologies, so it became difficult for website developers to maintain so many different skills. Content developers are specialized website developers who have content generation skills such as graphic design, multimedia development, professional writing, and documentation. They can integrate content into new or existing websites without using information technology skills such as script language programming and database programming.

Content developers or technical content developers can also be technical writers who produce technical documentation that helps people understand and use a product or service. This documentation includes online help, manuals, white papers, design specifications, developer guides, deployment guides, release notes, etc.

Content developers may also be search engine optimization specialists, or Internet marketing professionals. High quality, unique content is what search engines are looking for, and content development specialists, therefore, have a very important role to play in the search engine optimization process. One issue currently plaguing the world of web content development is keyword-stuffed content which are prepared solely for the purpose of manipulating a search engine. This is giving a bad name to genuine web content writing professionals. The effect is writing content designed to appeal to machines (algorithms) rather than people or community. Search engine optimization specialists commonly submit content to article directories to build their website's authority on any given topic. Most article directories allow visitors to republish submitted content with the agreement that all links are maintained. This has become a method of search engine optimization for many websites today. If written according to SEO copywriting rules, the submitted content will bring benefits to the publisher (free SEO-friendly content for a webpage) as well as to the author (a hyperlink pointing to his/her website, placed on an SEO-friendly webpage).

Overview

There are numerous methods on how to get started with web content development. However, it stands to reason that in a place (the World Wide Web) that had more than 250 million websites as of December 2010, with 21.4 million new sites launched in 2010 alone, that a website would have to either specialize in specific niche audience, have original content that stood out from its peers, or present common information in a new way, thereby making it standout among its peers.

Step one would be to determine the type of site you want to develop (and have a good understanding of why). On his eponymous web site, owner/developer John December, who describes a major focus of his site as "providing links to useful information sources, I continuously work to discover, evaluate, describe, organize, and link to online resources that can help my site visitors," offers the following first step for content development.

> "Because the content of a Web site is the substance that draws and keeps an audience, the composition of your content should follow directly from your stated Web site purpose and audience. As a first step, you can prepare a set of content features that relate to your audience's activities, interests, and concerns. For example, a site about a school science fair might list rules of the fair, the location and details about the upcoming events, statements by judges, and descriptions of past winning projects."

New Approach

Currently the web content is no longer restricted to text, but has expanded to engulf other audio visual media. This includes video clips, presentations, and a host of other interactive forms which can be picked up by the search engines. Content owners are also increasingly relying on content protection networks to check on plagiarism and achieve a greater assurance that their content remains unique and unduplicated on the web.

Web Navigation

Web navigation refers to the process of navigating a network of information resources in the World Wide Web, which is organized as hypertext or hypermedia. The user interface that is used to do so is called a web browser.

A central theme in web design is the development of a web navigation interface that maximizes usability.

A website's overall navigational scheme includes several navigational pieces such as global, local, supplemental, and contextual navigation; all of these are vital aspects of the broad topic of web navigation. Hierarchical navigation systems are vital as well since it is the primary navigation system. It allows for the user to navigate within the site using levels alone, which is often seen as restricting and requires additional navigation systems to better structure the website. The global navigation of a website, as another segment of web navigation, serves as the outline and template in order to achieve an easy maneuver for the users accessing the site, while local navigation is often used to help the users within a specific section of the site. All these navigational pieces fall under the categories of various types of web navigation, allowing for further development and for more efficient experiences upon visiting a webpage.

History

Web navigation came about with the introduction of the World Wide Web, in 1989 when Tim Burners-Lee invented it. Once the world wide web was available, web navigation increasingly became a major aspect and role in jobs and everyday lives. With one-third of the world's population now using the internet, web navigation maintains a global use in today's ever evolving international society. Web navigation is not restricted to just computers, either, as mobile phones and tablets have added avenues for access to the ever growing information on the web today. The most recent wave of technology which has affected web navigation is the introduction and growth of the smartphone. As of January 2014, 58% of American adults owned a smart phone, and that number is on the rise from previous years. Web navigation has evolved from a restricted action, to something that many people across the world now do on a daily basis.

Types of Web Navigation

The use of website navigation tools allow for a website's visitors to experience the site with the most efficiency and the least incompetence. A website navigation system is analogous to a road map which enables webpage visitors to explore and discover different areas and information contained within the website.

There are many different types of website navigation:

- Hierarchical website navigation

The structure of the website navigation is built from general to specific. This provides a clear, simple path to all the web pages from anywhere on the website.

- Global website navigation

Global website navigation shows the top level sections/pages of the website. It is available on each page and lists the main content sections/pages of the website.

- Local website navigation

Local navigation is the links within the text of a given web page, linking to other pages within the website.

Styles of Web Navigation

Web navigations vary in styles between different website as well as within a certain site. The availability of different navigational styles allows for the information in the website to be delivered easily and directly. This also differentiates between categories and the sites themselves to indicate what the vital information is and to enable the users access to more information and facts discussed within the website. Across the globe, different cultures prefer certain styles for web navigations, allowing for a more enjoyable and functional experience as navigational styles expand and differentiate. Zheng has summarized and compared some common navigation system designs from an information seeking perspective, including:

- Text links: The anchor text, link label, link text, or link title is the visible, clickable text in a hyperlink.

- Breadcrumbs: Breadcrumbs or breadcrumb trail is a navigation aid used in user interfaces. It allows users to keep track of their locations within programs or documents. The term comes from the trail of breadcrumbs left by Hansel and Gretel in the popular fairytale.

- Navigation bar: A navigation bar or (navigation system) is a section of a website or online page intended to aid visitors in travelling through the online document.

- Sitemap: A site map (or sitemap) is a list of pages of a web site accessible to crawlers or users. It can be either a document in any form used as a planning tool for Web design, or a Web page that lists the pages on a Web site, typically organized in hierarchical fashion.

- Dropdown menu: In computing with graphical user interfaces, a dropdown menu or dropdown menu or drop-down list is a user interface control GUI element ("widget" or "control"), similar to a list box, which allows the user to choose one value from a list.

- Flyout menu: In computing with graphical user interfaces, a menu that flies out (either down or to the side) when you click or hover (mouseover) some GUI element.

- Named anchor: An anchor element is called an anchor because web designers can use it to anchor a URL to some text on a web page. When users view the web page in a browser, they can click the text to activate the link and visit the page whose URL is in the link.

Design of Web Navigation

What makes Web design navigation difficult to work with is that it can be so versatile. Navigation varies in design through the presence of a few main pages in comparison to multi-level architecture. Content can also vary between logged-in users and logged-out users and more. Because navigation has so many differences between websites, there are no set guidelines or to-do lists for organizing navigation. Designing navigation is all about using good information architecture, and expressing the model or concept of information used in activities requiring explicit details of complex systems.

Future of Web Navigation

Adaptive Website Navigation

Adaptive web navigation describes the process of real-time changes in a website's navigation links and layout according to individual user preferences as they browse the site. Innovative websites are increasingly attempting to automatically personalize web sites based on a user's browsing pattern in order to find relevant information more quickly and efficiently. The usage of data analysis allows website creators to track behavior patterns of a user as they navigate a site. Adding shortcut links between two pages, rearranging list items on a page, and omitting irrelevant navigation links are all examples of adaptive changes that can be implemented in real-time. The advantage of utilizing adaptive technologies in web navigation is it reduces the time and navigational effort required for users to find information. A possible disadvantage of this is that users may get disoriented from global and local navigational changes from page to page.

Browser Integrated Web Navigation

To ensure cross-site navigational UI consistency, the navigation system can be integrated into the web browser itself. Standard sitemap navigator (standard-sitemap.org) and Sitemap Explorer are two examples that are specifically designed to provide easy access to sitemaps in a consistent and rich interaction model. Both systems feature an interactive sitemap client as a browser side panel (or other UI components), XML based sitemap files, standard commands for information seeking behaviors such as moving up/down a level, expanding/collapsing a level, searching within the structure file, etc.

Web Application

In computing, a web application or web app is a client–server software application in which the client (or user interface) runs in a web browser. Common web applications include webmail, online retail sales, online auctions, wikis, instant messaging services and many other functions.

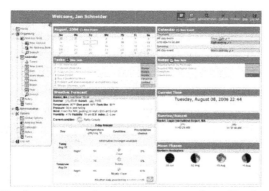

Horde groupware is an open-source web application.

Definition and Similar Terms

The general distinction between a dynamic web page of any kind and a "web application" is unclear. Web sites most likely to be referred to as "web applications" are those which have similar functionality to a desktop software application, or to a mobile app. HTML5 introduced explicit language support for making applications that are loaded as web pages, but can store data locally and continue to function while offline.

Single-page applications are more application-like because they reject the more typical web paradigm of moving between distinct pages with different URLs. Single-page frameworks like Sencha Touch and AngularJS might be used to speed development of such a web app for a mobile platform.

Mobile Web Applications

There are several ways of targeting mobile devices when making a web application:

- Responsive web design can be used to make a web application - whether a conventional web site or a single-page application viewable on small screens and work well with touch-screens.

- Native apps or "mobile apps" run directly on a mobile device, just as a conventional software application runs directly on a desktop computer, without a web browser (and potentially without the need for Internet connectivity); these are typically written in Java (for Android devices) or Objective C or Swift (for iOS devices). Recently, frameworks like React Native and Flutter allow the development of native apps for both platforms using languages other than the standard native languages.

- Hybrid apps embed a mobile web site inside a native app, possibly using a hybrid framework like Apache Cordova and Ionic or Appcelerator Titanium. This allows development using web technologies (and possibly directly copying code from an existing mobile web site) while also retaining certain advantages of native apps (e.g. direct access to device hardware, offline operation, app store visibility).

History

In earlier computing models like client–server, the processing load for the application was shared between code on the server and code installed on each client locally. In other words, an application had its own pre-compiled client program which served as its user interface and had to be separately installed on each user's personal computer. An upgrade to the server-side code of the application would typically also require an upgrade to the client-side code installed on each user workstation, adding to the support cost and decreasing productivity. In addition, both the client and server components of the application were usually tightly bound to a particular computer architecture and operating system and porting them to others was often prohibitively expensive for all but the largest applications. (Today, of course, native apps for mobile devices are also hobbled by some or all of the foregoing issues.)

In contrast, web applications use web documents written in a standard format such as HTML and JavaScript, which are supported by a variety of web browsers. Web applications can be considered as a specific variant of client–server software where the client software is downloaded to the client machine when visiting the relevant web page, using standard procedures such as HTTP. Client web software updates may happen each time the web page is visited. During the session, the web browser interprets and displays the pages, and acts as the *universal* client for any web application.

In the early days of the Web each individual web page was delivered to the client as a static document, but the sequence of pages could still provide an interactive experience, as user input was returned through web form elements embedded in the page markup. However, *every* significant change to the web page required a round trip back to the server to refresh the entire page.

In 1995 Netscape introduced a client-side scripting language called JavaScript allowing programmers to add some dynamic elements to the user interface that ran on the client side. So instead of sending data to the server in order to generate an entire web page, the embedded scripts of the downloaded page can perform various tasks such as input validation or showing/hiding parts of the page.

In 1996, Macromedia introduced Flash, a vector animation player that could be added to browsers as a plug-in to embed animations on the web pages. It allowed the use of a scripting language to program interactions on the client side with no need to communicate with the server.

In 1999, the "web application" concept was introduced in the Java language in the Servlet Specification version 2.2. [2.1?]. At that time both JavaScript and XML had already been developed, but Ajax had still not yet been coined and the XMLHttpRequest object had only been recently introduced on Internet Explorer 5 as an ActiveX object.

In 2005, the term Ajax was coined, and applications like Gmail started to make their client sides more and more interactive. A web page script is able to contact the server for storing/retrieving data without downloading an entire web page.

In 2011, HTML5 was finalized, which provides graphic and multimedia capabilities without the need of client side plug-ins. HTML5 also enriched the semantic content of documents. The APIs and document object model (DOM) are no longer afterthoughts, but are fundamental parts of the HTML5 specification. WebGL API paved the way for advanced 3D graphics based on HTML5 canvas and JavaScript language. These have significant importance in creating truly platform and browser independent rich web applications.

Interface

Through Java, JavaScript, DHTML, Flash, Silverlight and other technologies, application-specific methods such as drawing on the screen, playing audio, and access to the keyboard and mouse are all possible. Many services have worked to combine all of these into a more familiar interface that adopts the appearance of an operating system. General purpose techniques such as drag and drop are also supported by these technologies. Web developers often use client-side scripting to add functionality, especially to create an interactive experience that does not require page reloading. Recently, technologies have been developed to coordinate client-side scripting with server-side technologies such as ASP.NET, J2EE, Perl/Plack and PHP.

Ajax, a web development technique using a combination of various technologies, is an example of technology which creates a more interactive experience.

Structure

Applications are usually broken into logical chunks called "tiers", where every tier is assigned a role. Traditional applications consist only of 1 tier, which resides on the client machine, but web applications lend themselves to an n-tiered approach by nature. Though many variations are possible, the most common structure is the three-tiered application. In its most common form, the three tiers are called *presentation, application* and *storage*, in this order. A web browser is the first tier (presentation), an engine using some dynamic Web content technology (such as ASP, CGI, ColdFusion, Dart, JSP/Java, Node.js, PHP, Python or Ruby on Rails) is the middle tier (application logic), and a database is the third tier (storage). The web browser sends requests to the middle tier, which services them by making queries and updates against the database and generates a user interface.

For more complex applications, a 3-tier solution may fall short, and it may be beneficial to use an n-tiered approach, where the greatest benefit is breaking the business logic, which resides on the application tier, into a more fine-grained model. Another benefit may be adding an integration tier that separates the data tier from the rest of tiers by providing an easy-to-use interface to access the data. For example, the client data would be accessed by calling a "list_clients()" function instead of making an SQL query directly against the client table on the database. This allows the underlying database to be replaced without making any change to the other tiers.

There are some who view a web application as a two-tier architecture. This can be a "smart" client that performs all the work and queries a "dumb" server, or a "dumb" client that relies on a "smart" server. The client would handle the presentation tier, the server would have the database (storage tier), and the business logic (application tier) would be on one of them or on both. While this increases the scalability of the applications and separates the display and the database, it still doesn't allow for true specialization of layers, so most applications will outgrow this model.

Business Use

An emerging strategy for application software companies is to provide web access to software previously distributed as local applications. Depending on the type of application, it may require the development of an entirely different browser-based interface, or merely adapting an existing application to use different presentation technology. These programs allow the user to pay a monthly or yearly fee for use of a software application without having to install it on a local hard drive. A company which follows this strategy is known as an application service provider (ASP), and ASPs are currently receiving much attention in the software industry.

Security breaches on these kinds of applications are a major concern because it can involve both enterprise information and private customer data. Protecting these assets is an important part of any web application and there are some key operational areas that must be included in the development process. This includes processes for authentication, authorization, asset handling, input, and logging and auditing. Building security into the applications from the beginning can be more effective and less disruptive in the long run.

Cloud Computing model web applications are software as a service (SaaS). There are business applications provided as SaaS for enterprises for fixed or usage dependent fee. Other web applications are offered free of charge, often generating income from advertisements shown in web application interface.

Writing Web Applications

Writing a web application is often simplified by open source software such as Django, Ruby on Rails or Symfony called web application frameworks. These frameworks facilitate rapid application development by allowing a development team to focus on the parts of their application which are unique to their goals without having to resolve common development issues such as user management. While many of these frameworks are open source, this is by no means a requirement.

The use of web application frameworks can often reduce the number of errors in a program, both by making the code simpler, and by allowing one team to concentrate on the framework while another focuses on a specified use case. In applications which are exposed to constant hacking attempts on the Internet, security-related problems can be caused by errors in the program. Frameworks can also promote the use of best practices such as GET after POST.

In addition, there is potential for the development of applications on Internet operating systems, although currently there are not many viable platforms that fit this model.

Applications

Examples of browser applications are simple office software (word processors, online spreadsheets, and presentation tools), but can also include more advanced applications such as project management, computer-aided design, video editing and point-of-sale.

Web Application Development

Web application development is the process and practice of developing web applications.

Risk

Just as with a traditional desktop application, web applications have varying levels of risk. A personal home page is much less risky than, for example, a stock trading web site. For some projects security, software bugs, etc. are major issues. If time to market, or technical complexity is a concern, documentation, test planning, change control, requirements analysis, architectural description and formal design and construction practices can mitigate risk.

Technologies

- Ajax
- ASP
- ASP.NET
- ActionScript
- CSS
- ColdFusion
- CGI
- HTML
- Java
- JavaScript
- JSP
- Visual LANSA
- Lasso
- Node.js
- OSGI
- Perl
- PHP
- PSGI
- Python
- Ruby

Lifecycle Model

Time to market, company-growth and requirements churn, three things that are emphasized in web-based business, coincide with the principles of the Agile practices. Some agile lifecycle models are:

- Extreme programming
- Scrum

- Timebox development

- Feature-driven development

Testing

Web applications undergo the same unit, integration and system testing as traditional desktop applications. But because web application clients vary so greatly, teams might perform some additional testing, such as:

- Security

- Performance, Load, and Stress

- HTML/CSS validation

- Accessibility

- Usability

- Cross-browser

Many types of tests are automatable. At the component level, one of the xUnit packages can be a helpful tool. Or an organization can create its own unit testing framework. At the GUI level, Watir or iMacros are useful.

Tools

In the case of ASP.NET, a developer can use Microsoft Visual Studio to write code. But, as with most other programming languages, he/she can also use a text editor. Notepad++ is an example. WebORB Integration Server for .NET can be used to integrate .NET services, data and media with any web client. It includes developer productivity tools and APIs for remoting, messaging and data management.

For ColdFusion and the related open source CFML engines, there are several tools available for writing code. These include Adobe Dreamweaver CS4, the CFEclipse plugin for Eclipse (software) and Adobe CF Builder. You can also use any text editor such as Notepad++ or TextEdit.

For Java (programming language), there are many tools. The most popular are Apache Tomcat, GlassFish, JDeveloper and Netbeans but there are many others.

For PHP, the Zend Development Environment provides numerous debugging tools and provides a rich feature set to make a PHP developer's life easier. WebORB Integration Server for PHP can be used to integrate PHP classes and data with any web client. It includes developer productivity tools and APIs for remoting, messaging and data management. Tools such as Hammerkit abstract PHP into a visual programming environment and utilise component-based software methods to accelerate development.

Frameworks and Use

Practicing code reuse and using web application frameworks can greatly improve both productivity and time to market (McConnell 1996:537). Reusing externally developed components can allow an organization to reap the above benefits, while potentially saving money. However, for smaller components, it might be just as easy to develop your own components as it would be to learn new APIs. Also, if a component is essential to the business, an organization might want to control its development.

Web Usability

Web usability is the ease of use of a website. Some broad goals of usability are the presentation of information and choices in a clear and concise way, a lack of ambiguity and the placement of important items in appropriate areas. Another important element of web usability is ensuring that the content works on various devices and browsers. Another concern for usability is ensuring that the website is appropriate for all ages and genders.

The idea of Usability is centered on the concept of making the interface of the website more users friendly. Some of the common aspects of Usability are – simplicity, consistency, familiarity, clarity, credibility, relevancy and accessibility. The focus is to make users feel at ease and remove all the bottlenecks from the conversion path so that users don't have to deal with any inconvenience while browsing or purchasing a product online.

Methodology

As more results of usability research become available, this leads to the development of methodologies for enhancing web usability. There are a number of usability testing tools available in the market.

E-commerce

In the context of e-commerce websites, the meaning of web-usability is narrowed down to efficiency: triggering sales and/or performing other transactions valuable to the business.

Web usability received renewed attention as many early e-commerce websites started failing in 2000. Whereas fancy graphical design had been regarded as indispensable for a successful e-business application during the emergence of internet in the 1990s, web-usability protagonists said quite the reverse was true. They advocated the KISS principle (keep it simple, stupid), which had proven to be effective in focusing end-user attention.

Web Accessibility

Web accessibility refers to the inclusive practice of removing barriers that prevent interaction with, or access to websites, by people with disabilities. When sites are correctly designed, developed and edited, all users have equal access to information and functionality.

For example, when a site is coded with semantically meaningful HTML, with textual equivalents provided for images and with links named meaningfully, this helps blind users using text-to-speech software and/or text-to-Braille hardware. When text and images are large and/or enlargeable, it is easier for users with poor sight to read and understand the content. When links are underlined (or otherwise differentiated) as well as colored, this ensures that color blind users will be able to notice them. When clickable links and areas are large, this helps users who cannot control a mouse with precision. When pages are coded so that users can navigate by means of the keyboard alone, or a single switch access device alone, this helps users who cannot use a mouse or even a standard keyboard. When videos are closed captioned or a sign language version is available, deaf and hard-of-hearing users can understand the video. When flashing effects are avoided or made optional, users prone to seizures caused by these effects are not put at risk. And when content is written in plain language and illustrated with instructional diagrams and animations, users with dyslexia and learning difficulties are better able to understand the content. When sites are correctly built and maintained, all of these users can be accommodated without decreasing the usability of the site for non-disabled users.

The needs that Web accessibility aims to address include:

- Visual: Visual impairments including blindness, various common types of low vision and poor eyesight, various types of color blindness;

- Motor/mobility: e.g. difficulty or inability to use the hands, including tremors, muscle slowness, loss of fine muscle control, etc., due to conditions such as Parkinson's Disease, muscular dystrophy, cerebral palsy, stroke;

- Auditory: Deafness or hearing impairments, including individuals who are hard of hearing;

- Seizures: Photo epileptic seizures caused by visual strobe or flashing effects.

- Cognitive/Intellectual: Developmental disabilities, learning disabilities (dyslexia, dyscalculia, etc.), and cognitive disabilities of various origins, affecting memory, attention, developmental "maturity," problem-solving and logic skills, etc.

Assistive Technologies Used for Web Browsing

Individuals living with a disability use assistive technologies such as the following to enable and assist web browsing:

- Screen reader software, which can read out, using synthesized speech, either selected elements of what is being displayed on the monitor (helpful for users with reading or learning difficulties), or which can read out everything that is happening on the computer (used by blind and vision impaired users).

- Braille terminals, consisting of a refreshable braille display which renders text as braille characters (usually by means of raising pegs through holes in a flat surface) and either a mainstream keyboard or a braille keyboard.

- Screen magnification software, which enlarges what is displayed on the computer monitor, making it easier to read for vision impaired users.

- Speech recognition software that can accept spoken commands to the computer, or turn dictation into grammatically correct text - useful for those who have difficulty using a mouse or a keyboard.

- Keyboard overlays, which can make typing easier or more accurate for those who have motor control difficulties.

- Access to subtitled or sign language videos on the Internet for all deaf people.

Guidelines on Accessible Web Design

Web Content Accessibility Guidelines

In 1999 the Web Accessibility Initiative, a project by the World Wide Web Consortium (W3C), published the Web Content Accessibility Guidelines WCAG 1.0.

On 11 December 2008, the WAI released the WCAG 2.0 as a Recommendation. WCAG 2.0 aims to be up to date and more technology neutral. Though web designers can choose either standard to follow, the WCAG 2.0 have been widely accepted as the definitive guidelines on how to create accessible websites. Governments are steadily adopting the WCAG 2.0 as the accessibility standard for their own websites.

Criticism of WAI Guidelines

There has been criticism of the W3C process, claiming that it does not sufficiently put the user at the heart of the process. There was a formal objection to WCAG's original claim that WCAG 2.0 will address requirements for people with learning disabilities and cognitive limitations headed by Lisa Seeman and signed by 40 organisations and people. In articles such as "WCAG 2.0: The new W3C guidelines evaluated", "To Hell with WCAG 2.0" and "Testability Costs Too Much", the WAI has been criticised for allowing WCAG 1.0 to get increasingly out of step with today's technologies and techniques for creating and consuming web content, for the slow pace of development of WCAG 2.0, for making the new guidelines difficult to navigate and understand, and other argued failings.

Other Guidelines

Canada

In 2011, the Government of Canada began phasing in the implementation of a new set of web standards that are aimed at ensuring government websites are accessible, usable, interoperable and optimized for mobile devices. These standards replace Common Look and Feel 2.0 (CLF 2.0) Standards for the Internet.

The first of these four standards, Standard on Web Accessibility came into full effect on July 31, 2013. The Standard on Web Accessibility follows the Web Content Accessibility Guidelines (WCAG) 2.0 AA, and contains a list of exclusions that is updated annually. It is accompanied by an explicit Assessment Methodology that helps government departments comply. The government also developed the Web Experience Toolkit (WET), a set of reusable web components for building innovative websites. The WET helps government departments build innovative websites that are accessible, usable and interoperable and therefore comply with the government's standards. The WET is open source and available for anyone to use.

The three related web standards are: the Standard on Optimizing Websites and Applications for Mobile Devices, the Standard on Web Usability and the Standard on Web Interoperability.

Philippines

As part of the Web Accessibility Initiatives in the Philippines, the government through the National Council for the Welfare of Disabled Persons (NCWDP) board approved the recommendation of forming an adhoc or core group of webmasters that will help in the implementation of the Biwako Millennium Framework set by the UNESCAP.

The Philippines was also the place where the Interregional Seminar and Regional Demonstration Workshop on Accessible Information and Communications Technologies (ICT) to Persons with Disabilities was held where eleven countries from Asia - Pacific were represented. The Manila Accessible Information and Communications Technologies Design Recommendations was drafted and adopted in 2003.

Spain

In Spain, UNE 139803 is the norm entrusted to regulate web accessibility. This standard is based on Web Content Accessibility Guidelines 1.0.

Sweden

In Sweden, Verva, the Swedish Administrative Development Agency is responsible for a set of guidelines for Swedish public sector web sites. Through the guidelines, web accessibility is presented as an integral part of the overall development process and not as a separate issue. The Swedish guidelines contain criteria which cover the entire lifecycle of a website; from its conception to the publication of live web content. These criteria address several areas which should be considered, including:

- accessibility
- usability
- web standards
- privacy issues
- information architecture
- developing content for the web
- Content Management Systems (CMS) / authoring tools selection.
- development of web content for mobile devices.

An English translation was released in April 2008: Swedish National Guidelines for Public Sector Websites. The translation is based on the latest version of Guidelines which was released in 2006.

United Kingdom

In December 2010, the BSI (British Standards Institute) released the standard *BS 8878:2010 Web accessibility. Code of practice.* This standard effectively supersedes PAS 78 (pub. 2006). PAS 78, produced by the Disability Rights Commission and British Standards Institution, provided guidance to organisations in how to go about commissioning an accessible website from a design agency. It describes what is expected from websites to comply with the UK Disability Discrimination Act 1995 (DDA), making websites accessible to and usable by disabled people. The standard has been designed to introduce non-technical professionals to improved accessibility, usability and user experience for disabled and older people. It will be especially beneficial to anyone new to this subject as it gives guidance on process, rather than on technical and design issues. BS 8878 is consistent with the Equality Act 2010 and is referenced in the UK government's e-Accessibility Action Plan as the basis of updated advice on developing accessible online services. It includes recommendations for:

- Involving disabled people in the development process and using automated tools to assist with accessibility testing

- The management of the guidance and process for upholding existing accessibility guidelines and specifications.

BS 8878 is intended for anyone responsible for the policies covering web product creation within their organization, and governance against those policies. It additionally assists people responsible for promoting and supporting equality and inclusion initiatives within organizations and people involved in the procurement, creation or training of web products and content. A summary of BS 8878 is available to help organisations better understand how the standard can help them embed accessibility and inclusive design in their business-as-usual processes.

Japan

Web Content Accessibility Guidelines in Japan were established in 2004 as JIS (Japanese Industrial Standards) X 8341-3. JIS X 8341-3 was revised in 2010 to adopt WCAG 2.0. The new version, published by the Web Accessibility Infrastructure Commission (WAIC), has the same four principles, 12 guidelines, and 61 success criteria as WCAG 2.0 has.

Essential Components of Web Accessibility

The accessibility of websites relies on the cooperation of eight components:

1. the website itself - natural information (text, images and sound) and the markup code that defines its structure and presentation

2. user agents, such as web browsers and media players

3. assistive technologies, such as screen readers and input devices used in place of the conventional keyboard and mouse

4. users' knowledge and experience using the web

5. developers

6. authoring tools

7. evaluation tools

8. a defined web accessibility standard, or a policy for your organization (against which to evaluate the accessibility)

These components interact with each other to create an environment that is accessible to people with disabilities.

Web developers usually use authoring tools and evaluation tools to create Web content. People ("users") use Web browsers, media players, assistive technologies or other "user agents" to get and interact with the content."

Guidelines for Different Components

Authoring Tool Accessibility Guidelines (ATAG)

- ATAG contains 28 checkpoints that provide guidance on:
    - producing accessible output that meets standards and guidelines
    - promoting the content author for accessibility-related information
    - providing ways of checking and correcting inaccessible content
    - integrating accessibility in the overall look and feel
    - making the authoring tool itself accessible to people with disabilities

Web Content Accessibility Guidelines (WCAG)

- WCAG 1.0: 14 guidelines that are general principles of accessible design

- WCAG 2.0: 4 principles that form the foundation for web accessibility; 12 guidelines (untestable) that are goals for which authors should aim; and 65 testable success criteria. The W3C's Techniques for WCAG 2.0 is a list of techniques that support authors to meet the guidelines and success criteria. The techniques are periodically updated whereas the principles, guidelines and success criteria are stable and do not change.

User Agent Accessibility Guidelines (UAAG)

- UAAG contains a comprehensive set of checkpoints that cover:
    - access to all content
    - user control over how content is rendered
    - user control over the user interface
    - standard programming interfaces

Web Accessibility Legislation

Because of the growth in internet usage and its growing importance in everyday life, countries around the world are addressing digital access issues through legislation. One approach is to protect access to websites for people with disabilities by using existing human or civil rights legislation. Some countries, like the U.S., protect access for people with disabilities through the technology procurement process. It is common for nations to support and adopt the Web Content Accessibility Guidelines (WCAG) 2.0 by referring to the guidelines in their legislation.

Australia

In 2000, an Australian blind man won a court case against the Sydney Organizing Committee of the Olympic Games (SOCOG). This was the first successful case under Disability Discrimination Act 1992 because SOCOG had failed to make their official website, Sydney Olympic Games, adequately accessible to blind users. The Human Rights and Equal Opportunity Commission (HREOC) also published World Wide Web Access: Disability Discrimination Act Advisory Notes. All Governments in Australia also have policies and guidelines that require accessible public websites; Vision Australia maintain a complete list of Australian web accessibility policies.

Brazil

In Brazil, the federal government published a paper with guidelines for accessibility on 18 January 2005, for public reviewing. On 14 December of the same year, the second version was published, including suggestions made to the first version of the paper. On 7 May 2007, the accessibility guidelines of the paper became compulsory to all federal websites. The current version of the paper, which follows the WCAG 2.0 guidelines, is named e-MAG, Modelo de Acessibilidade de Governo Eletrônico (Electronic Government Accessibility Model), and is maintained by Brazilian Ministry of Planning, Budget, and Management.

The paper can be viewed and downloaded at its official website.

European Union

In February 2014 a draft law was endorsed by the European Parliament stating that all websites managed by public sector bodies have to be made accessible to everyone.

Ireland

In Ireland, the Disability Act 2005 requires that where a public body communicates in electronic form with one or more persons, the contents of the communication must be, as far as practicable, "accessible to persons with a visual impairment to whom adaptive technology is available" (Section 28(2)). The National Disability Authority has produced a Code of Practice giving guidance to public bodies on how to meet the obligations of the Act. This is an approved code of practice and its provisions have the force of legally binding statutory obligations. It states that a public body can achieve compliance with Section 28(2) by "reviewing existing practices for electronic communications in terms of accessibility against relevant guidelines and standards", giving the example of "Double A conformance with the Web Accessibility Initiative's (WAI) Web Content Accessibility Guidelines (WCAG)".

Israel

The Israeli Ministry of Justice recently published regulations requiring Internet websites to comply with Israeli standard 5568, which is based on the W3C Web Content Accessibility Guidelines 2.0. The main differences between the Israeli standard and the W3C standard concern the requirements to provide captions and texts for audio and video media. The Israeli standards are somewhat more lenient, reflecting the current technical difficulties in providing such captions and texts in Hebrew.

Italy

In Italy, web accessibility is ruled by the so-called "Legge Stanca" (Stanca Act), formally Act n.4 of 9 January 2004, officially published on the Gazzetta Ufficiale on 17 January 2004. The original Stanca Act was based on the WCAG 1.0. On 20 March 2013 the standards required by the Stanca Act were updated to the WCAG 2.0.

Norway

In Norway, web accessibility is a legal obligation under the Act June 20, 2008 No 42 relating to a prohibition against discrimination on the basis of disability, also known as the Anti-discrimination Accessibility Act. The Act went into force in 2009, and the Ministry of Government Administration, Reform and Church Affairs [Fornyings-, administrasjons- og kirkedepartementet] published the Regulations for universal design of information and communication technology (ICT) solutions [Forskrift om universell utforming av informasjons- og kommunikasjonsteknologiske (IKT)-løsninger] in 2013. The regulations require compliance with Web Content Accessibility Guidelines 2.0 (WCAG 2.0) / NS / ISO / IEC 40500: 2012, level A and AA with some exceptions. The Norwegian Agency for Public Management and eGovernment (Difi) is responsible for overseeing that ICT solutions aimed at the general public are in compliance with the legislative and regulatory requirements.

United Kingdom

In the UK, the Equality Act 2010 does not refer explicitly to website accessibility, but makes it illegal to discriminate against people with disabilities. The Act applies to anyone providing a service; public, private and voluntary sectors. The *Code of Practice: Rights of Access – Goods, Facilities, Services and Premises* document published by the government's Equality and Human Rights Commission to accompany the Act does refer explicitly to websites as one of the "services to the public" which should be considered covered by the Act.

Website Accessibility Audits

A growing number of organizations, companies and consultants offer *website accessibility audits*. These audits, a type of system testing, identify accessibility problems that exist within a website, and provide advice and guidance on the steps that need to be taken to correct these problems.

A range of methods are used to audit websites for accessibility:

- Automated tools are available which can identify some of the problems that are present. Depending on the tool the result may vary widely making it difficult to compare test results.

- Expert technical reviewers, knowledgeable in web design technologies and accessibility, can review a representative selection of pages and provide detailed feedback and advice based on their findings.

- User testing, usually overseen by technical experts, involves setting tasks for ordinary users to carry out on the website, and reviewing the problems these users encounter as they try to carry out the tasks.

Each of these methods has its strengths and weaknesses:

- Automated tools can process many pages in a relatively short length of time, but can only identify some of the accessibility problems that might be present in the website.

- Technical expert review will identify many of the problems that exist, but the process is time consuming, and many websites are too large to make it possible for a person to review every page.

- User testing combines elements of usability and accessibility testing, and is valuable for identifying problems that might otherwise be overlooked, but needs to be used knowledge-ably to avoid the risk of basing design decisions on one user's preferences.

Ideally, a combination of methods should be used to assess the accessibility of a website.

Remediating Inaccessible Websites

Once an accessibility audit has been conducted, and accessibility errors have been identified, the errors will need to be remediated in order to ensure the site is compliant with accessibility errors. The traditional way of correcting an inaccessible site is to go back into the source code, reprogram the error, and then test to make sure the bug was fixed. If the website is not scheduled to be revised in the near future, that error (and others) would remain on the site for a lengthy period of time, possibly violating accessibility guidelines. Because this is a complicated process, many website owners choose to build accessibility into a new site design or re-launch, as it can be more efficient to develop the site to comply with accessibility guidelines, rather than to remediate errors later.

Accessible Web Applications and WAI-ARIA

For a Web page to be accessible all important semantics about the page's functionality must be available so that assistive technology can understand and process the content and adapt it for the user. However, as content becomes more and more complex, the standard HTML tags and attributes become inadequate in providing semantic reliably. Modern Web applications often apply scripts to elements to control their functionality and to enable them to act as a control or other dynamic component. These custom components or widgets do not provide a way to convey semantic information to the user agent. WAI-ARIA (Accessible Rich Internet Applications) is a specification published by the World Wide Web Consortium that specifies how to increase the accessibility of dynamic content and user interface components developed with Ajax, HTML, JavaScript and related technologies. ARIA enables accessibility by enabling the author to provide all the semantics to fully describe its supported behaviour. It also allows each element to expose its current states and properties and its relationships between other elements. Accessibility problems with the focus and tab index are also corrected.

Adaptive Hypermedia

Adaptive hypermedia (AH) uses hypermedia which is adaptive according to a *user model*. In contrast to linear media, where all users are offered a standard series of hyperlinks, adaptive hypermedia (AH) tailors what the user is offered based on a model of the user's goals, preferences and knowledge, thus providing links or content most appropriate to the current user.

Background

Adaptive hypermedia is used in educational hypermedia, on-line information and help systems, as well as institutional information systems. Adaptive educational hypermedia tailors what the learner sees to that learner's goals, abilities, needs, interests, and knowledge of the subject, by providing hyperlinks that are most relevant to the user in an effort to shape the user's cognitive load. The teaching tools "adapt" to the learner. On-line information systems provide reference access to information for users with a different knowledge level of the subject.

An adaptive hypermedia system should satisfy three criteria: it should be a hypertext or hypermedia system, it should have a user model and it should be able to adapt the hypermedia using the model.

A semantic distinction is made between *adaptation*, referring to system-driven changes for personalisation, and *adaptability*, referring to user-driven changes. One way of looking at this is that adaptation is automatic, whereas adaptability is not. From an epistemic point of view, adaptation can be described as analytic, a-priori, whereas adaptability is synthetic, a-posteriori. In other words, any adaptable system, as it "contains" a human, is by default "intelligent", whereas an adaptive system that presents "intelligence" is more surprising and thus more interesting.

Architecture

The system categories in which user modelling and adaptivity have been deployed by various researchers in the field share an underlying architecture. The conceptual structure for adaptive systems generally consists of interdependent components: a user model, a domain model and an interaction model.

User Model

The user model is a representation of the knowledge and preferences which the system 'believes' a user (which may be an individual, a group of people or non-human agents) possesses. It is a knowledge source which is separable by the system from the rest of its knowledge and contains explicit assumptions about the user. Knowledge for the user model can be acquired implicitly by making inferences about users from their interaction with the system, by carrying out some form of test, or from assigning users to generic user categories usually called 'stereotypes'. The student model consists of a personal profile (which includes static data, e.g., name and password), cognitive profile (adaptable data such as preferences), and a student knowledge profile. Systems may adapt, depending on user features such as:

- goals (a feature related with the context of a user's work in hypermedia)

- knowledge (knowledge of the subject represented in the hyperspace)

- background (all the information related to the user's previous experience outside the subject of the hypermedia system which is relevant enough to be considered)

- hyperspace experience (how familiar is the user with the structure of the hyperspace and how easily can the user navigate it)

- preferences (the user can prefer some nodes and links over others and some parts of a page over others).

Domain Model

The domain model defines the aspects of the application which can be adapted or which are otherwise required for the operation of the adaptive system. The domain model contains several concepts that stand as the backbone for the content of the system. Other terms which have been used for this concept include content model, application model, system model, device model and task model. It describes educational content such as information pages, examples, and problems. The simplest content model relates every content item to exactly one domain concept (in this model, this concept is frequently referred to as a domain topic). More advanced content models use multi-concept indexing for each content item and sometimes use roles to express the nature of item-concept relationship. A cognitively valid domain model should capture descriptions of the application at three levels, namely:

- The task level which makes the user aware of the system purpose.

- The logical level which describes how something works.

- The physical level which describes how to do something.

Each content concept has a set of topics. Topics represent individual pieces of knowledge for each domain and the size of each topic varies in relation to the particular domain. Additionally, topics are linked to each other forming a semantic network. This network is the structure of the knowledge domain.

Interaction Model

The interaction or adaptation model contains everything which is concerned with the relationships which exist between the representation of the users (the user model) and the representation of the application (the domain model). It displays information to the user based on his or her cognitive preferences. For instance, the module will divide a page's content into chunks with conditions set to only display to certain users or preparing two variants of a single concept page with a similar condition. The two main aspects to the interaction model are capturing the appropriate raw data and representing the inferences, adaptations and evaluations which may occur.

Content-level and link-level adaptation are distinguished as two different classes of hypermedia adaptation; the first is termed *adaptive presentation* and the second, *adaptive navigation support*.

Adaptive Presentation

The idea of various adaptive presentation techniques is to adapt the content of a page accessed by a particular user to current knowledge, goals, and other characteristics of the user. For example, a qualified user can be provided with more detailed and deep information while a novice can receive additional explanations. Adaptive text presentation is the most studied technology of hypermedia adaptation. There are a number of different techniques for adaptive text presentation.

Adaptive Navigation Support

The idea of adaptive navigation support techniques is to help users to find their paths in hyperspace by adapting the way of presenting links to goals, knowledge, and other characteristics of an individual user. This area of research is newer than adaptive presentation, a number of interesting techniques have been already suggested and implemented. We distinguish four kinds of link presentation which are different from the point of what can be altered and adapted:

- Local non-contextual links – This type includes all kinds of links on regular hypermedia pages which are independent from the content of the page.

- Contextual links or "real hypertext" links – This type comprises "hotwords" in texts, "hot spots" in pictures, and other kinds of links which are embedded in the context of the page content and cannot be removed from it.

- Links from index and content pages – An index or a content page can be considered as a special kind of page which contains only links.

- Links on local maps and links on global hyperspace maps – Maps usually graphically represent a hyperspace or a local area of hyperspace as a network of nodes connected by arrows.

Methods

Adaptation methods are defined as generalizations of existing adaptation techniques. Each method is based on a clear adaptation idea which can be presented at the conceptual level.

Content Adaptation

- additional explanations – hides parts of information about a particular concept which are not relevant to the user's level of knowledge about this concept,

- prerequisite explanations – before presenting an explanation of a concept the system inserts explanations of all its prerequisite concepts which are not sufficiently known to the user,

- comparative explanations – if a concept similar to the concept being presented is known, the user gets a comparative explanation which stress similarities and differences between the current concept and the related one,

- explanation variants – assumes that showing or hiding some portion of the content is not always sufficient for the adaptation because different users may need essentially different information,

- sorting – fragments of information about the concept are sorted from information which is most relevant to user's background and knowledge to information which is least relevant.

Link Adaptation

- global guidance – the system suggests navigation paths on a global scale,

- local guidance – the system suggests the next step to take, for instance through a "next" or "continue" button,

- local orientation support – the system presents an overview of a part of the (link) structure of the hyperspace,

- global orientation support – the system presents an overview of the whole (link) structure of the hyperspace,

- managing personalized views in information spaces – each view may be a list of links to all pages or sub-parts of the whole hyperspace which are relevant for a particular working goal.

Techniques

Adaptation techniques refer to methods of providing adaptation in existing AH systems.

Content Adaptation

- conditional text – with this technique, all possible information about a concept is divided into several chunks of texts. Each chunk is associated with a condition on the level of user knowledge represented in the user model. When presenting the information about the concept, the system presents only the chunks where the condition is true.

- stretchtext – turns off and on different parts of the content according to the user knowledge level.

- page variants – the most simple adaptive presentation technique. With this technique, a system keeps two or more variants of the same page with different presentations of the same content.

- fragment variants – The system stores several variants of explanations for each concept and the user gets the page which includes variants corresponding to his or her knowledge about the concepts presented in the page

- frame-based techniques – With this technique all the information about a particular concept is represented in form of a frame. Slots of a frame can contain several explanation variants of the concept, links to other frames, examples, etc. Special presentation rules are used to decide which slots should be presented to a particular user and in which order.

Link Adaptation

- direct guidance – the "next best" node for the user to visit is shown, e.g. through a "next" or "continue" button,

- link sorting – all the links on a particular page are sorted according to the user model and to some goal-oriented criteria: the more towards the top of the page, the more relevant the link is,

- link hiding – hiding links to "non-relevant" pages by changing the color of the anchors to that of normal text),

- link annotation – to augment the link with some form of comment which tells the user more about the current state of the pages to which the annotated links refer,

- link disabling – the "link functionality" of a link is removed,

- link removal – link anchors for undesired links (non-relevant or not yet ready to read) are removed,

- map adaptation – the content and presentation of a map of the link structure of the hyper-space is adapted.

Authoring Adaptive Hypermedia

Authoring adaptive hypermedia uses designing and creation processes for content, usually in the form of a resource collection and domain model, and adaptive behaviour, usually in the form of IF-THEN rules. Recently, adaptation languages have been proposed for increased generality. As adaptive hypermedia adapts at least to the user, authoring of AH comprises at least a user model, and may also include other aspects.

Issues

Authoring of adaptive hypermedia was long considered as secondary to adaptive hypermedia delivery. This was not surprising in the early stages of adaptive hypermedia, when the focus was on research and expansion. Now that adaptive hypermedia itself has reached a certain maturity, the issue is to bring it out to the community and let the various stakeholders reap the benefits. However, authoring and creation of hypermedia is not trivial. Unlike in traditional authoring for hypermedia and the web, a linear storyline is not enough. Instead, various alternatives have to be created for the given material. For example, if a course should be delivered both to visual and verbal learners, there should be created at least two perfectly equivalent versions of the material in visual and in verbal form, respectively. Moreover, an adaptation strategy should be created that states that the visual content should be delivered to visual learners, whereas the verbal content should be delivered to the verbal learners. Thus, authors should not only be able to create different versions of their content, but be able to specify (and in some cases, design from scratch) adaptation strategies of delivery of contents. Issues with which authoring of adaptive hypermedia is confronted are:

- creation of exchange language for the content (some early examples are the CAM language),

- creation of exchange language for adaptation (with the LAG language and the LAG-XLS language as examples),

- creation of a framework for adaptation

- standardization of adaptation processes.

AH Authoring Frameworks

There already exist some approaches to help authors to build adaptive-hypermedia-based systems. However, there is a strong need for high-level approaches, formalisms and tools that support and facilitate the description of reusable adaptive hypermedia and websites. Such models started appearing. Moreover, recently have we noticed a shift in interest, as it became clearer that the implementation-oriented approach would forever keep adaptive hypermedia away from the 'layman' author. The creator of adaptive hypermedia cannot be expected to know all facets of the process as described above. Still, he/she can be reasonably trusted to be an expert in one of these facets. For instance, it is reasonable to expect that there are content experts (such as, e.g., experts in chemistry, for instance). It is reasonable to expect, for adaptive educational hypermedia that there are experts in pedagogy, who are able to add pedagogical metadata to the content created by content experts. Finally, it is reasonable to expect that adaptation experts will be the one creating the implementation of adaptation strategies, and descriptions (metadata) of such nature that they can be understood and applied by laymen authors. This type of division of work determines the different authoring personas that should be expected to collaborate in the creation process of adaptive hypermedia. Moreover, the contributions of these various personas correspond to the different modules that are to be expected in adaptive hypermedia systems.

AH Authoring Systems

- MOT (My Online Teacher)

- TANGOW

History

By the early 1990s, the two main parent areas – hypertext and user modeling – had achieved a level of maturity that allowed for the research in these areas to be explored together. Many researchers had recognized the problems of static hypertext in different application areas, and explored various ways to adapt the output and behavior of hypertext systems to suit the needs of individual users. Several early papers on adaptive hypermedia were published in the *User Modeling and User-Adapted Interaction* (UMUAI) journal; the first workshop on adaptive hypermedia was held during a user modeling conference; and a special issue of UMUAI on adaptive hypermedia was published in 1996. Several innovative adaptive hypermedia techniques had been developed, and several research-level adaptive hypermedia systems had been built and evaluated.

After 1996, adaptive hypermedia grew rapidly. Research teams commenced projects in adaptive hypermedia, and many students selected the subject area for their PhD theses. A book on adaptive hypermedia, and a special issue of the New Review of Hypermedia and Multimedia (1998) were published. Two main factors accounted for this growth. Due a diverse audience, the internet boosted research into adaptivity. Almost all the papers published before 1996 describe classic pre-Web hypertext and hypermedia; the majority of papers published since 1996 are devoted to Web-based adaptive hypermedia systems. The second factor was is the accumulation and consolidation of research experience in the field. Early papers provided few references to similar work in adaptive hypermedia, and described original laboratory systems developed to demonstrate and explore innovative ideas. After 1996, papers cite earlier work, and usually suggest either real world systems, or research systems developed for real world settings by elaborating or an extending techniques suggested earlier. This is indicative of the relative maturity of adaptive hypermedia as a research direction.

Research

Adaptive hypermedia and user modeling continue to be actively researched, with results published in several journals and conferences such as:

- User Modeling and User-Adapted Interaction (UMUAI)
- Adaptive Hypermedia

Multimedia

Multimedia is content that uses a combination of different content forms such as text, audio, images, animations, video and interactive content. Multimedia contrasts with media that use only rudimentary computer displays such as text-only or traditional forms of printed or hand-produced material.

Multimedia can be recorded and played, displayed, interacted with or accessed by information content processing devices, such as computerized and electronic devices, but can also be part of a live performance. Multimedia devices are electronic media devices used to store and experience multimedia content. Multimedia is distinguished from mixed media in fine art; by including audio, for example, it has a broader scope. The term "rich media" is synonymous for interactive multimedia. Hypermedia scales up the amount of media content in multimedia application.

Categorization

Multimedia may be broadly divided into linear and non-linear categories. Linear active content progresses often without any navigational control for the viewer such as a cinema presentation. Non-linear uses interactivity to control progress as with a video game or self-paced computer based training. Hypermedia is an example of non-linear content.

Multimedia presentations can be live or recorded. A recorded presentation may allow interactivity via a navigation system. A live multimedia presentation may allow interactivity via an interaction with the presenter or performer.

Major Characteristics

Multimedia presentations may be viewed by person on stage, projected, transmitted, or played locally with a media player. A broadcast may be a live or recorded multimedia presentation. Broadcasts and recordings can be either analog or digital electronic media technology. Digital online multimedia may be downloaded or streamed. Streaming multimedia may be live or on-demand.

Multimedia games and simulations may be used in a physical environment with special effects, with multiple users in an online network, or locally with an offline computer, game system, or simulator.

The various formats of technological or digital multimedia may be intended to enhance the users' experience, for example to make it easier and faster to convey information. Or in entertainment or art, to transcend everyday experience.

A lasershow is a live multimedia performance.

Enhanced levels of interactivity are made possible by combining multiple forms of media content. Online multimedia is increasingly becoming object-oriented and data-driven, enabling applications with collaborative end-user innovation and personalization on multiple forms of content over time. Examples of these range from multiple forms of content on Web sites like photo galleries with both images (pictures) and title (text) user-updated, to simulations whose co-efficients, events, illustrations, animations or videos are modifiable, allowing the multimedia "experience" to be altered without reprogramming. In addition to seeing and hearing, haptic technology enables virtual objects to be felt. Emerging technology involving illusions of taste and smell may also enhance the multimedia experience.

Terminology

History of the Term

The term *multimedia* was coined by singer and artist Bob Goldstein (later 'Bobb Goldsteinn') to promote the July 1966 opening of his "LightWorks at L'Oursin" show at Southampton, Long Island. Goldstein was perhaps aware of an American artist named Dick Higgins, who had two years previously discussed a new approach to art-making he called "intermedia."

On August 10, 1966, Richard Albarino of *Variety* borrowed the terminology, reporting: "Brainchild of songscribe-comic Bob ('Washington Square') Goldstein, the 'Lightworks' is the latest *multi-media* music-cum-visuals to debut as discothèque fare." Two years later, in 1968, the term "multimedia" was re-appropriated to describe the work of a political consultant, David Sawyer, the husband of Iris Sawyer—one of Goldstein's producers at L'Oursin.

Multimedia (multi-image) setup for the 1988 Ford New Car Announcement Show, August 1987, Detroit, MI

In the intervening forty years, the word has taken on different meanings. In the late 1970s, the term referred to presentations consisting of multi-projector slide shows timed to an audio track. However, by the 1990s 'multimedia' took on its current meaning.

In the 1993 first edition of McGraw-Hill's *Multimedia: Making It Work*, Tay Vaughan declared "Multimedia is any combination of text, graphic art, sound, animation, and video that is delivered by computer. When you allow the user – the viewer of the project – to control what and when these elements are delivered, it is *interactive multimedia*. When you provide a structure of linked elements through which the user can navigate, interactive multimedia becomes *hypermedia*."

The German language society, Gesellschaft für deutsche Sprache, decided to recognize the word's significance and ubiquitousness in the 1990s by awarding it the title of 'Word of the Year' in 1995. The institute summed up its rationale by stating "[Multimedia] has become a central word in the wonderful new media world."

In common usage, *multimedia* refers to an electronically delivered combination of media including video, still images, audio, text in such a way that can be accessed interactively. Much of the content on the web today falls within this definition as understood by millions. Some computers which were marketed in the 1990s were called "multimedia" computers because they incorporated a CD-ROM drive, which allowed for the delivery of several hundred megabytes of video, picture, and audio data. That era saw also a boost in the production of educational multimedia CD-ROMs.

Word Usage and Context

Since media is the plural of medium, the term "multimedia" is used to describe multiple occurrences of only one form of media such as a collection of audio CDs. This is why it's important that the word "multimedia" is used exclusively to describe multiple forms of media and content.

The term "multimedia" is also ambiguous. Static content (such as a paper book) may be considered multimedia if it contains both pictures and text or may be considered interactive if the user interacts by turning pages at will. Books may also be considered non-linear if the pages are accessed non-sequentially. The term "video", if not used exclusively to describe motion photography, is ambiguous in multimedia terminology. *Video* is often used to describe the file format, delivery format, or presentation format instead of *"footage"* which is used to distinguish motion photography from *"animation"* of rendered motion imagery. Multiple forms of information content are often not considered modern forms of presentation such as audio or video. Likewise, single forms of information content with single methods of information processing (e.g. non-interactive audio) are often called multimedia, perhaps to distinguish static media from active media. In the Fine arts, for example, Leda Luss Luyken's ModulArt brings two key elements of musical composition and film into the world of painting: variation of a theme and movement of and within a picture, making *ModulArt* an interactive multimedia form of art. Performing arts may also be considered multimedia considering that performers and props are multiple forms of both content and media.

The *Gesellschaft für deutsche Sprache* chose *Multimedia* as German Word of the Year 1995.

Usage/Application

A presentation using Powerpoint. Corporate presentations may combine all forms of media content.

Virtual reality uses multimedia content. Applications and delivery platforms of multimedia are virtually limitless.

VVO Multimedia-Terminal in Dresden WTC (Germany)

Multimedia finds its application in various areas including, but not limited to, advertisements, art, education, entertainment, engineering, medicine, mathematics, business, scientific research and spatial temporal applications. Several examples are as follows:

Creative Industries

Creative industries use multimedia for a variety of purposes ranging from fine arts, to entertainment, to commercial art, to journalism, to media and software services provided for any of the industries listed below. An individual multimedia designer may cover the spectrum throughout their career. Request for their skills range from technical, to analytical, to creative.

Commercial Uses

Much of the electronic old and new media used by commercial artists and graphic designers is multimedia. Exciting presentations are used to grab and keep attention in advertising. Business to business, and interoffice communications are often developed by creative services firms for advanced multimedia presentations beyond simple slide shows to sell ideas or liven-up training. Commercial multimedia developers may be hired to design for governmental services and non-profit services applications as well.

Entertainment and Fine Arts

In addition, multimedia is heavily used in the entertainment industry, especially to develop special effects in movies and animations(VFX, 3D animation, etc.). Multimedia games are a popular pastime and are software programs available either as CD-ROMs or online. Some video games also use multimedia features. Multimedia applications that allow users to actively participate instead of just sitting by as passive recipients of information are called *Interactive Multimedia*. In the Arts there are multimedia artists, whose minds are able to blend techniques using different media that in some way incorporates interaction with the viewer. One of the most relevant could be Peter Greenaway who is melding Cinema with Opera and all sorts of digital media. Another approach entails the creation of multimedia that can be displayed in a traditional fine arts arena, such as an art gallery. Although multimedia display material may be volatile, the survivability of the content is as strong as any traditional media. Digital recording material may be just as durable and infinitely reproducible with perfect copies every time.

Education

In education, multimedia is used to produce computer-based training courses (popularly called CBTs) and reference books like encyclopedia and almanacs. A CBT lets the user go through a series of presentations, text about a particular topic, and associated illustrations in various information formats. Edutainment is the combination of education with entertainment, especially multimedia entertainment.

Learning theory in the past decade has expanded dramatically because of the introduction of multimedia. Several lines of research have evolved (e.g. Cognitive load, Multimedia learning, etc.). The possibilities for learning and instruction are nearly endless.

The idea of media convergence is also becoming a major factor in education, particularly higher education. Defined as separate technologies such as voice (and telephony features), data (and productivity applications) and video that now share resources and interact with each other, media convergence is rapidly changing the curriculum in universities all over the world. Likewise, it is changing the availability, or lack thereof, of jobs requiring this savvy technological skill.

The English education in middle school in China is well invested and assisted with various equipments. In contrast, the original objective has not been achieved at the desired effect. The government, schools, families, and students spend a lot of time working on improving scores, but hardly gain practical skills. English education today has gone into the vicious circle. Educators need to consider how to perfect the education system to improve students' practical ability of English. Therefore, an efficient way should be used to make the class vivid. Multimedia teaching will bring students into a class where they can interact with the teacher and the subject. Multimedia teaching is more intuitive than old ways; teachers can simulate situations in real life. In many circumstances teachers do not have to be there, students will learn by themselves in the class. More importantly, teachers will have more approaches to stimulating students' passion of learning.

Journalism

Newspaper companies all over are also trying to embrace the new phenomenon by implementing its practices in their work. While some have been slow to come around, other major newspapers like *The New York Times*, *USA Today* and *The Washington Post* are setting the precedent for the positioning of the newspaper industry in a globalized world.

News reporting is not limited to traditional media outlets. Freelance journalists can make use of different new media to produce multimedia pieces for their news stories. It engages global audiences and tells stories with technology, which develops new communication techniques for both media producers and consumers. The Common Language Project, later renamed to The Seattle Globalist, is an example of this type of multimedia journalism production.

Multimedia reporters who are mobile (usually driving around a community with cameras, audio and video recorders, and laptop computers) are often referred to as mojos, from *mobile journalist*.

Engineering

Software engineers may use multimedia in computer simulations for anything from entertainment to training such as military or industrial training. Multimedia for software interfaces are often done as a collaboration between creative professionals and software engineers.

Industry

In the industrial sector, multimedia is used as a way to help present information to shareholders, superiors and coworkers. Multimedia is also helpful for providing employee training, advertising and selling products all over the world via virtually unlimited web-based technology.

Mathematical and Scientific Research

In mathematical and scientific research, multimedia is mainly used for modeling and simulation. For example, a scientist can look at a molecular model of a particular substance and manipulate it to arrive at a new substance. Representative research can be found in journals such as the *Journal of Multimedia*.

Medicine

In medicine, doctors can get trained by looking at a virtual surgery or they can simulate how the human body is affected by diseases spread by viruses and bacteria and then develop techniques to prevent it. Multimedia applications such as virtual surgeries also help doctors to get practical training.

Document Imaging

Document imaging is a technique that takes hard copy of an image/document and converts it into a digital format (for example, scanners).

Disabilities

Ability Media allows those with disabilities to gain qualifications in the multimedia field so they can pursue careers that give them access to a wide array of powerful communication forms.

Miscellaneous

In Europe, the reference organisation for Multimedia industry is the European Multimedia Associations Convention (EMMAC).

Structuring Information in a Multimedia form

Multimedia represents the convergence of text, pictures, video and sound into a single form. The power of multimedia and the Internet lies in the way in which information is linked.

Multimedia and the Internet require a completely new approach to writing. The style of writing that is appropriate for the 'on-line world' is highly optimized and designed to be able to be quickly scanned by readers.

A good site must be made with a specific purpose in mind and a site with good interactivity and new technology can also be useful for attracting visitors. The site must be attractive and innovative in its design, function in terms of its purpose, easy to navigate, frequently updated and fast to download.

When users view a page, they can only view one page at a time. As a result, multimedia users must create a "mental model" of information structure.

Conferences

There is a large number of multimedia conferences, the two main scholarly scientific conferences being:

- ACM Multimedia;
- IEEE ICME, International Conference on Multimedia & Expo.

References

- Mark Levene (18 October 2010). An Introduction to Search Engines and Web Navigation (2nd ed.). Wiley. p. 221. ISBN 978-0470526842. Retrieved 12 November 2012.

- Rozanski, Nick; Eóin Woods (April 20, 2005). Software Systems Architecture: Working With Stakeholders Using Viewpoints and Perspectives. Addison-Wesley Professional. p. 576. ISBN 0-321-11229-6.

- Leffingwell, Dean; Don Widrig (May 16, 2003). Managing Software Requirements: A Use Case Approach, Second Edition. Addison-Wesley Professional. p. 544. ISBN 0-321-12247-X.

- Vaughan, Tay, 1993, Multimedia: Making It Work (first edition, ISBN 0-07-881869-9), Osborne/McGraw-Hill, Berkeley, pg. 3.

- "Regulation for universal design of information and communication technology (ICT) solutions". Ministry of Local Government and Modernisation. Retrieved 10 November 2016.

- "The Government's Action Plan for Universal Design 2015–2019" (PDF). Norwegian Ministry of Children, Equality and Social Inclusion. Retrieved 10 November 2016.

- Jonathan Chetwynd (24 July 2007). "Putting the User at the Heart of the W3C Process". JISC CETIS. Retrieved 15 January 2015.

- "JIS X 8341-3:2010". waic.jp (in Japanese). Web Accessibility Infrastructure Commission. Retrieved 15 January 2015.

- Timothy Stephen Springer (2010-02-24). "Section 508 of the Rehabilitation Act". SSB BART Group. Retrieved 2015-08-24.

- Leibowitz. Brandon (21 February 2014). "Website Usability: Virtual Elephants of the Internet Room". Bosmol Social Media News. Retrieved 19 May 2014.

- Mark Rogers (2012-11-13). "Government Accessibility Standards and WCAG 2.0". Powermapper.com. Retrieved 2014-12-15.

- "Standard on Optimizing Websites and Applications for Mobile Devices". Government of Canada. Retrieved 2014-12-14.

- "MEPs vote to make online public services accessible to everyone". www.europarl.europa.eu. European Parliament. 26 February 2014. Retrieved 15 January 1205. Check date values in: |access-date= (help)

- Giannoumis, G. Anthony (2014). "Regulating Web Content: the nexus of legislation and performance standards in the United Kingdom and Norway". Behavioral Sciences & the Law. 32 (1): 52–75. doi:10.1002/bsl.2103.

- Lynch, Patrick J.; Horton, Sarah (1997). "Yale Style Manual-Site structure". Yale School of Medicine. Archived from the original on 16 October 2002. Retrieved 16 October 2014.

- Trenton Moss says:. "WCAG 2.0: The new W3C accessibility guidelines evaluated". Webcredible.co.uk. Retrieved 2013-07-28.

- Gian Sampson-Wild (2013-07-11). "Testability Costs Too Much • An A List Apart Article". Alistapart.com. Retrieved 2013-07-28.

- "World Wide Web Access: Disability Discrimination Act Advisory Notes ver 4.0 (2010) | Australian Human Rights Commission". Hreoc.gov.au. 2010-07-01. Retrieved 2013-07-28.

- "Code of Practice on Accessibility of Public Services and Information Provided by Public Bodies". Nda.ie. 2006-07-21. Retrieved 2013-07-28.

- Benyon, David; Murray, Dianne. "Applying user modelling to human-computer interaction design" (PDF). lucite. Retrieved 4 March 2013.

- De Bra, Paul; Houben, Geert-Jan; Wu, Hongjing. "AHA: AHAM: A Reference Model to Support Adaptive Hypermedia Authoring". Retrieved 1 April 2013.

Permissions

All chapters in this book are published with permission under the Creative Commons Attribution Share Alike License or equivalent. Every chapter published in this book has been scrutinized by our experts. Their significance has been extensively debated. The topics covered herein carry significant information for a comprehensive understanding. They may even be implemented as practical applications or may be referred to as a beginning point for further studies.

We would like to thank the editorial team for lending their expertise to make the book truly unique. They have played a crucial role in the development of this book. Without their invaluable contributions this book wouldn't have been possible. They have made vital efforts to compile up to date information on the varied aspects of this subject to make this book a valuable addition to the collection of many professionals and students.

This book was conceptualized with the vision of imparting up-to-date and integrated information in this field. To ensure the same, a matchless editorial board was set up. Every individual on the board went through rigorous rounds of assessment to prove their worth. After which they invested a large part of their time researching and compiling the most relevant data for our readers.

The editorial board has been involved in producing this book since its inception. They have spent rigorous hours researching and exploring the diverse topics which have resulted in the successful publishing of this book. They have passed on their knowledge of decades through this book. To expedite this challenging task, the publisher supported the team at every step. A small team of assistant editors was also appointed to further simplify the editing procedure and attain best results for the readers.

Apart from the editorial board, the designing team has also invested a significant amount of their time in understanding the subject and creating the most relevant covers. They scrutinized every image to scout for the most suitable representation of the subject and create an appropriate cover for the book.

The publishing team has been an ardent support to the editorial, designing and production team. Their endless efforts to recruit the best for this project, has resulted in the accomplishment of this book. They are a veteran in the field of academics and their pool of knowledge is as vast as their experience in printing. Their expertise and guidance has proved useful at every step. Their uncompromising quality standards have made this book an exceptional effort. Their encouragement from time to time has been an inspiration for everyone.

The publisher and the editorial board hope that this book will prove to be a valuable piece of knowledge for students, practitioners and scholars across the globe.

Index

www.ingramcontent.com/pod-product-compliance
Lightning Source LLC
Jackson TN
JSHW052205130125

77033JS00004B/211